AF877063

World Sustainability Series

Series editor

Walter Leal Filho, Hamburg, Germany

More information about this series at http://www.springer.com/series/13384

Walter Leal Filho · Paul Pace
Editors

Teaching Education for Sustainable Development at University Level

Springer

Editors
Walter Leal Filho
HAW Hamburg
Hamburg
Germany

and

Manchester Metropolitan University
Manchester
UK

Paul Pace
University of Malta
Msida
Malta

ISSN 2199-7373 ISSN 2199-7381 (electronic)
World Sustainability Series
ISBN 978-3-319-32926-0 ISBN 978-3-319-32928-4 (eBook)
DOI 10.1007/978-3-319-32928-4

Library of Congress Control Number: 2016936568

© Springer International Publishing Switzerland 2016
This work is subject to copyright. All rights are reserved by the Publisher, whether the whole or part of the material is concerned, specifically the rights of translation, reprinting, reuse of illustrations, recitation, broadcasting, reproduction on microfilms or in any other physical way, and transmission or information storage and retrieval, electronic adaptation, computer software, or by similar or dissimilar methodology now known or hereafter developed.
The use of general descriptive names, registered names, trademarks, service marks, etc. in this publication does not imply, even in the absence of a specific statement, that such names are exempt from the relevant protective laws and regulations and therefore free for general use.
The publisher, the authors and the editors are safe to assume that the advice and information in this book are believed to be true and accurate at the date of publication. Neither the publisher nor the authors or the editors give a warranty, express or implied, with respect to the material contained herein or for any errors or omissions that may have been made.

Printed on acid-free paper

This Springer imprint is published by Springer Nature
The registered company is Springer International Publishing AG Switzerland

Preface

It is widely known among educators and practitioners that among the many challenges to realise the goal of sustainable development, teaching education has been and still is one of the major areas to tackle. Indeed, there is a pressing need to strengthen and adapt the institutional framework of pre-service and in-service teacher training, especially at the regional and national levels. This need has been highlighted for many years now, for instance at the 2012 UN Conference on Sustainable Development held in Rio de Janeiro and at the UNESCO World Conference on Education for Sustainable Development (WCESD) hosted in Aichi-Nagoya in 2014. Paradoxically, despite the number of recommendations and suggestions made outlining the need to pursue sustainable development, many environmental problems have been exacerbated rather than solved. This state of affairs suggests that little progress can be made unless some basic needs are properly addressed.

One of these basic needs is to acknowledge that it is necessary to address the fragmented nature of the handling of sustainability issues at formal education programmes as a whole, and in teacher education in particular. Improvements are needed not only on the ways to cater for sustainability in the curriculum, but also on how to handle and promote issues related to sustainable development at multiple levels (e.g. community and family) with a focus on the interplay and interlinkages. Also, the development of flexible teaching methods capable of incorporating environmental, economic, societal and cultural elements is greatly needed.

But without a proper training of teachers on the principles and practices of sustainability, with which they can educate and raise awareness about sustainable development among schoolchildren and among students, there can be little hope that any of the changes outlined above can be achieved.

Among the various issues which deserve attention is the documentation and the dissemination of good practice in teaching for and about sustainable development at the institutions of higher education. Consistent with the perceived need for action in this field, the book “Teaching Education for Sustainable Development at University Level” has been prepared. It is divided into two parts.

Part I deals with curriculum elements, demonstrating curriculum innovation and new ways to make provisions for sustainable development in teaching practices.

Part II contains contextualised case studies, showing how the goal of making teacher education for sustainable development possible has been achieved.

We thank the authors for their willingness to share their knowledge, know-how and the information they have been able to obtain from their work and from their projects. We hope that the experiences gathered here can be useful to others interested at or working in the field of teacher education for sustainable development, and that they may support current and future efforts towards curriculum innovation on the one hand, and teaching practice on the other.

Enjoy the reading.

Spring 2016

Walter Leal Filho
Paul Pace

Contents

Teaching Education for Sustainable Development: Implications on Learning Programmes at Higher Education

Walter Leal Filho and Paul Pace

Abstract

This paper considers the basic elements associated with teaching education for sustainable development and outlines the implications on learning programmes at higher education institutions. In particular, the paper considers the extent to which the formation of educators influences this process, and defends the view that an emphasis on the long-term pre-service and in-service training of educators should be a top priority.

1 Teaching Education for Sustainable Development: More Than a Question of Definition

It is widely acknowledged that education is characterised as a future-facing activity. Learning processes start at very early childhood during which children develop basic skills and pick up basic knowledge, attitudes and values from their parents and other significant persons. These formative years have been defined as crucial in for ESD. Compulsory schooling—usually taking an average 12 years of intensive learning—is a period during which issues related to sustainable development (SD) are explored in more detail. The post-compulsory education phase is characterised by steps towards finding a job/profession. It is a phase during which

W. Leal Filho (✉)
HAW Hamburg and Manchester, Metropolitan University,
Hamburg, Germany
e-mail: walter.leal@haw-hamburg.de

P. Pace
University of Malta, Msida, Malta
e-mail: paul.j.pace@um.edu.mt

© Springer International Publishing Switzerland 2016
W. Leal Filho and P. Pace (eds.), *Teaching Education for Sustainable Development at University Level*, World Sustainability Series,
DOI 10.1007/978-3-319-32928-4_1

learners have an opportunity to apply any SD knowledge they might have received to their work place or opt for further training in specialised SD contexts.

This book will focus on the aspect of further training, i.e. in preparing professionals that are committed towards SD. It aims to provide examples of good practice—a varied testimony of the different ways Higher Education institutions are responding to the emerging needs for education for sustainable development (ESD).

There are many definitions for ESD. For the purposes of this paper it is regarded as the process of equipping students with the knowledge and understanding, skills and attributes needed to work and live in a way that safeguards their environmental, social and economic wellbeing, both in the present and for future generations (Longhurst 2014). It is also considered that ESD is part of the general educational remit to enable every new generation to humanise living conditions (Rauch 2008). According to "Guidance for UK Higher Education Providers" ESD means working with students to contextualise their learning to the realities of their own specialisation, profession and personal life by encouraging them to develop: (a) the notion of global citizenship; (b) a commitment towards environmental stewardship; (c) a reflection about the interaction between issues of social justice, ethics, wellbeing and ecological and economic factors; and (d) a future-facing outlook; learning to think about the consequences of actions, and how systems and societies can be adapted to ensure sustainable futures (Longhurst 2014).

The concept of sustainability, on the other hand, largely remains abstract despite the fact that there acceptable definitions. ESD is a process of learning how to make decisions that consider the long-term futures of the economy, ecology, the equitable development of all communities as well as the promotion of their cultures (Besong and Holland 2015).

The 1992 Rio Summit's drive to *reorient education towards sustainable development* was followed by a plethora of elaborations of the process of Environmental Education: Environmental and Development Education (EDE) (UNCED 1992); Environmental Education for Sustainability (EEfS) (Tilbury 1995); Education for Sustainability (EfS) (Huckle and Sterling 1996); Education for a Sustainable Future (ESF) (UNESCO 1997); Education as Sustainability (EaS) (Foster 2001); SD Education (SDE) (Smyth 2002), to cite just a few. This can be interpreted as an attempt to adapt the basic principles of Environmental Education, as outlined in the Tbilisi Conference of 1977, to the various contexts and educational realities that have evolved since (Pace 2010). Although the international community seems to have settled (for now) with the term Education for Sustainable Development (ESD), different authors in the different chapters of this book have preferred to use other terms which accentuate that "*What you call it*" is not that important, as long as what you are doing shares the same educational principles of ESD. Moreover, the chapters also evidence a preference of Higher Education (HE) institutions to develop programmes that are culturally sensitive to the contexts in which they are operating rather than settling for the importation of 'ready-made solutions' from other countries/regions.

2 The Complexity of Teaching Education for Sustainable Development

The current global economic problems, the unfair distribution of resources and ensuing conflicts, and the impacts of climate change and other environmental hazards evidence the complex web of unsustainable practices that characterise our global reality. The current paradigm of development is simply not delivering the wellbeing it has promised and consequently there is an emerging need for a shift in human mind-sets towards more sustainable values, behaviours and lifestyles that collectively improve both the environmental and human quality of life (Besong and Holland 2015). Although the UNDESD final report (UNESCO 2014) indicated a "*stepping up*" of efforts towards ESD in HE; the complexity of educational systems, the various levels of decision-making on educational policies, and traditional curricular structures are still presenting challenges for learners to develop (and transfer) competences in SD. The experiences cited in this book evidence that fast, effective and institution-wide change towards ESD in HE was always catalysed by legislation that spurred institutions to address their inertia and disciplinary traditions. Without this 'political' motivation systemic change towards ESD is a more laborious and isolated experience that is vulnerable to changes in administration, staff mobility and available resources.

Repeated declarations have pointed out multi- and inter-disciplinarity as a major characteristic of ESD as it reflects the complex issues raised when dealing with SD themes, and which in turn mirror the interconnectivity of the various dimensions of our surroundings (Tilbury et al. 2002). In the context of HE institutions, this has habitually raised implementation barriers mainly due to monodisciplinary structures predominant in these institutions (Moore 2005a). A way in between that retains the "*… traditional focus on individual subjects and at the same time open*(s) *the door to multi- and inter-disciplinary examination of real-life situations*" is proposed by the UNECE Strategy for ESD (UNECE 2005, p. 28). This continuum of curricular solutions is also evident in the programmes described in the chapters of this publication, with a particular bias to the development of integrated themes that are cross disciplinary.

In his reflection on the lack of effective preparation of graduates to address sustainability (survival) issues, Orr (1994) implies that the solution lies in a change in the way knowledge is defined and education is perceived, i.e. a departure from courses focussed on just the transmission of knowledge to *spaces for pedagogical transformation* that support transformative and transdisciplinary learning (Moore 2005b). This current publication proposes various contexts in which course design has a marked emphasis on the development of competences and autonomous learning rather than just on the acquisition of knowledge. Implicit in this development is a redefinition (or rather an evolution) of the roles of HE institutions, educators and learners.

Although preparing students for employment is a very important aspect of HE institutions, ESD programmes should focus on a wider target: preparing students for a future that is still unknown. This means providing learning experiences that develop *critical thinking, problem solving, creativity and innovation skills, collaboration skills, contextual learning skills, self-direction, as well as communication skills* (Iliško et al. 2014, p.100). The implication is that learners are no longer considered as passive consumers of knowledge, but active participants in their education and partners in learning. The UNECE strategy suggests the setting up of teams of educators and students that together develop learning programmes (UNECE 2005). The programmes presented in the chapters of this publication are characterised by conscious steps to increase student participation, not just during the learning sessions, but also in the design of the programme and its assessment. This increased participation did not just result in a change in students' mindsets, but also in the attitudes of their tutors and the management staff of their respective universities.

ESD also implies the widening of learners' perspectives that enable a deeper and wider analysis of life experiences. The current generation of young learners are the product of the Information Age, born to a multimedia world (Nurmilaakso 2015) where learning takes place independent of physical locations. Indeed, in today's interconnected and technology-driven world, a learning environment can be virtual, online or remote (Kay and Greenhill 2011). However, the current generation is less physically fit, less equipped to interact socially, and less able to concentrate and be effective in class than previous generations. Learners need action, challenges and opportunities based on real-life interactions to develop 21st century skills (Coyle 2010). This implies that learning is not the sole prerogative of formal education institutions and requires a widening of the base of HE and going beyond the confines of the walls of traditional lecture rooms and into the community. Besides enhancing learning, such experiences (if developed) can increase the social responsibility and commitment of HE institutions. The case studies included in this publication document efforts to adopt out-of-classroom sessions that involve moving out into nature and exploring community spaces (including the HE campuses themselves).

A common knee-jerk reaction, when confronted with the daunting issues related to SD, is to try to rely on scare tactics to mould behaviours into sustainable practices. Although this approach tends to be quite favourite with media which tend to skew information to sensationalise issues, experience and research have shown that it is ineffective. When faced with predications of impending disasters and uncertain futures, most people feel overwhelmed, powerless, frustrated and too discouraged to act. Iliško et al. (2014) have shown that providing bachelor's and master's degree students with opportunities to think about preferred futures had better results. Besides suggesting solutions, students felt personally responsible to be part of these solutions. The educational programmes described in the following chapters are characterised by a focus on positive solutions by featuring and critically reflecting on success stories and role models/examples that offer an antidote to the feelings of insecurity and despair.

Learning and teaching are intimately related. Effective educators know how to choose the most appropriate pedagogies to address different contexts and different learning needs (Nurmilaakso 2015). However, effective educators do not grow on trees, and while reorienting teacher education towards sustainability has been readily recognised as an important approach to address the urgent need for SD (Raus and Falkenberg 2014) the preparation of university lecturers has not received the same meticulous attention that is given to teachers. In this case, it seems that the major concern is just for a rigorous formation in the content dimension. Little, if any, importance is given to a candidate's communication and pedagogical skills when lecturers are employed with he institutions. It is no wonder that HE is mostly characterised by mastery of subject matter rather than the development of students as persons that are responsible for the wellbeing of Earth and its inhabitants (Orr 1994).

3 Conclusions

SD should no longer be interpreted solely as an academic subject, but as a participatory lifelong process which would involve all areas of civil society. Furthermore, ESD leads to an informed and involved citizenry having the creative problem-solving skills, scientific and social literacy, and commitment to engage in responsible individual and co-operative actions. These actions will help ensure an environmentally sound, socially just and economically prosperous future. ESD has the potential to serve as a tool for building stronger bridges between the classroom and business, and between schools and communities (UNESCO 2010). The "school of the future"—particularly HE institutions—should be a mission-driven goal in line with the goals of ESD and sustainable societies. The formation of educators is a pre-condition to achieve this goal, and therefore an emphasis on the long-term pre-service and in-service training of educators should be a top priority.

References

Besong, F., & Holland, C. (2015). The Dispositions, Abilities and Behaviours (DAB) Framework for profiling learners sustainability competencies in Higher Education. *Journal of Teacher Education for Sustainability, 17*(1), 5–22. doi:10.1515/jtes-2015-0001

Coyle, K. J. (2010). *Back to school: Back outside!* National Wildlife Federation.

Foster, J. (2001). Education as Sustainability. *Environmental Education Research, 7*(2), 153–165.

Huckle, J., & Sterling, S. (1996). *Education for sustainability*. London: WWF & Earthscan.

Iliško, D., Skrinda, A., & Mišule, I. (2014). Envisioning the future: Bachelors and Masters degrees students perspectives. *Journal of Teacher Education for Sustainability, 16*(2), 88–102. doi:10.2478/jtes-2014-0013.

Kay, K. & Greenhill, V. (2011). Twenty-first century students need 21st century skills. In G. Wan & D. Gut (Eds.). *Bringing schools into the 21st century*. Volume 13 of the series Explorations of Educational Purpose. Springer, Berlin.

Longhurst, J. (2014). *Education for Sustainable Development: Guidance for UK Higher Education Providers*. Gloucester, UK: The Quality Assurance Agency for Higher Education.

Moore, J. (2005a). Barriers and pathways to creating sustainability education programs: Policy rhetoric and reality. *Environmental Education and Research, 11*(5), 537–555.

Moore, J. (2005b). Seven recommendations for creating sustainability education at the university level: A guide for change agents. *International Journal of Sustainability in Higher Education, 6*(4), 326–339.

Nurmilaakso, M. (2015). How children can support their learning to write and read by computer in the early years of school. *Journal of Teacher Education for Sustainability, 17*(1), 98–106. doi:10.1515/jtes-2015-0008

Orr, D. W. (1994). *Earth in mind: On education, environment, and the human prospect.* Washington: Island Press.

Pace, P. (2010). Education for Sustainable Development: current fad or renewed commitment to action? *Journal of Baltic Science Education, 9*(4), 315–323.

Rauch, F. (2008). Action Research as Interventional Research in ESD. In W. Sleurs (Ed.), *Competencies for ESD (Education for Sustainable Development) Teachers: A framework to integrate ESD in the curriculum of teacher training institutes.* Belgium: Katholieke Hogeschool Leuven.

Raus, R., & Falkenberg, T. (2014). The journey towards a teacher's ecological self: A case study of a student teacher. *Journal of Teacher Education for Sustainability, 16*(2), 103–114. doi:10.2478/jtes-2014-0014

Smyth, J. C. (2002). *Are educators ready for the next Earth Summit? Millennium Papers Series, Issue 6*. London: Stakeholder Forum for Our Common Future.

Tilbury, D. (1995). Environmental Education for Sustainability: Defining the new focus of environmental education in the 1990s. *Environmental Education Research, 1*(2), 195–212.

Tilbury, D., Stevenson, R. B., Fien, J., & Schreuder, D. (Eds.). (2002). *Education and sustainability: Responding to the global challenge*. IUCN, Gland, Switzerland and Cambridge, UK: Commission on Education and Communication.

UNCED (United Nations Conference on Environment and Development). (1992). *The United Nations Conference on Environment and Development: A guide to Agenda 21*. Switzerland: UN Publications Office, Geneva.

UNECE. (2005). UNECE *Strategy for Education for Sustainable Development*. Adopted at the High-Level Meeting of Environment and Education Ministries (Vilnius, 17–18 Mar 2005). Retrieved from http://www.unece.org/fileadmin/DAM/env/documents/2005/cep/ac.13/cep.ac.13.2005.3.rev.1.e.pdf

UNESCO. (1997). *Educating for a Sustainable Future: A transdisciplinary vision for concerted action*. Paris: UNESCO.

UNESCO. (2010). *Teaching and learning for a sustainable future*. UNESCO, Paris. Retrieved from: http://www.unesco.org/education/tlsf/

UNESCO. (2014). *Shaping the future we want: UN Decade of Education for Sustainable Development (2005–2014) Final Report*. Paris: UNESCO.

Part I
Curriculum Elements and Innovation

An Approach to Embedding Sustainability into Undergraduate Curriculum: Macquarie University, Australia Case Study

Leanne Denby and Sara Rickards

Abstract

Universities have been identified as being critical in developing sustainability-focused skillsets and mindsets (UNESCO in United Nations Decade of Education for Sustainable Development 2004–2014, 2004; UNCSD in The future we want, 2012; UE4SD in The state of the art report 2014). A UK-based survey further identified that 80 % of students believe that universities should incorporate sustainable development. Additionally this percentage increases as students progress through their degree (LSIS in Embedding sustainability into teaching, learning and curriculum in the learning and skills sector, 2013). There is also a growing demand from business, for graduates to be sustainability literate, with company leaders increasingly seeing sustainability as one of the top 3 priorities (McKinsey in Sustainability's strategic worth McKinsey global survey results, 2014). Academic discussions around sustainability are often problematic due to many factors including understanding, relevance and time (LSIS 2013; Lozano 2010). The approach outlined in this chapter acknowledged barriers and utilised a method to mitigate these issues. The process focused on program level mapping and coverage of sustainability as an interdisciplinary concept, using the Macquarie University Sustainability Framework. The initial stages undertaken in 2014 investigated connections to sustainability in four undergraduate programs at Macquarie University: Bachelor of Media (Faculty of Arts); Bachelor of Human Science (Faculty of Human Science); Bachelor of Mechanical Engineering (Faculty of Science), and Bachelor of Business

L. Denby (✉) · S. Rickards
Sustainability Office, Macquarie University, Balaclava Rd, North Ryde, NSW 2109, Australia
e-mail: leanne.denby@mq.edu.au

S. Rickards
e-mail: sara.rickards@mq.edu.au

© Springer International Publishing Switzerland 2016

W. Leal Filho and P. Pace (eds.), *Teaching Education for Sustainable Development at University Level*, World Sustainability Series,
DOI 10.1007/978-3-319-32928-4_2

Administration (Faculty of Business and Economics). The programs involved in this phase were chosen because they were not typically 'sustainability-focused' degrees. However, mapping showed all programs demonstrated connections to sustainability learning at the program level, covering a minimum of 86 % of the Framework, with the Bachelor of Human Sciences demonstrating 100 % coverage. Evaluation as to whether graduates leave with sustainability skills and knowledge is yet to be completed. Providing evidence of teaching that not just informs, but transforms students will be vital to increasing employability of Macquarie University graduates. Going forward the authors aim to measure the transformational learning of both academics and students. Essentially, external circumstances at a global level dictate that embedding sustainability into the curriculum is a responsibility all universities must undertake. The evidence gathered to date indicates that this is not an impossible mission, so long as a considered methodology and adequate resourcing is in place to support often time-poor academics.

Keywords
Sustainability · Sustainable development · Curriculum · Higher education

1 Introduction

This chapter proceeds on the assumption there is general understanding that there is no doubt that today's students face some of the greatest challenges of our times as they enter a changing workforce, surrounded by a rapidly changing society and environment. Growing social and environmental pressures demand new skillsets, fostered through pedagogy that stimulates innovative, active and collaborative learning experiences (Tilbury 2011). Universities have been identified as being critical in developing sustainability-focused skillsets and mindsets (UNESCO 2014; UNCSD 2012; UE4SD 2014). However, academic discussions around sustainability are often problematic due to many factors.

Extensive research undertaken in 2013 on behalf of Learning Skills and Improvement Service (LSIS) looked at exploring and understanding the relationship and relevance of sustainability to education, including understanding the barriers to a broader uptake of Education for Sustainability (EfS) (LSIS 2013). The primary barrier related to a lack of sustainability understanding, and an inability on how to translate it into subject matter. Time was also cited, particularly concerning already busy classes, and a capacity to take time to learn about sustainability and its relevance to subject areas. Acknowledging known barriers provides a useful starting point for thinking about how to progress the EfS agenda.

To mark the end of the United Nations Decade of Education for Sustainable Development, a survey out of the United Kingdom found that 80 % of students believe that universities should incorporate sustainable development. Additionally this percentage increases as students progress through their degree (HEA 2014). There is also a growing demand from business, for students to be sustainability literate, with company leaders increasingly seeing sustainability as one of the top 3 priorities (McKinsey 2014).

Systemic educational change with respect to sustainability has been slow, primarily due to our inability to overcome institutional inertia and disciplinary traditions (Greig 2015).

> University leaders and staff must be empowered to catalyse and implement new paradigms, and ensure that Sustainable Development is the 'Golden Thread' throughout the entire university system (Lozano et al. 2013)

Essentially, embedding sustainability into curriculum cannot be left for one discipline or program[1] to implement if a shift towards a more equitable and ecologically just world is to occur—teaching what and how we have always taught only assists to maintain current unsustainable paradigms. Therefore, to achieve sustainability mindsets and skillsets, it is critical to consider process as well as content. But what does it mean to have a pedagogical process that encompasses sustainability? And what support is needed to assist academics[2] grappling with this all too nebulous concept?

A team from Macquarie University, Sydney, Australia, consisting of staff from Macquarie Sustainability (the authors), set about trying to answer these and other questions. The approach used at the University aims to demystify sustainability, using the Macquarie University Sustainability Framework (the Framework) to provide clear guidelines for identifying Education for Sustainability (EfS), and demonstrate how skills for sustainability are applicable in any program. This approach allows investigation as to whether such a framework is useful to academics, and what support is needed for program level, interdisciplinary concept learning.

The initial stages of the project investigated how sustainability is mapped and embedded into four undergraduate programs: Bachelor of Media (Faculty of Arts); Bachelor of Human Science (Faculty of Human Science); Bachelor of Mechanical Engineering (Faculty of Science), and Bachelor of Business Administration (Faculty of Business and Economics).

[1]In this context, 'program' is equivalent to 'degree'. Essentially, the grouping of individual units to make a program or degree, leading to a Bachelor qualification. Units are often called 'courses' elsewhere.

[2]'Academics' is the term used in Australia to define teaching staff. Often called 'Faculty' elsewhere.

Fig. 1 Macquarie University sustainability framework

2 Macquarie University Sustainability Framework

Macquarie University incorporated sustainability as an underlying principle of undergraduate capabilities in 2010. With quality assurance requirements coming to the fore in Australia in 2012, the University was prompted to demonstrate how graduate capabilities were being developed in-line with this guiding principle—and in a way that academics could relate to. A small project team consisting of academics across Macquarie's four faculties was brought together to develop a framework to clarify the 'what' and 'how' of sustainability in the curriculum (Fig. 1). This Framework was tested against 72 People and Planet units,[3] and

[3]People units are designed to give students an understanding of what it means to live in the social world, and to develop cultural or social literacy, while Planet units enable students to develop an

Table 1 Sub-themes of the sustainability framework

Harmony & Wellbeing	Economics & Economic Wellbeing	Natural Resources	Climate Change	Implementation & Governance	Learning Skills
Social justice & equity	Production, consumption & waste	Atmosphere	Science of climate change	Participation of stakeholders in decision making	Future thinking, visioning
Health	Trade & development systems	Biodiversity	Social, environmental & economic impacts of climate change	Communication	Responsible innovation (underpinned by ethical decision making)
Human rights	Sustainable economies	Oceans, seas and coasts	Adaptation & resilience	Promoting education, public awareness and training	Critical thinking: ability to challenge, 'find your voice'
Animal rights	Investment	Freshwater	Mitigation	Access to information, sharing of technology	Creative thinking
Cultural diversity	Financing	Management	Risk assessment	International, national & local governance	Clarification & activation of value systems
Poverty		Land use and tenure	Coastal management	Political dimensions	Leadership
Food Security		Planetary boundaries	Transport	Corporate social responsibility	Self-directed, autonomous & reflective learning
Cooperation				Integration of environment & social development in decision making	Practical, real world knowledge
Learning from history				Instruments & mechanisms	Systemic thinking
Disaster management				Capacity building	Consequential thinking
				Sustainable design – sustainable cities	Stakeholder, group collaboration & wider interpersonal skills
					Communication skills

workshopped at two international conferences for further input and feasibility testing. The authors are yet to determine how iterative the Framework should be in order to maintain relevance over time, without compromising any work completed using it as it currently exists.

The Framework consists of five primary content related themes (Harmony and Wellbeing; Economy and Economic Wellbeing; Natural Resources; Climate Change; Implementation and Governance), and pedagogy based on learning skills

(Footnote 3 continued)
understanding of science and the challenges and issues facing the world at present (http://handbook.mq.edu.au/2015/Units/People and http://handbook.mq.edu.au/2015/Units/Planet).

and value recognition in line with EfS principles. Each primary theme is underpinned by numerous sub-themes (see Table 1), with definition at both the primary and sub-theme level deriving from internationally recognised reference points. At present, the Framework provides Macquarie University with a consistent method for mapping EfS, with the added bonus of building understanding and knowledge of holistic sustainability.

3 Method

Research has shown there are a number of existing approaches to embedding sustainability into curriculum (LSIS 2013):

1. Adding sustainability topics to lectures in an opportunistic manner
2. Having a planned approach to include sustainability topic/s as part of lessons
3. Using existing programs that focus on sustainability in some capacity
4. Having a requirement specified by professional bodies to include sustainability topics in order to complete a degree
5. Developing an additional program or course that focuses on sustainability
6. Including sustainability topics in a capstone or other unit designated as compulsory for learning
7. Adopting different pedagogies to create a different way of working and learning, enabling the learner to understand themselves and the world
8. Including sustainability themes without actually highlighting them as 'Sustainability'
9. Including a combination of the approaches listed above

Informed by previous discussions with academics around the topic of sustainability in curriculum, the authors proceeded on the assumption that approach number 8 was common at the University: academics essentially needed a way to identify the connections with sustainability and their teaching, hence the use of the aforementioned Framework (Fig. 1). It was also acknowledged that approach number 9 would also be relevant, and capturing this element became part of understanding how academics were teaching where connections to the Framework existed (See Sustainability Mapping below).

Time was also spent researching and understanding barriers to engaging academics in sustainability discussions to assist in developing the appropriate way forward. By pre-empting barriers such as time, relevance, and lack of understanding (LSIS 2013; Lozano 2010), the approach was adapted accordingly, to increase likelihood of success. The primary insight gained from this research was ensuring there was a dedicated resource to complete the majority of work involved, rather than placing that burden onto the academics themselves: hence the appointment of an Education for Sustainability (EfS) Manager. This dedicated resource, in conjunction with the Framework, provided a way to alleviate the aforementioned barriers.

Consideration was further given to understanding existing and emerging trends within the University, to ensure that yet another level of complexity was not introduced into the academic workload, and to demonstrate alignment with the broader strategic direction. As it happened, changes were at hand, with the University moving towards better definition and mapping at the program level. Hence program level mapping, rather than sporadic individual unit mapping, became an integral part of the approach.

In order to incorporate the learning from the aforementioned conditions, the authors chose to utilise two methodologies: sustainability mapping and sustainability surveys. For the purpose of this chapter, only the mapping will be discussed.

3.1 Sustainability Mapping

Utilising the Framework, the authors worked with unit convenors to make implicit connections to EfS more explicit, whilst providing support to those who wished to enhance sustainability learning for themselves and/or their students. Table 2 outlines the stages involved for identifying and enhancing sustainability connections, noting that at the time of writing, the authors had only progressed to stage 2 for three programs, and stage 3 for one program (discussed in Results). Some unit convenors have also progressed to the post stage, though this will not be covered in this chapter.

Once mapping was completed, the compilations were given to Program Directors with recommendations. A post involvement focus group was also conducted with Program Directors to evaluate what worked, what didn't work, and any suggestions for improvement.

It should be noted that neither of the authors are employed at Macquarie University in an academic capacity. Both in fact sit within a professional or non-academic office. Recognising the potential friction that could be caused by having non-academic staff enter into the academic space, the authors spent a considerable amount of time undertaking a process of learning. This learning included better understanding the language and circumstance of academics (concerns such as workload and research pressures for example), whilst gaining trust through informal discussions and networking opportunities. There was also a certain amount of determination and passion required in order to make the case for EfS compelling. The fact that the authors also positioned themselves as providing service and support, rather than as 'experts' with all the answers, also seemed to allay concerns, which may have been held by academics.

Table 2 Integrating and mapping sustainability approach

Stage	Approach	Comments
Pre: set up	The authors met with Executive Deans and Associate Deans Learning and Teaching (AD L&T) to gain support and identify a non-traditional sustainability program to undergo mapping. AD L&T then approached the relevant Program Director[a] to ask if they would be involved, after which time, the authors made formal contact with the Program Director	It was essential to gain Executive buy-in, and have that level initially contact the Program Director, so that the Director had the right to veto without direct contact with the authors. Initial discussions with Directors outlined the methodology. Initial communications with Unit Convenors was generated by the Program Director Time impact: while the discussions themselves were not time intensive, coordinating to find suitable meeting times did take some effort on behalf of the authors
1. Preliminary mapping	With input from the Program Directors, the authors identified core units from each program that would be mapped. The authors then used unit outlines to do a preliminary mapping exercise against the Framework. Figure 5 demonstrates this mapping	Using the unit outline provided an opportunity for us to determine what impression a student might have regarding sustainability learning occurring within the program. The authors acknowledge that their in-depth knowledge of sustainability likely skewed the preliminary mapping, when comparing how someone with no sustainability knowledge may have interpreted learning outcomes for mapping Time impact: this stage had minimal impact on Program Directors, but was very time intensive on behalf of the authors, with each unit requiring 15 min to map, resulting in program mapping taking approximately 4 h each *N.B. After evaluation, it is unlikely that this stage will continue as validity vs time invested was not worthwhile*

(continued)

Table 2 (continued)

<table>
<tr><th>Stage</th><th>Approach</th><th>Comments</th></tr>
<tr><td>2. Convenor mapping</td><td>The authors facilitated workshops and one-on-one discussions with unit convenors to assist them in using a matrix template to populate where they felt they had connections with the Framework. Figures 2, 3, 4 and 6 demonstrate this mapping</td><td>Having the unit convenors undertake the mapping exercise themselves allowed gaps between preliminary mapping andv their own understanding of where connections occur to be revealed. It also provides a way to understand how the overall program maps with regards to EfS. To gain insight into how the Framework was assessed convenors identified how they were addressing the Framework using the following coding:
<table>
<tr><td>I</td><td>Implicit: Covered but not explicitly. Students may not recognise learning as EfS.</td></tr>
<tr><td>LTC</td><td>Lecture/Tut Content: Content connected to a theme/s is explicitly covered as content in a lecture/s and/or tutorial/s.</td></tr>
<tr><td>LTP</td><td>Lecture/Tut Pedagogical: Connections exist through the way in which learning occurs. For example Workplace Integrated Learning opportunities building Learning Skills.</td></tr>
<tr><td>CP</td><td>Lecture/Tut Content and Pedagogical: A combination of LTC and LTP occurs</td></tr>
<tr><td>LO</td><td>Learning Outcome: Stated learning outcome of engaging with a unit or program.</td></tr>
<tr><td>A</td><td>Assessment: Assessment task explicitly connects to EfS.</td></tr>
</table>
Time impact: Most of the impact was borne by the authors in trying to find suitable time to meet with convenors. Mapping by convenors usually took 30 minutes on average.</td></tr>
<tr><td>3. Levels of learning</td><td>The authors facilitated workshops and one-on-one discussions with unit convenors to assist them in providing details against levels of learning occurring in the mapping. The Bachelor of Human Sciences case study demonstrates this mapping</td><td>A rudimentary tick system was used to capture levels of learning:
√= Some discussion occurs, though not the main focus
√√= Covered in detail
√√√= Consistent theme throughout delivery of unit/major component
N.B.: capturing levels of learning is quite a difficult but essential process in establishing depth rather than just breadth. Much of this element is still underway, with the exception of Bachelor of Human Sciences (Fig. 7). At present, the tick system seems to work reasonably well, however further evaluation of effectiveness will occur over time
Time impact: as per other stages, most of the time impact was borne by the authors trying to find times convenors were available to meet. For the convenors themselves, this mapping exercise took about 30 min on average</td></tr>
</table>

(continued)

Table 2 (continued)

Stage	Approach	Comments
4. Supporting documentation	The authors facilitated workshops and one-on-one discussions with unit convenors to gather supporting documentation against mapping. This predominantly involves getting access to the online system used by convenors to disseminate information to their students (iLearn) to bring together 'evidence' to support stated claims, in line with quality assurance requirements	This element is still underway and is proving to be the most difficult and time consuming. Often convenors have difficulty determining what would be suitable as a supporting document, which often caused some distress and confusion. It is anticipated in the future authors will be enrolled in iLearn early, and work more closely and intensely with convenors Time impact: this is definitely one of the most time intensive stages for both the authors and convenors. Convenors need to be able to suggest appropriate documentation, which often requires them to revisit what resources, assessments, and tasks they provide to students. For the authors, it requires spending time sifting through the information provided in iLearn, connecting the dots to the mapping. Estimating time involved in this stage is difficult, and can range from 1 h to a full day
Post: continued development	Many unit convenors expressed an interest in further developing their unit to align with sustainability learning	Work will continue with unit convenors to develop appropriate teaching resources, whilst also assisting to bring identified connections to the fore. The post phase is a critical element in maintaining sustainability-learning connections Time impact: the impact in this stage is mostly on the authors, rather than the convenors, and is dependent on whether an appropriate resource already exists in the resource base or if more work needs to be done to develop an appropriate resource. Time required here is variable

The Program Director is a new position at Macquarie University, but essentially is a nominated academic responsible for representing the program, and working to build the program approach being adopted by the University

4 Results

4.1 Key Findings

- Of all the Framework themes from Fig. 1, Climate Change and Natural Resources had the least coverage (Tables 3, 5, 7 and 9)

- Learning Skills emerged as the primary EfS connection across all programs (see Table 1 for details of defined Learning Skills)
- Working with cross-faculty programs verses department based programs proved harder to collectively gather convenors for workshop participation, resulting in more one-on-one transactions (with time impact for the authors)
- The interdisciplinary Bachelor of Human Sciences program emerged as the program with the best overall coverage of sustainability themes (Fig. 6).

4.2 Sustainability Mapping Percentages

As part of the results presented, there are a number of percentages displayed within tables. Following is an explanation of these:

- 'Program theme level coverage' is a percentage of the total program coverage, by Framework theme (Fig. 1). For example in Table 3, Harmony and Wellbeing has 19 % coverage, which means that 19 % of possible sustainability connections with sub-themes (Table 1), at a program level are covered.
- 'Pedagogical coverage' relates to the spread as a percentage of how the Framework (Fig. 1) is being addressed. For example in Table 4 there is 28 % of the total Framework connections being covered Implicitly (I).

Table 3 Program level theme coverage

Harmony and wellbeing (%)	Economies and economic wellbeing (%)	Natural resources (%)	Climate change (%)	Implementation and governance (%)	Learning skills (%)
19	34	9	3	28	45

Percentage based on the total number of coloured squares within each theme from Fig. 2

Table 4 Pedagogical coverage

I	28 %
LTC	33 %
LTP	4 %
CP	3 %
LO	9 %
A	24 %

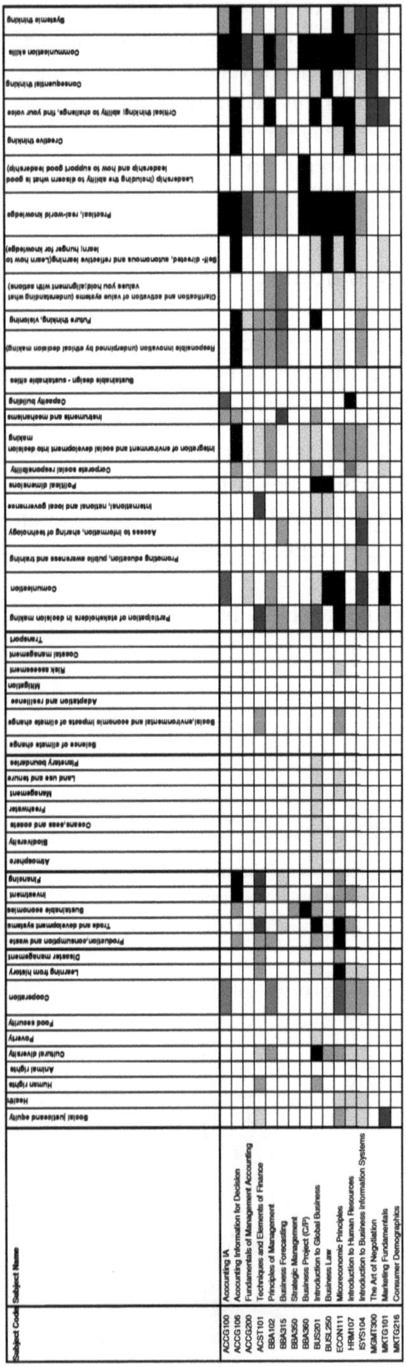

Fig. 2 Convenor mapping bachelor of business administration. Note for clarification of colour scheme see Table 2, Stage 2

4.3 Overview of Individual Program Findings

The following results present unit convenor mapping outcomes (Stage 2), and high-level analysis of this mapping. The case study on the Bachelor of Human Sciences gives a more in depth overview of Stages 1–3 mentioned in Table 2.

4.4 Bachelor of Business Administration

4.4.1 Key Findings

- 86 % of the Framework (Fig. 1) is taught at the program level (Fig. 2)
- Learning skills was the most highly covered area at 45 % (Table 3)
- Most learning occurred through Lecture and/or Tutorial content (LTC) at 33 % (Table 4).

4.5 Bachelor of Mechanical Engineering

4.5.1 Key Findings

- 96 % of the Framework (Fig. 1) is taught at the program level (Fig. 3)
- Learning skills emerged as the key area covered at 64 % (Table 5)
- Assessment (A) emerged as the primary manner by which learning occurred at 26 % (Table 6).

4.6 Bachelor of Media

4.6.1 Key Findings

- 86 % of the Framework (Fig. 1) is taught at the program level (Fig. 4).
- Learning Skills is the dominant path through which sustainability connections occur at 82 % (Table 7).
- Assessment (A) emerged as the primary delivery mechanism for sustainability learning at 53 % (Table 8).

4.7 Case Study

The authors chose to use the Bachelor of Human Sciences as the more in depth case study for two main reasons:

- The interdisciplinary nature of the program set it apart from the other programs;
- Of all the programs, this was the one that progressed the furthest in accordance with the stages outlined in Table 2.

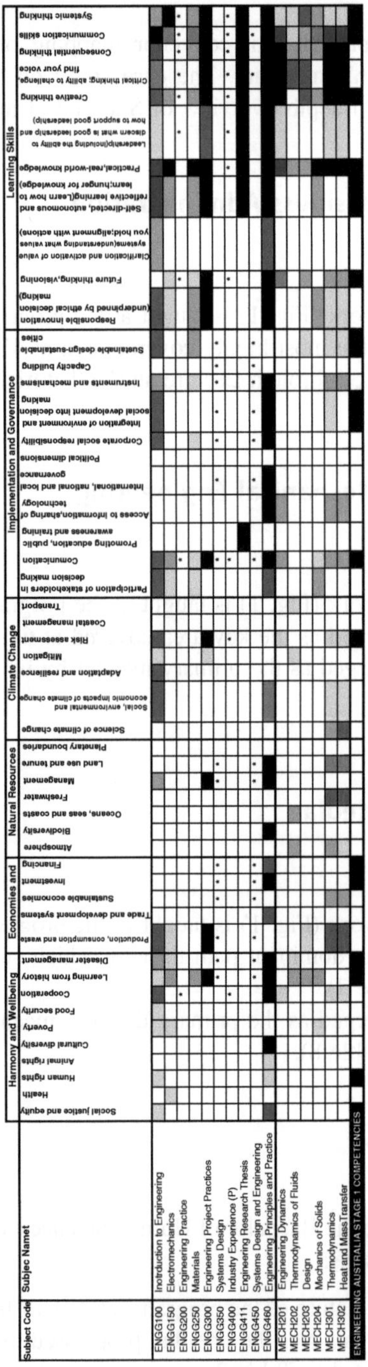

Fig. 3 Convenor mapping mechanical engineering. Note the *asterisk* mapping in this instance indicates that the sustainability sub-theme is covered (YES)—"how" it is covered is yet to be determined

Table 5 Program level theme coverage

Harmony and wellbeing (%)	Economies and economic wellbeing (%)	Natural resources (%)	Climate change (%)	Implementation and governance (%)	Learning skills (%)
21	24	15	14	30	64

Percentage based on the total number of coloured squares within each theme from Fig. 3

Table 6 Program level sustainability pedagogical coverage

YES	21%
I	20%
LTC	19%
LTP	3%
CP	8%
LO	3%
A	26%

4.8 Bachelor of Human Science

4.8.1 Key Findings

- 100 % of the Framework (Fig. 1) is taught at the program level (Fig. 6).
- Preliminary Mapping (Stage 1, Table 2) predicted 29 % Framework coverage, whilst convenor mapping determined coverage to be 79 %, indicating a large difference between what unit outlines are articulating and what is actually occurring (Figs. 5 and 6).
- At 93 %, Learning Skills dominated as the area through which connections and learning occurred (Table 9).
- 38 % of learning occurs where sustainability is a consistent theme throughout delivery of the unit or as a major component—indicated by 3 ticks (Fig. 7).

Assessment of the program level coverage revealed that Learning Skills (93 %), Harmony and Wellbeing (79 %) and Implementation and Governance (79 %), were the primary themes addressed across the program (Table 9).

4.8.2 Pedagogical Coverage

Coverage across all areas was fairly consistent, with the exception of Lecture and Tutorial Pedagogical (LTP), which was considerably low (Table 10). Likewise pedagogical approaches utilised to address themes was also spread across the program (Table 11).

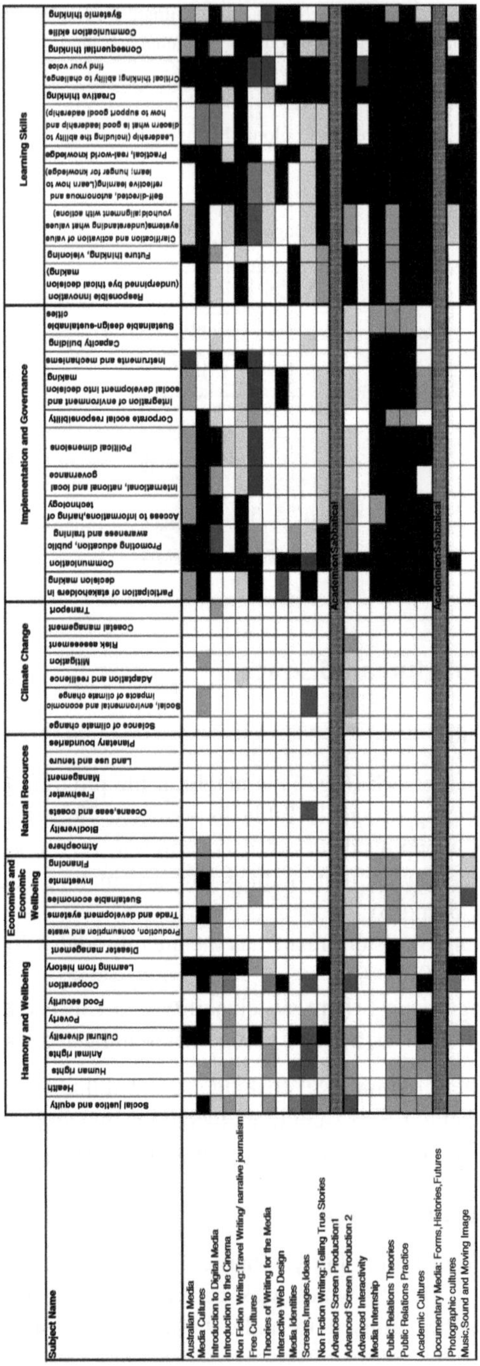

Fig. 4 Convenor mapping bachelor of media

Table 7 Program level theme coverage

Harmony and wellbeing (%)	Economies and economic wellbeing (%)	Natural resources (%)	Climate change (%)	Implementation and governance (%)	Learning skills (%)
43	25	1	7	34	82

Percentage based on the total number of coloured squares within each theme from Fig. 4

Table 8 Program level pedagogical coverage

I	16%
LTC	23%
LTP	2%
CP	3%
LO	3%
A	53%

4.8.3 Levels of Learning

More than a third of learning (38 %) saw sustainability emerge as a major component or consistent theme throughout delivery of units (defined as 3 ticks), while 30 % had sustainability covered in detail (2 ticks) and 31 % involved some discussion though sustainability is not the main focus (1 tick) (Stage 3, Table 2; Fig. 7).

5 Discussion

> Education is the most powerful path to sustainability. Economic and technological solutions, political regulations or financial incentives are not enough. We need a fundamental change in the way we think and act.
>
> Irina Bokova, Director-General of UNCSD (2012)

As societal challenges continue to grow, it is no longer sufficient for new graduates to rely on subject or discipline specific knowledge. Nor should it be acceptable for educational institutions to continue to teach the same knowledge and skills in the same way: as Einstein is famously quoted for saying "we cannot solve our problems with the same level of thinking that created them". Furthermore, students require skills that will enhance their chance of employability (Fallows and Stevens 2000), while encouraging them to break free from reinforcing current

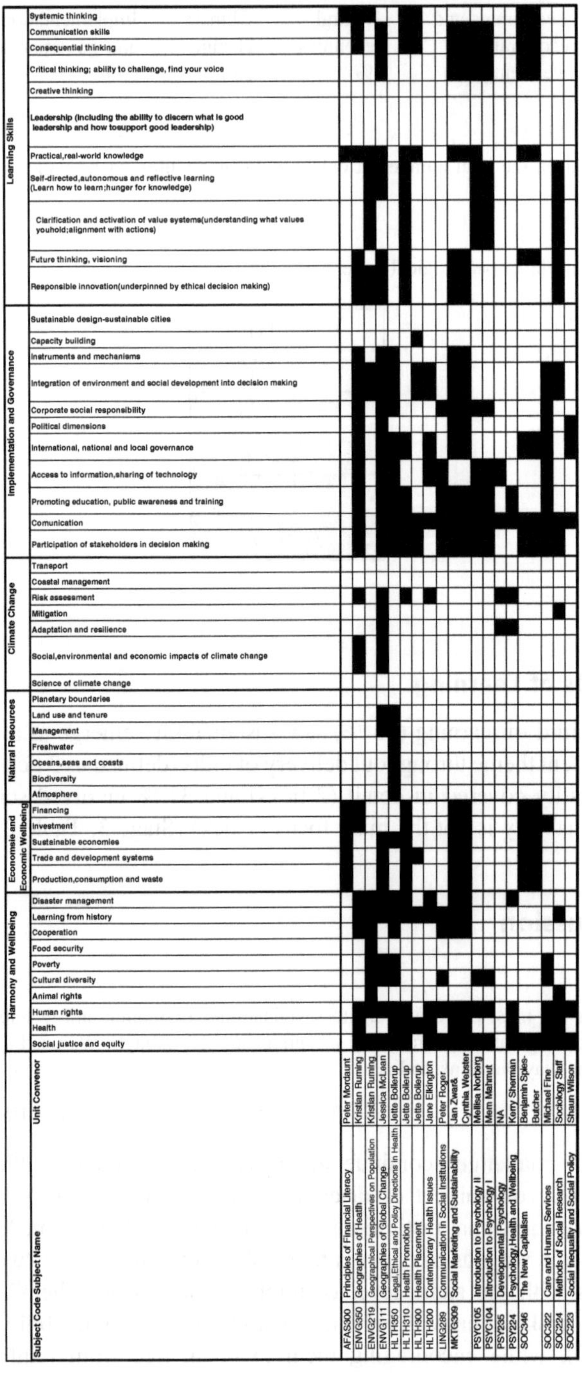

Fig. 5 Preliminary mapping bachelor human science

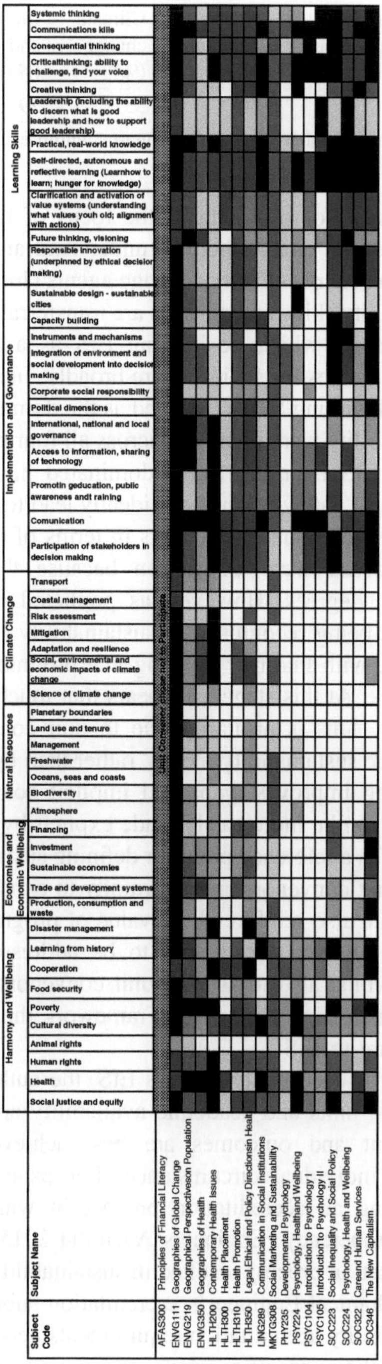

Fig. 6 Convenor mapping bachelor human science

Table 9 Program level theme coverage

Harmony and wellbeing (%)	Economies and economic wellbeing (%)	Natural resources (%)	Climate change (%)	Implementation and governance (%)	Learning skills (%)
79	52	30	33	79	93

Percentage based on the total number of coloured squares within each theme from Fig. 6

unsustainable paradigms. Not surprisingly, the focus of EfS is to equip students with skills and abilities that enable them to understand and resolve complex sustainability problems, to become effective change agents (Johnston 2013; Wiek et al. 2011). These sustainability skills and abilities are transferrable, therefore of value to any prospective employer, whilst positioning EfS as a transformative learning pathway with better outcomes for society more broadly. Interestingly, the results of this work showed that Learning Skills emerged as the dominant area through which connections to sustainability were identified across all four programs (Tables 3, 5, 7 and 9). The fact that EfS Learning Skills dominated highlights the opportunity universities have to create pathways that will ideally lead to a positive societal shift, whilst providing additional value for students in terms of employability.

The programs involved were all chosen because they were not typically 'sustainability-focused' degrees. However, as predicted earlier, sustainability is often included without being recognised as sustainability (LSIS 2013), and this is certainly the case here, with findings showing that programs cover a minimum of 86 % of the Framework. At this stage, it appears that much sustainability teaching is occurring implicitly. This is primarily due to unit convenors' lack of understanding of what holistic sustainability means, rather than by intent. It is anticipated that once understanding improves, gaps and implicit connections to sub-themes within the Framework can be more easily made explicit by design. Without doubt, having the Framework as a reference point for defining sustainability was extremely beneficial, as it gave unit convenors an opportunity to explore connections quickly and easily. Work to date also reinforced the value of program level approaches, as mapping at this level allowed for themes to be addressed in a more strategic scaffolded approach, whilst also reassuring unit convenors and program directors that not every unit had to align with every Framework theme, to provide students with consistent exposure to EfS.

In looking at how to successfully address EfS, the authors came to the understanding that programs, units and academic availability are intricately different—agreement, engagement and outcomes are best achieved through a tailored approach, specific to individual circumstance. For example: Mechanical Engineering was undergoing an accreditation process in which sustainability is an embedded Stage 1 Competency (Engineers Australia 2015). Linking work in this program to the accreditation process resulted in sustainability mapping being a clear value-add for the Mechanical Engineer's accreditation submission. However, programs with no sustainability accreditation requirements needed a different identified 'driver', tailored to their specific needs to encourage engagement. In all

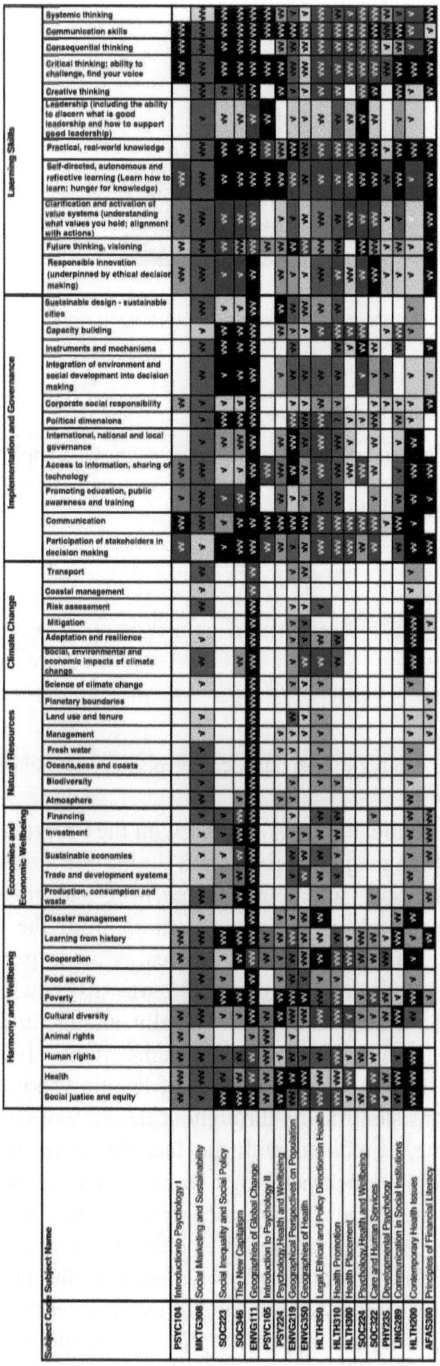

Fig. 7 Bachelor of human sciences levels of learning mapping

Table 10 Program level pedagogical coverage

I	17%
LTC	20%
LTP	3%
CP	18%
LO	17%
A	25%

Table 11 Pedagogical coverage by theme

	Harmony and wellbeing (%)	Economies and economic wellbeing (%)	Natural resources (%)	Climate change (%)	Implementation and governance (%)	Learning skills (%)
I	11	11	31	18	19	16
LTC	27	41	36	28	16	9
LTP	7	2	0	0	3	1
CP	18	23	14	21	20	17
LO	13	7	0	10	17	28
A	24	16	19	23	25	29

Percentage based on the number of individual coloured squares, within each theme from Fig. 6

circumstances, it was critical to work closely with the Program Director to establish the most appropriate language, approach and timing for moving forward. Program Directors were a necessary initial link to reaching and engaging core unit convenors, though interestingly, the unit convenors from the Bachelor of Human Science did not necessarily identify themselves as being part of a program. This situation may be specific to this program as it was just newly established.

The Bachelor of Human Science is actually an interesting case for another reason. Unlike any other participating programs, it has 100 % coverage of the Framework (Fig. 6). In fact, mapping levels of learning showed 38 % coverage of sustainability as a consistent theme throughout delivery of units (Stage 3, Table 2; Fig. 7). This outcome, combined with the fact that assessments emerged as the primary method through which pedagogy was covered (Table 10), is a fairly good indication that students should leave the program with enhanced sustainability knowledge and skills. Analysis of impact is yet to occur, as the program is yet to be delivered in totality. The broad spread could indicate the inherent diversity of an interdisciplinary program as a strength for addressing interdisciplinary concepts and the benefit of sustainability as an interdisciplinary concept and 'golden thread' in an interdisciplinary course. Additionally, disciplinary teaching must be supplemented by interdisciplinary education, to provide students with the ability to deal with issues that transcend disciplines (Gardner 2006).

Various research has indicated the primary barriers for embedding sustainability into curriculum, which includes: time; sustainability understanding; over-crowded curricula; relevance to course or discipline not being apparent, and lack of support. (LSIS 2013; Lozano 2010). As previously mentioned, prior to commencing work with these programs, the authors had given extensive consideration to addressing these barriers. Having dedicated staff members undertake a considerable amount of the work on behalf of unit convenors and coordinate the overall process was definitely one of the most important elements in breaking down identified barriers. The response from participating unit convenors supported this position stating that the process was not cumbersome. Having a clearly defined process and upfront expectation of time involved was also another positive, according to feedback.

Despite the progress achieved to date, there are still a number of areas for further research:

- Coding identified in Stage 2, Table 2 is open to interpretation, and as such could be construed as fairly subjective. This becomes problematic when comparing program results, and could also explain the differences in areas such as the Bachelor of Human Sciences where Lecture and/or Tutorial Pedagogy (LTP) was quite low (Table 10).
- Alignment with quality assurance processes to capture sustainability criteria through the introduction of new units and review of existing units is a critical element to ensuring sustainability is embedded regardless of what changes occur.
- Evaluation of student experience and learning is necessary, as is determining how this will actually occur. No baseline was established before changes were made to programs involved in this phase, making impact and comparison difficult.
- Capturing levels of learning, and gathering supporting documentation to 'evidence' unit convenor mapping is required. Addressing this aspect covers off assurance of learning elements and provides better understanding of breadth and depth of EfS coverage.
- Further work with units will continue, particularly to track changes unit convenors make as a result of involvement. Several convenors have expressed a keen interest to work closely with us to enhance their unit connectivity with sustainability learning.

Evidence to date indicates that embedding an interdisciplinary concept throughout curriculum is a challenging and time consuming effort, though certainly not impossible. Much of the work needs to occur in the set up—getting the support from appropriate stakeholders and participants, reassuring fears, and surmounting barriers.

6 Conclusion

External circumstances at a global level dictate that embedding sustainability into the curriculum is a responsibility all universities must undertake. The evidence from this initiative indicates that this is not an impossible mission, so long as a considered methodology is in place to support often time-poor academics. Indeed, the methodology outlined is one that could potentially be replicated in other institutions, perhaps with consideration to changes at the local context to ensure applicability and suitability, and take advantage of existing or occurring opportunities.

Having an approach that intended to address known barriers was definitely an advantage. In fact, without sufficient support and clear step progress, the authors question if there would have been as positive an outcome as has been seen to date. In moving forward, the authors believe that while it is a time and resource intensive process to address EfS across curriculum, it will undoubtedly have a positive outcome for Macquarie University, its academics and its students, particularly as employers realise that graduates have more to offer in this space.

References

Engineers Australia. (2015). *Stage 1 competency standard for professional engineer*. Available online at https://www.engineersaustralia.org.au/sites/default/files/shado/Education/Program%20Accreditation/110318%20Stage%201%20Professional%20Engineer.pdf. Accessed February 10, 2015.

Fallows, S., & Steven, C. (2000). Building employability skills into the higher education curriculum: A university-wide initiative. *Education+Training, 42*(2), 75–83. doi:10.1108/00400910010331620

Gardner, H. (2006). *Five minds for the future*. Boston, Mass: Harvard Business School Press.

Greig, A. J. (2015). Making sustainability part of every student's curriculum. In *Integrative approaches to sustainable development at university level* (pp. 27–41). New York: Springer International Publishing.

HEA: The Higher Education Academy. (2014). *Students want more on sustainable development from their higher education careers*. Available online at https://www.heacademy.ac.uk/about/news/10194. Accessed February 20, 2015.

Johnston, L. F. (2013). *Higher education for sustainability: Cases, challenges, and opportunities from across the curriculum*. Abingdon: Routledge.

Lozano, R. (2010). Diffusion of sustainable development in universities' curricula: An empirical example from Cardiff University. *Journal of Cleaner Production, 18*(7), 637–644.

Lozano, R., Lukman, R., Lozano, F. J., Huisingh, D., & Lambrechts, W. (2013). Declarations for sustainability in higher education: Becoming better leaders, through addressing the university system. *Journal of Cleaner Production, 48*, 10–19.

LSIS: Learning and Skills Improvement Service. (2013). *Embedding sustainability into teaching, learning and curriculum in the learning and skills sector*. Available online at http://webarchive.nationalarchives.gov.uk/20130802100617/http:/lsis.org.uk/publication-content/embedding-sustainability-teaching-learning-and-curriculum-learning-and-skills. Accessed February 17, 2015.

McKinsey. (2014). *Sustainability's strategic worth McKinsey global survey results*. Available online at http://www.mckinsey.com/insights/sustainability/sustainabilitys_strategic_worth_mckinsey_global_survey_results. Accessed February 20, 2015.

Tilbury, D. (2011). *Assessing ESD experiences during the DESD: An expert review on processes and learning for ESD*. Paris: UNESCO. Available online at http://unesdoc.unesco.org/images/0019/001914/191442e.pdf. Accessed February 21, 2015.

UE4SD: University Educators For Sustainable Development. (2014). *The state of the art report*. Available online at http://www.ue4sd.eu/images/RegionalMapping/UE4SD_State-of-the-art-report.pdf. Assessed February 17, 2015.

UNCSD: United Nations Conference on Sustainable Development. (2012). *The future we want*, paragraphs 229–235. Available online at http://sustainabledevelopment.un.org/futurewewant.html. Accessed May 12, 2014.

UNESCO: United Nations Educational, Scientific and Cultural Organization. (2004). *United nations decade of education for sustainable development 2004–2014*. Available online at http://portal.unesco.org/education/admin/ev.php?URL_ID=27279&URL_DO=DO_TOPIC&URL_SECTION=201. Assessed May 12, 2014.

UNESCO (2014) *Roadmap for implementing the Global Action Programme on Education for Sustainable Development*. UNESCO: France

Wiek, A., Withycombe, L., & Redman, C. L. (2011). Key competencies in sustainability: A reference framework for academic program development. *Sustainability Science, 6*(2), 203–218.

Author Biographies

Leanne Denby has been working at Macquarie University in Sydney as the Director of Sustainability since March 2008. Prior to this Leanne worked at the Australian Research Institute in Education for Sustainability (ARIES) as a Project Director responsible for two higher education focused projects looking to bring about change towards sustainability. Since taking on the role at Macquarie, Leanne has incorporated sustainability as a strategic direction for the University, growing from a single role to a team of nine. Leanne also holds the role of President of Australasian Campuses Towards Sustainability (ACTS).

Sara Rickards is the Sustainability Project Manager (Learning and Teaching) for Macquarie University and currently working on embedding and mapping sustainability the curriculum at the University. She has investigated the Ecological Footprint of Macquarie University's campus, buildings and faculties. Sara has benchmarked universities both nationally and internationally in terms of resource consumption and efficiency. She is a biomedical scientist and environmental engineer, which gives her the ability to develop transdisciplinary solutions to complex issues. Sara has worked in various capacities including; learning and teaching, consulting, facilities and operations.

Sustainability in the University Curriculum: Teaching Introductory Economics

Madhavi Venkatesan

Abstract

Economics is the study of human behavior in relation to a resource-constrained world. The discipline is a *behavioral* science. From this perspective, economics incorporates the evaluation of both individual and societal behavior within the context of prevailing cultural values to assess resource use, constraints and sustainability relative to *anthropomorphic* or human-focused resource utilization. However, many cultural values can be described as legacy, defined as an inheritance from a previous generation. Additionally and related, unless there is a continuous assessment and reassessment of and between social actions and societal frameworks, there can be a delay in the needed responsiveness to modify cultural values. The latter statement addresses the need for promoting awareness of the parameters that define sustainable consumption. This paper explores one example of how increasing awareness of the assumptions embedded within supply and demand, as overtly visible in "fair" market prices, can increase awareness of the inherent responsibility of consumption decisions. Using a replicable life cycle cost assessment assignment, the author provides a rationale and outcome for the incorporation of a sustainability project in the teaching of introductory economics.

Keywords

Education · Economics · Life cycle analysis · Sustainability · Consumption

M. Venkatesan (✉)
Department of Economics, Bridgewater State University, 131 Summer Street, Bridgewater, MA 02325, USA
e-mail: mvenkatesan@bridgew.edu

© Springer International Publishing Switzerland 2016

W. Leal Filho and P. Pace (eds.), *Teaching Education for Sustainable Development at University Level*, World Sustainability Series,
DOI 10.1007/978-3-319-32928-4_3

1 Introduction

By definition the concept of sustainability incorporates the intertemporal allocation of resources through a holistically assessed strategic utilization rate that includes environmental and social justice parameters. From the Brundtland Report (WCED 1987):

> Sustainable development is development that meets the needs of the present without compromising the ability of future generations to meet their own needs. It contains within it two key concepts:
>
> - The concept of **needs**, in particular the essential needs of the world's poor, to which overriding priority should be given; and
> - The idea of **limitations** imposed by the state of technology and social organization on the environment's ability to meet present and future needs. (p. 43)

Economics plays a significant role in the establishment of sustainable development. However, in viewing production and consumption from the perspective of supply, demand and market price, the assumptions related to consumer behavior theoretically enable sustainable outcomes to the extent that consumers are aware of the inherent responsibility of their consumption and are knowledgeable with respect to the impact of consumption on both the environment and social welfare.

In the United States, consumption contributes to over 65 % of gross domestic product (GDP), which since the 1940s has been the international metric for economic progress. Given this linkage and the corresponding focus on GDP growth as a proxy for progress, consumption decisions can have a significant ripple effect throughout a single economy and ultimately the finite global resource base, making consumption-led growth a potential limiting factor to sustainable development. Consider for example the use of milk cartons.

Lined, printed-paper cartons were created for the transport and preservation of beverages from the production to the consumption stage. However, the components of the carton were not developed with waste disposal in mind, rather increasing distribution, shelf life and ultimately sales were the rationale for the carton. As a result, largely due to the basis of its creation, the paper beverage carton serves a consumption purpose, consideration of the impact to the environment and potential future human and animal health as it relates to its composition and waste has largely been an after thought until the present period. This illustration on a broaderconsumption scale provides a simplified perspective to evaluate the underlying values captured in consumption decisions. From this perspective, production for consumption may be expressed as a myopic activity, focused on near-term satiation of a need or want to the exclusion of the evaluation of the impact or ripple effect of the satiation.

The values embedded and communicated within demand and supply, determine the manner in which a need or want is attained. To the extent that there is no discussion of the values and behavioral factors assumed and reflected in demand and supply, arguably, implicit values, the values and the subsequent behaviors become endogenous to the economic system. From this perspective, explicit awareness of present behavioral assumptions inclusive of the "unlimited wants" of consumers, profit maximization motivations of producers, and the understated resource depletion resulting from externalized or under enumerated costs, offer the potential to modify active and embedded behavior.

In this paper, the author addresses how the teaching of introductory economics can raise awareness of the significance of consumption behavior as the activity relates to sustainability, where the definition of sustainability is adopted from the United States Environmental Protection Agency (EPA) (n.d.): "Sustainability creates and maintains the conditions under which humans and nature can exist in productive harmony, that permit fulfilling the social, economic and other requirements of present and future generations." Following a brief review the present state of introductory economics instruction, the case is made and an example provided of how integration of sustainability as a value embedded within the consumption discussion can influence economic outcomes as these relate to the inter-temporal allocation of resources consistent with the EPA's definition of sustainability. The discussion and example are specific to a single case study involving the instruction of Principles of Microeconomics; however, the methods used are replicable across disciplines.

2 The Present State of Introductory Economics Instruction

Introductory economics is typically comprised of Principles of Microeconomics and Principles of Macroeconomics. The former course focuses on the rationale for decision-making behavior on the part of the consumer and the firm. The latter focuses on the aggregate factors that define economic progress as this concept relates to the "standard" expenditure-based variable of quantifying growth, gross domestic product (GDP). Both courses incorporate elements of Microeconomics to establish the foundation for the assumptions of individual and firm behavior where such behavior is guided by a "rational" agent assumption and the underlying premise of rational decision-making is defined as maximizing return while minimizing cost. The explicit discussion of the embedded assumptions guiding the behavior of the decision-maker is usually not a part of the teaching process. Typically as noted by Knoedler and Underwood (2003), that the assumption of insatiable want may be a taught and learned behavior, which is reinforced through the economic market model is not even addressed in economics. Additionally, alternative scenarios where satiation can be attained without maximization of consumption are not addressed. Nelson (1995) states, "The possibility that consumption should be reduced because the act of consumption is not good for the soul, or is not what actually makes people happy, has no place within the economic value system." As a result, to the extent that individual economic agents, producers or consumers of a good or service, are bounded by rationality that does not include addressing the impact of externalized (i.e. non-quantified costs) the economic discussion does not promote or position the assessment of alternative outcomes (Daly 1996, 2014; Dietz and O'Neill 2013). Implicitly and endogenously, the economic discussion establishes and maintains consumption to production circular flow, focusing on the gratification of consumption and profit taking from production, seemingly eliminating responsibility and assessment of externalities and holistic dynamics as a part of the cycle.

Returning to the beverage carton example, the economic discussion would be limited to the utility gained from consuming the beverage and the corresponding profit maximization of the producer. Waste would be regarded as an externality rather than an endogenous aspect of the decision making process. Additionally, production costs would be assumed to be priced into the product, through efficient market assumptions, to yield a fair market price that embodies the totality of the product life cycle cost (i.e. from the point of extraction to production distribution, consumption and waste). In net consumers would expect that the purchase price is indicative of the holistic cost of the product and producers would view production costs as being related to the market price of inputs not environmental impacts during or as part of the life cycle of the good. However, the assumption of the fairness of the market price would only be able to be evidenced in real terms if consumers were aware of the production process and policed the preference for the inclusion of externalities in demand, which is inconsistent with the present reality. As Nelson (1995) notes, the factors that are included in an economic evaluation are limited to the tangible quantifiable costs and costs are overlooked where either a market or regulatory oversight has not provided a monetary justification. From this perspective, the market mechanism disenfranchises the consumer from the welfare of those impacted by his/her consumption and promotes the perception that price alone is indicative of the true cost of a good.

3 Establishing a Foundation for the Incorporation of Sustainability in Introductory Economics

The failure in present market mechanisms as they relate to the outcome and promotion of sustainable development may be directly attributed to the cultural values that are embedded within consumer demand and producer supply. The significance of this affirmation rests in the potential for education to promote augmentation of cultural values to be consistent with sustainable outcomes. In essence, teaching sustainability requires guidance in adopting cultural changes, including social and lifestyle changes, necessary to achieve sustainability via sustainable economic development as noted by UNESCO (2000):

> Culture shapes the way we see the world. It therefore has the capacity to bring about the change of attitudes needed to ensure peace and sustainable development which, we know, form the only possible way forward for life on planet Earth. Today, that goal is still a long way off. A global crisis faces humanity at the dawn of the 21st century, marked by

> increasing poverty in our asymmetrical world, environmental degradation and short sightedness in policy-making. Culture is a crucial key to solving this crisis. (p. Preface).

A discussion related to the role of culture in fostering sustainability within higher education, provides context for an assignment, which is the focus of this paper, related to the integration of sustainability values within the Principles of Microeconomics curriculum. The assignment promotes an explicit understanding of consumerism and economic growth within the context of implicit values depicted in market pricing for goods and services. Further the assignment provides a foundation to students in how the implicit delegation of consumer responsibilities for responsible consumption have fostered the degradation, exploitation and depletion of global resources yielding the unsustainable outcomes presently observable. The assignment as has been deployed, engages students to realize the significance of market price on unsustainable consumption in conjunction with the power of consumer demand to foster and establish a sustainable future.

However, to facilitate the introductory background for the assignment, students are expected to be familiar with the following foundational economic concepts:

- Definition of economics;
- Definitions of supply and demand; law of supply; law of demand and embedded assumptions in supply and demand curves;
- Historic evolution of gross domestic product (GDP) from production capacity measure to an indicator of global economic progress;
- Definition of the expenditure equation of GDP;
- Assumptions of consumer and firm (i.e. business or producer) behavior;
- Assumption of equilibrium market price related to price accuracy and the cost of products and services;
- Potential for market prices to under-remunerate true costs and thereby allow for unsustainable consumption;
- Definition of externality and how externalizing of costs facilitates unsustainable consumption.

Additionally, students should be aware of the three assumptions embedded in the classical definitions of consumer, firm and market behavior: (1) "unlimited wants" on the part of the consumer, (2) market price efficiency, which is the implied view that market price at equilibrium adequately assesses production and consumption costs, and (3) producer motivation to minimize costs and maximize revenue (profit), in part by maximizing externalities, often with unsustainable outcomes. A key issue and focal point of the assignment is how externalities relate to the price of a good or service, whereby non-quantified costs (i.e., externalities) essentially subsidize (i.e., reduce) the market price, and thereby promote unsustainable resource utilization rates (Hards 2011; Fischer et al. 2012; Sen 2010; and Venkatesan 2015). In conjunction with the aforementioned concepts and the arguable endogeneity of the assumptions, an inclusion of the historical perspective of the classical principles is advocated for inclusion, to provide a contextual representation of the anachronistic capacity of the present state of the teaching of the principles of economics (Venkatesan 2015).

Evaluating the historical cultural progression of human society can promote a stronger understanding of the economic relationship with resource allocation, both intra- and inter- society, and most importantly provide insights with respect to how perceptions of the world are shaped through cultural frameworks at a given point in time. The pace at which cultural attributes evolve may also provide a deeper understanding of why institutional and social frameworks may be inconsistent with the manifestation of contemporary challenges.

4 Incorporating Sustainability Culture in Higher Education, Class by Class

Many educational institutions have started to integrate or create stand alone sustainability programs. Specific to the intent of the inclusion of sustainability, it would appear that the primary channel for promoting viable sustainability initiatives would include a holistic sustainability curriculum along with inclusion of institutionalized sustainability. There are many methods of establishing sustainability initiatives on a campus-wide basis and these can include formation of an oversight function for facilities and institutional integration related to a defined Sustainability Mission Statement via the creation of a Director of Sustainability to establishment and funding of student-led Green Teams charged with developing and deploying initiatives targeted at the student body. However, institutionalization, though advocated, is beyond the scope of the present discussion and is only presented here from the perspective of establishing a self-reinforcing culture that supports the curriculum in which sustainability values are implicitly incorporated and explicitly addressed. Further given that this paper addresses the incorporation of sustainability from a single course perspective, the inclusion of remarks related to a holistic deployment of sustainability serve to acknowledge the need for an overarching sustainability strategy. Having a stand alone program without a holistic support framework within the institution challenges the adoption of sustainability as an individual pursuit, while incorporating sustainability within the operational structure of an institution establishes a cultural value.

Consistent with the scope of this paper, development of a sustainability curriculum that incorporates cultural values is advocated on a discipline-by-discipline basis given each discipline's unique intersection with sustainability values. For example, the inclusion of sustainability within philosophy could include the transformation of moral philosophy as it relates to economic practices and intrinsic value of living resources, while the inclusion of sustainability in economics could incorporate an evaluation of the "fairness" of trade, the impact of the non-capture of externalities in pricing, and the assumptions of consumer insatiability. Creating curriculum where the value of and for sustainable outcomes is both implicit and explicitly compared to current practices will promote stronger awareness and the reinforcement of sustainable values across a student's course load. In turn this will promote a favorable environment for individual awareness and change, leading hopefully, to the potential for a coalescing of individuals to establish a cultural practice of campus sustainability. The inclusion of which could then either further enable institutional objectives or be a catalyst for the creation of the same.

5 Principles of Microeconomics: Sustainability Integration Case Study

As part of a semester long Principles of Microeconomics course, students were introduced to the economic concepts of supply and demand and the implicit assumptions embedded in each: the profit motivations of producers (supply) and the insatiable wants of consumers (demand). Included in the discussion were the characteristics that define supply and demand, such as, preferences and income on the part of the consumer, and resource access and production capacity on the part of the producer. In addition, students were familiarized with the concepts of *marketed demand* and the culture of *consumerism* which defines the U.S. economy to increase their conscious awareness that consumption decisions may not reflect need or even wants but manufactured wants stemming from marketing, advertising, and the media or cultural values that promote consumption as a leisure activity.

Specific to the assumption of consumer insatiability, through a discussion of the role of consumerism as part of a cultural foundation for consumption choices, students became explicitly acquainted with the values embedded in the exercising of demand and supply, the influence of marketing and advertising on demand, as well as, the potential inconsistency between producer incentives and consumer values as they may relate to sustainability. The guided discussion of these concepts promoted student engagement in self-evaluation of consumption decisions; assessment of the sustainability of consumption decisions; and promotion of the importance of consumer behavior in establishing sustainable consumption. The goal of this activity was to increase awareness of the implicit values promoted through present consumption behavior within the broader context of a consumerism-based culture. With a foundational understanding of the basis of individual consumption behavior, students were then challenged to evaluate and exercise the responsibility inherent in their consumption decisions within the context of the role of cultural influence.

5.1 Life Cycle Assessment Assignment

The life cycle assessment assignment was introduced following foundational understanding in economic theory and corresponding behavioral assumptions. The assignment's goal was to provide students with an opportunity to tangibly assess whether or not the market price of a beverage they routinely consumed represented a sustainable price or instead represented a net price after allocation of externalities to other societies and the environment. Students picked beverages from Red Bull to milk. The learning outcomes (LO) of the assignment were stated on the assignment and included in the syllabus description of the project. The learning outcomes included:

LO1: Recognize externalities incurred in the production of a product and relate these to the price paid for the product.
LO2: Question the sustainability of consumption choices through a life cycle evaluation of the costs of production, distribution, consumption and waste.
LO3: Explain the consumer's role in promoting a sustainable economic outcome.
LO4: Articulate potential inconsistencies between consumer and producer incentives.

The assignment, which was distributed with the course syllabus and was scheduled to be addressed mid-semester, explicitly engaged students in an analysis of their own consumption motivations (i.e. need, want, marketed demand, etc.) in conjunction with explicit evaluation of the sustainability of a specific consumption choice. The assignment was carried out through a qualitative assessment of the life cycle costs of a purchased good and by definition, evaluated environmental and social costs from production to waste. Students were expected to assess the qualitative life cycle cost in relation to the market price of the good to then determine if the price paid reflected subsidization by the environment and society. The assignment entailed three parts: outside class research and qualitative assessment of the environmental, social and health impact of the beverage; in class discussion of individual student findings—two weeks after assignment distribution; and a reflection paper, which addressed questions specific to the set learning outcome objectives:

- Does the market price reflect the cost of producing your beverage? (LO1)
- Has this activity modified how you will make consumption decisions in the future? (LO2)
- How can consumers impact sustainability? (LO3)
- Do consumers implicitly assume that producers are factoring sustainable values? Why or why not? (LO3, LO4)
- Which do you view as the most significant attribute to consumption: supply, demand, or price? Why? (LO4)

The life cycle assessment included addressing the life cycle impact of the beverage container as well as the environmental, social and health impact of the beverage. Given the duration and introductory nature of this assignment as well as the assignment's occurrence within an introductory economics course, student evaluation of the life cycle impact was limited to the health impact, water footprint and carbon footprint and students were provided with an Assessment Table to assist in facilitating their qualitative assessment of these factors (see Appendix A). Specific to the introduction of the life cycle of the beverage container, discussion centered on production costs (i.e. use of petroleum in production of plastic bottles) and then the impact of the disposal of the beverage container on the land and oceanic environments, culminating with the impact back to human health (i.e. impact to aquatic life harvested for food production).

The assessment of the environmental impact of the beverage entailed an evaluation of the ingredients in the beverage product, focusing on the assessment of potential adverse and beneficial health impacts, relative to water. This step was fostered by providing students with resources available from the United States Department of Agriculture (n.d.) where students were able either enter the name of their beverage or the beverage ingredient list to evaluate the nutritional benefit both singularly and relative to water.

The water footprint of the beverage was then assessed through the information and research available from public sources, including but not limited to independent research organizations and the beverage producer. This process introduced students to the fact that a water footprint not only includes the water in the beverage but also the water used to grow ingredients ultimately used in the production of the beverage, as well as, impact to water related to use of pesticides and herbicides in the production of the beverage ingredients.

Students also assessed the carbon dioxide footprint of their chosen beverage. This is an area where students made direct assumptions with respect to distance and use of transportation.

As in the case of all the assessments and as stated earlier, given the short duration of the assignment, students were not expected to quantify the health and environmental costs but instead used qualitative evaluation based on their research to assess the adverse impact related to the three areas of assessment: health impact, water footprint and carbon footprint. Two weeks following the distribution of the assignment, individual research and qualitative assessments were shared in class, along with resources discovered by the student as a means of fostering peer-to-peer learning while also enhancing student resources. Following the sharing and discussion of resources and assessments, students were expected to provide a written description of their life cycle assessment, via a reflection paper.

The reflection paper was directed through the use of questions, as provided above, which directly tied to the assignment's learning objectives and as a result, provided students with the ability to evaluate their own decision-making pre- and post- assignment specific to their chosen beverage. In answering the questions specified for the reflection paper students were prompted to use the outcome of their assessment including a review of their research process and their qualitative assessment of environmental factors to explain how they ultimately decided on the justification of the price of their beverage relative to the market price. Students were required to include their Assessment Table (see Appendix A) with the submission of their reflection paper.

5.2 Reflection Paper Perspectives

The reflection paper was limited to a length of three to five pages and students were directed to use APA style to format their documents, including citations and references. Additionally grading was dependent, as noted in the assignment rubric (see

Appendix B), on the quality of a student's response to the questions accompanying the life cycle project. The quality of response was assessed by the strength of the narrative construction, the evaluation process related to the question addressed, and the research detailed in the student response.

From the student responses and as these relate to forming a culture of sustainability, the outcome of the assignment appeared to increase overall student awareness of externalities involved in their consumption decisions. Out of 62 students participating in the assignment, all noted that they had gained greater awareness and 75 % noted an anticipated change in the consumption decisions as a result of the assignment. Student reflections included commentaries relaying specifics with respect to responsible consumption and their individual role in permeating the value. One student, who evaluated the impact of soda consumption noted, "While this assignment has not changed my behavior and choices, it has definitely increased my awareness of the true costs that go into each can, and I will be more mindful going forward." While another student who focused on the impact of price in consumption choices stated, "Before this assignment, while somewhat reserved in certain products for the most part I bought impulsively. Not thinking about what I was actually contributing to, that being the exhausting of the planets resources as well as my own health and the environment's health as a whole. After learning all of this information I plan on really putting in a committed effort to know not only what I'm buying, but what I'm buying into." Another student reflected:

> The way I made consumption decisions prior to Micro and Macroeconomics were careless and unknowing, like most of today's citizens in America. I bought a 1995 Toyota 4 runner instead of an eco-friendly car because I just wanted an SUV. Making the decision of owning a vehicle that chugs gasoline constantly was a consumption decision I was not aware affected anything other than myself. Now, I still want an SUV, but there are many hybrid models that I will consciously look for now that I know how much one person can affect the entire world, and hopefully by teaching the people around me of the same values, I can make at least a small change in our world's future.

6 Concluding Comments

The life cycle assignment as described, provided students with an ability to evaluate economic assumptions with respect to the relationship between assumptions and the prevailing economic framework, as well as the significance of consumption via a culture of consumerism with respect to resulting economic outcomes. An important component of the exercise was in establishing the relationship between individual consumption decisions and sustainable outcomes, essentially introducing to students the responsibility inherent in consumption. Though the outcomes as provided in student reflection papers were mixed with respect to the degree by which the increased awareness would augment present consumption patterns, all students recognized they had an ability to contribute to sustainable outcomes and all students stated that they would be more conscious of their consumption choices and their impact on the sustainability of the planet.

The assignment was designed with an expectation of making the course material more relevant to student interests by challenging assumptions of behavior to increase student critical thinking and thereby evolve individual assessment of values. The outcome of the class promoted the anticipated awareness and from the perspective of course objectives and assignment leanings outcome was a success. However, given the single course focus on sustainability relative to the entirety of a collegiate degree program, the traction of the awareness of students may be short-lived rather than habit forming. From this perspective, it is highly recommended that collegiate institutions adopt sustainability values within at minimum all core or required course work to ensure that students are at minimum being engaged in more than one classroom setting. In addition, it is recommended that institutions incorporate active facilities-based sustainability practices such that sustainability automatically is fostered as a campus cultural behavior.

As noted by UNESCO (2000) and evident in the historical progression of global consumerism, culture plays a significant role in fostering and maintaining sustainability. However, the education of the importance and significance of culture needs to be updated and routinely communicated to ensure the maintenance of sustainable practices.

6.1 Economics as a Catalyst

The present global status of recognized environmental degradation, exploitation and resource depletion tied to understating of resource costs and ultimately the pursuit of a narrowly defined consumption-based metric of economic progress, gross domestic product, has promoted an increased multidisciplinary interest in sustainability. By definition the concept of sustainability incorporates the intertemporal allocation of resources through a holistically assessed strategic utilization rate that includes environmental and social justice parameters. The curriculum exercise shared in this paper provides a significant step forward with respect to the explicit introduction of sustainability into Principles of Microeconomics curriculum. The results obtained are consistent with expectations and promote the creation of sustainable rational agent behavior.

The defining of sustainability is in close alignment with the objective of the discipline of economics. Economics is the study of human behavior in relation to a resource-constrained world. The ability of economics to add value to sustainability objectives requires the insertion of value parameter or normative thinking in conjunction with the positive or observational stance adopted by the discipline. The catalyst for the value based practice of economic rests with the ability to promote an understanding of the discipline, establish pervasive rational agent behavior in the economy and promote attainment of optimal social and environmental outcomes rather than observationally recording the realization of the theory of second best.

The assignment provided in this paper aligns with the ability of economics to provide a tangible student connection to the role, importance and significance of sustainable consumption; however, the life cycle approach is replicable across other disciplines as various components of the assignment can be stressed to promote an understanding of the interdisciplinary nature of sustainability. In a natural science course, for example, the externalities assessment could be broadened to more deeply explore the environmental footprint of production on both human and ecosystem health.

Though the case study provided here focused on a limited number of students within a requirement-fulfilling introductory course in the discipline of economics, the awareness that the assignment promoted should not be diminished. What was made evident through the assignment was that exercises, which promote tangibility to sustainability, can foster an understanding of the role of culture (values) to ultimately promote modification of behavior in favor of sustainable outcomes.

Appendix A: Assessment Table

Students are requested to populate the table below using a scale of 1 (minimal) to 3 (significant) where scoring is based on justifiable evaluation of the impact of the beverage on the stated category and impact grouping. For example, if the beverage uses 10 gallons of water in the production of an ounce, you may view this as a 3 for the category production and impact grouping water footprint. The table will be used in the in-class group discussion and should be attached to the student reflection essay.

Good: beverage—cola/soda	Water footprint	Carbon footprint	Human health impact	Natural resource impact
Production				
Distribution detail impacts specific to the distribution of the final good				
Consumption detail impacts from the point of consumer purchase to disposal				
Disposal detail impacts from the point of waste disposal; waste incineration or landfill; impact of packaging disposal-impact of recycling				

Appendix B: Assignment Learning Outcomes—Instructor Evaluation

The rubric provided below is to be used in evaluating the student reflection essay. All categories are tied to the stated learning outcomes of the assignment.

Learning outcome	Excellent score: 4	Good score: 3	Average score: 2	Poor score: 1
Recognize externalities incurred in the production of a product and relate these to the price paid for the product				
Question the sustainability of consumption choices through a life cycle evaluation that includes production, distribution, consumption and waste		.		
Explain the consumer's role in promoting a sustainable economic outcome				
Articulate the potential for inconsistency between incentives for the producer relative to the consumer				

References

Daly, H. E. (1996). *Beyond growth: The economics of sustainable development*. Boston, MA: Beacon.

Daly, H. E. (2014). *From uneconomic growth to a steady-state economy*. Northampton, MA: Edward Elgar.

Dietz, R., & O'Neill, D. W. (2013). *Enough is enough: Building a sustainable economy in a world of finite resources*. San Francisco, CA: Berrett-Koehler Publishers. Inc.

Fischer, J., Dyball, R., Fazey, I., Gross, C., Dovers, S., Ehrlich, P. R., et al. (2012). Human behavior and sustainability. *Frontiers in Ecology and the Environment, 10*(3), 153–160.

Hards, S. (2011). Social practice and the evolution of personal environmental values. *Environ. Values, 20*, 23–42.

Knoedler, J. T., & Underwood, D. A. (2003). Teaching the Principles of Economics: A Proposal for a Multi-Paradigmatic Approach. *Journal of Economic Issues, 37*(3), 697–725.

Nelson, R. H. (1995). Sustainability, Efficiency, and God: Economic Values and the Sustainability Debate. *Annual Review of Ecology and Systematics, 26*, 135–154.

Sen, A. (2010). Adam Smith and the contemporary world. *Erasmus Journal for Philosophy and Economics, 3*(1), 50–67.

UNESCO Culture Sector. (2000). *World culture report*. Paris: France.

United States Department of Agriculture. (n.d.). *SuperTracker*. Retrieved from https://www.supertracker.usda.gov

United States Environmental Protection Agency. (n.d.). *Sustainability*. Retrieved from http://www.epa.gov/sustainability/

Venkatesan, M. (2015). *Economic principles: A primer, A foundation in sustainable practices*. Mathews, NC: Kona Publishing.

World Commission on Environment and Development (WCED). (1987). *Our common future*. Oxford, U.K.: Oxford University Press.

Author Biography

Madhavi Venkatesan is a faculty member in the Department of Economics at Bridgewater State University. Her present academic interests are specific to the integration of sustainability into the economics curriculum and she is currently pursuing scholarly interests in sustainable development. Prior to re-entering academics, Madhavi held senior level positions in investor relations for three Fortune 250 companies. In this capacity she was a key point of contact for investors and stakeholders and was instrumental in the development of socially responsible investing strategies and corporate social responsibility reporting. Madhavi started her financial services career after completing her post-doctoral fellowship at Washington University in St. Louis. She has a PhD in Economics from Vanderbilt University and a Masters in Sustainability and Environmental Management from Harvard University.

Strengths and Weaknesses of an E-learning Program in Environmental Sciences at Universidade Aberta, Portugal

Ana Paula Martinho, Paula Vaz-Fernandes, Carla Padrel de Oliveira, Paula Bacelar-Nicolau, Ulisses Miranda Azeiteiro and Sandra Caeiro

Abstract

Earlier research studies have shown that e-learning higher education is a powerful system within teaching and education for sustainable development. In spite of the advantages of independency of time and place, compared to traditional face to face, some barriers are found showing the importance of evaluating the effectiveness of e-learning system. This paper aims to assess the strengths and weaknesses of the 1st cycle undergraduate program of environmental sciences at the Portuguese Distance Learning Education University

A.P. Martinho (✉) · P. Vaz-Fernandes · C.P. de Oliveira · P. Bacelar-Nicolau
U.M. Azeiteiro · S. Caeiro
Department of Sciences and Technology, Universidade Aberta, Lisbon, Portugal
e-mail: aptm@uab.pt

S. Caeiro
e-mail: scaeiro@uab.pt

A.P. Martinho
Laboratory of Distance Education and e-Learning, Universidade Aberta, Lisbon, Portugal

P. Vaz-Fernandes
Centre for Public Policy and Administration, ISCSP, University of Lisboa, Lisbon, Portugal

C.P. de Oliveira
Centro de Química Estrutural, IST, University of Lisboa, Lisbon, Portugal

P. Bacelar-Nicolau · U.M. Azeiteiro
Centre for Functional Ecology, Department of Life Sciences, University of Coimbra, Coimbra, Portugal

S. Caeiro
Center for Environmental and Sustainability Research, Faculdade de Ciências e Tecnologia, Universidade Nova de Lisboa, Lisbon, Portugal

© Springer International Publishing Switzerland 2016

W. Leal Filho and P. Pace (eds.), *Teaching Education for Sustainable Development at University Level*, World Sustainability Series,
DOI 10.1007/978-3-319-32928-4_4

(Universidade Aberta, Portugal). The methods included (i) data analysis relating to the candidate's enrolment and students' progression from the Academic Office registry of UAb; (ii) SWOT analysis (strengths, weaknesses, opportunities and threats) of the undergraduate program (iii) inquiry by interview to student's representatives of management councils and the university ombudsman to evaluate attitudes, barriers and motivators towards e-learning. Although higher levels of motivation, satisfaction and aptitude with e-learning of the 1st undergraduate program in environmental sciences at UAb were identified, weaknesses, namely the need to improve self-organization and time management. Recommendations to overcome the weakness found are given and new educational and teaching paths to achieve sustainability are discussed.

Keywords
Distance learning · Dropout rates · Sustainability · Higher education

1 Introduction

During the last decade, an increasing number of higher education institutions (HEIs) have been engaged in incorporating and institutionalizing sustainability into their curricula (Lozano 2011; Remington-Doucette et al. 2013). Nevertheless, and besides the United Nations Decade of Education for Sustainable Development 2005–2014 (UNESCO 2005), the Millennium Ecosystem Assessment states that Education for Sustainable Development is still insufficient and that more informed and strategic measures are needed to address goals such as environmental protection (Millennium Ecosystem Assessment 2005). The more recent proposal for sustainable development goals and targets of the United Nation (UN 2015), launched in 2015, following the Rio+20 UN conference, stresses that by 2030 all learners should acquire knowledge and skills needed to promote sustainable development, including through education for sustainable development (ESD), and also increase the supply of qualified teachers.

Many HEIs have integrated sustainable development into their educational activities by designing courses with learning objectives that are clearly focussed upon holistic approaches to sustainable societal development. This requires the development and testing of new types of student assessment methods and changing many of the teaching paradigms to help to overcome the mono-disciplinary barriers to change (Ramos et al. 2015). Lozano et al. (2015) emphasis the need for a more complete, systematic and focused approach to implementation of ESD, specifically on course design and delivery, by using theories of teaching and learning and linking the course objectives, delivery, and assessment to holistic integration of ESD in all courses and curricula.

Educational programs on offer in those scientific areas at the university level, together with novel information and communication technologies, demands of new competences, flexibility, and competition between institutions, created an educational niche opportunity for e-learning. In fact e-learning in Higher Education can give an important contribution for the effective lifelong learning education and teaching of sustainability, in particular for a population of students who are simultaneously full time employees (Azeiteiro et al. 2015).

E-learning is a teaching and learning process, that allows flexible learner-centred education since it is based on information and communication technologies. Those technologies allow e-learning to take place in virtual learning environments where multidirectional communication is possible (teacher-student and student-student) (Pereira et al. 2008). As highlighted by Diamond and Irwin (2013) e-learning is a fundamental area of interest and development that can provide effective and imaginative ways to embed Sustainability literacy through several teaching approaches. E-learning allows the guidelines recommended by Moore (2005) about creation sustainable education at Higher Education, like inclusion of reflective discussion, or problem-based learning; development of personal values of students and interdisciplinary learning (involving students from contrasting subjects) to promote deep and critical learning (Warburton 2003), and using real-world learning to reconnect learners with reality.

However for e-learning students, attitude towards e-learning, self-motivation as well as the scientific and pedagogical quality of degree programs assume considerable significance in their success learning path (Bacelar-Nicolau et al. 2015). In addition e-learning students have to face barriers like informatics' literacy and lack of e-skills (Panda and Mishra 2007), social interaction and cost to access to internet (Muilenberg and Berge 2005), excess of workload and time available to study (Bacelar-Nicolau et al. 2015), and skill development and professional confidence in applying skills in real-world contexts (Diamond and Irwin 2013).

Earlier studies conducted by the research team shown that e-learning for education and teaching for sustainable development is effective, and produce good results in terms of students competences, attitudes and behaviours (e.g. Amador et al. 2015; Azeiteiro et al. 2015; Bacelar-Nicolau et al. 2009, 2012, 2015; Martinho et al. 2014; Oliveira et al. 2012). Nevertheless, those studies also pointed out some weaknesses, namely the fact that e-learning students are mainly a working and adult population that have several barriers that need to be better identified and understood. Also the reasons and motivations for students to enrol courses within education for sustainable development are important to be addressed, so in overall teachers and program coordinator's are able to improve the effectiveness of those formal programs.

Within sustainable development teaching and learning process, this paper aims to assess the strengths and weaknesses of the 1st cycle undergraduate program of environmental sciences at the Portuguese Distance Learning University (Universidade Aberta, Portugal). Several data collection were used and assessed, namely student's data characterisation from official academic Office, teacher's focus groups, and interviews to student's representative of university management councils. The paper is structured in 4 parts: the case study characterization, followed by the methods, results and its discussion, and conclusions and future developments.

2 The Undergraduate Program in Environmental Science at Universidade Aberta, Portugal

Established in 1988, Universidade Aberta (UAb) is the only Distance Learning public higher education institution in Portugal. All pedagogical offers at UAb are integrated into the Bologna European Process and are taught via e-learning since 2008. UAb is a reference HE European institution in the area of online and advanced e-learning using the most advanced information and communication technologies, and a recognised Virtual Pedagogical Model (Pereira et al. 2008). The 1st cycle degree program in Environmental Sciences offered at UAb is a b-learning program, directed to an adult public (over 21 years old), who are mostly working-students seeking professional development. The general purpose of this undergraduate program is to promote and develop a set of professional skills and competences within the Environmental Sciences.

The Environmental Sciences undergraduate program integrates scientific courses in social-economics, law and politics, earth sciences, biology and environmental technology leading the students to the concept of sustainability science. The three years program is composed of 30 curricular units, and totals 180 European Credit Transfer System (ECTS). The first two years (*major*) are composed of 20 compulsory curricular units in science and environmental technologies (40 ECTS), biological sciences (22 ECTS), earth sciences (22 ECTS), mathematics (12 ECTS), chemistry (12 ECTS), physics (6 ECTS) and law and politics (6 ECTS).

This curricular structure provides the student with a broad-based curriculum. In the third curricular year, the student may choose one of three *minors* in an area of their preference: (i) Environmental Management and Sustainability, (ii) Natural Heritage, (iii) Environment and Health (Martinho et al. 2014).

The target audience for this program are all the individuals who are concerned with environmental topics and are interested in developing their knowledge and skills in these areas. It is also offered for technical staff from local and central governmental authorities, managers of tourism units, specially agro and sustainable tourism, managers of small enterprises involved in the production and commercialisation of biological products, employees of small private companies and public organisations that undertake environmental work, technical staff from museums, botanical gardens, natural heritage centres and local development organisations, tourism guides concerned with sustainable projects, people working in pedagogical farms and youth camps and NGO members that conduct environmental work and sustainable development.

The Environmental Sciences undergraduate program follows the UAb pedagogical model in its virtual class regime (Pereira et al. 2008), except for two curricular units (Fieldwork I and Fieldwork II), which include a face-to-face component. In this learner centred pedagogical model, based on the flexibility of access, without temporal or spatial constraints, the students are responsible for knowledge building. It also relies on diversified interactions between teacher and students, students and students as well as students and learning resources in a social context. Central to the functioning of each curricular unit there is an e-book Plan of Curricular Unit, prepared by the teacher. This document is structured into topics, outcomes, competences to be acquired or developed, learning methodology, list of e-activities, timetable for developing learning activities, and list of support learning materials. The semester is defined as a period of twenty weeks, where the five final weeks are dedicated to final assessment. The continuous assessment component (obtained through the e-activities) is weighted 40 % and a 60 % of the final mark (face-to-face final p-folio or exam). The open source Moodle (http://elearning.uab.pt/) is the course management systems used in all the programs. A two weeks online introductory module is available to students before the beginning of the 1st semester, which is intended to familiarise the students with the virtual environment and the e-learning tools, as well as promoting the acquisition of online communication and online social skills. All the courses have virtual class sites, a coordination site for student matters, a coordination site for the teacher's team, an online secretariat, and a virtual "*cafe*" (Azeiteiro et al. 2014).

3 Methods

Case study and grounded theory were used in this study according to a mixed method choice (see Saunders et al. 2007). This section explains the data analyses methods used to evaluate the strengths and weaknesses of the 1st cycle undergraduate program of environmental sciences at UAb, Portugal. Several types of data collection were used and assessed with different aims namely: (i) data from the official academic office of students' general characterisation, enrolment and progression, (ii) teachers' focus groups to discuss the main strengths and weaknesses of the undergraduate program, and (iii) interviews with students' representatives of university management councils to evaluate attitudes, barriers and motivators towards e-learning.

The limitations associated with interviewing, e.g. validity, reliability and generalizability, such as those associated with participant and observer error and bias (Saunders et al. 2007) were taken into account in the discussion of results, and when drawing conclusions.

3.1 Student's Data Analysis

Data were collected from the academic Office of UAb relating to the candidate's enrolment, and to the students progression in the environmental science under graduate program for the scholar years 2010/11 until 2013/14. The data included: (i) student's profile (nationality, region, gender); (ii) students enrolment per academic year and status (dropout, student, graduate); success rate per courses of the undergraduate program. Descriptive statistics and analysis of variance were performed on these data (Excel, Windows).

3.2 SWOT Analysis

A focus group with university stakeholders in terms of the Environmental Science program was conducted to identify Strengths, Weaknesses, Opportunities and Threats (Learned et al. 1969) of the program. The participants, chosen on the basis of their long familiarity with the program aims and functioning, were the program coordination team (two teachers), the director of the department, the president of pedagogical council and the vice-rector responsible by the quality assurance of formal programs at UAb. The following items were assessed in the SWOT: program aims, students and learning system and results. Those items were assessed based on student's data analysis (see heading 3.1) and earlier surveys conducted on student's satisfaction (UAb 2015) and graduates employability (Martinho et al. 2014).

3.3 Semi Structured Interviews

A survey with semi-structured interviews was applied to a non-probabilistic by judgement sample (Barnett 2002), composed of three students' representatives of the pedagogical council, the president of the student's association, and the university ombudsman, in a total of five interviewees. Respondents were chosen on the basis of their grounded knowledge of the University procedures and students profiles, as well as being delegates of the students in the different University management bodies. The semi-structured interview included a qualitative approach (open questions) to analyze 4 dimensions of student discourse: (i) reasons to do the e-learning environmental sciences undergraduate program at UAb; (ii) challenges, satisfaction and interaction; (iii) difficulties and barriers and ways to overcome them; (iv) e-learning experience. The interviews were conducted in face-to-face or using Skype software with an average duration of 30 min, and transcribed by direct note taking. A content analysis was conducted according to Bardin (1977) and discussed according to the theory and state of the art, allowing to develop from the data collected: (i) classification of the answers in categories, serving the survey questions as starting categories; and (ii) integrating categories and their meaning, or modifying the categories to provide new interpretations based on theory. The limitations associated with interviewing, e.g. validity, reliability and generalizability, such as those associated with participant and observer error and biased (Saunders et al. 2007) were taken into account in the discussion of results, and when drawing conclusions. The transcriptions of students open answers were translated from Portuguese to English for this manuscript.

4 Results

4.1 Student's Data Analysis

The analysis of data from the Academic Office for the 4 academic years, from 2010/2011 to 2013/2014, registered a total of 347 students enrolled in the program of Environmental Sciences, of which 29.5 % were female and 60.3 % were male. Their nationalities included Portuguese (95.8 %) and Portuguese speaking countries (Cape Verde, Mozambique; 4.18 %). Their region of provenance were 35.9 % from the Lisbon region; 16.7 % from insular Portugal; 15.7 % northern Portugal; 12.9 % centre of Portugal; 7 % southern Portugal; and 4.9 % from foreign countries.

The data relating to candidates enrolment (Fig. 1) showed an increase of students in regular situation on the Environmental Sciences program, throughout the last three academic years, and a decrease of cancelled enrolments. Suspension of enrolment and change of program were minor situations.

Data from the Academic Office also showed that the student's success rate for completion of the degree has continuously risen during the 4 academic years (Fig. 2). Among the graduates, globally, most took 4 years to complete the degree, although there has been also a continuous shift towards "longer time" (up to 7 years) to complete the degree (Fig. 3).

Regarding the global approval rate per curricular year of the degree (Fig. 4) there was an increase throughout the 3 years of program, from ca. 20 % (1st year), to 50 % (2nd year), and up to 75 % (3rd year). Among the 3 *minor* of the degree, GSA minor has slightly greater approval rates. There was a significant difference on the approval rate between the 3 years; there was no significant difference among the approval rate of the 3 *minor* (Anova, $P < 0.05$).

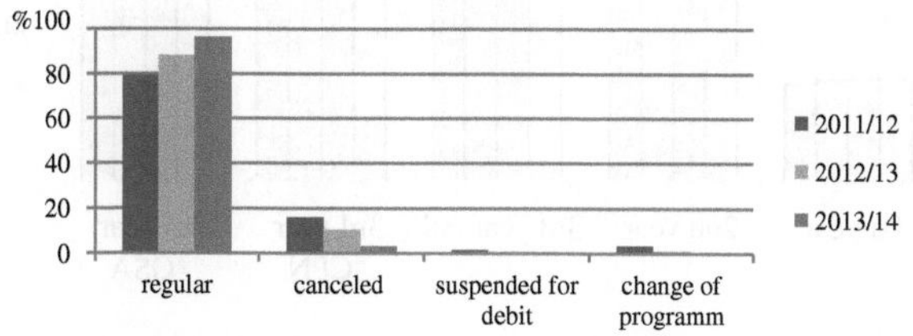

Fig. 1 Status of student's enrolments in the environmental science program

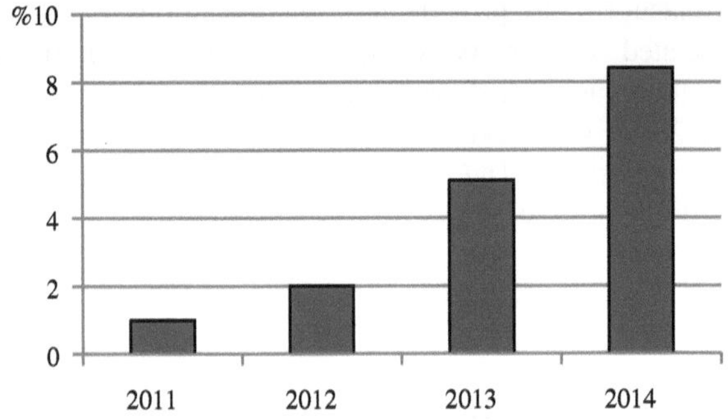

Fig. 2 Student's success rate in the environmental science program (number of graduates per total number of enrolled students, in each year)

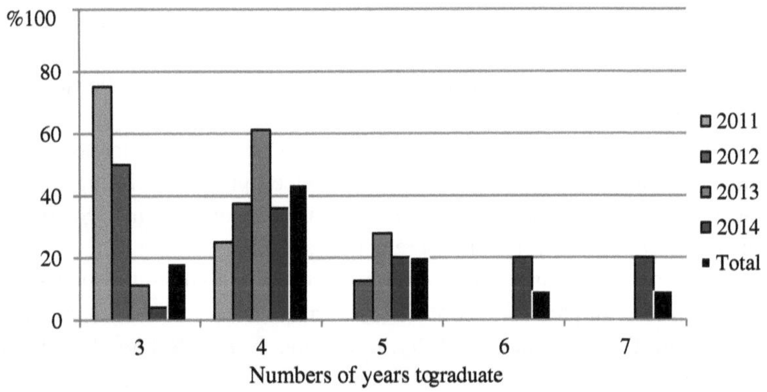

Fig. 3 Number of years to graduate on the environmental sciences program

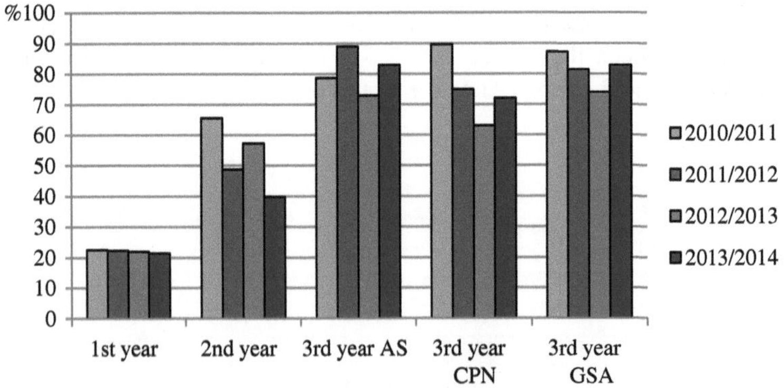

Fig. 4 Global approval rate per curricular year in the environmental sciences program

4.2 SWOT Analysis

Table 1 summarizes the main results of the workshop, which were in line with those shown so far.

Table 1 SWOT analysis related with general objectives of LCA program; the students and teaching learning environment and the results of LCA program

	Strengths	Weaknesses
Internal factors	**General objectives of the study cycle** • Based on the UAb Pedagogical Model, adjusted to current guidelines and international procedures, using the latest technologies and the possibility of network communication • The structure in *major* and *minor* allows students to deepen their studies in various subject areas, and also to continue their training in 2nd and 3rd cycle programs that are offered articulately at UAb • Flexibility of work associated with the e-learning becomes relevant to investment in this training regime, enabling the connection of students with many different cultures, backgrounds and experiences • Training of graduates with quality, at the level of skills acquired in the expertise areas, and at the level of transversal competences in science and technology (soft skills, particularly in the context of the project developed at Work Field II course) • Being a program where the issues environmental, social, economic and governance issues are all considered	**General objectives of the study cycle** • Careful planning and organisation of quality educational resources in digital format is one of the requirements associated with the operation and achievements of the overall objectives of a 1st cycle in e-learning. This may lead to a longer period between the conceptualisation and the achieving of updated resources • Need to improve the skills acquired by students in terms of employability and promotion of a more active citizenship
	Students and teaching/learning environments • Flexibility of distance learning, allowing for study independent of time and space; • The face-to-face weeks within the WF I and II courses increased the interaction already established during the asynchronous learning phase, and strengthen the exchange of knowledge and sharing of experiences of the students, since most are active professionals • Possibility of access to higher education by students with special needs, particularly those with reduced mobility	**Students and teaching/learning environments** • Insufficient comprehension of foreign languages (especially in English) which results in an additional effort to be able to provide bibliography and/or translated texts to diminish this barrier • Difficulty in preparing and organising written work, technical and scientific reports • Need of strong organisation by the students, who have to plan their time accurately, particularly given that the majority work full-time and have family, deciding when to perform the online

(continued)

Table 1 (continued)

	Strengths	Weaknesses
	• Student's integration and guidance/tutoring is achieved in the virtual space of each course, as well as on the Introductory Module (compulsory and free of charge); pedagogical and scientific guidance by the course coordinator, secretary administrative support and socialization space. virtual space of the courses	activities rather than simply present themselves in a classroom at a specific time • Need to improve the disclosure and recognition of the environmental science program at national and international level
	Results • The frequency of a program on e-learning regime is for these students, already in the labour market, important for their training and acquisition of skills and competences, as well as professional and personal development • The success rate of the environmental science program follows the same trend as the success rate of graduates in Portuguese higher education in the sciences and engineering, even in the case of an audience largely made up of working students with high workload and family commitments. This fact can be due to student motivation, the learning model and its flexibility and the multidisciplinary curriculum of the program • Teachers integrate several R&D centres, allowing for the publication, establishing partnerships and providing services to its scientific and pedagogical community activity	**Results** • The total number of students who complete the program is still low; this is linked to the fact that the program is still recent and that most students enrol the program in part time, so very few manage to complete the program within three years
	Opportunities	Threats
Exernal factor	**General objectives of the study cycle** • Contribute to the application of principles and practices of environmental science and sustainability in economic activities, including in public and private organizations, and non-governmental organizations, both scientific and professional or civic (e.g. projects prepared by students under the Work Field II, and within their professional activity in several organizations); • Ability to recruit students from Portuguese-speaking countries, namely Brazil, Angola, Mozambique and Cape Verde, but also other lusophone communities spread out • To deepen the international cooperation agreements for the development of joint	**General objectives of the study cycle** • Current economic crisis, including the labour market and socio-economic conditions of the target population • The biased perception that the area of environmental science is not a priority in economic, political and social unfavourable conditions, may contribute to the absence of students seeking higher education in these areas • The current budgetary constraints arising from the circumstances of the country limit the possibilities of hiring new teachers, which is likely to put in the future problems regarding the sustainability of the program and the renewal of the curricula

(continued)

Table 1 (continued)

	Opportunities	Threats
	programs of higher education, and exchange of teachers and students • In light of the new priorities arising from UN initiatives on higher education for sustainability, there is an opportunity to respond to new challenges at the level of curriculum, campus and community	
	Students and teaching/learning environments • Increase the number of students at international level, especially the Portuguese Speaking community • The current economic crises increase the need for training, particularly in emerging areas of environmental science • The learning model in distance education and e-learning is attractive to capture students located outside major urban centres, as well as those who, by virtue of their professional and family life, lack of time required to attend classroom courses • The fact that the environmental science students work in virtual environments allows them to develop some of the skills necessary to tackle the challenges posed by contemporary societies, whether in the field of active civic intervention, whether in deepening their digital skills • Increasing trend for people to work in virtual networks that enhance cultural exchange and sharing of professional experiences	**Students and teaching/learning environments** • The high cost or lack of quality of Internet access in parts of the non-urban world, precludes potential candidates, especially in the Portuguese speaking countries • Many students return to study after a long period without study habits. This fact causes an increased difficulty in learning and lack of bases, in the particular case of courses like mathematics, physics and chemistry. In turn this fact results in a lower success rate in these courses • Economic and logistical difficulties of students that need to participate in the face to face activities, in the same scholar year (2nd year) to attend WF I and II, although these are condensed into five days, including the weekend
	Results • Due to the characteristics of UAb students (adult populations already integrated in the labour market), the frequency of the program is an invaluable asset for the students themselves, in the acquisition of a diverse set of skills within their qualification and their self-esteem and professional development in the field of environmental sciences. In this way they give the possibility of employers to have qualified people in this area • Increase national and international dissemination (particularly in countries of Portuguese language and expression) of the reports produced under Field Work II	**Results** • Economic and financial constraints at national and global scale, have as consequence that students enrol in fewer courses, so take longer time to finalise the environmental science program • Since UAb has no *numerus clausus* and even with the entrance exams the diversity of students training at secondary school level, causes a low success rate at 1st year, associated with the basic courses of calculus, physics for environmental sciences and fundamental concepts of chemistry

4.3 Semi Structured Interviews

The main motivators that were pointed out by the interviewed student—representatives of management university councils and the university ombudsman—were mainly the e-learning time and space flexibility, the job improvement skills and competences, and the fact that the e-learning regime is adequate and gives sense of belonging to an adult and mature student group. Also, according to the respondents, the environmental science area has interesting and appealing contents. Other referred motivators were the personal satisfaction, the increasing of knowledge, the e-learning fees flexibilities ("you only pay the courses you want to do"; #interviewee 2) and the diversity of contents of the Environmental science program.

The main challenges pointed out by the interviewed students, representatives of management university councils and the university ombudsman, were (i) the student's self-organization and time management, (ii) the attendance of the face-to-face weeks, within Field-work I and Field-work II courses (particularly for foreign as well as for insular Portuguese students), (iii) the self-motivation and the (iv) financial constraints. Other challenges, also pointed out, were "fighting passivity" (#interviewee 2); related with not having studied for a long time, "filling of aloneness" (#interviewee 2), availability of a computer and internet, asynchronous communication ("due to delayed teacher's feedback"; #interviewee 3), putting into practice the acquired theoretical knowledge, in some basic courses such as chemistry, physics and mathematics, and the "need to find complementary materials in the internet to help the learning process of those courses, what is not easy" (#interviewee 5).

Respondents highlighted that the social networks and the face-to-face social activities among students motivated the spirit of helpfulness among them, and helped overcoming the filling of aloneness ("that is easier to happen in the mature and non-competitive environment of UAb students"; #interviewee 3). These interviewees also referred to others ways of overcoming the challenges of enrolling in the environmental science program, namely: studying more, relearning study methods and managing study time, or using the support given by the UAb Local Learning Centres (where students can meet up). The interviewees also suggested that more videos should exist to help studying the more difficult courses (e.g. mathematic and physic contents), as well as for replacing the face-to-face fieldwork weeks, with the support of network of Local Learning Centres. Among all challenges, only the financial constraint is the barrier, which is almost impossible to overcome, according to one of the respondents (#interviewee 3).

All the interviewees were e-learning enthusiasts, and characterised the e-learning program as a very enriching and positive experience, where a great spirit of helpfulness exists, time and space is flexible but also more demanding and where it is easy to share knowledge. One of the students emphasised that he shared his e-learning experience to others by saying "in the present I already find myself in the future" (#interviewee 3).

5 Discussion

Environmental professionals have to acknowledge the different dimensions and complexity of environmental issues, through a more proactive attitude and development of integrated solutions (Martinho et al. 2014). In a globalised context, environmental professionals have to develop social, ethical, creative, personal and interpersonal skills in addition to technical competences to be of value in attaining sustainability (Martinho et al. 2014). E-learning brings new dimensions to traditional education and increases the motivation to learn about environmental thematics. E-Learning for environment courses allows for new ways of exploring and solving environmental problems in an interactive way (Bacelar-Nicolau et al. 2009; Azeiteiro et al. 2014, 2015; Sibbel 2014). The course contents, organisation and learning regime allow students to change their attitudes about environmental domains and to feel they will contribute to others change of attitudes and behaviours. Moreover, it may increase the readiness to learn if the students are allowed to move into new social roles through the course (Bacelar-Nicolau et al. 2009). The results herein reported show a clear student satisfaction with the program they have enrolled in, which is also evidenced by the increasing success rates for completion of the degree, over the last 4 academic years. The low number of students that are completing the program, here identified as a weakness, is also linked to the fact that the program is still recent and the vast majority of the students are part time students, so they barely complete the program within the three years.

The trail to sustainability requires a significant reform on the way environmental professionals perceive and solve environmental problems and the challenge is to prepare those professionals to cope with societal, economic and technical changes, to maintain a job and to have a positive role in the quest for sustainability (Martinho et al. 2014). The environmental sector is gradually moving from an 'end-of-pipe' approach to environmental management holistic process-based approaches, which require an entire new set of technical, social and individual skills and competences (Martinho et al. 2014). The findings of this work linked, with those of Martinho et al. (2014), about the needs of the labour market and the development of key competences and skills for employability, gives very interesting insights for the future of this e-learning offer in the environmental area. In this context, the identified weaknesses "the need to improve the skills acquired by students in terms of employability and promotion of a more active citizenship" is being overcome.

The path to sustainability of higher education systems includes the need for high quality both in science and pedagogy and the need for effective institutional policies and technological initiatives that makes it possible to overcome barriers and enlarge the number and quality of the motivators (Bacelar-Nicolau et al. 2015). The present work clearly reinforces the conclusions from Bacelar-Nicolau et al. (2015) that student attitude and motivation assume considerable significance in overcoming barriers and succeeding training. Attitudinal pre-dispositions, institutional and allied barriers (including appropriate policy initiatives), besides the scientific and pedagogical quality of degree programmes are assumed to play a crucial role in sustainability of higher education systems namely in the environmental area.

To build sustainability thinking into an environmental science and sustainability curriculum, and thus encourage science students to deepen their thoughts of green/pro environmental issues, as well as be more sensitive on sustainability matters, further approaches need to be developed. As pointed out in previous studies the use of e-learning for sustainable development is effective, and produces results in terms of students competences, attitudes and behaviours (e.g. Amador et al. 2015; Azeiteiro et al. 2015; Bacelar-Nicolau et al. 2009, 2012, 2015; Martinho et al. 2014; Oliveira et al. 2012). This study reinforces the need for new e-learning materials for teaching environmental sustainability and this new materials should meet demand for distance/online Environmental Sustainability education in the near future (see Halog and Dishman 2014; Caird et al. 2014) bearing in mind the preparation of educators to teach sustainability topics in virtual spaces (online/e-learning) (see Archambault and Warren 2014).

6 Conclusions

This chapter aims to contribute to the global debate on the implementation of Education for Sustainability and Teaching Environmental Sustainability, by presenting a SWOT analysis performed on an e-learning program in environmental sciences offered at the Portuguese public distance university, UAb. It is also emphasised the role that e-learning can play in this process, by linking pedagogical concepts and curricular issues.

Almost three decades after the concept of sustainable development was formally put in the international agenda by the Brundtland Commission and the year 2014 that was the last year of the United Nations Decade on Education for Sustainable Development (UNDESD), e-learning is one of the areas where some developments have been seen, since it has become more widely accepted in formal and non-formal education settings, with a proven potential to be an effective tool towards promoting education for sustainable development. The use of Information and Communication Technologies (ICT) as a whole, and of e-learning in particular, presents many advantages. The delivery of content is flexible and can be adapted to various circumstances and settings. Furthermore, the use of the internet and social networks have helped to make e-learning on education for sustainable development more available, and also more present in learning and education processes. Finally, the time and space flexibility associated with e-learning contributes even more for its growing use (see Azeiteiro et al. 2014, 2015; Leal Filho 2014).

Attitudinal pre-dispositions (student attitude and motivation assume considerable significance in overcoming barriers and succeeding training), besides the scientific and pedagogical quality of degree programmes, are assumed to play a crucial role in sustainability of higher education systems. Changes to practice that should be made as a result of this research are to improve self-organization and time management by the course coordinators. The use of e-learning for sustainable development is effective, and produces results in terms of students competences, attitudes and behaviours and this study reinforces the need for new e-learning materials. This new material should meet demand for distance/online Environmental Sustainability education (together with the preparation of educators to teach sustainability topics in virtual spaces (online/e-learning).

The results herein presented complemented previous works relating to the sustainability of HE e-learning courses at UAb (see Azeiteiro et al. 2015 for a review), but raises more questions that need to be looked at in more detail. The candidate's and the graduate's socio-demographic and skills/competences profiles need to be investigated further, together with the expectations and needs of their employees, in order to better train for sustainability. Also on this work only representatives of the students and teachers were interviewed. Other data should be collected where a much larger and probabilistic sample should be used (e.g. randomly or stratified selected), namely in terms of students, to confirm the results obtained and to go deeper on the raised questions.

In addition, an alternative structure for the master course is been considered by the course coordination. In the present structure of the master course, content knowledge is presented in separate curricular units, which in core transversal issues of the course are developed in a multi/interdisciplinary way, e.g. including the development of learning activities and projects. The master course has recently gone over the formal evaluation procedure of the Portuguese Higher Education system and this course structure is being analysed again to make a change to a concept, structure and course dynamics presenting science topics in a multi/interdisciplinary way.

References

Amador, F., Martinho, A. P., Bacelar Nicolau, P., Caeiro, S., & Oliveira, C. M. B. (2015). Education for sustainable development in higher education: Evaluating coherence between theory and praxis. *Assessment and Evaluation in Higher Education, 40*(6), 867–882.

Archambault, L., & Warren, A. (2014). Leveraging e-learning to prepare future educators to teach Sustainability topics. In U. M. Azeiteiro, W. Leal Filho & S. Caeiro (Eds.), *E-learning and education for sustainability* (pp. 151–166). the series Umweltbildung, Umweltkommunikation und Nachhaltigkeit—Environmental Education, Communication and Sustainability, Peter Lang.

Azeiteiro, U. M., Bacelar-Nicolau, P., Caetano, F. J. P., & Caeiro, S. (2015). Education for sustainable development through e-learning in higher education: The Portuguese experience. *Journal of Cleaner Production, 106*, 308–319.

Azeiteiro, U. M., Leal Filho, W., & Caeiro, S., (Eds.). (2014). *E-learning and education for sustainability* (290p). In the series Umweltbildung, Umweltkommunikation und Nachhaltigkeit—Environmental Education, Communication and Sustainability, Peter Lang.

Bacelar-Nicolau, P., Caeiro, S., Martinho, A. P., & Azeiteiro, U. M. (2015). Attitudes, barriers and motivators as factors for sustainability of higher education e-learning programs at Universidade Aberta, Portugal. In W. Leal Filho, L. Brandli, O. Kuznetsova & A. Paço (Eds.), *Integrative approaches to sustainable development at university level: Making the links (part II)* (pp. 567–582). World Sustainability Series. Berlin: Springer.

Bacelar-Nicolau, P., Caeiro, S., Martinho, A. P., Azeiteiro, U. M., & Amador, F. (2009). E-learning for environment. The Universidade Aberta (Portuguese Open Distance University) experience in the environmental sciences post-graduate courses. *International Journal of Sustainability in High Education, 10*(4), 354–367.

Bacelar-Nicolau, P., Martinho, A. P., Amador, F., Caeiro, S., & Azeiteiro, U. M. (2012). Online learning for sustainability: The student perception in an environmental science post-graduation. In F. Gonçalves, J. Fernando, R. Pereira, W. Leal Filho & U. M. Azeiteiro (Eds.), *Contributions to sustainability* (pp. 281–294). In the series Umweltbildung, Umweltkommunikation und Nachhaltigkeit—Environmental Education, Communication and Sustainability, Vol. 33. Peter Lang.

Bardin, L. (1977). *Análise de Conteúdo*. Edições 70, Lisbon.

Barnett, V. (2002). *Sample survey principles and methods* (3rd ed.). London: Wiley.

Caird, S., Lane, A., & Swithenby, G. (2014). Developing e-learning materials for teaching industrial ecology. In U. M. Azeiteiro, W. Leal Filho & S. Caeiro (Eds.), *E-learning and education for sustainability* (pp. 105–116). In the series Umweltbildung, Umweltkommunikation und Nachhaltigkeit—Environmental Education, Communication and Sustainability, Peter Lang.

Diamond, S., & Irwin, B. (2013). Using e-learning for student sustainability literacy: Framework and review. *International Journal of Sustainability in Higher Education, 14*(4), 338–348.

Halog, A., & Dishman, G. (2014). Greeninh higher education qualification programmes with online learning. In U. M. Azeiteiro, W. Leal Filho & S. Caeiro (Eds.), *E-learning and education for sustainability* (pp. 83–104). In the series Umweltbildung, Umweltkommunikation und Nachhaltigkeit—Environmental Education, Communication and Sustainability, Peter Lang.

Leal Filho, W. (2014). E-learning for sustainable development: the way ahead. In U. M. Azeiteiro, W. Leal Filho & S. Caeiro (Eds.), *E-learning and education for sustainability* (pp. 151–166). In the series Umweltbildung, Umweltkommunikation und Nachhaltigkeit—Environmental Education, Communication and Sustainability, Peter Lang.

Learned, E. P. C., Christensen, R., Andrews, K., & William, D. (1969). *Business policy: Text and cases matrix* (revised edition, Ricahard D. Irwin).

Lozano, R. (2011). The state of sustainability reporting in universities. *International Journal of Sustainability in Higher Education, 12*(1), 67–78.

Lozano, R., Ceulemans, K., & Scarff Seatter, C. (2015). Teaching organisational change management for sustainability: Designing and delivering a course at the University of Leeds to better prepare future sustainability change agents. *Journal of Cleaner Production, 106*, 205–215.

Martinho, A. P., Caeiro, S., Caetano, F., Azeiteiro, U., & Bacelar-Nicolau, P. (2014). Training and employability, competences from an e-learning undergraduate program in environmental sciences. In U. Azeiteiro, W. Leal Filho, & S. Caeiro (Eds.), *E-learning and sustainability* (pp. 47–58). In the series Umweltbildung, Umweltkommunikation und nachhaltigkeit e environmental education, communication and sustainability, Peter Lang.

Millennium Ecosystem Assessment. (2005). *Ecosystems and human well-being: Synthesis*. Washington, DC: Island Press.

Moore, J. (2005). Seven recommendations for creating sustainability education at the university level: A guide for change agents. *International Journal of Sustainability in Higher Education, 6*(4), 326–339.

Muilenberg, L., & Berge, Z. (2005). Student barriers to online learning: A factor analytic study. *Distance Education, 26*(1), 29–48.

Oliveira, C. P., Martinho, A. P., Caeiro, S., Amador, F., & Caetano, F. (2012). Field activities within an undergraduate program of environmental sciences: A b-learning case study. In F. Gonçalves, J. Fernando, R. Pereira, W. Leal Filho & U. M. Azeiteiro (Eds.), *Contributions to sustainability* (pp. 255–280). In the series Umweltbildung, Umweltkommunikation und Nachhaltigkeit—Environmental Education, Communication and Sustainability, Peter Lang.

Panda, S., & Mishra, S. (2007). E-learning in a mega open university: Faculty attitude, barriers and motivators. *Educational Media International, 44*(4), 323–338.
Pereira, A., Mendes, A. Q., Morgado, L., Amante, L., & Bidarra, J. (2008). *Universidade Aberta's pedagogical model for distance education* © (109p). Lisbon: Universidade Aberta.
Ramos, T., Caeiro, S., van Hoof, B., Lozano, R., Huisingh, D., & Ceulemans, K. (2015). Experiences from the implementation of sustainable development in higher education institutions: Environmental management for sustainable universities. *Journal of Cleaner Production, 106*, 3–10.
Remington-Doucette, S., Connell, K., Armstrong, C., & Musgrove, S. (2013). Assessing sustainability education in a transdisciplinary undergraduate course focused on real-world problem solving. A case for disciplinary grounding. *International Journal of Sustainability in Higher Education, 14*(4), 404–433.
Saunders, M., Lewis, P., & Thornhill, A. (2007). *Research methods for business students* (4th ed., p. 624p). Harlow, England: Pearson Education Limited.
Sibbel, A. (2014). An experience in developing and implementing blended learning for sustainability. In U. M. Azeiteiro, W. Leal Filho & S. Caeiro (Eds.), *E-learning and education for sustainability* (pp. 15–28). In the series Umweltbildung, Umweltkommunikation und Nachhaltigkeit—Environmental Education, Communication and Sustainability, Peter Lang.
UAb. (2015). *UAb en numerous*. http://www.uab.pt/web/guest/uab/uab-em-numeros/inqueritos/ciclo1-2013-2014. Retrieved May 10, 2015.
UN. (2015). *Full report of the open working group of the general assembly on sustainable development goals*. A/68/970. United Nations, http://undocs.org/A/68/970. Accessed September 10, 2015.
UNESCO. (2005). *United nations decade of education for sustainable development (2005–2014)*. International implementation scheme. Section for education for sustainable development (ED/PEQ/ESD). Division for the promotion of quality education. France: UNESCO.
Warburton, K. (2003). Deep learning and education for sustainability. *International Journal of Sustainability in Higher Education, 4*(1), 44–56.

Author Biographies

Ana Paula Martinho Ph.D. in Environmental Engineering (2003), at Universidade Nova de Lisboa, Portugal. She is currently Assistant Professor in the Department of Science and Technology at Universidade Aberta and a senior researcher at LEAD, Laboratory of Distance Education and e-learning, Universidade Aberta, Portugal. Her main research and teaching areas include environmental impact assessment, integrated waste management, environmental ethics and environmental citizenship and participation, and e-learning in science education. She is now the Coordinator of B.Sc in Environmental Sciences.

Paula Vaz-Fernandes Ph.D. in Biology (2008) speciality in Microbiology, at Universidade Nova de Lisboa, Portugal. She is currently assistant professor in the Department of Science and Technology at Universidade Aberta and a senior researcher at CAPP, Centre for Public Policy and Administration, ISCSP, University of Lisboa, Portugal. Her main research and teaching areas include Health Promotion, Nutrition, Food Security and Sustainability and e-learning in science education. Currently is the President of the Pedagogical Council at Universidade Aberta.

Carla Oliveira Ph.D. in Chemical Engineering from Imperial College of Science, Technology and Medicine, London, UK (1991). Currently is an Associate Professor in the Department of Science and Technology at Universidade Aberta and a researcher at the Centro de Química Estrutural from Universidade de Lisboa, Portugal. The main research interests include sustainability sciences and sustainable development and e-learning in science. Currently coordinates the Doctoral program in Social Sustainability and Development and is Vice Rector of Universidade Aberta.

Paula Bacelar Nicolau Ph.D. in Microbial Ecology at University of North Wales, Bangor, UK, is Assistant Professor at Universidade Aberta, Portugal. Her main research interests are e-learning in biological and environmental sciences, and microbial ecology in marine/coastal zones. She is the scientific and pedagogical coordinator of the MSc in Environmental Citizenship and Participation at Universidade Aberta.

Ulisses Miranda Azeiteiro was educated at the Aveiro University, Portugal, from which he received his Master Science Degree in 1994, Coimbra University, Portugal, where he received his Doctorate (Ph.D.) in Ecology in 1999 and Universidade Aberta, Portugal, where he received his Aggregation in Biology in 2006. He holds an Assistant Professor teaching position at the Universidade Aberta (Assistant Professor with Aggregation and Tenure), Portugal, in the Department of Exact Sciences and Technology, where he teaches Environmental Education, Education for Sustainable Development, Biology, Biodiversity and Research Methodologies. He is the vice-coordinator of the MSc in Environmental Citizenship and Participation and also the Vice-Coordinator of the Master in Biostatistics and Biometry at UAb and has mentored over 50 Master's students, 20 Ph.D. students, and 5 postdoctoral researchers.

He is Senior Researcher at the Centre for Functional Ecology of Coimbra University where he is the Coordinator of the Group HISTORY OF SCIENCE, SCIENTIFIC COMMUNICATION AND DISSEMINATION. In the area of Sustainability he is Associate Editor of the International Journal of Sustainability in Higher Education. He published several books in Sustainability Science and Education for Sustainable Development.

Sandra Caeiro Ph.D. on Environmental Engineering at the New University of Lisbon (2004), Portugal. She is currently Assistant Professor in the Department of Science and Technology at Universidade Aberta, where she teaches in the field of environmental sciences and sustainability, and a senior researcher at CENSE—Center for Sustainability and Environmental Research from New University of Lisbon, Portugal. She is the coordinator of the European Virtual Seminar in Sustainable Development.

Future Generations: Developing Education for Sustainability and Global Citizenship for University Education Students

Philippa Watkins and Alison Glover

Abstract

Education for Sustainability and Global Citizenship is a module currently taught to final year students studying for an undergraduate Early Years degree at the University of South Wales. Initially the module focused on giving information about Welsh Government policy on Education for Sustainable Development and Global Citizenship (ESDGC) and similar policies from across the developing world. The focus was academic with some attention given to practical links between government policy and practice. The module has evolved to include greater understanding of ESDGC as a key element in fostering and promoting 21st century skills to Early Years students; such as problem solving, thinking skills and effective communication. This was achieved through links with Zelyn Academy, a school in the Kibera Slums of Nairobi and participation workshops. ESDGC is to be a key component of a new B.A. (Hons) Early Years Education and Practice degree at the university. It will continue to develop links between the school in Nairobi and a local high school, and will be taught through dynamic use of Information Technology, strategies from the 'flipped classroom' and participatory workshops. At its heart is a commitment to the fundamental importance of ESDGC not only as an ethos, but as a core practice.

Keywords

Early years · Education for sustainability · Global citizenship · Pedagogy · Wales

P. Watkins (✉) · A. Glover
Faculty of Life Sciences and Education, University of South Wales, Caerleon, Newport NP19 3QT, UK
e-mail: philippa.watkins@southwales.ac.uk

A. Glover
e-mail: alison.glover@southwales.ac.uk

© Springer International Publishing Switzerland 2016

W. Leal Filho and P. Pace (eds.), *Teaching Education for Sustainable Development at University Level*, World Sustainability Series,
DOI 10.1007/978-3-319-32928-4_5

1 Introduction

The Talloires Declaration (ULSF 1990) and the launch of the 1993 Copernicus Charter highlighted the role of universities to empower people for their role in society, acknowledging the highly skilled graduates, teachers among them, who along with other graduates will "develop the capacity and analytical skills that drive local economies, support civil society, teach children, lead effective governments, and make important decisions which affect entire society" (Copernicus Campus 2005, p. 10). The important role of universities in addressing this agenda has been revisited many times (Cortese 2003; Gough and Scott 2007; Jones et al. 2010; Leal Filho 2011; Ryan and Tilbury 2013).

This chapter focuses on the introduction and development of a module for Early Years students at the University of South Wales, United Kingdom, demonstrating the importance of addressing Education for Sustainability and Global Citizenship (ESDGC) and the journey one university is undergoing regarding this evolving agenda. Sterling (2001) highlighted the role and significance of education as a "transformative agent", with a participative transformative approach and values as opposed to adopting an imposed, transmissive focus (Sterling 2001, p. 38). According to Andersson et al. (2013) and Kennelly et al. (2012) assigning attention to the effective inclusion of education for sustainable development within teacher education can lead to improvements in school education in this field. With teacher education recognised as key in achieving a sustainable society, initial, or pre-service, teacher education provide a strategic opportunity to ensure "all teachers are ready, willing and able to teach for sustainability when they begin their teaching careers" (Ferreira et al. 2007, p. 227).

2 Education for Sustainability and Global Citizenship in UK Universities

The devolved administrations of the United Kingdom, Northern Ireland, Scotland and Wales, all support the UK's shared framework for sustainable development (Department for Environment, Food and Rural Affairs 2005) within their own strategies. Universities in the United Kingdom receive some of their funding via respective funding councils. The Higher Education Funding Council for England (HEFCE) also promotes universities in England and sustainable development provides a focus for challenge across the university sector; encouraging the development of new curriculum approaches and the sharing of emerging practice (HEFCE 2014). Another initiative supported by HEFCE is the Revolving Green Fund established to provide recoverable grants for English universities to reduce carbon dioxide levels and save money; several rounds of funding have proved successful (Blue Alumni 2014).

The importance of embedding education for sustainable development into the academic infrastructure was also prioritised as HEFCE funded a project on '*Leading curriculum change for sustainability*', which produced practical and strategic guidance for higher education (University of Gloucestershire 2015). This project also worked in collaboration with the UK Quality Assurance Agency for Higher Education (QAA) recognising that 'for ESD to navigate in higher education, more powerful ships are needed and they can be constructed using quality assurance and quality enhancement' (Ryan and Tilbury 2013, p. 237). The opportunity to use quality assurance as a tool to enhance the integration of education for sustainable development was discussed by Martin et al. (2010) concluding with a strong message that the priority of education to prepare people for work should be replaced to enable a more "transformative educational experience" (Martin et al. 2010, p. 452). In 2014 the QAA and the Higher Education Academy (HEA) published '*Education for Sustainable Development Guidance for UK higher education providers*' focusing on the skills, aptitudes and knowledge that graduates from all disciplines need, thus providing continuity of learning, as schools also address ESDGC across all areas of the learning environment and curriculum delivery (Estyn 2006).

3 The Welsh Context

The drive from the devolved Welsh Government to integrate sustainability as a key principle for all organisations across Wales (Welsh Assembly Government 2009a), and the recent '*Well-being of Future Generations (Wales) Bill*' provides context for the appetite for initiatives to drive sustainability across Wales. Figure 1 illustrates strategy developments focusing on, and influencing ESDGC, in Wales since power was devolved to the Welsh Assembly Government in 1999.

The '*Well-being of Future Generations (Wales) Bill*' aims to secure the sustainable development principle in law with the governance of public bodies to target improvement in well-being for Wales (National Assembly for Wales 2014). However, although the Higher Education Funding Council for Wales (HEFCW) and local authorities are listed as public bodies within the bill, there are no specific expectations required from schools and universities. HEFCW supports the ESDGC agenda within Welsh universities having delivered several initiatives in recent years, including the implementation of environmental management systems and energy improvements, an audit of university curricula ESDGC content (Higher Education Academy 2009; Glover et al. 2011; Lozano and Peattie 2011) and the development of ESDGC indicators for Welsh universities (Swansea University and University of Wales, Newport 2011). The HEA and HEFCW both assist the ESDGC higher education network that aims to support Welsh universities with ESDGC initiatives.

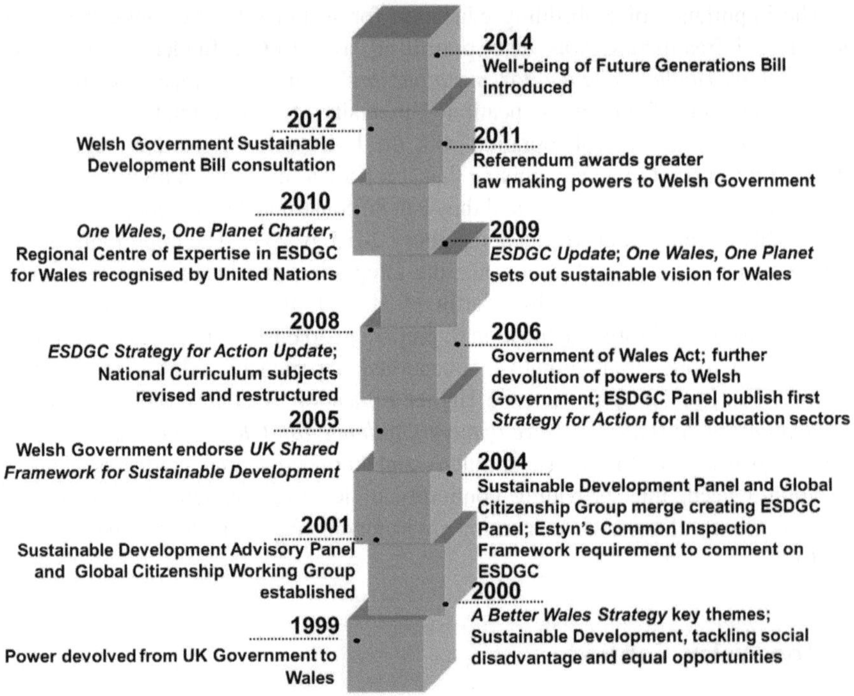

Fig. 1 Welsh strategy and policy influencing Education for Sustainability and Global Citizenship (Updated from Glover and Peters 2013, p. 207)

The Welsh ESDGC Panel that formed in 2004 has influenced the development of support material for the Welsh education sector (Norcliffe and Bennell 2010), and the Welsh Assembly Government issued a range of strategies for the education sectors between 2006 and 2009, as well as funding an ESDGC Champion to drive the agenda. The '*ESDGC Strategy for Action*' (Welsh Assembly Government 2006) discussed each education sector, identified targets and those responsible within the five common areas of commitment and leadership; teaching and learning; school management; partnerships; and research and monitoring. Two update reports recorded progress (Welsh Assembly Government 2008a, 2009b). However, although the ESDGC Champion was funded 2006–2009, the post was not financed beyond 2009. Since 2009 responsibility for EDSGC in the Welsh Government is no longer a stand-alone, but considered to be mainstreamed (Martin et al. 2013, p. 1528). Despite this apparent cooling of impetus from the Welsh Government, ESDGC activities within schools and colleges across Wales reflect development of practice (Martin et al. 2013), this is also supported by findings published by the education inspectorate in Wales (Estyn 2014).

4 Teacher Training and ESDGC

Individuals may enter the teaching profession via different routes; studying for an undergraduate or postgraduate degree, or employment based training; those wishing to teach in state-funded schools in Wales have to achieve Qualified Teacher Status (QTS). The QTS Standard must be reached and presents the knowledge, understanding and skills required of trainee teachers to enter the profession. Two of the QTS Standards in Wales directly address ESDGC:

> S2.2 – they are familiar with the most recent national guidance on the promotion of ESDGC;
>
> S3.3.15 – they take appropriate opportunities to promote and teach ESDGC in all relevant aspects of their teaching
> (Education Wales 2009).

To support the '*ESDGC Strategy for Action*' (Welsh Assembly Government 2006) Estyn carried out a baseline survey (Estyn 2006), followed by a progress report in 2014 (Estyn 2014). Progress since 2006 is apparent in the 2014 report with a clearer understanding of ESDGC evident, despite this further training was proposed for most of the schools visited (Estyn 2014, p. 5). With ESDGC part of the inspection framework it is vital that teacher trainees are not only familiar with, but skilled at embedding ESDGC in their delivery. As discussed, support and guidance is provided for teachers: '*ESDGC A Common Understanding for Schools*' (Welsh Assembly Government 2008b) and '*ESDGC Information for teacher trainees and new teachers in Wales*' (Welsh Assembly Government 2008c). At a UK level TEESNet (Teacher Education for Equity and Sustainability Network) aims to develop a UK wide community of practice in Education for Sustainable Development and Global Citizenship within teacher education in higher education and schools, sharing research and practice with a recently published summary of possible tools to assist teachers in evaluating and auditing EDSGC delivery (Belgeonne et al. 2014).

5 ESDGC at the University of South Wales

The University of Wales, Newport and the University of Glamorgan formed a new university—University of South Wales in April 2013. The university currently consists of several campuses across south east Wales; Treforest, Glyntaff, Cardiff, Newport City and Caerleon with approximately 30,000 full and part time students. There are plans to close the Caerleon Campus in 2016 with courses to relocate across the remaining campuses. Prior to the merger both universities were making excellent progress with sustainability initiatives (Higher Education Academy 2014). For example the University of Wales, Newport, was the first university in the UK to set up an on-site plant for turning waste cooking oil into eco-friendly biodiesel. Since 2007, the university has processed waste cooking oil from its catering facilities into biodiesel. The biodiesel has been used in maintenance vehicles, on campus, and in the post bus, which travels on the public highway between two of the campuses (Glover and Diniz 2010). Following the curricula audit of ESDGC content in 2009 at the university, Learning and Teaching Strategies and course requirements now refer to ESDGC (Glover et al. 2011; Higher Education Academy 2014).

In participating in the Green Academy organisational change programme the University of South Wales increased its drive towards awareness and impact of sustainability initiatives including ESDGC. Existing university activities cover areas as diverse as allotments, green communication technology and student volunteering (Higher Education Academy 2014). The curriculum delivered to students is increasingly expected to cover sustainability, with 80 % of students believing that sustainable development should be promoted and incorporated at their university (Drayson et al. 2013). With teachers educating the next generation it is vital that they are informed and skilled regarding ESDGC. The following example presents an important element of the Undergraduate experience for those wishing to embark on a career in teaching and is informative for others wishing to develop their ESDGC content for early years' practitioners and teacher trainees.

6 Future Generations: Developing Education for Sustainability and Global Citizenship at the University of South Wales, City Campus

Provision of Education for Sustainable Development and Global Citizenship has been a significant element of the B.A. (Hons) Education and Linked Name Awards degree which has been running at the University of South Wales for over ten years. The aim of the degree is to prepare students for a career in the field of education, with specific pathways offered in Education, Inclusive Education and Early Years. At the heart of the course is a commitment to link students' academic learning with consistent, meaningful experience in a number of educational settings. As well as some specific modules tailored to each pathway, all students take a professional practice module which involves spending one day a week, throughout the academic year, in a local educational setting. The students also undertake two 'block practice' weeks each year, where they spend the full week in the setting. This enables students to develop their understanding of the links between the theory studied on campus and the practice observed in settings.

In accordance with the Welsh Government's agenda, ESDGC is embedded in both the learning and teaching of the B.A. (Hons) Education and Linked Named Awards degree on campus, with a specific module dedicated to ESDGC in Year 3 of the degree, and with the practice observed in settings, where ESDGC forms an integral component of the statutory curriculum for all 3–7 year olds in Wales.

Initially, the Year 3 ESDGC module focused on the Welsh Assembly Government's policy for Early Years' education and was taught through a traditional academic approach. While it was underpinned by the Welsh Government's commitment to sustainable development as a "central organising principle" (Welsh Assembly Government 2009a, p. 8), the objective of this module was to deliver a theoretical and critical understanding of the ESDGC element of the Foundation Phase curriculum. This entailed informing students of the implications that ESDGC policy had for wider school issues in areas such as the environment, purchasing, transport policy and links with stakeholders, and ways to deliver lessons on issues such as recycling and healthy eating. Lectures were a mixture of the dissemination of current Welsh Government policy and how it had evolved, as well as examples of how effective learning activities could be provided in line with the ethos of the Foundation Phase. ESDGC is inherent in the aims and objectives of the Foundation Phase as its emphasis is "on experiential learning activities both indoors and outdoors and developing an awareness of the environment and the diversity of people who live there, through Lifelong Learning" (Welsh Assembly Government 2008b, p. 12). Students were provided with guidance regarding good practice through national case studies and encouraged to compare these with a critical examination of similar policies in other parts of the world, particularly "developed countries with different approaches to ESDGC" (SQW Consulting 2009, p. 25). The delivery method remained firmly rooted in a traditional 'lecture-based' teaching model, important for the dissemination of information and policy requirements, but requiring very little interaction between the students and their own engagement with ESDGC.

On reflection it became clear that while the lectures were informative, the approach taken to deliver the module was not adhering to the ethos of ESDGC policy in Wales and the intention of the course to prepare students for life in the 21st century. While lectures did encourage discussion, there was very little experiential learning and with such a didactic method of delivery, very little opportunity for students to develop key 21st century skills such as creativity, problem solving and thinking skills. It was clear that for ESDGC to be understood and engaged with in the spirit intended by the Welsh Assembly Government, and in line with ESDGC policy for Higher Education, the module had to taught in such a way that it was more than just the dissemination of information to students but "an ethos that can be embedded throughout schools, an attitude to be adopted, a value system and a way of life" (Welsh Assembly Government 2008b, p. 4). The role of universities is key in the development of ESDGC "since the students passing through it include a significant percentage of young society, of an age where questioning and forming views is critical, and of those who will be tomorrow's leaders" (Welsh Assembly Government 2006, p. 32). With this in mind it became clear that ESDGC should not be confined to the Early Years pathway, but should also be introduced as an element of other modules that all students on the B.A. (Hons) Education and Linked Named Awards studied. The firm belief that ESDGC "is more than a body of knowledge as it is about values and attitudes, understanding and skills" (Welsh Assembly Government 2008b, p. 4) encouraged a new approach to be taken.

One way this challenge was addressed was through the use of participatory workshops. Students were shown how to incorporate ESDGC into other important areas of learning; particularly in terms of Literacy and Numeracy, and Leadership and Management. These workshops developed the learning skills of students so that the students' approach to ESDGC was seen not just in terms of integrating "ESDGC into classroom practice" (Norcliffe and Bennell 2010, p. 1), but also about the skills they needed for their personal and professional development: skills related to the needs of emerging models of economic and social development which involve critical thinking, problem solving, communication, collaboration and innovation (OECD 2009).

For students, ESDGC has a significant impact on their future employability. A survey commissioned by the HEA, found that 80 % of first year students "believe sustainability skills are going to be important to their future employer" (Bone and Agombar 2011, p. 3). For those students seeking work in the teaching profession, whether it is at graduate or postgraduate level, the study of ESDGC provides them with the qualities and transferable skills necessary for employment (Welsh Assembly Government 2008b). According to the Organisation for Economic Co-operation and Development (OECD) "preparing for the modern labour market requires being able to manage uncertainty and change" with an emphasis not on what people know but what can be done with that knowledge (OECD 2011, p. 3). Combined with this is the requirement in *The UK Quality Code for Higher Education* for students to show initiative and personal responsibility, and to be able to make decisions in complex and unpredictable contexts (QAA 2014).

With the participatory workshops as the first step in terms of teaching and learning, the next step was to ensure the student experience of ESDGC was more in line with the Welsh Assembly Government's statement that ESDGC involves:

> … the things we do every day. It is about the big issues in the world - such as climate change, trade, resource and environmental depletion, human rights, conflict and democracy - and how they relate to each other and us. It is about how we treat the earth and about how we treat each other, no matter how far apart we live (Welsh Assembly Government 2008b, p. 4).

The challenge was to find an approach that would enable students to develop their own 21st century skills as they continued to develop their knowledge and understanding of ESDGC in the Foundation Phase. To achieve this, 'Wealth and Poverty', one of the seven themes of ESDGC (Welsh Assembly Government 2008b), provided the focus. For students for whom sustainability and global citizenship often lacks "a clear and widely accepted definition" (Welsh HE Institutional ESDGC Group 2010, p. 3) personal engagement with the subject is fundamental to ensure "a re-sensitised relationship" (Stevenson 2003, p. 92).

Inspired by the important role Wales plays in the National Regional Governments for Sustainable Development (NRG4SD) and the established global links through Wales for Africa and the Gold Star Communities to strive to achieve the Millennium Development Goals (Welsh Assembly Government 2008b), collaboration was sought with a school in the heart of the Kibera slums in Nairobi, Kenya. Zelyn Academy is a school that feeds, clothes and educates entirely through charitable contributions, 253 of Kibera's most vulnerable children. Taking advantage of technology in terms of video clips (filmed on a camera for which students raised funds) and via email and other social media, students were introduced to the life of some of children who live in a world of extreme poverty. The 're-sensitised relationship' began with one of the directors of Zelyn Academy, Elisha Ooga, filming the journey some of the pupils take to get to the school, allowing University of South Wales students to see not only the levels of poverty, but also the power of creative thinking, ingenuity and entrepreneurship. For example, there is a small road-side hardware business in Kibera, stocked with items recovered from the drains and sewers, which have been cleaned, polished and then put on sale for re-use. This picture of life for children in the Kibera slums made real for the students the importance of other issues of democratic responsibility, linking powerfully to the assertion that "ESDGC seeks to find ways to raise awareness and action to address the consequences of our life style choices and prepare us for sustainable living in the 21st century as global citizens" (Welsh Assembly Government 2008b, p. 3). As a result of Elisha's film, students reflected on their perceptions and the assumptions they had made about their ability to impact on other's lives. For example, a key focus of the Foundation Phase is recycling and students had prepared a lesson on recycling to send to Zelyn Academy. Once they had seen Elisha's film, they recognised their lessons on recycling were not needed.

While the partnership with Zelyn raised awareness, students expressed a desire to be more pro-active in their relationship with the school. They decided to engage with a local High School, rather than the more familiar setting of their practice with younger children, as it would allow them to develop their own skills of collaborative working. A partnership was formed between the university students, the leadership of Llanwern High School, Newport, their Year 8 (aged 12–13) pupils and the pupils of Zelyn Academy. The university students delivered an assembly to approximately 200 Year 8 pupils; introducing Zelyn Academy and the intended 'Lesson in a Shoebox' project. Pupils planned and prepared appropriate literacy/numeracy lessons, in line with the Welsh statutory National Literacy and Numeracy Framework, for which all resources needed to teach and participate in the lesson were to fit 'in a shoebox'. The subject of the project was chosen because it required critical thinking, problem solving and creativity; not simply in terms of what might be important to the children of Kibera for their education, what experiences they might share, but also how the resources might be delivered. The project was a success and a number of very effective lessons for literacy and numeracy were developed. However, problems of posting resources to Nairobi, such as cost, customs and taxes in Kenya, had to be solved, and are still an on-going issue. In terms of skills for the university students, as well as the appropriate communication and collaborative skills, the project helped develop their employability skills, providing them with the opportunity to deliver an assembly to a group of students they normally did not come into contact with and work with other professionals.

7 Development

In September 2015, the B.A. (Hons) Early Years Education and Practice degree replaced the current B.A. (Hons) Education and Linked Named Awards degree at the University of South Wales. In refining a course from three separate pathways into a single degree, the newly validated course has been able to focus on the age that the Welsh Government describes as the critical part of childhood (Welsh Government 2013). The new degree has attracted a high number of students who have an interest in learning about and working with children in the Early Years and has been created with the purpose of developing a highly employable Early Years' workforce possessing the knowledge and practical skills to underpin the Welsh Government's commitment to providing every child with the best possible start in life. The newly validated degree is underpinned by the firm commitment to building 21st century skills into the whole qualification, through content, pedagogy and a firm belief in creative learning. For each module throughout the three year course, clear links are made to Education for Sustainability. For example, the 'Words Matter, Numbers Count' module delivered in Year 1 embeds digital literacy into teaching and learning as well as discreet lectures on how literacy and numeracy are taught in the developing world. In Year 2 the 'Learning for Sustainability' module builds on much of the good practice already established in the current Year 3 ESDGC module, but with a clear objective to develop proficiency in 21st Century skills vital to support a sustainable future. Clear emphasis is placed on digital learning, effective communication skills and innovative entrepreneurship (in the field of education) as core components of learning for sustainability. It is the acquisition of these skills that will create active global citizens, who are able not only to recognise the challenges of the 21st Century, but also be able to offer solutions. For undergraduate students on the BA Early Years Education and Practice degree, these skills will form part of their own learning, but also inform their practice with Early Years' pupils.

The vision to create, innovative, digitally literate, creative and globally aware students demands a re-evaluation of how these skills are taught in the university context. Traditionally, university teaching and learning has been through lectures and seminars. Recently there has been a growing consensus that to suitably prepare students for a world that is developing at exponential speed, universities need to rethink their own pedagogies (Beetham 2008). Reflection on the now closed degree, feedback from stakeholders and students, and the vision of the Welsh Assembly Government have directed the department to rethink how Early Years' education is taught at the University of South Wales. For example good practice observed in the primary and secondary sectors, as well as advice from practitioners through social media (e.g. Twitter) have prompted an evolution in approach. Although elements of lecture based teaching will remain, the majority of the teaching will take on the principles of a 'flipped learning' approach. Flipped learning is defined as a

> pedagogical approach in which direct instruction moves from the group learning space to the individual learning space, and the resulting group space is transformed into a dynamic,

interactive learning environment where the educator guides students as they apply concepts and engage in the subject matter (FLN, cited in Arfstrom et al. 2014, p. 5).

With relocation from a semi-rural campus to a new city campus that has considerable technical support and allocated spaces for Early Years' students, the environment provides solid support for a more interactive, experiential learning experience. Inspired by good practice from the foundation phase, rooms will be set up to support students' learning as well as their creative thinking. For example, each semester, a class room is prepared with a variety of learning resources suitable for Early Years' teaching, which students will be able to use during directed time, but also independently, to analyse and then develop learning resources to suit a variety of audiences and purposes. At the centre of this will be the use of digital technologies, specifically the role of the iPad, enabling students to extend their information technology skills and engage in activities (such as creating digital interactive apps) that can develop questions of identity, access and power, judgement and criticality (Gillen and Barton 2010). One of the underlying purposes of the development of digital skills will be to consider how to keep the resources sustainable, current and suitable for use in the developing parts of the world. The aim is that these activities will encourage independent, creative and 'global' thinking and embed these practices in each student's approach to teaching and learning, or indeed any other career path they choose. It is through the principles of flipped learning, and the wide ranging support that technology offers, that students will become more independent as learners able to develop and refine the higher order skills of problem solving, thinking skills and creativity, all of which are vital if universities are to provide graduates with the attitude, skills and beliefs needed to face the issues of the 21st century.

8 Conclusion

The constant need to improve the teaching and learning experiences of students studying on the B.A. (Hons) Early Years Education and Practice, as well as firm commitment to the principles and ethos of ESDGC, were the main drivers behind the development of the 'Learning for Sustainability' module. The existing pedagogy and mind-set, with its focus on knowledge acquisition rather than skills was no longer suitable if the course was to produce students with the employability skills demanded for 21st century life. It was, and still remains, vitally important to provide an experience for students that meets their needs and aspirations and challenges them to be globally aware. The early developments of the teaching of ESDGC did go some way to meeting these needs, especially with the lessons learnt from collaborative working with Llanwern High and Zelyn Academy. However, despite these early small successes, including the key perception changes of students, there are still other lessons to be learnt. For example avenues need to be explored in terms of being more significant in helping the pupils and staff of Zelyn

Academy and there is a clear need for more joined up thinking and more comprehensive links with others working in the slums.

The writer and scholar, John Schaar wrote 'The future is not some place we are going to, but one we are creating. The paths to it are not found but made, and the activity of making them changes both the maker and the destination' (cited in JISC 2009, p. 4). It is this belief that guides the pedagogy of the B.A. Early Years Education and Practice degree and confirms the importance of ESDGC as an underpinning principle of all we do. Understanding the breadth and depth of what it means to be sustainable is vital if Wales is to face the challenges of the 21st century and meet the goals for the Well-being of Future Generations (Wales) Act 2015. By designing a degree that equips students with the knowledge and skill set needed to meet the well-being goals set out in the 2015 Act, the course will remain vibrant, current and sustainable. This will impact on the individual and create the kind of citizens needed to enhance national and global well-being.

References

Andersson, K., Jagers, S. C., Lindskog, A., & Martinsson, J. (2013). Learning for the future? Effects of education for sustainable development (ESD) on teacher education students. *Sustainability, 5*, 5135–5152. doi:10.3390/su5125135

Arfstrom, K., McKnight, K., Mcknight, P., & Yarbro, J. (2014). *Extension of a review of Flipped Learning. Flipped Learning Network.* Pearsons and George Mason University. http://flippedlearning.org/cms/lib07/VA01923112/Centricity/Domain/41/Extension%20of%20FLipped%20Learning%20LIt%20Review%20June%202014.pdf. Last accessed April 14, 2015.

Belgeonne, C., Clough, N., Inman, S., Rogers, M., Warwick, P., Baughen, M., et al. (2014). Education for Sustainable Development and Global Citizenship: Evaluating and auditing ESDGC in teacher education (Teacher Education for Equity and Sustainability Network). Higher Education Academy, United Kingdom.

Beetham, H. (2008). Review: Design for learning programme. JISC. http://www.jisc.ac.uk/media/documents/programmes/elearningpedagogy/helenbeethamreviewphase2.doc. Last accessed 02 September 2015.

Blue Alumni. (2014). *Evaluation of Rounds 1 to 3 of HEFCE's Revolving Green Fund*. Blue Alumni, United Kingdom. http://www.hefce.ac.uk/media/hefce/content/pubs/indirreports/2014/Evaluation,of,RGF,rounds,1,to,3/2014_rgf1to3.pdf. Last accessed April 14, 2015.

Bone, E., & Agombar, J. (2011). *First-year attitudes towards, and skills in, sustainable development*. United Kingdom: Higher Education Academy.

Copernicus Campus. (2005). Copernicus Guidelines for Sustainable Development in the European Higher Education Area. Copernicus Campus Sustainability Center at the Carl von Ossietzky University Oldenburg and the Copernicus Campus University Alliance for Sustainability. http://www.unece.org/fileadmin/DAM/env/esd/information/COPERNICUS%20Guidelines.pdf. Last accessed April 14, 2015.

Cortese, A. (2003). The critical role of higher education in creating a sustainable future. *Planning for Higher Education, 33*(1), 15–22.

Department for Environment, Food and Rural Affairs. (2005). *One future—different paths The UK's shared framework for sustainable development*. United Kingdom: Defra.

Drayson, R., Bone, E., Agombar, J., & Kemp, S. (2013). *Student attitudes towards and skills for sustainable development*. United Kingdom: Higher Education Academy.

Education Wales. (2009). Qualified Teacher Status Standards Wales 2009. Welsh Government, United Kingdom. http://gov.wales/legislation/subordinate/nonsi/educationwales/2009/3220099/?lang=en. Last accessed March 25, 2015.

Estyn. (2006). *Establishing a position statement for Education for Sustainable Development and Global Citizenship in Wales*. Estyn, Wales.

Estyn. (2014). *ESDGC Progress in education for Sustainable Development and Global Citizenship*. Estyn, Wales.

Ferreira, J., Ryan, L., & Tilbury, D. (2007). Mainstreaming Education for Sustainable Development in Initial Teacher Education in Australia: A review of existing professional development models. *Journal of Education for Teaching: International Research and Pedagogy, 33*(2), 225–239.

Gillen, J., & Barton, D. (2010). Digital Literacies: A research Briefing by the Technology enhanced Learning phase of the Teaching and Learning programme. London Knowledge Lab, Institute of Education, University of London, United Kingdom. http://www.tlrp.org/docs/DigitalLiteracies.pdf. Last accessed September 02, 2015.

Glover, A., & Diniz, T. (2010). Future is due: Reflecting on local and global practice to discover effective sustainability. In S. K. Haslett, & R. Rowlands (Eds.), Enhancing Research-Teaching Links in Higher Education. In *Proceedings of the Newport NEXUS Conference Centre for Excellence in Learning and Teaching Special Publication, No. 3, 2010* (pp. 59–69). Newport, United Kingdom: University of Wales.

Glover, A., Peters, C., & Haslett, S. K. (2011). Education for Sustainable Development and Global Citizenship: An evaluation of the validity of the STAUNCH auditing tool. *International Journal of Sustainability in Higher Education, 12*(2), 125–144.

Glover, A., & Peters, C. (2013). A whole sector approach: Education for Sustainable Development and Global Citizenship in Wales. In S. Caeiro, L. Filho, C. Jabbour, & U. Azeiteiro (Eds.), *Sustainability assessment tools in higher education* (pp. 205–222). Switzerland: Springer Publishing.

Gough, S., & Scott, W. (2007). *Higher education and sustainable development, paradox and possibility*. Oxford, United Kingdom: Routledge.

HEFCE. (2014). *Sustainable development in higher education, HEFCE's role to date and a framework for its future actions*. United Kingdom: Higher Education Funding Council for England.

Higher Education Academy. (2009). *Education for Sustainable Development and Global Citizenship (ESDGC): Review of a curriculum audit in Wales*. United Kingdom: Higher Education Academy.

Higher Education Academy. (2014). *Green Academy 2 change programme 2013–14, An overview of the programme, participating institutions and case studies*. United Kingdom: Higher Education Academy.

JISC. (2009). Effective practice in a digital age. JISC, United Kingdom. http://www.jisc.ac.uk/media/documents/publications/effectivepracticedigitalage.pdf. Last accessed September 02, 2015.

Jones, P., Selby, D., & Sterling, S. (Eds.). (2010). *Sustainability education, perspectives and practice across Higher Education*. United Kingdom: Earthscan Ltd.

Kennelly, J., Taylor, N., & Serow, P. (2012). Early career primary teachers and education for sustainability. *International Research in Geographical and Environmental Education, 21*(2), 139–153.

Leal Filho, W. (2011). About the role of Universities and their contribution to sustainable development. *Higher Education Policy, 24*, 427–438.

Lozano, R., & Peattie, K. (2011). Assessing Cardiff University's curricula contribution to sustainable development using the STAUNCH system. *Journal of Education for Sustainable Development, 5*(1), 115–128.

Martin, S., Dillon, J., Higgins, P., Peters, C., & Scott, W. (2013). Divergent evolution in education for sustainable development policy in the United Kingdom: Current status, best practice, and opportunities for the future. *Sustainability, 5*, 1522–1544.

Martin, S., Jucker, R., & Martin, M. (2010). Quality and education for sustainable development: Current context and future opportunities. In L. E. Kattington (Ed.), *Handbook of curriculum development*. USA: Nova Science Publishers, Inc.
National Assembly for Wales. (2014). Well-being of Future Generations (Wales) Bill. National Assembly for Wales. http://www.assembly.wales/laid%20documents/pri-ld9831%20-%20well-being%20of%20future%20generations%20(wales)%20bill/pri-ld9831-e.pdf. Last accessed April 05, 2015.
Norcliffe, D., & Bennell, S. (2010). Analysis of views on the Education for Sustainable Development and Global Citizenship Policy in Wales. *International Journal of Development Education and Global Learning, 3*(1), 39–58.
OECD. (2009). 21st century skills and competences for new millennium learners in OECD countries, EDU working paper No. 41. Organisation for Economic Co-operation and Development. http://www.oecd.org/officialdocuments/publicdisplaydocumentpdf/?cote=EDU/WKP%282009%2920&doclanguage=en. Last accessed April 13, 2015.
OECD. (2011). *The OECD Skills Strategy*, Organisation for Economic Co-operation and Development. http://www.oecd.org/edu/47769132.pdf. Last accessed April 15, 2015.
QAA. (2014). UK quality code for higher education part A: Setting and maintaining academic standards; the frameworks for higher education qualifications of UK degree-awarding bodies. QAA, United Kingdom. http://www.qaa.ac.uk/en/Publications/Documents/qualifications-frameworks.pdf. Last accessed April 12, 2015.
Ryan, A., & Tilbury, D. (2013). Uncharted waters: Voyages for Education for Sustainable Development in the higher education curriculum. *The Curriculum Journal, 24*(2), 272–294.
SQW Consulting. (2009). ESDGC: Analysis of good Practice in Welsh Higher Education Institutions—A report to the Higher Education Funding Council for Wales. Hefcw, https://www.hefcw.ac.uk/documents/about_he_in_wales/wag_priorities_and_policies/HEFCW%20ESDGC%20%20-%20final%20report%20to%20client%20May%202009v2.pdf. Last accessed April 15, 2015.
Sterling, S. (2001). *Sustainable education re-visioning learning and change*. United Kingdom: Green Books.
Stevenson, N. (2003). *Cultural Citizenship*. Maidenhead, United Kingdom: Open University Press.
Swansea University and University of Wales, Newport. (2011). 'Baselining' for ESDGC—piloting an approach: Education for Sustainable Development and Global Citizenship (ESDGC) Development Framework (EDF) Report to HEFCW. Hefcw, https://www.hefcw.ac.uk/documents/about_he_in_wales/wag_priorities_and_policies/Baselining%20for%20ESDGC%20EDF%20-%20final%20report%20to%20HEFCW%20310311.pdf. Last accessed April 04, 2015.
ULSF. (1990). *The Talloires Declaration*. Association of University Leaders for a Sustainable Future. http://www.ulsf.org/pdf/TD.pdf. Last accessed February 15, 2015.
University of Gloucestershire. (2015). Guide to Quality and Education for Sustainability in Higher Education. University of Gloucestershire, http://efsandquality.glos.ac.uk/project_overview.htm . Last accessed April 05, 2015.
Welsh Assembly Government. (2006). *Education for Sustainable Development and Global Citizenship A Strategy for Action. DELLS Information Document 017-06*. Department for Education, Lifelong Learning and Skills, Welsh Assembly Government, Wales.
Welsh Assembly Government. (2008a). *Education for Sustainable Development and Global Citizenship A Strategy for Action. Updates January 2008, Information Document No: 055/2008*. Department for Children, Education, Lifelong Learning and Skills, Welsh Assembly Government, Wales.
Welsh Assembly Government. (2008b). *Education for Sustainable Development and Global Citizenship a Common Understanding for Schools, Information Document No: 065/2008*. Department for Children, Education, Lifelong Learning and Skills, Welsh Assembly Government, Wales.

Welsh Assembly Government. (2008c). *Education for Sustainable Development and Global Citizenship Information for teacher trainees and new teachers in Wales, Information Document No: 066/2008.* Department for Children, Education, Lifelong Learning and Skills, Welsh Assembly Government, Wales.

Welsh Assembly Government. (2009a). *One Wales: One Planet. The Sustainable Development Scheme of the Welsh Assembly Government.* Department for Children, Education, Lifelong Learning and Skills, Welsh Assembly Government, Wales.

Welsh Assembly Government. (2009b). *Education for Sustainable Development and Globak Citizenship A Strategy for Action. Updates January 2009, Information Document No: 077/ 2009.* Department for Children, Education, Lifelong Learning and Skills, Welsh Assembly Government, Wales.

Welsh Assembly Government. (2013). *Building a Brighter Future: Early Years and Childcare Plan.* Department for Children, Education, Lifelong Learning and Skills, Welsh Assembly Government, Wales.

Welsh HE Institutional ESDGC Group. (2010). Towards a Common Understanding for Sustainable Development and Global Citizenship. Hefcw. http://www.hefcw.ac.uk/documents/about_he_in_wales/WG_priorities_and_policies/Common%20Understanding%20of%20ESDGC%20.pdf. Last accessed April 13, 2015.

Author Biographies

Philippa Watkins is currently a lecturer at the University of South Wales and a fellow of the Higher Education Academy. She worked for 12 years as a High School English teacher, and was Head of English for four years before moving to the higher education sector. She is responsible for the development of ESDGC on the Early Years degree in the Faculty of Life Sciences and Education.

Alison Glover received her doctorate in Education from the University of Wales, Newport where she investigated the impact of strategies and policies on Education for Sustainable Development and Global Citizenship in higher education in Wales. She has taught Geography in the United Kingdom and overseas. She currently works as a researcher and contributes to courses in the Faculty of Life Sciences and Education at the University of South Wales.

Basic Teacher Training Oriented Toward Sustainability: Why and How to Carry It Out Today?

Pedro Vega-Marcote and Mercedes Varela-Losada

Abstract

The environmental deterioration of the planet, caused by unsustainable development and an unfair model, requires a global change on a political, social, and environmental level. To boost this change it is necessary to redirect education, and specifically Environmental Education for Sustainable Development, to educate citizens so that they are capable of making responsible, solidary and sustainable decisions. This requires educational initiatives promoted by higher education institutions for reorienting teacher education towards sustainability. With this aim we present and substantiate an educational teacher training model based on the development of sustainable competencies and on the solving of environmental problems, bridging the gap between theory and practice. Its purpose is to enable future teachers to participate, individually and collectively, in the improvement of social-environmental problems, local and global, fostering sustainable life-styles, through teaching material designed for this purpose. Its implementation and evaluation shows that this experiential educational model promotes and favors sustainable actions in Faculties of Educational Science, responsible for basic teacher training in Spain. It also carries a multiplying effect, due to students' professional perspectives, and it could be the basis for future proposals elsewhere.

P. Vega-Marcote (✉)
Department of Didactics and Pedagogy, Faculty of Educational Sciences,
University of A Coruña, A Coruña 15071, Spain
e-mail: pedro@udc.es

M. Varela-Losada
Department of Special Didactics, Faculty of Educational Sciences,
University of Vigo, Pontevedra 36005, Spain
e-mail: mercedesvarela@uvigo.es

© Springer International Publishing Switzerland 2016

W. Leal Filho and P. Pace (eds.), *Teaching Education for Sustainable Development at University Level*, World Sustainability Series,
DOI 10.1007/978-3-319-32928-4_6

Keywords
Educational model · Sustainable competencies · Teacher training

1 Introduction

Recent reports from prestigious international organizations (GEO-5 2012; Worldwatch Institute 2013) point to the rapid environmental deterioration that is currently taking place in our planet. The underlying causes of these problems are related to human lifestyles. Linked to this is the push for continuous economic growth, based on the developed world's hyper-consumption, which continues to increase as if the capacities of the Earth were infinite (Giddens 2009; Latouche 2011). As Klein (2014) points out, our economic and planetary systems are currently at war.

In an attempt to put a stop to this deterioration, the need for Sustainable Development was proposed, and defined as a way of meeting the needs of the present generation without compromising the ability of future generations to meet their own needs (Brundtland Report 1987). At the turn of the century, the United Nations set forth the Millennium Development Goals and even went a step further by pointing out that development must be socially fair, financially feasible and must not exceed the environmental limits; indicating, also, that Sustainable Development must be global—in order to prevent certain parts of the planet from growing at the expense of others—and all-inclusive, integrating the cultural and political spheres (UN 2000). The solutions to the environmental problems must be sought in the cultural, socio-economic, and political spheres of living conditions, through education (Carlsson and Jensen 2006).

Thus, interest in education, and, in particular in Environmental Education, is growing, as illustrated by the reviews of the field (Hines et al. 1986/1987; Rickinson 2001; Heimlich and Ardoin 2008; Gifford 2014). After forty years of research in the field there are still unanswered questions, aspects needing further study, and some gaps (Reid and Scott 2013). Achieving sustainable development requires communities to change habits and lifestyles, and achieving environmentally significant behavior is dauntingly complex, both in variety and causal influences (Stern 2000).

This necessary change has to take place by empowering people to become citizens who are informed and environmentally active, which should lead to the transformation of the behavior of entire communities and societies (Ferreira 2013). Consequently, schools are an opportunity for developing fair and responsible communities that are respectful with their surroundings. To achieve this, a transformation process has to take place as part of a wider social change that is necessary to address environmental issues (Tilbury 1995).

The role of education is now conceptualized to provide opportunities to develop the capacity to think critically, ethically, and creatively in appraising environmental situations; to make informed decisions on those situations; and to develop the capacity and commitment to act individually and collectively in ways that sustain and enhance the environment (Hicks and Holden 1995; Stevenson and Stirling 2010). This requires approaches: (i) based on students' real participation; (ii) that encourage reflecting on the complexity of environmental issues; (iii) that foster critical thinking on the role of people in the system and the influence of the socio-cultural and economic factors in their lifestyles; (iv) that promote the adoption of autonomous and responsible decisions and (v) that enable the integration of the knowledge acquired in the classroom and in the real life of the communities (Varela-Losada et al. 2015). These approaches have to pay special attention to the factors related to the information that people have for reorienting their way of life and on the possible strategies to follow in order to solve a specific environmental problem. That is to say, their knowledge on environmental action and their capacity (necessary skills) to execute it (Alvarez and Vega 2009). This topic was already addressed at the end of the eighties (Hines et al. 1986/1987), and is being studied more and more due to its incidence in the didactic methodology usually used in EE, and where teacher training plays a fundamental role.

Thus, teachers are an essential pillar to lead this change, for they are directly responsible for the teaching and learning process. There is plenty of literature on the impact on the teacher-student relationship in the classroom (Forbes and Zint 2010; Roorda et al. 2011; García Bacete et al. 2014) as well as on the importance of teachers and other adults as role models for the development of environmental literacy (Rickinson 2001; Stern et al. 2010). Notwithstanding, previous studies also reveal the insecurity and low level of knowledge teachers have on the environment or on educational strategies in the field of EE (Forbes and Davis 2008; Eurydice 2011). Additionally, teachers tend to reproduce previously experienced teaching models, which refer to a transmitting type of methodology (Varela-Losada et al. 2014).

This is due to the scarce attention that education pays to preparing citizens to achieve a sustainable future (Berryman and Sauvé 2013). The effect of university studies in student environmental literacy shows that it is normally very limited (Rideout 2005; Yavetz et al. 2009). Therefore, the majority of the members of the university community are not trained in the principles that Sustainable Development preaches and therefore they are neither aware nor prepared to act sustainably, that is, to acquire sustainable competencies (Tilbury 2012).

Consequently, there is a need for teachers who are committed to environmental education, through the use of uncommon pedagogical methods that are not commonly seen in traditional classes. Teachers need to understand the interdisciplinary and globalized nature of environmental situations and have to be able to place themselves within a critical paradigm (Varela-Losada et al. 2014). Thus, the role of the University in the achievement of the objectives related to EE, as the figure responsible for the proper training of teachers, is quite significant, for it is faced with a profound review of its curricular activities, its management tasks and its research works (Aznar-Minguet and Ull 2009). Teacher training should become a means of information and communication for Sustainable Development, also making it possible to implement it.

2 How Can Sustainable Skills in Initial Teacher Training Be Developed?

To respond to the demands of today's society, the European Union is promoting a new educational model linked to the development of competencies, in our case focused on University level teacher training (EU 1999). These competencies are seen as the ability to respond to complex demands and adequately carry out a variety of tasks, combining practical skills, knowledge, motivation, ethical values, attitudes, emotions and other social components and behaviors that come together to achieve efficient action (OECD 2005). This movement, a feature of the competencies, implies the importance of developing activities linked to reality, the need for social interaction, and the challenging of models based exclusively on the transmission of knowledge (Stiefel 2008). It is not enough to acquire concepts; it is necessary to learn to put them into action, integrate them, and use them adequately under different real-life circumstances. Thus, competencies turn into learning achievements, instead of the mere acquisition of knowledge, fully affecting the teaching and learning process (Bolívar 2009), and particularly the role of the teacher.

In the field of Environmental Education many authors (Jensen and Schnack 1997; Mogensen and Schnack 2010; NAAEE 2011; UN 2011) also point out the need to focus Environmental Education toward the development of sustainable, based on a critical, active and participative view, which can result in citizens who are informed, responsible and committed with the environment and with people, and who can act to solve present-day and future problems.

From this viewpoint, sustainable competencies can be defined as complexes of knowledge, skills, and attitudes that enable successful task performance and problem solving with respect to real-world sustainability problems, challenges, and opportunities (Wiek et al. 2011). But the integration of this new viewpoint is not exempt of difficulties (Barth et al. 2007; Mogensen and Schnack 2010; Wiek et al. 2011), it is necessary to clarify what these sustainable competencies are, and design educational proposals that contribute toward their development in order to evaluate their achievement.

Therefore, we must search for educational models based on knowledge, where not only skills surface, but also commitments and the willingness to act, through educational activities that allow us to (Vega and Álvarez 2011):

(a) build a new model based on the principles of sustainability;
(b) understand the connection between the environmental, social, economic and cultural processes;
(c) be aware of the local and global (glocal) social and environmental problems and their relationships;
(d) train students to analyze socio-environmental conflicts, during the debate to find alternatives and in individual and collective decision-making;
(e) promote the extension of "sustainable best practices" in different contexts and cultures.

Thus, the development of sustainable practices should be part of a framework of research on sustainability and problem-solving (Jensen and Schnack 1997; Mogensen and Mayer 2005) giving priority to the acquisition of an environmental literacy based on critical thinking. Moreover, it should contribute to the development of people who make knowledgeable decisions on their behavior, basically in relation to the main environmental problems (Boyes and Stanisstreet 2012). This would consequently relate critical thinking with an efficient use of decision-making skills (Kincheloe 2008).

Therefore, the design of educational proposals, in addition to favoring a profound understanding of the problem and the search for possible action strategies (Räthzel and Uzzell 2009), should favor decision-making and the ability to act as per the sustainability criteria adopted. This perspective implies that the educational actions should seek the development of specific skills that foster sustainable actions based on sensible decisions for real-world and complex situations. The review of the literature on this subject by Wiek et al. (2011) indicates five basic competencies that should be combined significantly and effectively to reach this aim:

- Systems-thinking competence is the ability to collectively analyze complex systems across different domains (society, environment, economy, etc.) and across different scales (local to global), thereby considering cascading effects, inertia, feedback loops and other systemic features related to sustainability issues and sustainability problem-solving frameworks.
- Anticipatory competence is the ability to collectively analyze, evaluate, and craft rich "pictures" of the future related to sustainability issues and sustainability problem-solving frameworks
- Normative competence is the ability to collectively map, specify, apply, reconcile, and negotiate sustainability values, principles, goals, and targets
- Strategic competence is the ability to collectively design and implement interventions, transitions, and transformative governance strategies toward sustainability
- Interpersonal competence is the ability to motivate, enable, and facilitate collaborative and participatory sustainability research and problem solving.

In this new framework, teacher training is a basic pillar. If we want education to have the dual social function, to educate future generations through an integral model of sustainability (synchronic and diachronic support) and to contribute to changes in lifestyles, a reference framework for teacher training that backs up and specifies the educational proposals will be necessary (Novo 2009). The introduction of sustainable competencies in its curriculum implies a change in the teaching culture, which lays down the foundations to achieve the model of human being and society that we want to establish (UNESCO 2005).

In summary, specific actions in teacher training which help promote sustainable lifestyles are required. Therefore, an educational model based on the development of sustainable competencies is founded, designed and implemented, that seek to produce an improvement in the knowledge, attitudes and intention of pro-environmental behavior (directed at sustainability) of the aspiring teachers.

3 Methodology

An educational model is proposed with a research-based nature and a socio-ecological approach (Kyburz-Graber 2013), for the resolution—albeit not the "solution"—of socio-environmental problems (which are *real, complex, global, local, and systemic* problems). It is addressed from a participative and multi-disciplinary perspective and its final aim is to contribute to their ability to act on these problems following sustainability criteria. Through it, we attempt to show the "applicability" of Environmental Education that is directed toward sustainability and the resolution of real and specific problems; bridging the gap between theory and practice and encouraging the development of sustainable competencies.

This model was carried out with a selection on socio-environmental actions that have to do with improving the sustainability of the Faculty of Education and of the campus (Vega Marcote and Álvarez Suárez 2011). The chosen themes dealt with daily issues in student life, seeking certain personal and social behaviour and the achievement of lifestyles that improve the environment, for in all of them it is to be established their relation with the excessive consumption of the aspects analyzed and their overall influence on environmental deterioration in other parts of the planet. An exemplification of the approach used may be seen in Table 1. Others proposals can be the study of the problem of the loss of diversity or acoustic contamination, as well as the performance of school environmental audits, which are also reported in other works by the authors (Vega and Alvarez 2012; Álvarez-Suárez et al. 2014).

As the example shows, the educational experience begins by providing each group with a text-summary of the specific problem that is going to be "researched", the goals of the "research" and a list of the activities to be carried out that deal with a specific aspect of the problems involved, and, if applicable, the prior considerations that need to be taken into account to carry them out. The research is executed by distributing the task among the different groups. This means that the teams work monographically on various sustainable management indicators, set forth with the final aim of drafting a report, to later hold a debate and share them in a large group. The entire process involves the students' autonomous work supervised by the teachers.

Of special relevance during the development process was the study of the multi-causal complexity of environmental problems, which involves three main tasks or procedures for its handling and resolution: (i) identify the intervening factors, distinguishing them from other relevant facts; (ii) analyze the network of connections among those factors; and (iii) evaluate their relative importance, that is, determine the importance of each one as they occur in the situation studied. This requires social and scientific criticism and is complemented by a reflection on the process, where the data collected is analyzed, and, if applicable, whether it is necessary to reconsider the activity plan (feedback), and the development of a set of contents agreed upon, based on the information regarding the problems studied.

Table 1 Example of a research project: "PROBLEMS GENERATED BY SOLID URBAN-WASTE (SUW)

<table>
<tr>
<td rowspan="2">Text promoting the research (Summary)
During its everyday activities, humans generate large amounts of different types of waste. Domestic waste is that which originates in our own households
It is true that in nature is a variety of organisms (bacteria and fungi) that can break down and transform organic matter, thus completing cycles of matter. However, the introduction, especially as of the 50s, of non-biodegradable synthetic products resulted in their remaining "indefinitely" in nature. Due to a series of factors, which include the rapid increase in population that, moreover, resides mainly in city centers, the use of rapidly ageing products and the widespread use of non-returnable containers and, above all, the production and consumption of different no biodegradable synthesis products, the amount of waste has increase exponentially over the past years, becoming a serious problem to eliminate it in a clear and eco-friendly was. These factors have also contributed toward the emission of gases responsible for climate change. In our territory, an average of 900,000 tons of Solid Urban Waste (SUW) is produced per year
There are different technical solutions that, to a certain extent, minimize the problem. However, they require facilities (controlled dumps, incinerators, composting or recycling plants, etc.), that very often arc rejected by the public opinion. To try to find a solution to this problem in our city, two treatment systems were launched: an incineration plant and a composting and recycling complex. Notwithstanding, dumps still exist, and many are uncontrolled</td>
<td>Aims
• Determine the importance of reducing consumption and reusing/recovering SUW
• Analyze the amount and type of waste produced locally and nationally
• Relate the amounts produced and the characteristics of the SUW to lifestyles
• Acquire critical judgment on the suitability of the different methods used to eliminate SUW
• Assess the environmental and economic aspects on health related to the management of SUW
• Develop and apply individual and collective strategies for solving environmental problems caused by SUW
• Use different documentary sources to obtain precise information that permits the establishment of criteria based on the management of SUW
• Relate the production of waste (consumption, socio-economic models), to sustainable development and lifestyles
• Apply the acquired knowledge to the study of the problems generated by SUW, both locally and globally (for example in relation to climate change)
• Propose actions for the preservation and improvement of the environment and its relation to SUW
• Design didactic approaches directed at citizens in general and Primary School students</td>
</tr>
<tr>
<td>Group distribution anil activities
Group A: SUW, what do we throw out? Quantitative and qualitative composition, impact
Group B: SUW, how is it managed? Treatment, environmental impact and economic management
Group C: SUW, what do we recycle? Quantitative and qualitative composition, saving of resources
Group D: Visit to an uncontrolled dump. Environmental impact
Group E: Visit to an incineration plant Management and environmental impact
Group F: Visit to a composting and recycling complex. Waste management and treatment
Group G: Other waste. Types and treatment, environmental impact
Group H: Action proposals aimed at solving the problems posed
Group I: Compilation of information from the different groups and drafting of a joint report (it can be a summary poster) that includes a glossary and bibliography used
All (GG): Decision matrix
Role play. What to do with waste?
Design of an agreed "concept map"
Debate and proposal of individual and group actions
Individual (TI): Design of a teaching proposal</td>
</tr>
</table>

The didactic model posed requires for its development a series of stages, both for on-campus and off-campus classes, where different activities are carried out as part of the learning sequence, that make it possible to apply the different aspects of the model (Álvarez and Vega 2009; Vega and Álvarez 2011). Their stages and their main activities are described in Table 2 where the sustainable competencies dealt with at all times are also described.

The initial stages of the experience are designed so that students may practice scientific and environmental literacy in order to achieve knowledge building, which involves the setting out and questioning of former ideas to analyze and resolve a real problem. During these early phases, the development of the competency of systems thinking and the strategic and anticipatory competency through the global analysis of the theme that is the object of the study are particularly important.

It is not sufficient, however, to find solutions to specific environmental problems, for what is considered finding an adequate solution depends on one's own values, especially if we bear in mind that these problems could change in the future. Thus, the final stages of the experience are directed towards addressing the development of competencies that favor decision-making based on sustainability criteria and responsible behavior. For this reason, they are formulated to apply the contents to real-life situations, so as to foster skills for the use of knowledge, decision-making, and acting in different contexts, both individually and collectively. This would encourage the application of the themes studied to real-life situations. These stages deal, above all, with the development of strategic competence, anticipatory competence and legislative competence through the process of identifying the conditions to be changed, the study of the different solutions and of the priorities to act sustainably on a local and global level.

It is also necessary to take into account that the Environmental Education model that we defend includes a positive approach to collective decision-making, respect for democracy, for different cultures, and the understanding of participation processes. So, to develop this experience, the students must be divided into small teams (4–5 students/group). For, although environmental and social responsibility must be undertaken individually, it must develop into group-oriented actions. The aim is for students to act as a community that produces and mobilizes its own knowledge (Uskola et al. 2010) and is aware and responsible of its learning, with the purpose of acting sustainably. Therefore, the development of interpersonal competency is encouraged during the entire process.

Group work must be periodically coordinated in established supervised modules and large group meetings. The role of the teachers is to guide the learning process of the students, monitoring the work of each group, coordinating information, providing feedback on the learning process, presented in such a way that the difficulties which could arise during the application of this type of methodologies could be solved.

As this is an educational model for teachers in training, the teaching proposal could include a final stage consisting on the design of a teaching action based on the problem under study. This last phase conveys a reflection upon the experience carried out in the context of a transforming Environmental Education, where the

Table 2 Stages in educational action

Stages	Main activities in each stage	Competencies
0. Selection of socio-environmental problems	Formulation of a problem: – meaningful (with logical coherence, that awakens students' interest and activates their knowledge in a new situation, which requires the learning of new knowledge and its transfer to a real context) – open (based on the complexity, with multiple solutions, that encourage debate and that involve the use of scientific data)	
1. Formulation of the problems object of the study	Identification and formulation of the problem based on students' previous knowledge Selection of meaningful content for students Establishment of an initial work plan	– Systems thinking competence – Interpersonal competence
2. Identification of causes and consequences	Preparation of strategies to incorporate information that leads us to the identification of the causes and consequences of the problem situation posed, taking into account the different points of view on the conflicts and weighing the different factors that affect them (social, cultural and economic) Information handling, selected to address the learning obstacles that appear during the research and that come close to their level of knowledge	– Systems thinking competence – Strategic competence – Interpersonal competence
3. Identification of the conditions to change	Definition of lines of action, establishing criteria for the selection and sequencing of proposed actions, which give rise to questions such as: what can be done through technology and science; what has been done previously under similar conditions and what was the result; who is responsible for providing solutions; to what extent can citizens participate; what can we do	– Strategic competence – Anticipatory competence – Interpersonal competence
4. Specification of the difficulties and establishment of priorities for action	Feasibility study of the proposals to be carried out—what blocks and obstacles we can come across during the solution processes—to direct and change them if necessary, establishing different levels of complexity to consider them feasible and prepare a calendar of actions. Consideration of the lines of research aimed at looking for formulas for the resolution of conflicts, mediation methods and new directions and participation mechanisms	– Strategic competence – Interpersonal competence
5. Carrying out of appropriate and sustainable actions	Application of the concepts learned to real-life situations, fostering the ability to make sustainable decisions	– Strategic competence – Normative competence – Interpersonal competence

Adapted from (Alvarez and Vega 2009)

principles, aims and methodological guidelines reflected in the task that they have carried out are different from the transmitting type traditional model. The purpose of this final stage is to also contribute to the development of teaching skills in the corresponding areas of knowledge.

4 Conclusions for Sustainability-Oriented Teacher Training

The importance of addressing environmental issues in teacher training is highlighted from the European Union (Council of the European Union 2010: 327/12), urging Member States to equip teachers, school staff and school leaders with the awareness, knowledge and competences required to promote and include the principles underlying Education for Sustainable Development in their approaches to teaching and management. Thus, academic development is necessary to provide educators with the capacity for understanding sustainability as an overarching conceptual framework, which can be used to reconsider the way we think and act toward each other and the planet, and to provide them with the capacity to undertake sustainability educational praxis (Holdsworth et al. 2013).

Accordingly, in order to check out the effectiveness of the model presented, this proposal was evaluated comparing the effect of the educational model based on the development of sustainable competencies as opposed to a traditional model based on an expository teaching methodology. Thus, a study of the students' initial situation was carried out, regarding their knowledge, attitudes and their intention of behaviour toward the environment, not only as a starting point for their learning, but also as a reference to evaluate the change produced. The evaluation indicates that this is a highly effective resource for working from the point of view of Environmental Education focused at sustainability—at least at a university level—in so far as it favours significantly the development of knowledge, attitudes and pro-environmental intentions of behaviour (aimed at sustainable) of aspiring teachers, as can be seen in other works by the authors (Vega and Alvarez 2012; Álvarez-Suárez et al. 2014). This has significant implications for the teaching practice, since a more autonomous and collaborative learning are promoted on the basis on skills development as learning objectives.

The proposed model is based on solving social and environmental problems, local and global in nature, and therefore, that can be adapted and used in other contexts. The proposal also involves an educational component that introduces the contents of sustainable management in the curriculum and combines the practice and teaching of sustainability. In this way, it facilitates the transfer of learning toward individual and social life and enables future teachers to experiment methodologies that are quite removed from the traditional model.

Similarly, it promotes participation, reflecting on the complexity of environmental issues, critical thinking with regard to the role of people in the system and the adoption of individual decisions that are reflexive and responsible toward the environment and others, which are all essential requirements for an Environmental

Education that is targeted toward action. Thus, this formulation can foster behaviour that is more respectful with sustainability and it also includes a multiplying effect, due to the students' professional outlook (teachers in training).

But we must point out that the results obtained could present difficulties to become real behavioural changes (Gifford 2014). Therefore, new studies are being performed to evaluate the duration of the results and the reality of the changes obtained, along with a qualitative research regarding to the developing of competencies that would make it possible to expand and delve into its conclusions.

In short, it is necessary to redirect education toward the literacy of citizens and communities who are not only informed and sensitized, but also capable of adopting responsible decisions and acting sustainably before genuine and complex situations. Teacher training is a fundamental pillar in this change in the educational culture. Therefore, this educational model can serve as a basis for future proposals in this field, favoring the training of citizens and communities so that they are capable of tackling present-day and future environmental problems.

References

Alvarez, P., & Vega, P. (2009). Actitudes ambientales y conductas sostenibles: Implicaciones para la Educación Ambiental. *Psicodidactica, 14*, 245–260.

Álvarez-Suárez, P., Vega-Marcote, P., & García-Mira, R. (2014). Sustainable consumption: A teaching intervention in Higher Education. *International Journal of Sustainability in Higher Education, 15*(1), 3–15.

Aznar-Minguet, P., & Ull, M. A. (2009). *La formación de competencias básicas para el desarrollo sostenible: El papel de la Universidad* (pp. 219–237). Special issue: Revista de Educación.

Barth, M., Godemann, J., Rieckman, M., & Stoltenberg, U. (2007). Developing key competences for sustainable development in higher education. *International Journal of Sustainability in Higher Education, 8*, 416–430.

Berryman, T., & Sauvé, L. (2013). Languages and discourses of education, environment, and sustainable development. In R. B. Stevenson, M. Brody, J. Dillon, & A. E. J. Wals (Eds.), *International handbook of research on environmental education* (p. 591). New York: Routledge.

Bolívar, A. (2009). *Deseñar e Avaliar por Competencias na Universidade*; O EEES como reto. Vicerreitoría de Formación e Innovación Educativa, Universidade de Vigo, Vigo, Spain, 195 p.

Boyes, E., & Stanisstreet, M. (2012). Environmental education for behaviour change: Which actions should be targeted? *Journal of Science Education, 34*, 1591–1614.

Carlsson, M., & Jensen, B. B. (2006). Encouraging environmental citizenship: The roles and challenges for schools. In A. Dobson & D. Bell (Eds.), *Environmental citizenship* (p. 292). Cambridge: MIT Press.

Council of European Union. (2010). Council conclusions on education for sustainable development. European Union, Brussels. http://www.consilium.europa.eu/uedocs/cms_data/docs/pressdata/en/educ/117855.pdf. Last accessed September 1, 2015.

EU. (1999). The Bologna Declaration of 19 June 1999. Joint Declaration of the European Ministers of Education. European Union, Brussels.

Eurydice. (2011). *La enseñanza de las Ciencias en Europa: políticas nacionales, prácticas e investigación.* Agencia Ejecutiva en el ámbito educativo, audiovisual y cultural, Brussels.

Ferreira, J. (2013). Transformation, empowerment, and the governing of environmental conduct: Insights to be gained from a "history of the present" approach. In R. B. Stevenson, M. Brody,

J. Dillon, & A. E. J. Wals (Eds.), *International handbook of research on environmental education* (p. 591). New York: Routledge.

Forbes, C. T., & Davis, E. A. (2008). Exploring preservice elementary teachers' critique and adaptation of science curriculum materials in respect to socioscientific issues. *Science Education, 17*, 829–854.

Forbes, C. T., & Zint, M. (2010). Elementary teachers' beliefs about, perceived competencies for, and reported use of scientific inquiry to promote student learning about and for the environment. *The Journal of Environmental Education, 42*(1), 30–42.

García Bacete, F. J., Ferrá, P., Monjas, M. I., Marande, G. (2014). Las relaciones del profesorado con el alumnado en aulas del ciclo inicial de Educación Primaria. Adaptación del Questionnaire on Teacher Interaction-Early Primary (QTI-EP), 19, 1, 211–231.

GEO-5. (2012). *Fifth Global Environment Outlook: Summary for Policy Makers*. United Nations Environment Programme, Nairobi. http://www.unep.org/geo/geo5.asp. Last accessed March 1, 2015.

Giddens, A. (2009). *The politics of Climate Change*. London: Wiley & Sons. 276 p.

Gifford, R. (2014). Environmental psychology matters. *Psychology, 65*, 541–585.

Heimlich, J., & Ardoin, N. (2008). Understanding behavior to understand behavior change: A literature review. *Environmental Education Research, 14*(3), 215–237.

Hicks, D., & Holden, C. (1995). Exploring the future: A missing dimension in environmentaleducation. *Environmental Education Research, 1*(2), 185–193.

Hines, J.M., Hungerford, H. R., & Tomera, A. N. (1986/1987). Analysis and synthesis of research on responsible environmental behavior: a meta-analysis. *The Journal of Environmental Education 18*, 1–8.

Holdsworth, S., Thomas, I., & Hegarty, K. (2013). Sustainability education: Theory and practice. In R. B. Stevenson, M. Brody, J. Dillon, & A. E. J. Wals (Eds.), *International handbook of research on environmental education*. NewYork: Routledge.

Jensen, B. B., & Schnack, K. (1997). The Action Competence approach in environmental education. *Environmental Education Research 3*(2), 163–178.

Kincheloe, J. L. (2008). *Knowledge and critical pedagogy: An introduction*. London: Springer. 296 p.

Klein, N. (2014). *This changes everything: capitalism vs. the climate*. Simon and Schuster, Otawa, 576 p.

Kyburz-Graber, R. (2013). Socioecological approaches to environmental education and research: A paradigmatic response to behavioural change orientations. In R. B. Stevenson, M. Brody, J. Dillon, & A. E. J. Wals (Eds.), *International handbook of research on environmental education* (p. 591). New York: Routledge.

Latouche, S. (2011). *Vers une société d'abondance frugale: Contresenset controverses de la décroissance*. Fayard: Mille et une Nuits. 180 p.

Mogensen, F., & Mayer, M. (2005). *Eco-schools: Trends and divergences. A Comparative Study on ECO-school development processes in 13 countries*: Austrian Federal Ministry of Education, Science and Culture, Viena, 51 p. http://www.ubu10.dk/downloadfiles/comparative2.pdf. Last accessed May 1, 2015.

Mogensen, F., & Schnack, K. (2010). The action competence approach and the 'new' discourses of education for sustainable development, competence and quality criteria. *Environmental Education Research, 16*(1), 59–74.

NAAEE. (2011). *Developing a framework for assessing environmental literacy: executive summary*. North American Association for Environmental Education, Washington. http://www.naaee.net/sites/default/files/framework/DevFramewkAssessEnvLitOnlineEd.pdf. Last accessed March 12, 2015.

Novo, M. (2009). La Educación Ambiental: Una genuina para el desarrollo sostenible Revista de Educación, Special issue, 219–237.

OECD. (2005). *Definition and selection key competencies; executive summary*. http://www.oecd.org/pisa/35070367.pdf. Last accessed April 1, 2015.

Räthzel, N., & Uzzell, D. (2009). Transformative environmental education: A collective rehearsal for reality. *Environmental Education Research, 15*(3), 263–277.

Reid, A., & Scott, W. (2013). Identifying needs in environmental education research. In R. B. Stevenson, M. Brody, J. Dillon, & A. E. J. Wals (Eds.), *International handbook of research on environmental education* (p. 591). New York: Routledge.

Rickinson, M. (2001). Learners and learning in environmental education: A critical review of the evidence. *Environmental Education Research, 7*(3), 207–320.

Rideout, B. E. (2005). The effects of a brief environmental problems module on endorsement of the New Ecological Paradigm in college students. *Journal of Environmental Education, 37*, 3–11.

Roorda, D. L., Koomen, H., Spilt, J. T., & Oort, F. J. (2011). The influence of affective teacher-student relationships on students' school engagement and achievement: A meta-analytic approach. *Review of Educational Research, 8*(4), 493–529.

Stern, P. C. (2000). Toward a coherent theory of environmentally significant behaviour. *Journal of Social Issues, 56*, 407–424.

Stern, M. J., Powell, R. B., & Ardoin, N. M. (2010). Evaluating a constructivist and culturally responsive approach to environmental education for diverse audiences. *Journal of Environmental Education, 42*(2), 109–122.

Stiefel, B. M. (2008). *Competencias Básicas: Hacia un Nuevo Paradigma Educativo*. Madrid: Narcea. 201 p.

Stevenson. R. & Stirling, C. (2010). Environmental learning agency in diverse cultural contexts. In R. Stevenson, & J. Dillon, *Engaging environmental education: Learning, culture and agency* (254 p.). Rotterdam: Sense Publishers.

Tilbury, D. (1995). Environmental education for sustainability: Defining the new focus of environmental education in the 1990s. *Environmental Education Research, 1*, 195–212.

Tilbury, D. (2012). Higher education for sustainability: A global overview of commitment and progress. In *Higher Education in the World*; *Higher Education's Commitment to Sustainability: from Understanding to Action*. Hampshire: Palgrave MacMillan (185 p.).

UN. (2000). *55/2. United Nations Millennium Declaration*. General Assembly of United Nations. http://www.un.org/millennium/declaration/ares552e.htm. Last accessed May 1, 2015.

UN. (2011). *Learning for the future: Competences in education for sustainable development*; Economic Commission for Europe, Geneve. http://www.unece.org/fileadmin/DAM/env/esd/ESD_Publications/Competences_Publication.pdf. Last accessed March 21, 2015.

UNESCO. (2005). *Decade for sustainable development United Nations Decade (2005–2014). Vision and definition of ESD*. http://portal.unesco.org. Last accessed April 22, 2015.

Uskola, A., Maguregi, G., & Jiménez-Aleixandre, M. P. (2010). The use of criteria in argumentation and the construction of environmental concepts: A university case study. *International Journal of Science Education, 32*, 17.

Varela-Losada, M., Pérez-Ródríguez, U., & Álvarez-Lires, M. (2014). Desarrollo de competencias docentes a partir de metodologías participativas aplicadas a educación ambiental. *Formación Universitaria, 7*(6), 27–36.

Varela-Losada, M., Vega-Marcote, P., Pérez-Rodríguez, P., & Álvarez-Lires, M. (2015). Going to action? A literature review on educational proposals in formal Environmental Education, Environmental Education Research, doi:10.1080/13504622.2015.1101751

Vega Marcote, P., & Álvarez Suárez, P. (2011). La Agenda 21 y la Huella Ecológica como instrumentos para lograr una Universidad Sostenible. *Enseñanza de las Ciencias, 29*(2), 207–220.

Vega, P., y Álvarez, P. (2012). Training of teachers in Spain towards sustainability. Implementation and analysis of "ecometodología". European Journal of Teacher Education, *35*(4), 494–510.

Wiek, A., Withycombe, L., & Redman, C. L. (2011). Key competencies in sustainability: A reference framework for academic program development. *Sustainability, 6*, 203–218.

Worldwatch Institute. (2013). *State of the World: Is sustainability still possible?* Washington: The Worldwatch Institute. 200 p.

Yavetz, B., D. Goldman, & Pe'er, S. (2009). Environmental literacy of pre-service teachers in Israel: A comparison between students at the onset and end of their studies. Environmental Education Research *15*(4), 393–415.

Author Biographies

Pedro Vega-Marcote is a full Professor in the Faculty of Educational Sciences at the University of Coruña. Currently his research interests focus on the field of: Teacher training in Environmental Education and Sustainable Development, the Ecological Footprint and reduction of emissions of Greenhouse Gases, the implementation of Agenda 21 at the University and Municipalities (A21L) and in Experimental Science Teaching.

Mercedes Varela-Losada is a lecturer in the Faculty of Educational Sciences and Sport at the University of Vigo (Spain). She is currently working on her PhD on Environmental Education and Sustainable Development. Her research interests also focus on Experimental Science Teaching and teaching methodologies.

The University as a Site of Socialisation for Sustainability Education

Jennie Winter, Debby Cotton and Paul Warwick

Abstract
This chapter reports on an innovative approach to in-service teacher education focusing on Education for Sustainable Development (ESD) aimed at faculty in a UK university. Building on the underpinning philosophies that characterise sustainability education: participation, experiential learning and authenticity, a module on ESD was designed which at first flipped and then moved beyond the classroom. An online resource was developed to house the necessary declarative content which student-teachers accessed before the class. Class time was then spent within deliberative, dialogic and 'walkabout' learning spaces. These included a critically informed tour of the university campus and community exploring the 'unseen university', following energy and waste processes, evaluating accessibility and inclusivity and considering the university as an example of an organisation in transition. They also afforded the opportunity for student-teachers to meet key sustainability individuals from procurement, estates, marketing and finances, as well as curriculum champions and of course students themselves. Discussions took place in boiler rooms, on stairwells, in coffee shops and in parks. Following an action research strategy for change leadership, student-teachers collaboratively and critically dissected these experiences and negotiated assignments which were not only informed by these experiences but that sought to address specific sustainability needs identified on our journeying through the university as a manifold learning space. At the end of the course, student-teachers used the UNECE (Learning for the future: competencies in education for sustainable development. UNECE, Geneva, 2012) framework for Competences in Education for Sustainable Development to assess what had been learnt and where to focus ongoing CPD. The course has

J. Winter (✉) · D. Cotton · P. Warwick
PedRIO, Plymouth University, 3 Endsleigh Place, Drake Circus,
Plymouth PL4 8AA, UK
e-mail: jennie.winter@plymouth.ac.uk

© Springer International Publishing Switzerland 2016

W. Leal Filho and P. Pace (eds.), *Teaching Education for Sustainable Development at University Level*, World Sustainability Series,
DOI 10.1007/978-3-319-32928-4_7

proved popular in its home institution and has been showcased as an example of good practice by the European Communion through their 'Lifelong Learning Programme' (Mader et al. in State of the Art report: mapping opportunities for developing education for sustainable development competences in the UE4SD partner countries. University Educators for Sustainable Development, Cheltenham, 2014).

1 Introduction

The United Nations 'Decade of Education for Sustainable Development' (DESD) (2005–2014) has provided a focus for the development of a variety of educational activities around sustainability. The United Nations Educational, Scientific and Cultural Organisation stated that the over-arching goal of the DESD was to integrate the values of sustainable development into all aspects of education and learning in every education sector (UNESCO 2014). In the UK, although support for ESD in Higher Education (HE) has been both spatially and temporally piecemeal, there is evidence both of demand from students (Drayson et al. 2012), and enthusiasm from staff (Cotton et al. 2007). The Higher Education Funding Council for England produced its first sustainability policy and strategy in 2005 (HEFCE 2005) and although later HEFCE publications were somewhat less wholeheartedly supportive of sustainability in the curriculum, the UK Quality Assurance Agency have also taken up the mantle, producing a Guidance document for UK HE providers on ESD (QAA 2014). Thus, sustainability issues have been moving towards the mainstream of academic discussions, aided by the development of People and Planet's 'Green League', which has reported annually since 2007, and the rapid growth of the 'Green Gown Awards' (reflecting ESD innovation amongst other aspects of sustainability).

However, despite a global movement that has highlighted the need for sustainable development and emphasised the role that HE could play—through research, improving environmental management on campuses, and ESD (Sterling et al. 2013; Wals 2014), progress in campus greening continues to be more rapid—and less contested—than embedding sustainable development in the HE curriculum (Tilbury 2011). The reasons for the slow pace of change in teaching and learning have been widely discussed in the literature, and a key limiting factor is expertise of teaching staff and conceptual confusion. Research has established that both staff and students struggle to understand the range of the term, 'sustainability', focusing primarily on the environmental dimensions rather than integrating this with social and economic aspects (Bone and Agombar 2011; Kagawa 2007). In addition, there are considerable difficulties associated with helping students to develop the personal and social capacities which are important in ESD, especially when desired outcomes are complex and unpredictable (Cotton et al. 2012). Perhaps because of these barriers, there is little evidence that ESD is routinely embedded across HE curricula or in academic staff development programmes—although clearly pockets of good practice in both exist.

In order to prompt a step-change in ESD activities within HE, considerable efforts need to be expended in the sphere of teacher education aimed at in-service HE teaching staff (often termed faculty development or educational development). Innovative practices are needed to overcome the limited perspectives of ESD commonly constrained by disciplinary silos. The emergent nomenclature around sustainability, sustainable development and ESD suggest these are contested conceptual territories tightly constrained by socio-political geographical context (Blewitt 2008). However, increasing consensus that ESD is an important vehicle for pursuing sustainability has emerged and over time greater understanding of the cultural implications of sustainability has led to opportunities for innovation. Educators have started to move away from the confines of positivist, transmissive forms of pedagogy to explore interpretivist and socially critical approaches which better engender the characteristics of a sustainability orientated population (Robottom and Hart 1993); declarative and metacognitive competencies, self-reflection and awareness of the inter-connectedness of human and natural systems (Sterling 2004). In an HE context, this involves the development of systemic and epistemic thinking skills; responses that transcend discipline and other models of institutional organisation and call for institutional and organisational transformation founded on participation, experiential learning and authenticity (Winter et al. 2015a).

The significant consequences of such a change in perspective—were it to be widely adopted—indicate the need for increasing support for HE educators tasked with enthusing and creating a sustainability-cognisant graduate population. As well as suggesting a shift in pedagogic approach, there are increasing international efforts to generate taxonomies of knowledge, values and skills which can be used as measurable outcomes of ESD across disciplinary divides. In the UK these are commonly referred to as 'literacies' and salient examples have been developed by scholars including Dawe et al. (2005), Parkin et al. (2004), and Stibbe and Luna (2009). Underpinning these taxonomies are ideas about appropriate educator aptitudes and capabilities (Mader et al. 2014; Willy 2008). In the UNESCO report 'Learning: the treasure within', Delors et al. (1996) recognize four pillars for education of 21st Century: learning to know, learning to do, learning to be and learning to live together. These have been re-worked as a framework of competencies for educators in ESD by UNECE (2012) (Fig. 1) and have been widely communicated throughout the global HE sector.

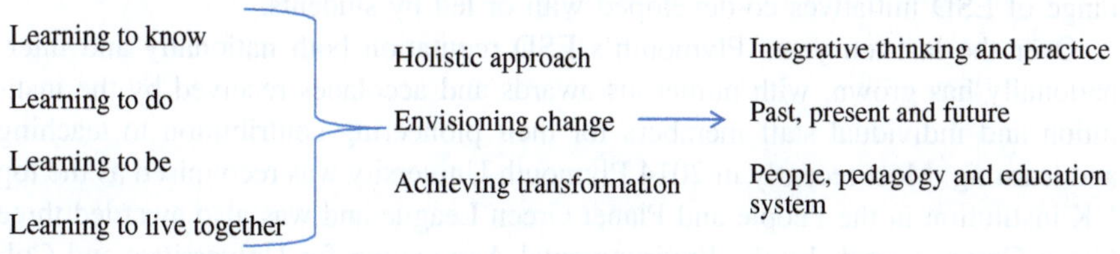

Fig. 1 Competencies for educators in ESD (abridged version–full model available at http://insight.glos.ac.uk/sustainability/Education/Pages/UNECE.aspx)

In UK HE, however, calls for ESD educator competencies must compete with other drivers for enhancing teaching quality, as well as the potentially conflicting interests of research and enterprise. Awareness of the value of continuing professional development (CPD) for teachers in HE has increased in response to a changing landscape motivated in part by policy developments and paralleled by changes to fee structures which position students as 'consumers' of HE. This has led to the growing provision of faculty or educational development in UK Higher Education Institutions (HEIs) which consists of a range of activities including introducing new lecturers to 'best' practice in teaching and learning, to pedagogic activities and themes, and to pedagogic research. As yet there is no nationally recognised mandatory accreditation of new university educators although recognition opportunities do exist through organisations like the Higher Education Academy (HEA), the professional association for Staff and Educational Developers (SEDA) and various other bodies. Provision and content of teaching-related CPD—including consideration or embedding of ESD—is currently dependent on local institutional priorities and the capacity/willingness of the CPD provider.

2 The Plymouth Context

Throughout the UNDESD, Plymouth University has worked towards becoming an international leader in ESD at HE level. In 2005 the University benefited from significant funding from HEFCE and was able to establish the Centre for Sustainable Futures (CSF) as a Centre for Excellence in Teaching and Learning in ESD. The CSF built on well-established ESD research and teaching practice at Plymouth University in order to advance ESD through an integrated approach to curriculum innovation. It developed a holistic model for whole institutional change that has been referred to as the 4 C's model of Campus, Curriculum, Community and Culture. From its start, the bold vision of the CSF has been to "develop a strategy and activities that could transform the university towards a state where sustainability permeated the curricula, physical campus, and the whole institutional culture" (Sterling et al. 2013 p. 41). Pursuing this vision has led to a range of positive steps towards the sustainable university including the creation of the University's sustainability strategy in 2008. CSF has been able to serve as a hub supporting a wide variety of faculty from across all departments in pioneering curriculum change and associated research. More recently it has also resulted in a range of ESD initiatives co-developed with or led by students.

Over the last ten years Plymouth's ESD reputation both nationally and internationally has grown, with numerous awards and accolades received by the institution and individual staff members for their pioneering contribution to teaching and learning. Most recently in 2014 Plymouth University was recognised as the top UK institution in the People and Planet Green League and was also awarded three Green Gown Awards by the Environmental Association for Universities and Colleges (EAUC), in recognition of exceptional sustainability initiatives.

- Identify an appropriate topic and explain its significance in relation to academic or professional practice
- Construct theoretically-informed arguments about the topic and critically analyse its relationship to academic or professional practice
- Generate new ideas or connections and reflect on their impact on your own academic or professional practice earning outcomes

Fig. 2 Learning outcomes for the ESD Negotiated Study Module

Throughout this time, internal reviews have highlighted the vital role of a broad suite of CPD opportunities for academic staff in ESD. Increasingly emphasis has been placed on training that engages staff in apt ESD pedagogies; supporting the active, participatory, experiential and interdisciplinary engagement of students (Peterson and Warwick 2015). Within this aspect of work it has also been recognised that it is vital that formal and accredited pathways are provided for new staff to engage in ESD. This leads us to innovative work in the area of Educational Development.

For the most part Educational Development in the UK has not embraced ESD tending to focus on instead on generic concepts of teaching and learning. Yet in Plymouth the holistic approach taken by the university necessitated a response from the Educational Development unit. This began a conversation of where and how to fit ESD into an already crowded curriculum which (with good fortune) ran parallel to like discussions about other teaching and learning topics which led to transformation of the curriculum.

There is a long history of Educational Development at Plymouth which is manifest in the current offer of an accredited teaching course for new lecturers, the Postgraduate Certificate in Academic Practice (PGCAP). This is a level 7 course which consists of a core module (30 credits) and either a pedagogic research module (30 credits) or two 'Negotiated Study Modules' (NSM) at 15 credits each (20 h contact time and a further 180 h independent study time). The NSM is an umbrella module which houses a range of important HE topics which share learning outcomes and quality assurance processes but differ in terms of content. This is where the ESD Module discussed in this chapter sits, which inevitably impacts on how it has been conceptualised: for example, the learning outcomes (Fig. 2) are necessarily generic to allow for the diversity of the topics studied through the NSMs, and the negotiated element of the module means that students have an input into the assessment criteria and format for their assignment.

3 The Sustainability Education Negotiated Study Module

The module was initially designed to provide an introduction and toolkit for the new educator interested in embedding sustainability into their teaching and student learning. The learning outcomes were addressed through a series of topics around which teaching was organised:

- Introduction to the historical context of ESD and its diffusion through to contemporary policy and practice in HE.
- Exploring different paradigms and positions.
- Learning theories and pedagogy; exploring experiential, transformative, individual and social approaches.
- Implementation; critically evaluate whole institution responses, the formal, informal and campus curricula and interdisciplinarity.

The first year the module ran it was taught in a classroom, using PowerPoint to convey information to participants but with a heavy emphasis on peer discussion to share knowledge and ideas about the content. The module was therefore interactive to some extent; students led elements of the discussion and were instrumental in choosing the form of assignment, however, despite being offered the opportunity to select an alternative form of assessment, they unanimously chose to submit essays. Although participants met the learning outcomes and passed the assessment—questions arose in the tutor's mind about the extent to which content and delivery could be 'transformed' within the context of the current system. This motivated a process of reflection and curriculum change which began with considering the module's learning outcomes, content, teaching/learning activities and assessment criteria to ascertain the extent to which these were constructively aligned (Biggs and Tang 2007). It was recognised through this process that the philosophies underpinning the content of the module sat uneasily with the pedagogies employed in its delivery; there was little to differentiate the delivery from traditional HE pedagogy or to align it with the philosophical and applied underpinnings of ESD. Where there had been opportunities for risk taking and modelling good practice there were instead tensions and dissonance. This formed the basis for curriculum change, the aim of which was to reflect better the principles of ESD in the module teaching.

Through considering the literature about educator competencies and sustainability literacies, we decided to align the content of the module with the underpinning philosophies of ESD. The existing academic content would be used to underpin a pedagogic approach which utilised the University campus and operations to provide an immersive experience encompassing the critical elements of 'learning to know, learning to do, learning to be and learning to live together' (Delors et al. 1996). The university is an excellent example of an organisation in sustainability transition (Jones et al. 2010) and includes elements which are successfully drawn together—as well as those which remain in tension. In effect, the campus was utilised as the classroom and provided authentic learning opportunities arising out of participant interactions with their environment through a genuine, exploratory and situated experience. Although fieldwork is an oft-utilised pedagogy in HE (Hill and Woodland, 2002) the university campus and organisation are not commonly used as vehicles for learning. However, using the campus as a way of building on existing connections to place can provide an enhanced learning experience. "Place is … a way of seeing, knowing and understanding the world. When we look at the world as a world of places we see different things. We see attachments and connections between people and place (Cresswell 2004 p. 11)."

Kagawa (2007 p. 320) suggests the campus as a possible catalyst for exemplifying "the interconnectedness of social, economic and environmental interests creating a 'sustainability orientated pedagogy of place." The campus can provide a subject-neutral forum through which sustainability can be experienced, discussed, critiqued and reflected upon regardless of the "limitations of [disciplinary] tunnel vision (Jucker 2002 p. 13)."

In moving out of the classroom and into the campus environment, an alternative pedagogic approach was needed. In this example, the new model drew on recent developments focused on 'flipping' the classroom (Berrett 2012; Mazur 2009) where participants gain first-exposure learning prior to class and focus on the processing part of learning (synthesizing, analysing, problem-solving, etc.) in class with the support of peers and the tutor (Brame ND). The content that had informed the original lectures was used to create a series of online resources in 'Xerte' (Nottingham University ND) which presented information relevant to the learning outcomes. The resource also presented interactive activities which the tutor linked to the face-to-face sessions. These activities encouraged participants to engage prior to the sessions, and come prepared with some content knowledge, questions and comments. (This resource has also been used by academics at Plymouth and beyond as a stand-alone introduction to ESD).

The face-to-face sessions were then freed up to pursue the holistic and experiential introduction to Plymouth University as a sustainability community. This was undertaken through a series of meetings, discussions and activities as presented in Fig. 3. Participants undertook pre-class activities which helped them prepare for the sessions. The first part of the teaching session was used to discuss new knowledge and place it into the Plymouth context by designing questions and themes to use with the significant individuals and activities that were scheduled for the day. Discussions with university staff took place in situ depending on the individual and theme, so for example the discussion with the Head of Estates took place on a tour of the university taking in boiler rooms, kitchens, recycling and waste facilities etc. The Student Union officer was met in the Student Union where a tour of progress in sustainability took place including a coffee and chat with students involved in sustainability-themed volunteering. Sometimes we made it back to the classroom to regroup and reflect; sometimes we did this in coffee shops or corridors. As we explored the university we observed the formal informal and hidden aspects of the sustainability curriculum (Cotton et al. 2013; Winter and Cotton 2012; Winter et al. 2012) and the day always ended with a reflective discussion to summarise our experiences and prepare next steps.

Through provision of content, activities and discussions, participants were able to gain an understanding of the strengths, weaknesses, links and complexities inherent in creating and maintaining a sustainability university and link this to curriculum opportunities. This better aligned ESD and academic development highlighting that "In general, good sustainable development pedagogy is often simply good pedagogy (HEFCE 2008 p. 34)," and provided participants with first-hand experience of the sustainability community of the university. Assignments became much more innovative and applied, and students were encouraged to

Pre-class activity	In-class activity
Introduction to the historical context of ESD Xerte URL - https://xerte.plymouth.ac.uk/xerte/play.php?template_id=151 Background research on significant individuals and roles in the university Suggested reading Xerte activities	**Significant Individuals–** • Head of ESD in the curriculum • Educational Developers **In-class activities -** • Defining Sustainability Exploring sustainability through everyday objects • SD in HE – strengths and weaknesses • Visiting the Centre for Sustainable Futures
Exploring different paradigms and positions on ESD Xerte URL – https://xerte.plymouth.ac.uk/xerte/play.php?template_id=158 Background research on significant individuals and roles in the university Suggested reading Xerte activities	**Significant individuals –** • Head of ESD in the curriculum • Previous students **In-class activities -** • Exploring personal values and their impact on teaching • Discussing links between content and pedagogy • Personal reflection on competencies as an ESD educator (UNECE 2012)
Learning theories and pedagogy* Xerte URL – https://xerte.plymouth.ac.uk/xerte/play.php?template_id=160 Background research on significant individuals and roles in the university Suggested reading Xerte activities	**Significant individuals –** • Head of ESD in the curriculum • Previous students • Student Union Environmental Officer **In class activities -** • Designing curriculum change – taking current teaching practice and making more sustainable • Teaching outside - moving the classroom to the park - benefits and disadvantages • Making connections with the informal
	curriculum – designing links with student groups • Walkabout of university making videos of evidence of sustainability and exploiting learning opportunities
Implementation** Xerte URL – https://xerte.plymouth.ac.uk/xerte/play.php?template_id=213 Background research on significant individuals and roles in the university Suggested reading Xerte activities	**Significant individuals –** • Sustainability Manager • Head of Estates • Head of Procurement • Head of Marketing • Student Union Environment Officer • Students **In class activities -** • Walkabout of university visiting boiler rooms, waste processing plant/ catering sites/student union/ outdoor learning spaces/ institute supporting sustainability research with relevant significant individuals discussing links between the different processes, event and activities • Working in interdisciplinary teams to develop briefs for teaching sustainability together • Analysing how the University markets its sustainability credentials alongside other competing agendas

*These elements were supported by Sterling (2012), Winter (2015) and Winter et al. (2015b).

Fig. 3 Detail of flipped classroom by teaching theme

consider submitting alternative assessment formats by a formative assignment which tasked them with making a short video about their position on sustainability education and what it meant for their teaching. Video is a useful way to capture and discuss learning and is increasingly accessible to students through the ubiquity and affordability of personal technologies (Attwell and Hughes 2010).

The videos were uploaded to the Digital Learning Environment (Moodle) where an online discussion about each one took place with critical commentary provided to guide final submissions. Summative assignments were much more varied and included; the redesign of a programme in architecture, a music concert using a junk orchestra, a conference presentation, a briefing paper on using the campus for learning in Geography and a draft journal article.

The module is now in its fourth year and continued evaluation has generated evidence about strengths and weaknesses. Feedback from students has been very positive, with satisfaction for the module consistently high (100 %) as is participant engagement and perceived contribution to professional development (both 100 %). Participants have offered the following statements around which highlight how the module impacts on lecturers' professional development:

Their experience of sustainability pedagogies

- 'The module opened my eyes, it was lively and real, it was not process driven and unrelated to real people'.
- It was wonderful to have some freedom in the assignment'.
- 'Group formative discussion, based on videos produced by NSM students, led to something of an epiphany. It became clear that, in interdisciplinary interactions around sustainability, involving my own discipline requires the twofold case to be clearly made that: philosophical realism is indispensable to engineering and the physical sciences; but philosophical realism does not inevitably mean a positivist epistemology, with all the difficulties that the latter would raise for experts in the humanities and social sciences'.

Embedding ESD into current curricula

- 'This course enabled me to integrate sustainability as part of the curriculum'.

Developing a community of practice

- 'Interviewing and interacting with key stakeholders across Plymouth University had the most significant impact on me'.

Interdisciplinarity

- 'The module helped me to approach pedagogy and research in a much more interdisciplinary way and to learn from others' experiences'

Innovation

- 'Doing the video prep for this module encouraged me to set a podcast for 100 students which I would not have done otherwise'.
- 'Writing the assignment has helped in an ongoing process of clarifying my thinking about how undergraduate teaching in fluid mechanics can be rearrange to make available information on the use, for building ventilation and other fluid delivery systems, of renewable energy sources, particularly the buoyancy associated with naturally-occurring temperature differences and with waste heat from machinery, as an alternative to turbo-machinery powered by grid electricity. As a result, I now believe I may be able to implement this reform in time for delivery in stage 4 in the 2016–2017 academic year'.

In addition to this positive feedback it is evident that many students went on to undertake other ESD-related CPD including attending conferences, running workshops and publishing papers. However, tutor reflections and participant feedback have also led to recommendations for future change. For example, at present participants elect to take the module and so engagement with the ESD agenda remains largely optional. This could be addressed by articulating the close links between ESD and academic development within the core offer. In addition, more work with experienced academics and teaching teams with regard to embedding sustainability across the curriculum is planned and in progress. Working with staff at a range of levels within the institution is important to ensure that change is not left to lone enthusiasts and that those faculty inspired by the ESD module are supported to make further changes to the curriculum. This does however require buy in from what are already very busy people and this is brokered through good will and the increasing involvement of the CSF. We see this as a crucial area for future development so that relationships between CSF and new lecturing staff are formed and the suite of CSF funding, resources and personnel to support future research and innovation are made more easily accessible to the participants once they have completed the course.

4 Conclusion

UNESCO's Global Action Plan for ESD, following on from the UNDESD, continues the call for universities to lead on the sustainability agenda and emphasises the ongoing need for whole institutional change. This chapter has argued that a key aspect in this mandate to transform the university towards sustainability is teacher education aimed at new and existing HE teaching staff. As highlighted by the UNECE (2012), ESD requires educators to have a broad range of competencies that are not easily or quickly developed. At Plymouth University our experiences have revealed the importance of HE professional development opportunities that embody the participatory, experiential and interdisciplinary pedagogical approaches that are congruent with the aims of ESD. Focusing on a specific accredited ESD teacher education module we have seen the value of changing the very fabric of the course so that its aims and content could shift from an academic perspective on ESD to a holistic, systemic and experiential introduction to the University as a sustainability community and an organisation in sustainability transition. It has encouraged module participants to engage in ESD as 'critical creatives'; identifying where and how their teaching, and more importantly their students' learning, could contribute to the University moving ever closer towards its sustainability aspirations.

References

Attwell, G., & Hughes, J. (2010). Pedagogic approaches to using technology for learning: Literature review. Lifelong Learning UK. http://webarchive.nationalarchives.gov.uk/20110414152025/. http://www.lluk.org/wp-content/uploads/2011/01/Pedagogical-appraches-for-using-technology-literature-review-january-11-FINAL.pdf. Accessed May 20, 2015.

Berrett, D. (2012). How 'flipping' the classroom can improve the traditional lecture. *The Chronicle of Higher Education,* Accessed Febuary 19, 2012.

Biggs, J., & Tang, C. (2007). *Teaching for Quality Learning at University* (3rd ed.). Maidenhead: Open University Press.

Blewitt, J. (2008). *Understanding Sustainable Development.* London: Earthscan.

Brame, C. (ND). Flipping the classroom. http://cft.vanderbilt.edu/guides-sub-pages/flipping-the-classroom/. Accessed May 29, 2015.

Bone, E., & Agombar, J. (2011). *First-year attitudes towards, and skills in, sustainable development.* York: Higher Education Academy.

Cotton, D., Warren, M., Maiboroda, O., & Bailey, I. (2007). Sustainable Development, Higher Education and Pedagogy: A study of lecturers' beliefs and attitudes. *Environmental Education Research, 13*(5), 579–597.

Cotton, D., Sterling, S., Neal, V., Winter, J. (2012). *Putting the 'S' into ED: Education for sustainable development in educational development.* SEDA special 31.

Cotton, D. R. E., Winter, J., & Bailey, I. (2013). Researching the hidden curriculum: Intentional and unintended messages. *Journal of Geography in Higher Education, 37*(2), 192–203.

Cresswell, T. (2004). *Place: A short introduction.* Oxford: Blackwell Publishing.

Dawe, G., Jucker, R., & Martin, S. (2005). *Sustainable development in higher education: Current practice and future developments.* HEA, York: A report for the Higher Education Academy.

Delors, J., et al. (1996). Learning: The treasure within. Paris: UNESCO. http://unesdoc.unesco.org/images/0010/001095/109590eo.pdf. Accessed May 29, 2015.

Drayson, R., Bone, E., Agombar, J. (2012). Student attitudes towards and skills for sustainable development. NUS/HEA, York. http://www.heacademy.ac.uk/assets/documents/esd/Student_attitudes_towards_and_skills_for_sustainable_development.pdf. Accessed May 20, 2015.

Higher Education Funding Council for England (HEFCE). (2005). *Sustainable development in higher education.* Bristol: HEFCE.

Higher Education Funding Council for England (HEFCE). (2008). *Strategic review of sustainable development in higher education in England.* Bristol: HEFCE.

Hill, J., & Woodland, W. (2002). An evaluation of foreign fieldwork in promoting deep learning: A preliminary investigation. *Assessment and Evaluation in Higher Education, 27*(6), 539–555.

Jones, P., Selby, D., & Sterling, S. (Eds.). (2010). *Sustainability education: Perspectives and practice across higher education.* London: Earthscan.

Jucker, R. (2002). *Our common illiteracy: Education as if earth and people mattered.* Frankfurt: Peter Lang.

Kagawa, F. (2007). Dissonance in students' perceptions of sustainable development and sustainability. *International Journal of Higher Education, 8*(3), 317–338.

Mader, M., Michelsen, M., Mader, C., Burandt, S., Tilbury, D., Ryan, A., et al. (2014). State of the Art Report: Mapping opportunities for developing education for sustainable development competences in the UE4SD partner countries. University Educators for Sustainable Development, Cheltenham. http://www.sustainabilityexchange.ac.uk/files/ue4sd_state-of-the-art-report_final_2.pdf Accessed May 25, 2015.

Mazur, E. (2009). Farewell, Lecture? *Science, 323*, 50–51.

Nottingham University. (ND) "The Xerte Project". http://www.nottingham.ac.uk/xerte/index.aspx. Accessed May 02, 2015.

Parkin, S., Johnson, A., Buckland, H., & White, E. (2004). *Learning and skills for sustainable development: Developing a sustainability literate society*. London: HEPS.

Peterson, A., & Warwick, P. (2015). *Global learning and education*. Oxon: Routledge.

Quality Assurance Agency (QAA). (2014). *Education for sustainable development: Guidance for UK higher education providers*. Gloucester: QAA.

Robottom, I., & Hart, P. (1993). *Research in environmental education: Engaging the debate. The Deakin-Griffith Environmental Education Project*. Australia: Deakin University.

Sterling, S. (2004). Higher education, sustainability and the role of systemic learning, In: P. Blaze Conran A. Wals (Eds.) *Higher education and the challenge of sustainability: Problematics, promise and practice*. London: Kluwer Academic Publishers, pp. 347–348.

Sterling, S. (2012). *The future fit framework—An introductory guide to teaching and learning for sustainability in HE*. New York: Higher Education Academy.

Sterling, S., Maxey, L., & Luna, H. (2013). *The sustainable university: Progress and prospects*. London and New York: Earthscan/Routledge.

Stibbe, A., & Luna, H. (2009). Introduction. In A. Stibbe (Ed.),. The handbook of sustainability literacy: Skills for a changing world. Totnes: Green Books.

Tilbury, D. (2011) Higher education for sustainability: A global overview of commitment and progress. In GUNI (Ed.) *Higher Education's Commitment to Sustainability: From Understanding to Action,* Higher Education in the World 4, GUNI: Barcelona. pp. 18–28.

UNECE. (2012). *Learning for the future: Competencies in education for sustainable development*. Geneva: UNECE.

UNESCO. (2014). *Shaping the future we want: UN decade of education for sustainable development (2005-2014) Final Report*. Paris: UNESCO.

Wals, A. (2014). Sustainability in higher education in the context of the UN DESD: A review of learning and institutionalization processes. *Journal of Cleaner Production, 62*, 8–15.

Willy, S. (2008). Competencies for ESD (education for sustainable development) teachers. A framework to integrate ESD in the curriculum of teacher training institutes. CSCT, Brussels. http://www.unece.org/fileadmin/DAM/env/esd/inf.meeting.docs/EGonInd/8mtg/CSCT%20Handbook_Extract.pdf. Accessed May 28, 2015.

Winter, J. (2015) Taking an institutional approach to learning about sustainability. Educational Development, Plymouth University. https://www.plymouth.ac.uk/uploads/production/document/path/3/3410/596109_261397__Steps_to_Taking_an_institutional_approach_to_learning_about_sustainability_bold.pdf. Accessed May 02, 2015.

Winter J., Barton G., Allison J., Cotton, D. (2015a). Learning Development and Education for Sustainability: what are the links? Journal of Learning Development in Higher Education, 8, pp 1–23.

Winter, J., & Cotton, D. (2012). Making the hidden curriculum visible: sustainability literacy in higher education. *Environmental Education Research, 18*(6), 783–796.

Winter, J., Sjerps-Jones, H., Dexter, B., Klaff, J. (2012). Informal learning for sustainability. In D. Cotton S. Sterling V. Neal J. Winter (Eds). *Putting the 'S' into ED: Education for sustainable development in educational development*. SEDA, London. pp. 27–32.

Winter, J., Sterling, S., Cotton, D. (2015b). 7 Steps to embedding sustainability into student learning. Educational Development, Plymouth University. Available online. https://www.plymouth.ac.uk/uploads/production/document/path/3/3409/595997_261396_7_Steps_to_Embedding_Sustainability_into_Student_Learning_1214_BOLD.pdf. Accessed May 02, 2015.

Teacher Education for Sustainable Development: Past, Present and Future

Annette Gough

Abstract

Since the earliest formulations of the UN goals for environmental education (EE) at the Belgrade conference (1975), through the reconceptualization of education for sustainable development (ESD) at the World Summit on Sustainable Development in Johannesburg (2002), to *The Future We Want* (2012), teacher education—at pre-service and in-service levels and across primary and secondary education—has been regarded as being essential for achieving sustainable development. In response, the UNESCO-UNEP International Environmental Education Programme (IEEP) published prototypes for teacher education at elementary and middle school levels in the 1980s, and UNESCO published *Guidelines and Recommendations for Reorienting Teacher Education to Address Sustainability* (Hopkins and McKeown 2005) and continues to support related programmes. However, despite these many attempts, there is recurring testimony to the almost universal lack of success in introducing coherent or consistent programmes of EE/ESD into teacher education courses. This essay discusses these and other strategies for re-orienting teacher education through pedagogy and whole school system approaches while acknowledging that the teacher education institutions themselves are often the biggest obstacles.

Keywords

Teacher education • Sustainable development • Environmental education • Mainstreaming

A. Gough (✉)
School of Education, RMIT University, Bundoora Victoria,
PO Box 71, Melbourne, VIC 3083, Australia
e-mail: annette.gough@rmit.edu.au

© Springer International Publishing Switzerland 2016

W. Leal Filho and P. Pace (eds.), *Teaching Education for Sustainable Development at University Level*, World Sustainability Series,
DOI 10.1007/978-3-319-32928-4_8

1 Introduction

Teachers have long been identified as a major target audience for environmental education: The Belgrade Charter (1975) and recommendations 17 and 18 from the 1977 Tbilisi Intergovernmental Conference on Environmental Education (UNESCO 1978) specifically refer to pre-service teacher education and in-service teacher education and call for teacher education to include environmental education. These early recommendations were framed around the belief that all teachers need "to understand the importance of environmental emphasis in their teaching" and so "environmental sciences and environmental education [need to] be included in curricula for pre-service teacher education" and that "the necessary steps [are taken] to make in-service training of teachers in environmental education available for all who need it" (UNESCO 1978, pp. 35–36).

There is no doubt that teacher education is essential to achieving ESD. With about 59 million teachers worldwide, and an annual turnover rate of 5–10 %, teachers are an obvious significant target group. The issue is, however, how to reach them and what to teach them as part of the ESD agenda. The UN Decade of Education for Sustainable Development implementation scheme (UNESCO 2005) recognized that educators and trainers needed to be assisted with the relevant knowledge and information to address ESD. However, the *Review of Contexts and Structures for Education for Sustainable Development 2009* (Wals 2009, pp. 50–51) noted that

> The extent to which ESD has been integrated into teacher education programmes is unclear as: 1) limited knowledge of ESD at all levels is still a fundamental challenge and, in many cases, ESD has yet to move beyond a focus on the environment in many training programmes; 2) ESD is still often carried out by a limited number of teacher training institutions at the national level and needs to be further mainstreamed; and 3) more policy support is needed to guide ESD in teacher education and professional development.

The follow-up report on the Decade (Wals and Nolan 2012) did not have teacher education as part of its monitoring and evaluation brief, but it still noted the importance of teacher education to primary and secondary education.

Teacher education, and curriculum, continued to be a focus in the *Future We Want,* the outcomes document from the 2012 Rio+20 United Nations Conference on Sustainable Development: "We therefore resolve to improve the capacity of our education systems to prepare people to pursue sustainable development, including through enhanced teacher training, [and] the development of sustainability curricula" (United Nations 2012, p. 44).

Teacher educators who were conscious of and engaged with the environmental education movement responded to these calls for environmental education in teacher education through a range of individual and group projects for both pre-service and in-service teacher education (see, for example, Fien 1998; McKeown and Hopkins 2002; Kyburz-Graber et al. 2006; Ferreira et al. 2006; McKeown and Nolet 2013). Many of these initiatives had a curriculum focus on increasing teachers' awareness of environmental issues and environmental content knowledge, but a few were concerned with pedagogy and recognizing the need for changing worldviews.

However, teacher education institutions are generally autonomous in what they teach, within the confines of the accreditation requirements of their context, and they often play games with the rules. In Scotland, for example, there are guidelines that teachers are required to be "knowledgeable about sustainable development and competent to contribute to ESD" (Higgins and Kirk 2002, p. 9), but it is an *option* for teacher education institutions to teach ESD and to determine how much emphasis is given to it. If teachers, and ultimately their students, are to understand ESD then there is a need for more stringent policies and guidance to ensure that teacher education programmes everywhere include ESD in their core content.

This essay reviews a range of international and local initiatives and strategies for re-orienting teacher education to address ESD, through curriculum, pedagogy and whole school system approaches, from the 1980s through to future directions; it is not an empirical study.

2 Early Initiatives

At an international level, in the 1980s the UNESCO-UNEP International Environmental Education Programme (IEEP) commissioned and published the thirty volumes of its Environmental Education Series (the "Green Books") to support various aspects of teacher education. These include pre-service or in-service teacher training modules and programmes (11 of the 30 volumes), education modules for classroom use (7), guides and approaches to various aspects of environmental education (9), and trend paper or surveys (3). These volumes were intended to support the implementation of environmental education in member countries.

The Environment and Schools Initiative (ENSI) Project started in 1986, initially funded by the Organisation for Economic Co-operation and Development (OECD), was an in-service-like teacher education project. However, this project was different from the usual series of workshops for classroom teachers that comprise in-service teacher education in that it was action research based where teachers and schools worked with researchers in developing their practice. The initial ENSI Project has gone on to be a decentralized international network that brings together school initiatives, educators and other stakeholders in several countries to promote and understand activities promoting sustainable development in schools and their communities. It has sponsored a number of projects, including *Quality Criteria for ESD-Schools: Guidelines to enhance the quality of Education for Sustainable Development* (Breiting et al. 2005), which are useful in both pre-service and in-service teacher education settings. For example, the Breiting et al. (2005) document presents a non-exhaustive list of 'quality criteria' to be used as a starting point for reflections, debates and further development regarding future work on ESD among educational officials, teachers, headmasters, parents, and students, and it has been translated into numerous European languages. The on-going ENSI activities, which generally draw on experiences from across a range of countries, are mentioned here as they provide resources for both pre-service teacher education and in-service teacher education (see, for example, Kyburz-Graber et al. 2006).

National projects for incorporating environmental education into teacher education have been developed and implemented in a number of countries at both pre-service and in-service education levels over many years. The Australian *Teaching for a Sustainable World*, subtitled "A New Agenda in Teacher Education" (Fien 1995, subsequently disseminated internationally by UNESCO 2002 as *Teaching and Learning for a Sustainable Future*) was designed as a pre-service teacher education project, but the modules could also be used in in-service teacher education contexts. Interestingly, this project was funded by the Australian development assistance agency, AIDAB, and the modules attempted to integrate environment and development issues, which makes them an early example of materials consistent with an Education for Sustainable Development agenda. Also in the early 1990s, there was a European Union initiative on environmental education within pre-service teacher education programmes which addressed pedagogical, assessment, implementation, curriculum and school aspects of what makes an "environmentally educated teacher" (Brinkman and Scott 1996). There was no national approach in the United States and a survey conducted by McKeown-Ice (2000) found that the environmental education component of preservice teacher education programmes varied, where they existed at all.

Indeed, across many countries, at individual teachers' college or university level there were numerous initiatives to incorporate environmental education into teacher education programmes. However, these usually took the form of an elective programme rather than being part of the core teacher education programme (Gough 1998; Ferreira et al. 2006).

Although the possible breadth of re-orienting teacher education for ESD could (and should) include both pre-service and in-service teacher education, for the remainder of this essay I am only focusing on pre-service teacher education because in-service teacher education is so diverse and ephemeral, and it is generally provided outside higher education contexts. Pre-service teacher education programmes have parameters and controls generally associated with the accreditation requirements for these programmes, however this does not mean that re-orienting them for ESD is simple, and the remainder of this essay focuses on strategies and barriers for re-orienting teacher education programmes for ESD.

3 Effectiveness of Early Initiatives to Incorporate Environmental Education into Teacher Education

The environmental education research literature of the 1990s provides a recurring testimony to the lack of success in introducing coherent or consistent programmes of environmental education into teacher education courses, despite many efforts (Gough 1998). Reviews of environmental education in teacher education from around this time tended to find that

- All universities offered some form of EE at some stage in their pre-service teacher education programmes
- Not all programmes are implemented in a manner consistent with the EE literature
- EE is often offered as an elective and is frequently only included in a course because of a lecturer's individual efforts
- EE is sometimes not offered until the final year of a teacher education programme
- There are substantial number of teachers who enter the teaching profession without any formal training in EE
- Where EE is taught as an integrated subject it is most likely associated with science or social studies subjects.

With respect to interventions such as the UNESCO-UNEP International Environmental Education Programme (IEEP), while produced with the very best of intentions, the exact audience for these volumes was not always clear. The volumes raised particular concerns because of the universalized nature of the statements made in them which do not recognize the diversity of cultures, environments, languages, religions, stages of 'development', and politics within the world, as well as differing stages of colonization and post-colonization. In addition, the volumes also overlooked or negated the social context and expertise of the teacher educator through statements such as, "When implemented as intended, these guidelines will, in fact, result in teachers who are sufficiently competent and skilled to offer instruction in environmental education that will clearly contribute to the development of environmentally literate students" (Marcinkowski et al. 1990, p. 1). Statements like this raise questions about what makes such prototype programmes for an environmental education curriculum appropriate for places other than where they have been developed and whether the major components and guidelines they have identified are also appropriate. This could well explain the low level of usage of these volumes by teacher educators, as more recent research in non-Western countries such as Malawi (Glasson et al. 2006) and the Pacific region (Thaman 2010) indicates. The findings from these studies suggest that teacher education programmes that are grounded in local culture and environment are more relevant and effective.

However, there are other aspects of teacher educators and teacher education institutions that require elaboration at this point to better clarify their responses to the calls for the incorporation of environmental education into teacher education.

4 Understanding the Response of Teacher Educators and Teacher Education Institutions

The calls for teacher education to include environmental education were heeded by those who were engaged with the area, but for others, the calls fell on deaf ears because environmental education was seen as a political priority rather than an educational one. The calls for its inclusion came from government level meetings and from activists outside of education—often environment groups and government environmental agencies—rather than from within education bureaucracies. As such, it was seen as yet another pressure for inclusion of an area into an already overcrowded curriculum—along with such things as driver education, sex education, multicultural education, and so on.

With a few exceptions—such as Oman (Mulà and Tilbury 2011), South Africa (Lotz-Sisitka 2012) and Vietnam (UNESCO 2013)—within governments, the policy pushes and statements in favour of environmental education were forthcoming from environment agencies and were thus distanced from the education authorities—and as such did not carry any requirement to comply.

Another significant issue in some countries is, exactly what constitutes pre-service teacher education. This can vary from being 1 year of training after a high school certificate for primary teachers in Bangladesh to a 2 year Master of Education programme following an undergraduate degree for secondary teachers in Finland and Australia—and in some countries there are many unqualified teachers.

Apart from different lengths in qualifying courses there are also differences between primary teacher education and secondary teacher education in terms of the content and focus of the programmes. Primary teachers are educated to be generalists, and are often expected to be experts in everything. Their programmes often specifically focus on literacy and numeracy as the basics of education because, in some countries, many students do not even reach these basic levels before they stop coming to school. Secondary teachers are trained to be specialized subject teachers rather than generalists and this too can militate against them being able to take on board environmental education because of their own preferences and the pressures of content for their specializations.

Thus the range of options for the inclusion of ESD in teacher education programmes that can be found in practice include:

- Struggling to be recognized as core curriculum alongside literacy and numeracy in early childhood and primary teacher education programmes,
- Being offered as an elective, which results in a few teachers specializing in ESD,
- Being mainstreamed across the teacher education programme so that a genuine 'whole-of-system' approach to ESD can be developed, or
- A combination of the above (adapted from Ferreira et al. 2006, p. 13).

The extent to which any teacher education institution takes up one or all of these options is usually within the control of the institution. As Higgins and Kirk (2002, p. 9) note with respect to Scotland,

> While the structure of programmes is determined by regulatory bodies, teacher education institutions can be as innovative and flexible as they wish, so long as their programmes are fully compatible with the national guidelines… it is left to individual teacher education institutions to determine how much emphasis is to be given to ESD.

Hopkins and McKeown (2005, pp. 30–32) identified a number of challenges to re-orienting teacher education for ESD which build on this comment from Higgins and Kirk. Within the teacher education institutions these include:

- Official national and provincial curriculum rarely mandates sustainability.
- Teacher certification guidelines do not mention sustainability.
- Lack of or inadequately trained professionals who are knowledgeable about ESD.
- Lack of or inadequate funding and material resources.
- Lack of or inadequate national, provincial and local policy to support ESD.
- Lack of or inadequate institutional climate that supports the creativity, innovation, and risk-taking necessary to support transformative efforts to re-orient education to address sustainability.
- Lack of, or inadequate, reward for institutions or faculty members who undertake ESD programmes.

I discuss the addressing of these challenges in the following sections.

5 Implications of the Shift from EE to ESD for Teacher Education

While the focus in this essay is on teacher education and education for sustainable development rather than environmental education, it is important to acknowledge the similarities and differences between the two areas. Education for sustainable development is seen by some as having grown out of environmental education, given that the characteristics of environmental education described in the Tbilisi recommendations (UNESCO 1978) are almost identical with those describing ESD (United Nations 1993, 2012; UNESCO 2005). However, there is a major difference in that the Tbilisi recommendations were generally interpreted as a drive to change the nature of the knowledge conveyed (for example, by introducing environmentally related topics into the school curriculum) whereas ESD is concerned with changing the way education is conceived. There are therefore significant differences as a result of the linking of education for sustainable development with other international initiatives in the international implementation scheme for the United Nations Decade of Education for Sustainable Development (UNESCO 2005). These initiatives—the Millennium Development Goal (MDG) process, the Education for All (EFA) movement and the United Nations Literacy Decade (UNLD)—are much more obviously linked to Education for Sustainable Development than environmental education, which did not, for example, overtly acknowledge the importance of gender equality (Gough 1999).

According to the implementation scheme, all of these initiatives

> aim to achieve comparable impacts: an improvement in the quality of life, particularly for the most deprived and marginalised, fulfilment of human rights including gender equality, poverty reduction, democracy and active citizenship. There is also a common consensus around the central importance of basic education and the need to extend it and enhance its quality (UNESCO 2004, p. 9).

This aim shares with the earlier description of environmental education a focus on quality of life and active citizenship, however, protecting the environment is no longer mentioned even though environmental stewardship is one of the underlying ideals of sustainable development (along with social equity, justice and tolerance and quality of life) (UNESCO 2005).

It has long been recognised that women's illiteracy is a major obstacle to them achieving full participation in sustainable development (see, for example, *Agenda 21* from the United Nations Conference on Environment and Development (UNCED) (United Nations 1993) so it is not surprising to see gender, literacy and sustainable development linked in the international implementation scheme for the United Nations Decade of Education for Sustainable Development. The Education for All report, for example, notes that "Progress towards the EFA goals is being undermined by a failure of governments to tackle persistent inequalities based on income, gender, location, ethnicity, language, disability and other markers for disadvantage" with an estimated 776 million adults lacking basic literacy skills in 2006, and two thirds of these are women (UNESCO 2008, pp. 4–5). However, the inclusion of Education for All into the agenda for the United Nations Decade of Education for Sustainable Development makes the re-orientation of teacher education for Education for Sustainable Development much more complicated than just re-orienting it to incorporate environmental education. Can the call to "re-orient teacher education for ESD" be interpreted as simply increasing the emphasis on educating teachers to address basic literacy, has the emphasis shifted to one of improving quality of life for all, or is there still an environmental agenda?

The remainder of this essay will discuss these new visions and some initiatives to support them, together with possible strategies for achieving a re-orientation of teacher education.

6 Recent Initiatives to Overcome Obstacles

In 2005, after much international consultation, UNESCO published *Guidelines and Recommendations for Reorienting Teacher Education to Address Sustainability* (Hopkins and McKeown 2005). Unlike the earlier UNESCO-UNEP International Environmental Education Programme (IEEP) series, these *Guidelines* recognized the importance of teacher education institutions developing "their own thematic guidelines based on descriptions and ideals of sustainability" (Hopkins and McKeown 2005, p. 15). To provide some guidance, nine criteria (seven positive and two negative) for creating and evaluating new ESD projects are proposed (Hopkins and McKeown 2005, p. 16):

- ESD is locally relevant and culturally appropriate.
- ESD is based on local needs, perceptions, and conditions, but recognizes fulfilling local needs often has global effects and consequences.
- ESD engages formal, non-formal, and informal education.
- ESD is a life-long endeavor.

- ESD accommodates the evolving nature of the concept of sustainability.
- ESD addresses content, context, pedagogy, global issues, and local priorities.
- ESD deals with the well being of all three realms of sustainability—environment, society, and economy.
- ESD is not imported from another cultural, economic or geographic region.
- ESD is not "one size fits all", but must be created to account for regional differences.

The *Guidelines* document also recognizes that "addressing ESD will require student teachers to think about their profession differently and learn skills that perhaps, teachers in previous eras did not learn or use" as well as understanding the interrelatedness of the environment, society, and economy and having this interrelatedness "evident in their teaching and their lives as community members" (UNESCO 2005, p. 43). However, by having the guidelines so broad there is the risk that teacher educators, and those who determine the content of teacher education programmes, could well continue to overlook ESD because the agenda has become much more complicated and they do not know what to do, so they continue to operate in ignorance until required to act.

Nevertheless, several initiatives took up the challenge posed by the UNESCO *Guidelines*—including, in Australia (Ferreira et al. 2009; Gooch et al. 2008), Canada (Beckford 2008; Dippo 2013), Jamaica (Down 2006), South Africa (Lotz-Sisitka 2012), the United States of America (Nolet 2013) and Vietnam (UNESCO 2013).

The Australian Government, through its Department of the Environment, Water, Heritage and the Arts, funded the "Mainstreaming Education for Sustainability within Teacher Education in Australia" research project (Ferreira et al. 2009). This project piloted a model for whole-of-system change as recommended in Ferreira et al. (2006), which adopted a participatory action research approach to mainstream Education for Sustainability (EfS) within and across a whole pre-service teacher education system. Findings from the pilot study indicate that ESD can be mainstreamed within teacher education by:

- capacity building within the teacher education community by
  - developing competencies in education for sustainability;
  - establishing more effective interactions between decision-makers and other stakeholders;
  - establishing a community of inquiry for participants; and
  - developing an appreciation of whole-school approaches to sustainability
- engaging with policy developers to:
  - enable a realignment of current policies; and
  - make changes to accreditation processes within education departments, teacher registration authorities and curriculum bodies;
- thinking broadly about the teacher education, so that all stakeholders are engaged in the change process; and

- improving networks across the teacher educator systems by: identifying and supporting key agents of change within the sector and by developing new, and utilizing existing, partnerships between schools, teacher education institutions and government agencies in the area of education for sustainability and whole-school approaches.

Similar conclusions emerge from the other studies across six different countries, thus providing some guidance on how to address obstacles to the successful implementation of ESD teacher education.

In the Jamaican study, Down (2006) describes how issues of sustainability were integrated into two different subjects (a basic computer course in the primary programme and a specialist course on Caribbean literature in the secondary programme) teacher education programmes. Down concluded that challenges to the mainstreaming of ESD in teacher education programmes are related to staff, students, syllabuses, policy and support. She noted the need for capacity building of stakeholders, for institutional policy to support such initiatives, for the development of local, regional and international networks to support teacher educators in re-orienting their practices for ESD, and the need for ESD to be conceptualized as locally relevant.

Achieving the goals of education for sustainability requires a very different approach to learning and teaching from that currently practiced in most schools and teacher education institutions. This is not a new observation—it has been signalled since the UNESCO meetings on environmental education of the 1970s. However, after the United Nations Decade of Education for Sustainable Development (2005–2014) brought together the Millennium Development Goal (MDG) process, the Education for All (EFA) movement and the United Nations Literacy Decade (UNLD)—there was a stronger connection with socially transformative education and the importance of universal literacy and social equity. Changing the content of and pedagogical approaches in teacher education is a challenge, but it is one that teacher education institutions can no longer ignore, as several researchers have described through case studies (including Dippo 2013; Ferreira et al. 2009; Lotz-Sisitka 2012; McKeown and Hopkins 2002; McKeown 2014; Stephens 2012). Nolet (2013, p. 4), for example, suggests four strategies for re-orienting teacher education programs in the United States:

- Focus on improving outcomes for all students
- Embed ESD in the process of learning to be a teacher
- Use existing structure, processes, and local resources
- Provide professional development for faculty and administrators.

Some guidance for teacher education institutions is forthcoming from the example of Teacher Education given in the document *Asia-Pacific Guidelines for the Development of National ESD Indicators* for monitoring and assessing progress during the United Nations Decade of ESD in the Asia-Pacific Region (UNESCO Bangkok 2007, p. 4). In particular, the guidelines recommend that each country has national education policy that requires pre-service teacher education courses to provide training in ESD and that all pre-service teacher education courses provide training on ESD-related content and pedagogy.

According to Gooch et al. (2008, p. 185), more guidance needs to be given to the pre-service teachers about "how to teach critical thinking skills and how to formulate plans to address issues such as comparing alternatives, rating suggestions for costs and effectiveness, and anticipating long and short-term consequences of each alternative". They also note the need for the development of networks between pre-service teachers and local communities, for developing exemplars of unit plans as models to guide the pre-service teachers, and for re-orienting "the ways in which teachers think about, and actively plan to teach for sustainability" (Gooch et al. 2008, p. 184).

In addition, teacher education institutions, as higher education institutions, need to be a catalyst for sustainability progress in academic and practical innovation because "The strategic implications of sustainability reach far beyond individual curriculum changes, isolated environmental practices and signatures on international declarations, and require adjustments to academic priorities, organizational structures, financial and audit systems" as well as requiring "considerable innovation for HE institutions to evolve as 'learning organizations'; advancing strategic integration, staff development, collaborative partnerships, and effective stakeholder dialogue" (Ryan et al. 2010, p. 113).

This convergence around strategies for overcoming obstacles provides useful directions for the future implementation of ESD in teacher education.

7 Conclusion

This review of the past thirty or so years of incorporating environmental education into teacher education reveals that there have been many efforts at many levels—so the fact that there are still no consistent or coherent programmes in many institutions is not for want of trying. The approach being taken in recent times is a more comprehensive one, attempting whole system (institution) approaches, and the results from the recent initiatives are encouraging. However, it is likely that these efforts will still struggle to be implemented in many places until ESD becomes an educational priority rather than a political one and it is wholehearted embraced by ministries of education and teacher education institutions.

According to McKeown (2014), the situation is improving and ESD is being woven into teacher education programmes in many ways. For example,

- ESD is being infused into existing coursework—also called embedding or mainstreaming ESD—is a common strategy for beginning to reorient teacher education to address sustainability.
- New courses, and certificate and degree programmes are being created.
- Teacher educators are weaving themes of sustainability and ESD pedagogies into the existing courses.

However, many of these initiatives rely on single enthusiastic individuals and teacher education institutions still need to work with their ministries of education and accept ESD as an educational priority within their teacher education programmes and thereby increasing the percentage of new teachers who understand and can implement ESD-related content and pedagogy. This content needs to be a mandatory component of teacher accreditation, not an option, as teachers have a pivotal role in the education of future generations.

Acknowledgement An earlier version of this essay was presented at the 12th UNESCO-APEID International Conference, Bangkok, Thailand, 24–26 March 2009.

References

Beckford, C. (2008). Re-orienting environmental education in teacher education programs in Ontario. *Journal of Teaching and Learning, 5*(1), 55–66.

Breiting, S., Mayer, M., & Mogensen, F. (2005). *Quality criteria for ESD-schools: Guidelines to enhance the quality of education for sustainable development.* Vienna: Austrian Federal Ministry for Education, Art and Culture.

Brinkman, F. G., & Scott, W. A. H. (1996). Reviewing a European union initiative on environmental education within programmes of pre-service teacher education. *Environmental Education Research, 2*(1), 5–16.

Dippo, D. (2013). Preservice teaching and pedagogies of transformation. In R. McKeown & V. Nolet (Eds.), *Schooling for sustainable development in Canada and the United States* (pp. 69–78). Dordrecht: Springer.

Down, L. (2006). Addressing the challenges of mainstreaming education for sustainable development in higher education. *International Journal of Sustainability in Higher Education, 7*(4), 390–399.

Ferreira J., Ryan L., Davis J., Cavanagh M., & Thomas J. (2009). *Mainstreaming sustainability into pre-service teacher education in Australia.* Canberra: Australian Research Institute in Education for Sustainability for the Australian Government Department of the Environment, Water, Heritage and the Arts.

Ferreira, J., Ryan, L., & Tilbury, D. (2006). *Whole-school approaches to sustainability: A review of models for professional development in pre-service teacher education.* Sydney: Australian Research Institute in Education for Sustainability for the Australian Government Department of the Environment and Heritage.

Fien, J. (1995). Teaching for a sustainable world: The environmental and development education project for teacher education. *Environmental Education Research, 1*(1), 21–33.

Fien, J. (1998). Sustaining action research and professional development in teacher education for sustainability: A case study from Asia and the Pacific. *International Research in Geographical and Environmental Education, 7*(3), 251–254.

Glasson, G. E., Frykholm, J. A., Mhango, N. A., & Phiri, A. D. (2006). Understanding the earth systems of Malawi: Ecological sustainability, culture and place-based education. *Science Education, 90*(4), 660–680.

Gooch, M., Rigano, D., Hickey, R., & Fien, J. (2008). How do primary pre-service teachers in a regional Australian university plan for teaching, learning and acting in environmentally responsible ways? *Environmental Education Research, 14*(2), 175–186.

Gough, A. (1998). Researching environmental education in teacher education: Initiating and sustaining student interest. *International Research in Geographical and Environmental Education, 7*(3), 260–264.

Gough, A. (1999). Recognising women in environmental education pedagogy and research: Towards an ecofeminist poststructuralist perspective. *Environmental Education Research, 5*(2), 143–161.

Higgins, P., & Kirk, G. (2002). Teacher education, outdoor education and sustainability in Scotland. *Planet, 4*, 8–11.

Hopkins, C., & McKeown, R. (2005). *Guidelines and recommendations for reorienting teacher education to address sustainability*. Education for Sustainable Development in Action Technical Paper No.2. Paris: UNESCO.

Kyburz-Graber, R., Robottom, I., Posch, P., & Hart, P. (Eds.). (2006). *Reflective practice in teacher education learning from case studies of environmental education*. Bern: Peter Lang.

Lotz-Sisitka, H. (2012). National case study: Teacher professional development with an education for sustainable development focus in South Africa: Development of a network, curriculum framework and resources for teacher education. In Working Document Presented at the Triennale on Education and Training in Africa, Ouagadougou, Burkina Faso, 7–12 February.

Marcinkowski, T. J., Volk, T. L., & Hungerford, H. R. (1990). *An environmental education approach to the training of middle level teachers: A prototype programme*. UNESCO-UNEP International Environmental Education Programme Environmental Education Series No. 30. Paris: UNESCO.

McKeown, R. (2014). The leading edge of teacher education and ESD. *Journal of Education for Sustainable Development, 8*(2), 127–131.

McKeown, R. & Hopkins, C. (2002). "Weaving sustainability into pre-service teacher education programs". In W. Leal Filho (Ed.), *Teaching sustainability at universities: Towards curriculum greening* (pp. 251–274). Frankfurt: Peter Lang.

McKeown, R., & Nolet, V. (2013). Education for sustainable development in Canada and the United States. In R. McKeown & V. Nolet (Eds.), *Schooling for sustainable development in Canada and the United States* (pp. 3–21). Dordrecht, The Netherlands: Springer.

McKeown-Ice, R. (2000). Environmental education in the United States: A survey of preservice teacher education programs. *The Journal of Environmental Education, 32*(1), 4–11.

Mulà, I., & Tilbury, D. (Eds.). (2011). *National journeys towards education for sustainable development 2011: Reviewing national ESD experiences from Chile, Indonesia, Kenya, The Netherlands, Oman*. Paris: UNESCO.

Nolet, V. (2013). Teacher education and ESD in the United States: The vision, challenges, and implementation. In R. McKeown & V. Nolet (Eds.), *Schooling for sustainable development in Canada and the United States* (pp. 53–67). Dordrecht: Springer.

Ryan, A., Tilbury, D., Corcoran, P. B., Abe, O., & Nomura, K. (2010). Sustainability in higher education in the Asia-Pacific: Developments, challenges, and prospects. *International Journal of Sustainability in Higher Education, 11*(2), 106–119.

Stephens, D. (2012). A critical overview of education for sustainable development with particular focus upon the development of quality teacher education in sub-Saharan Africa. In R. Griffin (Ed.), *Teacher education in sub-saharan Africa: Closer perspectives* (pp. 91–109). Oxford: Symposium Books.

Thaman, K. H. (2010). Teacher capacities for working towards peace and sustainable development. *International Journal of Sustainability in Higher Education, 11*(4), 353–364.

The Belgrade Charter. (1975). Reprinted in Connect, *I*(1), 1–8.

UNESCO. (1978). *Intergovernmental Conference on Environmental Education: Tbilisi (USSR)*, 14–26 October 1977. Final Report. Paris: UNESCO.

UNESCO. (2002). *Teaching and learning for a sustainable future*. Paris: UNESCO.

UNESCO. (2004). *United nations decade of education for sustainable development 2005–2014*. Draft international implementation scheme. October 2004.

UNESCO. (2005). *United nations decade of education for sustainable development (2005–2014): International implementation scheme*. ED/DESD/2005/PI/01.

UNESCO. (2008). *Overcoming inequality: Why governance matters*. EFA Global Monitoring Report 2009 summary. Paris: UNESCO.

UNESCO. (2013). *National journeys towards education for sustainable development 2013: Reviewing national ESD experiences from Costa Rica, Morocco, South Africa, Sweden, Vietnam*. Paris: UNESCO.

UNESCO Bangkok. (2007). *Monitoring and assessing progress during the UNDESD in the Asia-Pacific region: A quick guide to developing national ESD indicators*. Bangkok: UNESCO Bangkok.

United Nations. (1993). *Agenda 21: Earth summit: The united nations programme of action from rio*. New York: United Nations.

United Nations. (2012). *The future we want: Outcomes document adopted at Rio+20*. Rio de Janeiro: United Nations.

Wals, A. (2009). *Review of contexts and structures for education for sustainable development 2009*. Paris: UNESCO.

Wals, A., & Nolan, C. (2012). *Shaping the education of tomorrow: 2012 report on the UN decade of education for sustainable development, abridged*. Paris: UNESCO.

Author Biography

Annette Gough has been working in the field of environmental education since she conducted Australia's first needs for environmental education survey in 1974. She received her doctorate in education from Deakin University in 1995 where she researched the foundations of environmental education. She first taught at Deakin University but has been Professor of Science and Environmental Education the School of Education at RMIT University in Melbourne, Australia since 2005. She has been an adjunct or visiting professor at universities in Canada, South Africa and the Hong Kong Institute of Education, and has worked with UNESCO, UNEP and UNESCO-UNEVOC on research and development projects. She is a life fellowship of the Australian Association for Environmental Education. Her research interests include curriculum policy and development in science and environmental education, feminist, posthuman, critical and poststructuralist research, and research methodologies. She has written over 120 books, reports, essays, articles and curriculum materials in science and environmental education and related areas.

Part II
Contextualised Case Studies

Inquiry-Based Educational Course in Higher Education Towards Sustainable Communities: A Case Study

Dzintra Iliško

Abstract

Universities play a crucial role in educating a new generation in dealing with the concerns of global sustainability and assisting change towards sustainable development. Various attempts have been made to integrate sustainability into the University's agenda. Many higher institutions have included sustainability in their mission statements and adopted a whole institutional approach of integrating sustainability; many universities have designed study courses with the aim to promote learners' knowledge and understanding about environmental and societal issues. This article reflects efforts of a small scale University study course carried out with the aim to empower learners to change their behaviour and to take action for sustainable development by dealing with real cases. This article reflects an attempt to engage students in the inquiry based research projects as a part of a study course with the aim of promoting education for sustainable development. Students were asked to engage in an action research as an inquiry based learning process to locate the sites of unsustainable governance in the city level and beyond, and to design a project plan for transforming the selected case of governance/business into a more sustainable one by planning multi-stakeholder collaboration. Students designed a hypothetical plan for a change of situations that are contested, uncertain and complex. Traditional top-down management approaches in those cases are often insufficient. Instead, new forms of governance based on improved collaboration between stakeholders have proved its potential for dealing with complex and contested problems (Westin et al. 2014). By engaging in action research, the students are involved in a process of planning and reflection on strategies in order to transform the chosen case of an inquiry. The learning takes place by changing a focus from the

D. Iliško (✉)
Daugavpils University, Daugavpils, Latvia
e-mail: dzintra.ilisko@du.lv

© Springer International Publishing Switzerland 2016

W. Leal Filho and P. Pace (eds.), *Teaching Education for Sustainable Development at University Level*, World Sustainability Series,
DOI 10.1007/978-3-319-32928-4_9

problem to possible solutions, as well as by exploring how multiple stakeholders' collaboration can transform the situation of inquiry. The potential of this study is to build a capacity for university staff to engage students in evaluation of unsustainable practices, to discover examples of sustainable governance, and to develop a sustainable vision on the issue being investigated.

Keywords
Inquiry based projects · Sustainability · Multiple stakeholders · Action research · Transformation

1 Introduction: Sustainability Framework

The notion of sustainability has evolved since the Brundland Commission report "*Our Common Future*" in 1987. Since the end of the United Nation's (UN) *Decade of Education for Sustainable Development* (DESD) in 2014 much has been achieved in reorienting education towards the aim of sustainable development, still much is left to be done for building a more sustainable society. During the Decade as a result of international cooperation, a number of international networks and joint research projects have been carried out and interdisciplinary publications have been written with the aim to implement the ideals set by the Decade. Sustainable development become a central priority in educational research The analyses of results achieved during a Decade, allowed Universities to set the aim for further work outlined in the *Global Action Program* (GAP 2014). It incorporates a large scale post-2015 framework for accelerated progress towards sustainable development. As this has been emphasized in *the Roadmap for Implementing the Global Action Programme on Education for Sustainable Development* (2014), higher education plays a major role in enhancing changes in society, particularly by introducing whole scale changes "in a way we think and act," thus increasing a capacity of educators, youth and multiple stakeholders to promote sustainable development (UNESCO 2014, p. 7).

GAP has emphasized the need of reorienting educational paradigms leading to the use of more sustainable pedagogies, such as, an inquiry based, exploratory, and action oriented learning approaches with the aim to inspire learners to act in a more sustainable way by taking a responsibility for their actions. Sustainability in higher education is not a buzz word anymore but has its meaning in shaping study courses. Sustainability is also an organic notion in countries' and city's major strategic and development plans, such as *Sustainable Development Strategy of Latvia until 2030* (2010) that was formulated as a long term challenge for Latvia that covers regional, spatial, energy and environmental issues. It has a reference to a number of significant EU documents which have been ratified and contextualized for the specific context of the country. Still, the challenge remains to translate those strategic documents into tangible actions on individuals' and organizations at the community level.

As Wals and Jickling (2002) argue, sustainability brings together different groups of society and stakeholders with an opportunity for a dialogue. Therefore, the concept of sustainability should be seen not as a static but a dynamic concept open to diverse interpretations. Sustainability measuring indicators should be adjusted to a local contexts and situations. Filho (1999) asserts that embraced University wide sustainability policies will bring into dialogue stakeholders who are interested in fostering a sustainability agenda.

2 Pursuing Sustainable Pedagogies: The Role of Universities

The rationale of implementing sustainable pedagogies set by GAP (Global Action Plan) requires universities to focus on educating students about becoming agents of change in their societies and in their job placements. Quite a number of studies were devoted to ways and strategies for implementing education for sustainable education at the university setting, starting from embedding sustainability as a whole institutional approach to integrating sustainability on the level of study courses. Sustainability has been defined in a number of international documents and declarations (UN "*Decade of Education for Sustainable Development*") (DESD) and OECD (2008) and it became a core agenda in many universities as well. The mission of any university needs to be one step ahead in the processes that are taking place in the society and to contribute to sustainability agenda in the society. European Commission (2013) asserts that the task of higher education is to educate critical thinkers and problem solvers and doers, as well as to educate environmentally responsible citizens. Barth et al. (2007) stress that universities need to develop students' competencies or dispositions that lead to actions in line with the aim of a sustainable development. The complexity of real world challenges requires developing core competencies for education of a sustainable development.

This paper highlights the experience of good practice of university-based actions for facilitating the transition toward sustainable societies by educating students as agents of change (Ferrer-Balas et al. 2008). A sustainability—oriented University curriculum needs: to engage students in complex analyses of reality, to create space for democratic participation and decision making processes, to use sustainable and participative methodologies, and to provide training for individuals committed to a sustainable future (Junyent and Geli de Ciurana 2008). This is a reflexive pedagogy (Savin-Baden 2000) that teaches students that there are valid perspectives other than their own. This allows the students to examine critically their personal knowledge and engages in a questioning process.

There are lot of cases of good practice on the use of action research on the level of a study course in order to enhance teachers' professional level and ESD competencies (Badjanova and Drelinga 2013; Gedžune et al. 2011) and how to nurture values and develop skills that contribute to a sustainable development (Tilbury 2004; Kravale-Paulina and Olehnovica 2014). By doing so, universities educate future professionals to explore critical features of unsustainability in the community and teaches how to deal with it constructively (Bath and Rieckmann 2012).

Numerous scholars (Brundiers et al. 2010; Dale and Newman 2005) emphasize a value of integrating real world learning opportunities in a course work. As Meridith and Stubbs (2014) conclude, although universities have always played the leading role in initiation change processes in the society, they have not achieved a whole institutional approach. Among the factors of success they have mentioned committed, dedicated people, and local leadership.

Among various studies and policy papers education is also seen as "one of the most powerful tools for providing individuals with the appropriate skills and competencies" in order to become sustainable citizens (OECD 2008, 25). Still, universities need to implement a multi-faceted approach in providing leadership and support to their communities by improving their understanding about current sustainability principles, directions and policy (Justice et al. 2009).

3 Rationale and a Design of an Inquiry-Based Study Course

The university-based study courses designed for the youth specialists and career counsellors' entitled "*Leadership for a sustainable development of a community*" and the course "*Education for the Sustainable cultural and societal changes*" designed for the professional Master program students were designed as a part of curriculum in one of the regional university of Latvia. These study courses offers the students opportunities to engage in an exploratory inquiry of formal and informal youth community organizations by evaluating the educational contribution of their actions for bringing sustainable changes in the community.

Course participants were asked to identify and critically explore themes related to ESD, as well as to apply findings to their own life and their future work through conducting an enquiry in the locality of Latgale region. People from Latgale region experience high levels of unemployment and poverty. Students chose the focus for their study themselves, formulated a research question, decided where they would conduct the enquiry, explored the methods of data collection, and worked on set tasks. The expected outcome of the study course was to raise students' awareness about unsustainability cases in the community, as well as to develop a more balanced and holistic perspective of sustainability comprising ecological, social, economic, culture, and political aspects of their cases. They explored how to deal with unsustainability issues by the involvement of multiple stakeholders.

Steyaert and Jiggins (2007) argue about the need of intervention of multiple stakeholders in order to bring in innovation and to apply various forms of knowledge in order to jointly construct and deconstruct a current practice. The students involved in this study course are trained to be future leaders who will work in youth organizations; therefore, they need to acquire competencies of ESD in order to be more efficient agents of change in their sphere of work. The course work engaged the students to discuss issues related to sustainability, such as value education, equity, justice, intrinsic value of all species, and issues on cultural identity. As Biggs and Watkins (2001) assert, such individuals will be capable to reform unsustainable practices and try out new ideas and to explore contradictions as they appear.

The expectation of the study course is that students will develop collaborative problem solving capacity by addressing real sustainability issues. Students were encouraged to apply knowledge learned in the classroom to address the sustainability issues to real cases by searching for workable contribution and learning how they can have a positive impact in their community. The students planned a joint ownership of stakeholders over the process, common goals and objectives, societal relevancy and collective learning as the recommendations in their cases of study. The students were engaged in the process of evaluating their taken-for-granted assumptions and undertook a journey of constructing alternative, new and expanded frames of reference. Engaged in exploring real cases, the students learned from unfamiliar experiences instead of acquisition of imparted knowledge and developed communicative competency to negotiate and to examine critically their feelings, values and assumptions.

4 Design of the Study

The course is designed for the Master program students in Latvia. The course covered theory on diverse leadership models, approaches, and competences required for the sustainable leadership, and it covered the issue of holistic understanding of sustainability. The students developed criteria of measuring sustainability and strategies for building a collaborative framework with multiple stakeholders. The course was not taught in a traditional didactic teacher-centred way but rather was built on the use of group work, discussions, active students' participation, and the exploration of students' experiences. The course structure was based on engaging the students in action research by engaging the students in the cycle of reflection.

After short introductory lectures, followed by the course readings, students were engaged in a discussion of materials in the class. Reaching a holistic understanding of sustainability and understanding the meaning of sustainable leadership was a central focus of this course. The course was designed in a way that the students were provided with the opportunity to make decisions; therefore the content was built around the ideas, values, and interests expressed by the learners themselves. The students who were engaged in the study at the beginning of the study were asked to describe their intention of the project, the history, mission and the goal of the organization, as well as their concerns and expectation about their chosen case study.

The course integrates theoretical content, collaboration between students and community. Student engagement with the individual inquiry based projects aimed to foster their understanding about the relationships that exist between theory and practice. The organization of the course allowed the students to link their project ideas to their individual interests. The students were encouraged to take an ownership of their own learning, thus, developing their cognitive learning skills. During the project the students attended weekly seminars where they could raise questions and share problems. At the end of the project students were challenged to reflect upon all stages of the project work. Therefore, the course provided a hospitable space for learning and reflection for further action.

During the seminar workshops students were invited to explain their experience related to the course objectives; they were asked to reflect upon the observed data, their learnings, the experience gained in the fieldwork as related to the course readings, the possible improvement of the situation and the contribution of various stakeholders to a chosen case. Finally, at the end of the semester the students were asked to reflect upon their learnings, their values, believes and attitudes that have changed, a contribution of a chosen case to the environmental, culture, and social sustainability. They were asked to design recommendation for the improvement of the situation and collaboration among multiple stakeholders, as well as to evaluate an overall satisfaction with the project. The students were required to identify multiple stakeholders and to evaluate their involvement in their case as well.

Students were asked to evaluate what impact the chosen case/organization had on the participants' behaviour and local community. The students were provided with an opportunity to learn from the stories of hope of leaders from the chosen organization. They were encouraged to carry out life story interviews in order to learn personal and professional agendas of leaders and how they built collaboration with multiple stakeholders leading towards sustainable changes in the community. They were asked to evaluate what was missing in a more sustainable work of a chosen organization and were asked to design an action plan and strategies for the more efficient management of a chosen organization in building a more efficient collaboration with multiple stakeholders.

In order to clarify students' initial understandings of sustainability the tutor has carried out pre-course survey. Students learned which ESD competencies were needed for their future work and were given a task to identify any site in the city or an organization and to explore features of sustainable and unsustainable governance. They did an exploratory study by identifying further improvements by the involvement of multi stakeholders. At the end of the course for their final presentation the students were asked to present their investigated case and to argue about further developments of the case. This paper focuses on the analyses of students' reports on their learnings and enriched understandings. Post-course survey (students' reports) have helped to identify changes in learners' understanding about sustainability and their self-evaluation of their ESD competencies for the further work in fostering sustainability agenda.

4.1 Methodology of the Study

At the beginning of the course the students were engaged in focus group discussion and wrote about their prior understanding of sustainability. This was done with the purpose to identify students' shallow or deep understanding of sustainability and ability to trace the sign of un/sustainability in their lives and in the local community.

Afterwards they were engaged in the spiral process of doing action research (AR) by engaging in identifying the issue, planning the steps for themselves and the process of their inquiries in the community, and developing a plan of introducing changes in the chosen site of the inquiry by the participation of multiple stakeholders.

At the end of the course the students were invited to provide written feedback about the gains and new learning in a post-course inquiry about what they had gained as a result of undertaking this study course. The group of students were also invited to participate in focus group interviews sharing feedback of the process of doing their cases and inquiries.

The main methodology employed is an action research (AR). The transformative power of action research was emphasized in a number of studies (Kemmis and McTaggart 2000; Reason and Bradbury 2008; Phelps and Hase 2002). The reason for the selection of action research is based on its aim "*to develop participants' practical knowing in the pursuit of worthwhile human purposes, grounded in a participatory worldview*" (Reason and Bradbury 2008, p. 1). The author has used dialogic AR that involves undertaking action oriented investigation into organization issues that involves critical reflection of current practices, beliefs, values, and assumptions. In this case the presence of various stakeholders involved a variety of value orientations and assumptions. When engaging with various multiple stakeholders, a researcher acquires different horizons of understanding.

Students were engaged in doing qualitative research that is value-bound and subjective in its essence and that does not intend for any generalizations. There are many researchers who call into question the true objectivity of statistical measures and the possibility of attaining pure objectivity at all (Eisner 1991).

Action research was carried out in an open and non-linear way. It plays its role in disturbing traditional ways of doing things and in facilitating evolutionary possibilities by expanding the spaces of possibilities (Davis and Sumara 2005). The choice of action research as a research methodology was made because of its potential to provoke changes in participants' understandings. It was carried out in cycles of action–reflection that involved experiential learning amongst the research participants by transforming both individuals and their culture. AR developed new understanding for the participants through solving practical issues. Besides, action research expands the borders of discipline oriented conventional science.

Participatory enquiry approaches are integral parts of the exploratory study leading the students to make enquiries about issues identified by themselves in the local community. Reason and Bradbery (2006) argue that inquiry based approaches form the bases of action research in an interactive process. It balances problem solving, action implementation in collaboration in order to understand underlying causes, enabling future prospectus about personal and institutional change. As Wals (2007) argue, the process allows participants to deconstruct the ideas and the assumptions they have held and to embrace new understanding of the case. Practical value of AR is seen in its evolutionary character that allows the research participants to learn skills of inquiry, to deepen one's understanding of societal processes, in opening the space for the participants to articulate their vision and concerns.

4.2 The Sample

This is a small case study that was carried out within the framework of regional University's study course. The participants engaged in this course were eight (N = 8) youth specialists and career counsellors' from the study course entitled "*Leadership for a sustainable development of a community*" and twelve (N = 12) students from the course "*Education for the Sustainable cultural ad societal changes*" designed for the professional Master program students who represented different backgrounds and work experiences. Among the participants were eighteen female and two male students. Eight of them had some work experience in teaching, career counselling, work in youth organizations, small business, and in the sport sector as well. Ten of them were practicing teachers at the secondary school level. The average age of participants was between 25 and 29 years. Six of all the students had a work experience in the state sector and 6 had an experience of work in various youth organizations directly after the completing the undergraduate programs; some of them were involved in the private sector.

4.3 Research Findings

The analyses of the pre-course students' survey and focus group reflections:

Almost all twelve students had some vague understanding about sustainability, and it was mainly related to the environmental aspects. Many of them were not able to relate sustainability to real life situations and did not relate it to education and politics. For many students the understanding was very ambiguous:

One of the students has commented: "*I think sustainability need to be both the governmental priority and priority of every institution. This should not be only a part of bureaucratic papers, but it should be implemented in reality.*"

Another comment: "*We do hear about sustainability almost every day in media. We hear it in government's strategic announcements, but I am not quite sure how to define it. It is all about the development of the country, people, the environment and the things we have a concern about. Most probably sustainability is in all the things around.*"

Another student's focuses on social aspects of sustainability "*To my mind sustainability is mostly related to the way we live and consume, but we consume more than the planet can restore its resources. If we continue doing so, there will be limit of natural resources even for us.*"

The analyses of the post course students' survey and group reflections:

After completing the course the students were engaged in a focus groups interview and were required to write a post-course reflection on their gains and new leanings. It is evident from the post-course survey that the students had developed a much broader understanding of sustainability and evaluated their agency in pursuing sustainable changes. As one of the students has written in his report, "*I am eager to bring a sustainability message to youth with whom I will be working.*" Another student has written: "*I will use my skills and newly acquired knowledge for a well-being of the community.*" This comment indicates willingness of course participants to introduce some changes in the community. Some students were more engaged; some displayed a lower level of commitment and were less engaged in doing a fieldwork. The level of the engagement in the project work depends on interest and intrinsic motivation for the topic of each individual student. After the completion of their projects the students understood more clearly about the unsustainability causes and the need to change habitual patterns of living by engaging every single individual in building a better future.

As one of the participants wrote: "*Most of the population lives in the cities of high concentration of transportation which is the main source of pollution. That's why people and organizations living in the cities need to make commitments in favor of sustainable development.*"

Engagement in a deeper learning:

A majority of students displayed intrinsic motivation and engaged in deep learning of the chosen topic.

"*By exploring real life cases I have developed a deeper understanding of sustainability issues. The course opened me to new ideas about issues studied. The course was really challenging. It was not about learning theories but interacting with real people.*" Another student commented: "*At the beginning of the course I thought that sustainability was mainly concerned about the environmental issues and governmental policies. Now I see that it is all about real people doing real things in the community.*"..."*I became aware about unsustainable practices in my community and learned about the diverse ways to tackle it.*"

Another student also commented: "*While doing research I have realized that sustainability is not an abstract notion but it is part of my life and lives of others, as well as part of the organizations where you work.*"

Supportive learning community for exercising agency:

A supportive learning community was mentioned among the contributing factors for deep and transformative learning: "*There was always a possibility to express an opinion, to ask question and to know that all your concerns will be attended.*"

Safe spaces for making sense of one's experience:

"*While coming back from the* sites *of inquiry, our mentor invited us to share concerns we have encountered and to discuss with the classmates. Feedback and suggestions received from the instructor of the course enriched my understanding and helped me to shape further stages of my inquiry.*"

"We all were given an opportunity to take charge of our learning, to choose a site of inquiry, to set a question that was a real challenge that I was not provided in other courses."

Meta analyses of students' oral and written feedback—gains and difficulties:

Among the gains of enquiry-based learning one can mention the following: the importance of students' experience, students' ownership over the learning process, crossing boundaries among the disciplines, interrelatedness of theory and practice, the focus on the process rather than learning results. Students' participation is more meaningful if they take initiative and responsibility over the research process. The agenda prescribed by the teacher and the denial that youth is productive in generating new ideas results in passivity and a low participation of youth. By being engaged in the inquiry based learning the students have understood that learning takes place in the context of real life situations.

Students learned that there are various ways of knowing and they have questioned what counts as valid knowledge. They were framing their experiences and simultaneously were challenging the institutions and socio-political contexts in which they live, work and learn. They have engaged deeply in what has been learned and have challenged the validity of that understanding as well.

One of the main difficulties the students came across is that the students who have experienced lecture based methods of learning in their schools and university where they are required to acquire 'right answers', find this difficult to engage in the enquiry based learning process that requires critical thinking. While being engaged in researching complex situation, they need to decide what information and new sills are needed to deal with the situation of inquiry.

The **limitation** of this study:

The limitation of this study is that the evaluation of the course was only within one institution of higher education. The expansion of the sample to various institutions can certainly be beneficial for the evaluation of results. The comparative sample between institutions would give more insights into the issue of a study. Feedback received from the students was of a qualitative character and can be biased towards a positivist perspective. The choice of a qualitative research methodology as a dialogical inquiry requires one to question dominant norms and assumptions in real cases rather to respond to the pre-defined goals. Qualitative research can produce generalizations and ultimate answers. It focuses on hermeneutic knowledge of everyday life situations (Reason and Bradbury 2001, p. 2). It can provide clear answers and it does not generate "ultimate and verified knowledge" but rather contributes to a social dialogue and praxis in the society (Flyvbjerg 2001, p. 139). It generates shared understanding by learning together and points to importance of transforms individuals values and belief. As Gadamer (1992) asserts, we can never achieve a complete understanding of an issue of study. Instead, he views a value of engagement in the inquiry in reaching new understanding and questioning current understandings.

Validity of the use of AR is determined not merely by measured outcome or solved problem but in articulating subtle ways in which the inquiry is affecting our world and one' value system and assumptions, and deeper articulation of a more sustainable world.

5 Finding Meaning in the City: Locating Indicators of Un/Sustainability

There is still no consensus neither how to define sustainability nor what makes community sustainable. Research carried out by Meridith and Stubbs (2014) and Ferrer-Balas et al. (2008) indicates that organization that embraced a sustainability agenda can be described in a following way: it has a vision that expresses commitment to sustainability; it translates strategies of sustainability into practice and is aware of an ecological footprint it leaves, together with sustainable policies and practices that minimise a footprint. The indices of a sustainable city are water, transport management, composting, green areas, and policy of saving natural resources for the future generations, reduction waste production in the residential area. Exploration of sustainability in the city residential area involves a study of interconnectedness of social, economic, culture and environmental aspects.

The choice of a site of an inquiry made by the students was wide, considering the diversity of students' backgrounds and interests. Key themes identified from the students' field work of inquiry based approaches were a gas/oil station, a culture palace, youth organizations, and farmer's estate as an example of sustainable governance. One of the students chose to explore a case on a sustainability of her own parents' farmer's estate. She has identified the interconnectedness of political, economic, culture, environmental aspects as related to this particular case. After completing the course reading and class discussions she was surprised that "*sustainability is all around, you simple need to be aware how everything is interconnected: politics, environmental aspect, the way you think and plan your business; this all has a significant influence on a local and global environment.*" This student who chose to explore farmer's estate, in her report wrote: "*I clearly see how the governmental policy influences the development and the survival of an idea of sustainable governance and culture beyond the city.*" The development of small farming businesses becomes attractive for many young entrepreneurs who made a decision to move out of the city and settle in the suburbs.

Sustainability involves thinking about the future impacts of actions and investments one performs today and their impact tomorrow, as well as about social and environmental aspects of an issue of study, that has an expression as an efficient use of resources, waste management, sustainable buildings and social inclusion. Among the other indicators of sustainability students have explored environmental aspects, interconnectedness with the nature, resilient economy, community health, responsible regionalism, and intergenerational interconnectedness.

In the reflection about the case of a small farmer's estate the student wrote: "*When I began to investigate the case, It seems that this case is mainly to do with economic factors, but, when in engaging in the course readings, exploring the case in depth and discussing with the course participants, I have discovered strong links of all the sustainability factors in my case.*"

The students have identified the strength and weaknesses of management in a chosen organization, as well as interconnectedness of all dimensions of sustainability. The students have explored the contextual factors of their case, and the involvement of multiple stakeholders.

In the case of Youth Centre the student wrote: "*My case of study illustrates more vividly the importance of a negotiation among all the stakeholders in meeting the needs of contemporary youth.*"

The students were asked to imagine and to design a farsighted strategy and action for the improvement of their case by the involvement of multiple stakeholders. The strategy needed to take into account environmental, economic, culture and political requirements for its success and the impacts of actions on the ecosystem. Social dimension (Does the program provide opportunities for creative self-expression, meeting one's basic needs, encourages diversity, fosters strong intergenerational ties, fosters culture of place (maintenance of traditions, openness of novelty), political dimension (collective decision making through cooperation); economic dimension (reusing resources and reducing waste).

The student who chose the case of farmer's estate as an example of sustainable governance have examined wise use of resources, actions carried out by the farmer to satisfy the needs of the family members in harmony with the surrounding environment. The student wrote: "*In my case I see how a farmer meets one's basic needs, fosters strong intergenerational ties; I observe the culture of place* (*interplay of maintaining traditions and openness of novelty*), *which is an example of wise governance.*" Among the potential stakeholders she has named local municipality and the state that need to provide more support to small farming businesses.

The other student who chose to explore a gas station from the insiders' perspective pointed to the attempts of the gas station management team to create "*an ecologically sustainable space within by providing ecological services to its customers, by creating space of intergenerational encounters and advertising a strategy of reusable cups.*" Still he has noticed some contradiction between the officially declared ecologically friendly mission of an organization and real praxis of implementing this strategy. He has identified interconnectedness of sustainability dimensions and has noticed how this organization is seeking ways to become ecologically sustainable by practicing new organizational narrative and introduced changes that occurred within the internal physical environment of the facilities.

6 Community Involvement

Students reflected on the need of community involvement for a sustainable change to occur: "*I think that laws and declaration will not make people to act in a sustainable way, it's up to all community members to make wise everyday choices.*"

The community's involvement was well pronounced in the cases of Youth Club and culture place that provided the space for the intergenerational encounters and exchange that had a great potential for creativity to meet the needs within the limits of the environment.

As the student has commented "*I was surprised how the wisdom of older generation can be of great benefit for a younger generation.*"

The case of Youth Club chosen by one of the students is a good example of community involvement. This case represents a high adaptivity to the needs of youth, a rich repertoire of responses, accumulation of diverse variations of responses to those needs and flexibility. The case is a good representation of a complex adaptive system, the members of which easily work under uncertainty; it has an inherent capacity to be adaptable, serve multiple purposes and to maintain a balance between tradition and innovation, stability and instability.

"*I have learned how flexible and sensitive could be the leaders of a youth club towards the needs young people. This case is a good example of wise leadership. Even in poor economic circumstances the leader could attract financing from the diverse sources by arguing the needs of youth.*"

The case of youth organizations demonstrated the case of an attractive and responsive organization to the needs of youth, and served an example of an adaptive leadership. As Goldstein et al. (2010) argue, successful management in an adaptive organization requires 'positive interaction and interdependence' (p. 42) which was a case in this youth organization. Adaptive management in this organization indicates the adaptive actions made based on the situational possibilities and community needs. As described by the student, maintenance of traditions and openness to innovative experience is another feature that characterizes the sustainable governance in this organization. The students also reported about the barriers and difficulties of communicating sustainability messages within an organization.

6.1 Involvement of Multiple Stakeholders

Another aspect that the students have explored was the involvement of multiple stakeholders in bringing sustainability vision alive: "*Sustainable society cannot be created without the involvement of all members of the society.*" While doing their inquiries the students pointed out that in some cases the stakeholders are more actively involved in a decision making processes than in others. They have identified who the stakeholders really are in their specific case, explored how the specific goal and the strategic environment of a chosen organization allow the involvement of specific stakeholders, as well as have explored the impact of interactions between multiple stakeholders. They have identified a position of stakeholders on a grid (scale) representing varying degrees of power and interest of the investment of stakeholders in a chosen organization, ranging from low involvement to leading position in a chosen organization. Defining those relations participants have learned more about stakeholders and their influence upon the organization's strategic development.

The student who chose the Youth organization, wrote: "*I have observed how the charismatic leadership and democratic power sharing has attracted stakeholders, their diverse views and values were taken into account.*"

The students have explored regulations, implicitly and explicitly embedded practices and routines, culture and norms in a chosen organization. They have explored stakeholder's relationships that included a history of collaboration, types of relationships, and stakeholder's agendas. The other aspect of exploration was stakeholders' agency: receptiveness and commitment to collaboration with others, scope and goals set by the stakeholders to reshape the situation for better. Stakeholder's agency included commitment to collaboration with others, decision-making capacity, and time allocated to this process. They have discovered diverse views and values of stakeholders, their joint ownership of the decisions made in a certain case, as well as about their collective responsibility in a certain case. The students closely examined issues of power, control and stakeholder's involvement in all stages of the case.

In the particular case of a small farmer's governance the student has emphasized the need for a more favourable governmental policy in supporting and promoting sustainable farming. The other aspects explored in this particular case were ownership, sustainable leadership, farmer's agency and decision making agency to make changes in transforming environment for better, as well as unconditional devotion of one's time for one's own and consumers' benefit.

The student wrote: "*In my case I see that for many stakeholders sustainability is only a buzz word written in the official declaration. When this comes to reality and a real support to a small farming business some governmental stakeholders turn out to be deaf and blind. …The whole burden lies on the shoulders of the farmer. And sometimes this seems that he is left all alone Nowadays farmers become more courageous to apply to the EU funds and succeed in getting this support, still, the governmental support is almost invisible. Therefore, many farmers give up building their sustainable business. Instead of getting help from the governmental stakeholders, they put more obstacles and inspections.*"

The other significant aspect that was analysed was different aspects of power in the inquiry situation and the expressions of power as a power over, a power with and a power within, by taking into account different values and interests among the stakeholders. One of the course students has provided an excellent case of shared power relationships among various stakeholders by describing the case of Center for Youth as an example of multifunctional regional Culture Centre that fostered intergenerational cooperation, cooperation between multiple stakeholders built on trust, co-creation of knowledge, reaching out to new stakeholders and deepening understanding of the situation to transform it for better. That was a good example of practicing power with others by acting together and bringing knowledge, resources and strategies towards a sustainable goal. As a desired vision was an involvement of governmental stakeholders to provide financial support needed to support the activities organized by the centre.

Particular interest of another student was a study of a pollution of water in the city lakes and rivers, as well as a shared responsibility of various stakeholders to control and to improve water quality. The student has analysed the causes of deterioration of the environment. Among the causes she has listed the unsustainable pattern of consumption and production as well as citizen's and government's irresponsibility and the absence of a reliable and comprehensive system of monitoring of industrial emissions in compliance with the environmental standards.

While doing the case, the student has reflected: "*During my discovery I have discovered that there is gap between written declarations and practice. The government does not implement all those declarations of taking protective measures of water pools in practice. Also, the society needs to be educated of far reaching consequences of water pollution. This work need to start already at the kindergarten stage and in the families. Municipalities need to arrange educational programs for the community. Talkas (annual societal involvement in cleaning the surrounding environment) is not enough to change the situation. This should become a habit of mind of each inhabitant.*"

Several studies were designed to explore the food quality in educational institutions and shared responsibility of multiple stakeholders of ensuring the food quality in kindergartens and schools. The cases that represented the stories of efficient leadership proved to be the cases of teams of stakeholders striving for development of common understanding and policies. The students described how the organizations maintain their relationships with their various external stakeholders.

Two cases were designed to study consumption patterns and choices of city's customers in the supermarkets, as well as availability of ecological food in the stores. The students have explored consumption patterns of citizens as an aspect of their sustainable lifestyle that relates to the nature and amount of the different goods and service which they choose. For the purpose of their studies the students carried out online surveys, interviews and observation. The student has concluded: "*Unfortunately, poor economic situation the country is the main factor determining consumers' patters of choice of cheaper and more often unhealthy food.*"

The student wrote: "*This was painful to observe how the customers were choosing cheap and low quality food in the supermarkets. There were not many people who made their purchases in the food stores based to critical reasoning. The most vulnerable group is retired people and people from the low income families who chose low quality food.*"

Among the conclusions made by the students was as following: "*People need to be educated in sustainable life styles but government also need to support the most disadvantaged groups of people. The most disadvantaged people are forced to grow their own vegetables. They do this not because of sustainability reasons but as a result of poor economic conditions. Of course, there is a good tendency among the middle class to grow their own vegetables and to build a small sustainable farming out of sustainable considerations.*"

Consumption is critical for sustainable development since food belong to one of the basic human needs. The student has linked food sustainability to sustainable agriculture (way of raising and producing food, organically produced food, regional and seasonal products as well to packaging of food and fair trade issues). This case contributed to the increase of student's consumption awareness and competence as well as developed a better understanding of contributions of stakeholders in fostering sustainable consumer learning.

The students wrote: "*We need to join our effort in building a sustainable society of raising each individual's consciousness about the urgent need and a benefit of a sustainability in everyday situations.*"

7 Suggestions for Higher Institutions for Building Inquiry-Based Study Courses

Sustainability has been integrated in higher educational courses worldwide though, in most cases, the traditional format of the courses did not have impact on students' attitudes and behaviour regarding sustainability issues (Azapagic et al. 2005). Therefore, the study courses should aim to engage students in solving real transdisciplinary case studies or ill-defined problems by interacting with multiple stakeholders.

Single university courses do not capture the complexity of the concept of sustainability; therefore, this is advisable to adopt a holistic view of sustainability by engaging students in real life situations in the society. This way, university will gain from the expertise of multiple stakeholders. By engaging in complex life situations, theoretical knowledge will have its practical application. As a result, graduates need to adopt a vision of sustainable development which they can implement in their life and professional sphere of work.

Integrating sustainability in the university setting requires restructuring of didactic arrangements from teacher centred to inquiry based and experiential learning arrangements. It does not require recipes how to do it, but rather understanding of sustainability as a complex concept, involving ethical, moral, spiritual issues and its openness to different interpretations.

This is advisable that University's educational programs increase not only theoretical knowledge of sustainability but also focus on the impact of the programme on students' behaviour and attitudes, since the purpose of education is to acquire "values, behaviours and lifestyles required for sustainable development" (UNESCO 2006, p. 3). Acquired knowledge need to be applied in real-life cases, where it becomes sustainable.

Sustainable pedagogies challenge both, what is taught and how sustainability is taught in higher education (Cortese 2003; Rowe 2007). Students can learn how to deal with complex problems successfully if they are exposed to those problems and are encouraged to look for innovative ways to deal with them. Though, not all real-world learning opportunities are appropriate for sustainability programs. Some opportunities are more appropriate, some are less suitable for learning about sustainability, since they do not reflect key features of sustainability.

Inquiry based and experiential learning contributes more efficiently to transformations at the individual level when the students engage in a reflection on complex systems within themselves. Reaching individual level of sustainability is a starting point that carries along societal transformations. It includes awareness of ones values, behaviours and actions, as well as aspects of emotional, social, spiritual and intellectual aspects of one's life. As Papas et al. (2015) argue, transformations at the individual level potentially guides humans' responsibilities to collaborate with others and to make 'life-affirming decisions' (p. 324).

Development of deeper University's relations with various profit, non-profit and municipal organizations through these research projects fostered further collaboration and cooperation that helped in placement of students for jobs and internships. While doing enquiry, the students identify connections and interdependencies, participate in critical questioning on unsustainable systems, policies and practices. Therefore, teacher training programs need to focus on building a holistic picture on understanding any issue by the students, communities and stakeholders.

8 Concluding Remarks

Action research (AR) methodology was used to facilitate transformation of students' prior understandings of sustainability in the local community towards developing a broader and richer understanding. The course leader as engaged them in a reflexive and inquiry based learning process by inviting them to reconsider assumptions that underline their interpretation of the cases they chose. Inquiry method as an open ended and reflexive process used in the course allowed space for building new knowledge that is central in action research process which is carried out in the community of practice. It provided the students the opportunity to participate in the process of designing desirable changes in the nearest community.

AR was aimed to facilitate changes in students' perspectives on a more personal level leading that becomes a ground for a commitment to undertake a responsibility and leadership to bring along changes in the local community. By participating in group discussions and sharing their understandings with their classmates, the students formulated their perspectives on the issue of study, became acquainted with the perspectives of their co-learners, received a feedback both from the course mentor and the other classmates.

While doing action research few aspects must be underlined: identification of un/sustainability aspects in real world situations, emotional responsiveness, concern displayed towards the issue of study, and a professional responsibility and commitment to change the issue. Engagement in with the real world case allowed students to discuss and to reflect on the dominant modes of governance and leadership, stakeholders' involvement in their cases, to deepen their interpretations, as well as to plan strategies for its improvement.

The students discovered that those stakeholders, who are committed to building a more sustainable community, play a vital role in the change processes. The students have identified that the factors critical to enable stakeholders the transformational changes include: a strong sustainability policy and an awareness of other stakeholders about the importance of implementing sustainability agenda as a key to a successful leadership strategy.

Students who were engaged in the course were involved in visionary and imaginative work of thinking about sustainability problems in different and new ways. It was discovered that the students came to the course with the environmental focus on sustainability issues and gradually expanded their focus on sustainability as a complex and all-encompassing concept. The students have developed a more balanced and a holistic perspective of sustainability comprising ecological, social, economic, culture and political aspects and future oriented vision dealing with unsustainability issues.

The arrangement of the course indicates that when the students are actively engaged in learning and exploration, they become advocates of sustainability. Learner-cantered, participatory and interactive context was among the factors fostering deep learning. The inquiry done by the students proved to be a powerful method in broadening students' understanding of sustainability and their role as agents of change and future leaders. By engaging in addressing real world problems students have learned to identify, to evaluate and to carry out stakeholders' analysis.

Complexity of lens the students' used to understand their case extended to abstract thinking moving beyond their habitual ways of viewing phenomena. By providing 'thick descriptions', the students tried to increase their awareness of the contextual factors of their study. They paid deeper and more detailed attention to the case of their study by moving beyond a conventional way of seeing their cases. By undertaking the project the students were seeking the answers in real life situations from people, places and events. By finding the features of unsustainable governance they also generated new understanding of a sustainable governance and leadership.

References

Azapagic, A., Perdan, S., & Shallcross, D. (2005). How much do engineering students know about sustainable development? The findings of an international survey and possible implications for the engineering curriculum. *European Journal of Engineering Education, 30*(1), 1–19.

Badjanova, J., Iliško, Dz., & Drelinga, E. (2013). Holistic approach in reorienting teacher education towards the aim of sustainable education: The case study from the regional university in Latvia. In *Procedia-Social and Behavioural Journal.* ISSN: 1877-0428.

Barth, M., Godemann, J., Rieckmann, M., & Stoltenberg, U. (2007). Developing key competencies for sustainable development in higher education. *International Journal of Sustainability in Higher Education, 8*(4), 416–430.

Bath, M., & Rieckmann, M. (2012). Academic staff development as a catalyst for curriculum change towards education for sustainable development: An output perspective. *Journal of Cleaner Production, 26*, 28–36.

Biggs, J., & Watkins, D. (Eds.), Classroom Learning: Educational Psychology for the AsianTeacher. Singapore: Prentice Hall.

Brundiers, K., Wiek, A., & Redman, C. L. (2010). Real world opportunities in sustainability: From classroom into the real world. *International Journal in Higher Education, 11*(4), 308–324.

Cortese, A. D. (2003). The critical role of higher education in creating a sustainable future. *Planning for Higher Education, 31*(3), 15–22.

Dale, A., & Newman, L. (2005). Sustainable development, education and literacy. *International Journal of Sustainability in Higher Education, 6*(4), 351–362.

Davis, B., & Sumara, D. (2005). Complexity science and educational action research: Towards a pragmatics of transformation. *Educational Action Research, 13*(3), 453–464.

Eisner, E. W. (1991). *The enlightened eye: Qualitative inquiry and the enhancement of educational practice*. New York: Macmillan Publishing Company.

European Commission (EU) (High Level Group on the Modernization of Higher Education). (2013). *Improving the quality of teaching and learning in Europe's Higher Education Institutions, Report to the European Commission*. Accessed in August, 2013, http://ec.europa.eu/education/library/reports/modernisation_en.pdf

Ferrer-Balas, D., Adachi, J., Banas, S., Davidson, C. I., Hoshikoshi, A., Mishra, A., et al. (2008). An international comparative analyses of sustainability transformations across seven universities. *International Journal of Sustainability in Higher Education, 9*(3), 295–316.

Filho, W. L. (1999). Sustainability and university life: Some European perspectives. In W. L. Filho (Ed.), *Sustainability and university life* (pp. 19–30). New York: Peter Lang.

Flyvbjerg, B. (2001). *Making social science matter*. Cambridge: Cambridge University Press.

Gadamer, H. G. (1992). *Truth and method* (2nd ed.). New York: Crossroad. (transl. By J Weinsheimer & D. G. Marshall).

GAP. (2014). *Global action program*. Paris: UNESCO.

Gedžūne, G., Gedžūne, I., Salīte, I., & Iliško, Dz. (2011). Exploring pre-service teachers' frames of reference and their orientation towards inclusion or exclusion: Educational action research journey. In *Proceedings of the 9th JTEFS/BBCC conference Sustainable Development. Culture*. Education: BBCC Mission - Reorientation of Teacher Education and Research in Education for Sustainable Development, 18–21 May 2011 (pp. 80–102). Siauliai: Vš Šauli universiteto leidykla. ISBN 978-609-430-077-6.

Goldstein, J., Hazy, J. K., & Lichtenstein, B. B. (2010). *Complexity and the nexus of leadership*. New York: Palmgrave Macmillan.

Junyent, M., & Geli de Ciurana, A. (2008). Education for sustainability in university studies: A model for reorienting the curriculum. *British Educational Research Journal, 34*(6), 763–782.

Justice, C., Rice, J., Roy, D., Hudspith, B., & Jenkins, H. (2009). Inquiry-based learning in higher education: Administrator's perspectives on integrating inquiry pedagogy into curriculum. Higher Education: Administrators' perspectives on integrating inquiry pedagogy into the curriculum. *Higher Education, 58*, 841–855.

Kemmis, S., & McTaggart, R. (2000). Participatory action research. In N. K. Denzin & Y. S. Lincoln (Eds.), *Handbook of quantitative research* (pp. 567–605). Thousand Oaks: Sage.

Kravale-Paulina, M., Iliško, Dz., & Olehnovica, E. (2014). Values orientation approach to the educational process: The temporal dimension. In A. C. Sexton, T. Franklin, & A. Eskicumali (Eds.), *Proceedings of the 4th International Conference on New Horizons in Education*, Social and Behavioural Sciences, Elsevier, Webuser ID: 12880518, Vol. 106, pp. 3285–3290.

Meridith, R., & Stubbs, W. (2014). Integrating environmental sustainability into universities. *Higher Education, 67*, 71–90.

OECD—Organization for Economic Co-Operation and Development. (2008). *Promoting sustainable consumption. Good Practices in OECD Countries*. http://www.oecd.org/greengrowth/40317373.pdf (Last accessed in 10.02.2015).

Our Common Future. (1987). *Brundtland report*. World Commission on Environment and Development (WCED): United Nations.

Papas, E., Papas, P., & Sweeney, D. (2015). Walking the walk: Conceptual foundation of the sustainable personality. *Journal of Cleaner Production, 86*, 323–334.
Phelps, R., & Hase, S. (2002). Complexity and action research: Exploring the theoretical and methodological connections. *Educational Action Research, 10*(3), 503–519.
Reason, P., & Bradbury, H. (2001). Introduction: Inquiry and participation in search of a world worthy of human aspiration. In P. Reason & H. Bradbury (Eds.), *Handbook of action research: Participative inquiry and practice* (pp. 1–14). London: Sage.
Reason, P., & Bradbury, H. (2006). *The handbook of action research*. London: Sage.
Reason, P., & Bradbury, H. (2008). *The Sage handbook of action research: Participative inquiry and practice*. London: Sage.
Roadmap for Implementing the Global Action Programme on Education for Sustainable Development. (2014). Paris: ENESCO, Accessed at June, 2015 http://unesdoc.unesco.org/images/0023/002305/230514e.pdf
Rowe, D. (2007). Education for a sustainable future. *Science, 317*(5836), 323–324.
Savin-Baden, M. (2000). *Problem-based learning in higher education: Untold stories*. The Society for Research into Higher Education: Open University Press.
Steyaert, P., & Jiggins, J. (2007). Governance of complex environmental situations through social learning: A synthesis of SLIM's lessons for research, policy and practice. *Environmental Science & Policy, 10*, 575–586.
Sustainable Development Strategy of Latvia until 2030. (2010). Latvia: Saima of the Republic of Latvia. Accessed at July 30, 2015, http://www.cbs.nl/NR/rdonlyres/B7A5865F-0D1B-42AE-A838-FBA4CA31674D/0/Latvia_2010.pdf
Tilbury, D. (2004). Rising to the challenge: Education for sustainability in Australia. *Australian Journal of Environmental Education, 20*(2), 103–114.
UNESCO. (2006). *Framework for the UNDSD international framework scheme*. UNESCO, Accessed at July 30, 2015, www.unesco.org/new/en/education/themes/leading-the-international-agenda/education-for-sustainable-development/mission/
UNESCO. (2014). *Roadmap for implementing the global action programme on education for sustainable development*. Paris: UNESCO, Accessed at July 20, 2015, http://unesdoc.unesco.org/images/0023/002305/230514e.pdf
Wals, A. E. (Ed.). (2007). *Social learning towards a sustainable world*. Wagening: Academic Publisher.
Wals, A. E., & Jickling, B. (2002). "Sustainability" in higher education. From doublethink and newspeak to critical thinking and meaningful learning. *International Journal in Higher Education, 3*(3), 221–232.
Westin, M., Calderon, C., & Hellquist, A. (Eds.). (2014). *The inquiry based approach—A facilitator's handbook* (2014). SWEDEST (Swedish International Centre for Sustainable Development). Sweden: Swedish International Centre of Education for Sustainable Development, Uppsala University. Accessed at July, 2015, http://uu.diva-portal.org/smash/get/diva2:768134/FULLTEXT01.pdf

Author Biography

Dzintra Iliško PhD., Asoc. Professor at Daugavpils University, Institute of Humanities and Social Sciences, the Head of the Center of Sustainable Education. She is a member of a number of international networks, like, Teacher Education Network (TEN); International Network of Teacher Education Institutions Associated with the UNESCO Chair on Reorienting Teacher Education to Address Sustainability, BBCC network (*Baltic and Black Consortium in Educational Research*); She is an active participant in numerous international projects, for example, "*Lifelong Learning*

Programme Erasmus projekts" *University Educators for Sustainable Development* "(UE4SD)" 2013–2016; NORDPLUS project's intensive program: "Mythology culture and identity in the Nordic and Baltic Countries" (NPHE-2015/10077) 2013–2015 and others. She is a member of UNESCO/UNITWIN network, ISREV (International Society of Religious Education and Values) and ESWTR (European Society of Women in Theological Research). Her research interests are: reorienting teacher education towards the goal of sustainable education, gender issues, and inclusive education.

Students' Engagement in an Extension Program in Agroecology for Subsistence Farmers at the Universidad Católica Santa Maria La Antigua (USMA), Panamá

Bruno Borsari, Nuria Peréz De Gracia and Jorge Castro Peralta

Abstract

Experiential learning complements an education for sustainability that aims at becoming transformative in fostering students' competencies in sustainable development. In this work we assessed the experience of a private institution of higher education in Panamá where a sample of its students was engaged in an extension program for farmers, during the academic year 2014–2015. As part of course work in agroecology, students assisted the investigators with the development of topics and materials to be employed for five one-day workshops that were taught at the university farm, located in Las Minas (Herrera province). In this region, also known as 'Arco Seco' or 'Dry Arc' region of Panamá the dry season causes severe water stresses. The chronic poverty in the farming communities nearby is strongly related to deforestation and amplified by its effects on the hydrologic water cycle and climate change. These factors put at risk food production and quality of life for the inhabitants in most parts of the region. USMA's philosophy of education predicates that every student can be a vector (teacher) of positive change in sustainable development. Through this program we were able to put into practice the tenets of USMA's vision and experience its educational power and benefits.

B. Borsari (✉)
Department of Biology, Winona State University, 175 West Mark Street, Winona, MN 55987, USA
e-mail: bborsari@winona.edu

N.P. De Gracia · J.C. Peralta
Universidad Catolica Santa Maria La Antigua (USMA-Azuero), Chitré, Republic of Panamá
e-mail: NPerez@usma.ac.pa

J.C. Peralta
e-mail: Jorge.castroperalta@gmail.com

© Springer International Publishing Switzerland 2016

W. Leal Filho and P. Pace (eds.), *Teaching Education for Sustainable Development at University Level*, World Sustainability Series,
DOI 10.1007/978-3-319-32928-4_10

Keywords
Agroecology · Curriculum evaluation · Extension education · Food security · Panamá · Sustainable development

1 Education for Sustainable Development in Panamá with Focus in Agroecology

Panamá is a world hot-spot for biological diversity which intermingles with a variety of human cultures and approaches to life styles, farming and quality of life. At the end of the 19th century its rapid population growth, amplified by the construction of the canal, spurred the number of inhabitants a ten-fold increase, beginning to trigger inevitable environmental changes (Heckadon-Moreno and Espinosa-Gonzàlez 1985). Current human pressures continue to be exerted through a steady immigration flux that for the last decade has been attracting even more people to settle in Panamá (INEC-Panamá 2010). Romero and Quental (2014) explained this trend as Panamá's entrance into a prosperous phase, prompting growth and making its robust economy a possible reason for attracting foreign settlement and investments, despite present needs and challenges to enhance innovation, research and a development veering towards sustainability. Despite this rising affluence however, agriculture continues to play a very important role in panamenian economy, employing a majority of its rural population, outside of Panamá city. These are mainly small farmers who hold on to subsistence agricultural practices and a native, rural heritage and culture of doing agriculture. Also, the pressure of expanding farming operations to market agricultural products outside the national borders poses continue threats to land degradation, biodiversity loss, environmental and public health (Mozejko 2009), suggesting an urgent need for promoting a more sustainable development, with an emphasis on food production.

Although an education for sustainable development has already been predicated for a few decades as the successful approach in preparing future generations to cope with the management of declining resources (Onwueme and Borsari 2008), only since the summit Rio + 20 in 2012, the concept of sustainable development has become an integral framework geared towards enhancing a culture for sustainability in higher education (Beynaghi et al. 2014). Numerous academic programs exist already, yet, it appears that curricula often diverge in their breadth and depth of content in sustainability (especially at the graduate level), suggesting the need for a better integration across disciplines (O'Byrne et al. 2014). According to Borsari (2012) societal and institutional barriers continue to challenge an establishment of curricula in sustainability and Panamá is no exception, due also to its limited public spending on education, which appears to be the lowest on record for all of Central America (Mozejko 2009). Consequently, the preparation of panamenian agriculturists may remain void of courses with focus in sustainable development. There is a compelling need to lead education towards sustainable food production and security especially, with increasing unpredictability of weather patterns that more frequently threat to jeopardize agricultural outputs in vast regions of the world, including Panamá (Borsari et al. 2014b). At stake appears to be primarily the livelihood of poor farmers, where increasing population pressures, low level of technology and modest means of intervention, if a crisis occurs, often exacerbate the situation for many. Therefore, an agricultural education founded solidly on ecological principles and theory as proposed by agroecology is a curriculum imperative (Onwueme et al. 2008) that could become applicable to every level of instruction and for any learner in Panamá and elsewhere.

Agroecology is a scientific approach to agriculture that builds on the resource-conserving aspects of traditional, local, and small-scale agriculture while drawing on modern ecological knowledge and methods (Altieri 1995; Gliessman 2007). The resiliency of farming systems depends on agrobiodiversity (Borsari et al. 2014a; Altieri 1995; Altieri and Toledo 2011) making agroecology an approach to sustainable food production and development that could be beneficial to agriculture and quality of life in Panamá. Main emphasis is given to the study of soil management and water, in order to maintain diverse and productive plant and animal communities. An integration of livestock is very important to produce protein-rich foods, and recycling animals' waste (manure) supports more ecologically the fertility of soils, making farming systems integrated and, consequently, more sustainable (Jackson and Jackson 2002). Therefore, an education in agroecology could prepare students of agriculture to move farming toward a more holistic and pragmatic approach to sustainable food production, which is necessary to address declining resources and increasing human needs. In order to do this, it is necessary to address the properties of living systems first, while convincing ourselves that sustainability in agriculture is achievable through cautionary planning and ecologically-informed decision making (Wes Jackson, personal communication, 2012). At the same time, an increasing human population pressure has reduced biodiversity and depleted soil and water resources in Los Santos and Herrera provinces, in the Azuero peninsula of Panamá. The dry season occurring between January and May causes severe water stresses affecting this area, also known as 'Arco Seco' or 'Dry Arc' region (Desrochers 2004). Chronic poverty in this region is strongly related to deforestation and amplified by its effects on the hydrologic water cycle and climate change. These factors put at risk food production and quality of life for the inhabitants in most parts of the Azuero peninsula (Fischer and Vasseur 2000).

The need of insuring food production in Panamá inspired the authors to pursue this study as a demonstration of sustainable development education effort. Thus, the purpose of this work consisted in designing, teaching and evaluating an extension curriculum in agroecology to strengthen the technical skills of small-scale farmers in the Azuero peninsula of Panamá, through a direct engagement of agriculture students enrolled at the Universidad Católica Santa Maria La Antigua (USMA) during the academic year 2014–2015. Specifically, this program aimed at responding to the urgent need of improving the management of soil fertility and water use in the region to the benefit of peasant agriculture.

2 Methodology: Curriculum Development

The focus of this work was directed towards developing, teaching and assessing an outreach curriculum of five workshops for farmers to be taught at the USMA farm (Herrera province), in early 2015. The outreach/extension curriculum we proposed emphasized on hands-on, experiential, participatory learning as proposed by Méndez et al. (2013). The topics for these workshops were selected by the investigators with the assistance of fifteen USMA students majoring in animal science, who were enrolled in the agroecology course taught by the senior author, at USMA-Azuero, between August and December 2014. The students (who are also farmers in the region) were engaged as part of classwork to participate in the selection process for the workshops as members of a jury panel system, as suggested by Patton (1990) and also Glesne (1999). Initially, the investigators proposed fifteen topics to the students/panelists and these had to discuss and select the five themes to be considered for the workshops program (Table 1). The last three class meetings of the term were devoted to accomplish this important task, until a

Table 1 Proportion scores yielded by the panel jury system to select the extension curriculum topics for subsistence farmers

Proposed topics	Most significant	Somewhat significant	Least significant	Selected topics
Improved pasture systems and cattle nutrition	0.81	0.19	0.00	
On-farm renewable energy	0.375	0.125	0.5	
Water and soil conservation practices	0.875	0.00	0.125	Water and soil conservation practices
Evaluating soil quality in the field	0.81	0.125	0.075	Evaluating soil quality in the field
Small-scale poultry production	0.5	0.5	0.00	
Chicken tractor	0.125	0.5	0.375	Chicken tractor
Leadership and cooperation in food production	0.00	0.31	0.69	
Silviculture and reforestation	0.375	0.25	0.375	
Ecological management of Soil fertility	0.375	0.5	0.125	Ecological management of Soil fertility
Organic vegetable production	0.1	0.1	0.8	
Integrated pest management	0.07	0.11	0.82	
Biointensive agriculture and agroforestry	0.78	0.14	0.08	Biointensive agriculture and agroforestry
Apiculture	0.125	0.25	0.625	
Vermicomposting	0.4	0.25	0.35	
Women's role in food production	0.1	0.1	0.8	

consensus was achieved to select five priority topics. It was not difficult to reach a consensus about topics dealing with: soil conservation, fertility and water, being these two resources at greatest risks of depletion, due to deforestation and slash and burn agriculture practices in this region of Panamá (Fischer and Vasseur 2000; Desrochers 2004). The 'chicken tractor' workshop was selected by the student-panelists after learning in the agroecology class the benefits (economic and ecological) of raising hens in movable cages and the advantages of this approach to poultry keeping in the enhancement of soil fertility (Hilimire et al. 2013), in addition to the production of quality foods (eggs and meat). Between January and March 2015 the investigators developed the curriculum materials and field activities for the five chosen workshop themes.

2.1 Subjects and the Study Site

The subjects (n = 200) of this workshops program were local food producers who manage small, family farms near Las Minas (where the USMA farm is located) and nearby communities, USMA students and a few agriculture professionals, working for governmental organizations, or the Panamanian Ministry of Agriculture (MIDA).

The site for this investigation was the farm of the Universidad Católica Santa Maria la Antigua (USMA), which is an excellent facility (Casiciaco Haren Alde Farm School), of about 20 ha, located on the outskirts of the town of Las Minas, in Herrera province.

3 Evaluation Instruments

The nature of our study focused on assessing the curriculum of workshops and yielded a mixture of quantitative and qualitative data that were triangulated (Popham 1993) to measure the worth of the proposed extension curriculum. Workshops participants (local farmers, students and agriculture professionals) served as subjects of this investigation, yielding quantitative data that were collected from a purposefully designed survey, which was administered at the end of every workshop. The survey considered demographic queries to learn about the characteristics of participants. It also proposed 13 questions aimed at assessing the workshop objectives, critical thinking, learning environment and an overall evaluation of the program, on a Likert-scale. A final open-ended question solicited information from workshop participants on how to improve the program and asked for suggestions about future topics to be taught (Fig. 1). The protection of human subjects was ensured through approval by the Institutional Review Board (IRB) of the Universidad Santa Maria la Antigua and Winona State University. All workshops were taught by the same instructor.

Universidad Católica Santa María La Antigua

Primera Universidad privada debidamente acreditada por pares internacionales y certificada por el Consejo Nacional de Evaluación y Acreditación Universitaria de Panamá (CONEAUPA).

50 años USMA 1965–2015

Experiential Workshop in Agroecology
April, 2015

This survey is part of an effort to improve the quality of this workshop and some of the best data that we can gather about this program come from you. The information that you provide on this survey can help us modify the workshop to make it more effective. Because your responses on this survey are so important, please answer each question carefully and thoughtfully. In order to maintain confidentiality, this survey is anonymous. Please indicate how much you agree or disagree with each statement by marking one choice only per question, with an "X" on the selected space, to the right of each question here below:

Demographic information

I am: __ a man __ a woman Age: ________ year old
Profession: __ farmer __ student __ USMA employee __ Other
I have a farm of............hectares, located in:...................................., Province:..
The most important products of my farm are:..
My products are: __ only for use/consumption of my family __ Family use and local sale in my village
__ sale to towns in the region (Chitre') __ sale in Panamá city and/or abroad

Workshop Goals and Outcomes:	Strongly Agree	Agree	Disagree	Strongly Disagree	N/A
1. Workshop objectives/ goals were clearly explained at the beginning of the program.					
2. The workshop had a clear purpose.					
Independent Thinking					
3. The training opportunities presented at the workshop I attended helped me to develop critical thinking.					
4. The training opportunities presented at the workshop I attended stimulated me to want to pursue more knowledge and experience about this topic.					
Learning Environment					
5. The instructor attempted to create an atmosphere that encouraged participants' expression of ideas.					
6. I felt comfortable asking the instructor for assistance, if I needed it.					
7. I felt comfortable asking questions to the instructor.					
8. The instructor attempted to involve all participants in workshop activities.					
9. The practical demonstrations were effective to enhance my learning about the topic being taught.					
10. I took home a lot of valuable information that I will be able to apply to the management of my farm.					
Overall Evaluation					
11. The teaching in this workshop was effective.					
12. I have learned a lot in this workshop and the knowledge gained is valuable to me.					
13. I will participate again to an agroecology workshop offered by USMA.					

OPEN-ENDED QUESTION. **(Please answer on the back of this form):** Please state what you think are the strengths of this workshop and why you think so. Also how do you think this workshop may be improved? What more topics would you like to include if this program was going to be offered again at the USMA farm?

Fig. 1 Evaluation instrument

Qualitative data were obtained through six stakeholders (three farmers and three professional agriculturists who did not participate to the workshops program) via phone interviews that were recorded (with the permission of each respondent), on magnetic tape, as suggested by Glesne (1999) to reduce investigators' bias. Four interview questions were used in this evaluation:

- What are the challenges but also the opportunities for a successful agriculture in the Azuero peninsula?

- What is your personal definition of agroecology?
- What are priority needs to enhance farmers' education in sustainable food production?
- How effective is the preparation of agriculture and natural resources professionals working in the field in educating farmers to achieve sustainability?

A document analysis review of available materials (web sites, brochures, manuals and literature in extension education in Central America) for fostering farmers' education in agroecology and similar agricultural topics was carried out and this yielded more qualitative data. Thus, a triangulation of the results enabled the authors to draw conclusions about the efficacy of the curriculum. Groups of three students each who had enrolled in the agroecology course assisted the investigators during workshops instruction and also with the collection of survey data.

4 Results: Quantitative Data

Each workshop was capped at a maximum of 40 participants therefore, 200 learners in total attended the program (182 men and 18 women). One-hundred and two evaluations were returned yielding a 51 % assessment rate. A majority of the participants' responses were in the 'strongly agree' (M = 0.846) and/or 'agree' (M = 0.118) categories (Fig. 2).

In addition to this, a chi-square calculation ($\chi^2 = 13.039$, $P = 0.669904$) for the contingency table of the proportion scores of responses on the Likert-scale of the evaluation survey (Table 2), suggested that there was no significant difference in the efficacy of instruction among the workshops that had been taught ($p > 0.05$).

A 1.3 % of participants answered the open-ended question of the evaluation survey indicating that the workshops were well taught and organized, substantiating from a similar experience with Spanish organic growers (Cuellar and Calle 2011),

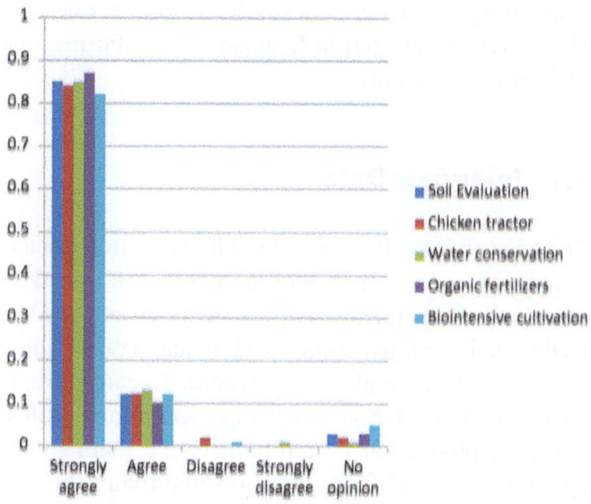

Fig. 2 Distribution of the evaluation scores (proportions) for every workshop

Table 2 Proportion scores yielded by the evaluation instrument

Workshop theme	Strongly agree	Agree	Disagree	Strongly disagree	No opinion
Soil evaluation	0.85	0.12	0.00	0.00	0.03
Chicken tractor	0.84	0.12	0.02	0.00	0.02
Water conservation	0.85	0.13	0.00	0.01	0.01
Organic fertilizers	0.87	0.1	0.00	0.00	0.03
Biointensive cultivation	0.82	0.12	0.01	0.00	0.05

that a more direct participation achieved through practical demonstrations and field work, was appreciated and effective in fostering learning in agroecology. Concerning ideas for the need of developing new workshop topics in the future, 6 % of the subjects who returned the evaluation at the end of each workshop proposed permaculture, 52 % proposed agroforestry themes (especially silvopasture), whereas 42 % indicated an interest to wanting to learn about the process to earn organic certification for their products.

5 Interviews Protocol and Respondents

In order to collect data through an interview, there is a rapport that must be established between the researcher and the respondent (Glesne 1999; Patton 1990). A preliminary contact was established with the respondents in February 2015 through an invitation to be interviewed that was made by the principal investigator with phone calls to a list of respondents that had been identified/suggested by some of the agroecology students who assisted with this project. This initial procedure allowed time for the investigator who conducted the interviews to introduce himself to the potential respondents and to discuss briefly with each interviewee the needs and purposes of the research. The interviews were conducted by telephone in March 2015. Every attempt to maintain a neutral stance in asking the questions and responding to any interviewee concerns or questions was considered. The interviews were conducted in Spanish, with 3 farmers and 3 professional agriculturists (4 men and 2 women).

5.1 Interview Data

The answer to the first part of the first question (What are the challenges but also the opportunities for a successful agriculture in the Azuero peninsula?) was consistent among the respondents. All six interviewees (100 %) indicated the need for protecting soil fertility from erosion and conserving water as these are principal challenges to agriculture in Azuero. Regarding opportunities, the opinions were split with three farmers and one agriculture professional (67 %) indicating that livestock production is traditionally the main farming activity in the region and agriculture should focus more on improving this sector because there is a steady market demand for beef. However, one farmer and one agriculture professional (33 %) pointed out that cattle production is the main cause of land degradation, fomenting the unsustainable practice of slash and burn practices to 'clean' pastures, which amplifies the loss of soil and the removal of trees, so important for protecting soil and water. For the second question (What is your personal definition of agroecology?) none of the respondents (100 %) could define agroecology, although the agriculture professionals (50 %) indicated succinctly, that the word must imply a more sustainable approach to farming. For the third question (What are priority needs to enhance farmers' education in sustainable food production?) all six respondents answered that alternative approaches must be taught to land owners to stop the practice of slashing and burning the fields during the dry season. One farmer suggested that more education is needed about water conservation and management and, he added, that replanting the trees that he remembered when he was a child has become (in his opinion), a very urgent need of present times. The three farmers (50 %) added also that they need more education on alternative methods to fertilize their fields and protecting their crops from weeds and pathogens as most farmers use agrichemical inputs causing often major damage to the environment, like the contamination of the Rio (river) La Villa with the herbicide atrazine, which occurred in early 2014. The fourth question asked how effective was the preparation of agriculture and natural resources professionals in providing leadership and technical assistance among farmers to achieve sustainability. One farmer and three agriculture professionals (67 %) indicated that the idea of sustainable agriculture is new in Panamà. One respondent said: "We hear about it [sustainable agriculture] many times, however we do not have clear production protocols from our government and therefore, there is a lack for guiding agriculture towards becoming more sustainable". One farmer added also that the demand of organic produce in Panamà city is driven by an increasing number of foreign residents (mainly US and Canadian retirees) and (in her opinion) this is the driving force for agricultural sustainability in the country, which justifies the training needs in organic farming many growers would like to pursue. The agriculture professionals (50 %) said that they need more training to do their job, yet there are scarce opportunities for professional development in their profession.

6 Agroecology in Extension Education: A Document Analysis

A robust body of literature exists already to document the benefits of agroecology when it is practiced in the tropics of Latin America (Altieri et al. 2012; Gliessman 2007; Isakson 2009; Ferguson and Morales 2010; Wezel et al. 2009). Emphasis on agroforestry (Camara-Cabrales 1999), especially in Panamà (Fischer and Vasseur 2000; Cochran and Bonnell 2005) is justified by the fact that the 95 % of Panamà was covered by different kinds of forests before human settlement (Heckadon-Moreno and Espinoza-González 1985). The primary focus in developing countries of the tropics is to reduce poverty (Pretty et al. 2003), through an agriculture that is conservative of its natural resource base, while reducing, or better eliminating the practice of slash and burn agriculture (Harwood 1996), and rich with more ecologically based farming approaches. Valuable information that served to prepare the workshops was downloaded from the National Sustainable Agriculture Information Service (https://attra.ncat.org/) and The Land Stewardship Project (http://landstewardshipproject.org/) web sites. Instead, the web site (http://www.agroecology.org/Links.html) offered information about curricula in agroecology in the US that with appropriate modifications, could become very valuable to enhance the preparedness in sustainable development to agriculture professionals in Panamá. Also, the Latin American Society of Agroecology (SOCLA) was another important resource. It will soon offer in Spanish, on its web site (http://www.socla.co/) more technical information to foster agroecology principles and practices in south and Central America.

7 Discussion and Conclusion

The assistance provided by the fifteen agroecology students with the selection of the curricular topics and the collection of quantitative data from workshop participants was an original learning experience, which hopefully, complemented the education they gained during course work in agroecology and beyond. The quantitative data indicated that the workshops program was effective to demonstrate ecologically based practices to local farmers in Azuero. In addition to this, respondents (87 %) pointed out that the learning environment was conducive to apply what was being taught and farmers felt comfortable to participate and contribute with their own experience, to the learning of the whole group of attendees. It is known that this kind of participatory research benefits all parts involved in the investigation/education process (Martin and Sherington 1997). Through extension education efforts like the one carried out at the USMA farm in 2015, subsistence farmers and their families became the primary beneficiaries of instruction and also the source of additional knowledge and learning for students, and other agriculture professionals who took part to the workshops program. Two hundred participants were in attendance and of this population, one-hundred twenty six (63 %) were USMA students (from freshmen to seniors), in pursuit of their Bachelor's degree in animal science. The authors did not have the opportunity to evaluate at this time the learning achieved by students who assisted with the design, implementation and evaluation of the extension curriculum however, the senior researcher observed that these were more engaged in the learning process than when the same took place in the classroom. Also, students who attended the workshops interacted collaboratively with all other learners in active discussions facilitated by their instructor. Learners in this program participated actively in all field activities, instruments use, measurements and problem-solving exercises that were proposed for each one of the five selected topics (Fig. 3).

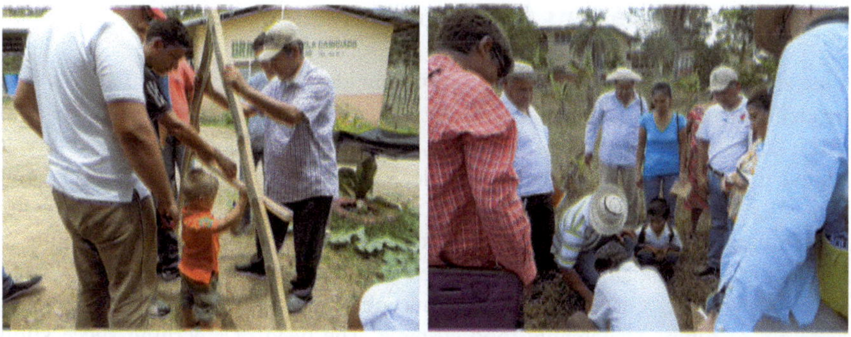

Fig. 3 Calibrating the Level-A, a simple instrument used to trace contour lines on a sloping terrain (*left*), and evaluating soil compaction in the field (*right*)

The qualitative data were valuable to complete the assessment of the curriculum and were triangulated with the quantitative data yielded by the administration of the survey instrument, to enhance the trustworthiness of the study (Patton 1990; Popham 1993). More specifically, the data yielded from the interviews suggested that agroecology has not become yet a well-established subject of study in agriculture, or sustainable development curricula in Panamá. Deforestation and slash and burn practices remain a pervasive *modus operandi* in panamenian agriculture, despite a broad recognition of their detrimental consequences on the environment. Although the benefits of slash and burn agriculture are outnumbered by many limitations, tangible measures for adopting alternative approaches to avoid expansions of land degradation, as these may lead quickly to the desertification of the Azuero region are still lacking. In sum, the need for embracing sustainable development in food production appears to be understood across the strata of the agricultural community in Panamá, yet, a limited preparedness of a majority of its agricultural professionals, scarcity of funds available for better conservation practices, and limited leadership impede the needed leaps towards an implementation of policies, education, and research efforts for establishing a more sustainable food production system. The qualitative data yielded by the document analysis review suggested that the information about agroecology and sustainable food production abounds in the literature and on the Internet. However, the scarcity of studies carried out in Panamá reiterated that sustainable development of food systems is a relatively new concept in this Central American country. Nonetheless, taught within this, or a similar framework, the proposed extension education curriculum proved to be an effective model of instruction to respond effectively to farmers' needs, while exposing (and hopefully, improving) the preparedness of students of agriculture at USMA, when these are engaged directly in resolving problems and challenges together with food producers. This and similar educational experiences can become excellent learning opportunities for students who prepare to enter soon their professional career paths.

8 Recommendations for Future Studies

A steady increase in human population worldwide is not exempting Panamá from the challenge of having to increase its agricultural outputs by 2050 as Tilman et al. (2011, 2002) have predicated, to satisfy a rise in food demand. The ability to achieve this goal will require an unprecedented wisdom and knowledge to avoid an exhaustion of our natural resource base (soil, water, energy, biodiversity). To this end, Ruttan (2000) made a clear case for proposing 'regenerative agriculture' a compelling and mandatory need for future efforts in sustainable development, while Altieri (1995) and Gliessman (2007) conceded that agroecology is the winning paradigm of future, sustainable food systems. The need of emerging successfully from the challenges of present, extractive agriculture can be pursued also through a mobilization and empowerment of rural communities (Bell et al. 2010) with education programs like the one that was presented in this evaluation study. The engagement and commitment of USMA students who assisted with this research endeavor implied that leadership skills were also gained by these soon-to-be professionals, who participated in developing the proposed extension curriculum. From the limitations that affected our assessment emerged some recommendations that could be considered in future and similar studies, to foster sustainable development in agricultural education in Panamá and these could consider the following foci:

- Evaluating students' educational benefits from this, or similar extension programs as such an effort would have beneficial implications for an improvement towards sustainability of academic curricula in the agricultural sciences in Panamá.
- Continue offering this curriculum to local farmers in the provinces of Herrera and Los Santos through the years and study how and whether food production becomes more diversified in this region and whether natural resources (soil, water and biodiversity primarily) recover their quality while continuing to fulfill the ecological services they provide to Azuero.
- Develop and offer workshops in: permaculture, agroforestry (with emphasis on silvopasture) and organic certification protocols for locally grown foods, while continuing assessment studies.
- Adapt and implement this curriculum for more regions of the country through a collaboration with more universities in Panamá who offer study programs in the agricultural sciences.

Finally, the authors would recommend and support the continuation of a direct involvement of students like the one that was experienced with this program, should the Universidad Católica Santa Maria La Antigua continue to appreciate the innovative pedagogy that was employed in this study. Over time, the experience gained by USMA with this approach to education could become an attractive model of instruction in sustainable development for more universities in the country and applicable also to more curricula, within the university.

Acknowledgements This work was supported by a Fulbright grant (award #: 48142622) that was awarded to the senior author in 2014. The authors are grateful to the criticism and thoughtful comments of two anonymous reviewers who helped improve the quality of this manuscript.

References

Altieri, M. A. (1995). *Agroecology. The science of sustainable agriculture*. Boulder, Colorado, USA: Westview Press Inc.

Altieri, M. A., Funez-Monzote, F. R., & Petersen, P. (2012). Agroecologically efficient agricultural systems for smallholder farmers: Contributions to food sovereignty. *Agronomy for Sustainable Development, 32*, 1–13.

Altieri, M. A., & Toledo, V. M. (2011). The agroecological revolution in Latin America: rescuing nature, ensuring food sovereignty and empowering peasants. *The Journal of Peasant Studies, 38*(3), 587–612.

Bell, M., Lloyd, E., & Vatovec, C. (2010). Activating the countryside: Rural power, the power of the rural and the making of rural politics. *Sociologia Ruralis, 50*(3), 205–224.

Beynaghi, A., Moztarzadeh, F., Maknoon, R., Waas, T., Mozafari, M., Hugé, J., et al. (2014). Towards an orientation of higher education in the post Rio + 20 process: How is the game changing? *Futures, 63*, 49–67.

Borsari, B. (2012). Curriculum framework for sustainability education. *Academic Exchange Quarterly, 16*(1), 74–78.

Borsari, B., Espinosa, J., & Hassán, J. (2014b). Agroecology and a vision for sustainable agriculture in spite of global climate change. *Investigación y pensamiento critico., 2*(5), 63–69.

Borsari, B., Neri. D., Ferretti, G., Tavoletti, S., & Wei-Choun Y. (2014a). Critical evaluation of genetic manipulation for improved productivity: Is this a sustainable agenda? In W. B. Campbell & S. Lopez-Ortiz (Eds.), *Sustainable food production includes human and environmental health*. Springer, Berlin, 233p.

Camara-Cabrales, L. (1999). Small farmer migration and the agroforestry alternative in the Panamá Canal Watershed. *Journal of Sustainable Forestry, 8*(3/4), 11–22.

Cochran, J. B., & Bonnell, R. (2005). Patterns of sustainable agriculture adoption/non-adoption in Panamá. *Journal of Sustainable Agriculture, 23*(3), 147–162.

Cuellar, M., & Calle, A. (2011). Can we find solutions with people? Participatory action research with small organic producers in Andalusia. *Journal of Rural Studies, 27*, 372–383.

Desrochers, A. (2004). Water harvesting through ponds in the Arco Seco region of the Republic of Panamá; decision support system for pond storage capacity estimation. Montreal, Canada: Macdonald Campus of McGill University (Masters' thesis).

Ferguson, B. G., & Morales, H. (2010). Latin American agroecologists build a powerful scientific and social movement. *Journal of Sustainable Agriculture, 34*, 339–341.

Fischer, A., & Vasseur, L. (2000). The crisis in shifting agriculture practices and the promise of agroforestry: A review of the Panamanian experience. *Biodiversity and Conservation, 9*, 739–756.

Glesne, C. (1999). *Becoming qualitative researchers: An introduction* (2nd ed., 336 p). White Plains, NY: Longman.

Gliessman, S. R. (2007). *Agroecology*. The ecology of food systems: CRC Press, Boca Raton, Florida, USA. 371p.

Harwood, R. R. (1996). Development pathways toward sustainable systems following slash-and-burn. *Agriculture, Ecosystems & Environment, 58*, 75–86.

Heckadon-Moreno, S., & Espinoza-González, J. (Eds.), (1985). *Agonia de la Naturaleza.Ensayos sobre el costo ambiental del desarrollo panameño*. Panamá: Instituto de Investigacion Agropecuaria de Panama and Smithsonian Tropical Research Institute, 327p.

Hilimire, K., Gliessman, S. R., & Muramoto, J. (2013). Soil fertility and crop growth under poultry/crop integration. *Renewable Agriculture and Food Systems, 28*(2), 173–182.

Instituto Nacional de Estadistica y Censo (INEC), Panamá. Censo Nacional de Poblacion y Vivienda: Año (2010). Available at: http://www.contraloria.gob.pa/INEC/Publicaciones/Publicaciones.aspx?ID_SUBCATEGORIA=59&ID_PUBLICACION=362&ID_IDIOMA=1&ID_CATEGORIA=13

Isakson, S. R. (2009). No hay ganancia en la milpa: the agrarian question, food sovereignty, and the on-farm conservation of agrobiodiversity in the Guatemalan highlands. *The Journal of Peasant Studies, 36*(4), 725–759.

Jackson, D. L., & Jackson, L. L. (2002). *The farm as natural habitat. Reconnecting food systems with ecosystems* (297 p). Washington D.C., USA: Island Press.

Martin, A., & Sherington, J. (1997). Participatory research methods implementation, effectiveness and institutional context. *Agricultural Systems, 55*(2), 195–216.

Méndez, V. E., Bacon, C. M., & Cohen, R. (2013). Agroecology as a transdisciplinary, participatory, and action-oriented approach. *Agroecology and Sustainable Food Systems, 37*, 3–18.

Mozejko, A. (2009). *Sustainability, climate change, and carbon sequestration in Panama master's thesis*. Bern, Switzerland: Faculty of Science, University of Bern.

O'Byrne, D., Dripps, W., & Nicholas, K. A. (2014). Teaching and learning sustainability: An assessment of the curriculum content and structure of sustainability degree programs in higher education. *Sustainability Science, 10*(1), 43–59.

Onwueme, I., & Borsari, B. (2008). Empowering universities and colleges to become dynamic actors for driving sustainable development. In C. H. Daub, P. Burger & Y. Sherrer (Eds.), Creating Values for Sustainable Development, p. 265. *Proceedings of the 2nd International Sustainability Conference*, pp. 115–117. Basel, Switzerland. (Extended Abstract).

Onwueme, I., Borsari, B., & Leal Filho, W. (2008). An analysis of some paradoxes in alternative agriculture and a vision of sustainability for future food systems. *International Journal of Agricultural Resources, Governance and Ecology, 7*(3), 199–210.

Patton, M. Q. (1990). *Qualitative evaluation and research methods* (532 p). Newbury Park, CA: Sage.

Popham, J. W. (1993). *Educational evaluation* (3rd ed.). MA, Prentice Hall: Needham Heights. 235p.

Pretty, J. N., Morrison, J. I. L., & Hine, R. E. (2003). Reducing food poverty by increasing agricultural sustainability in the development countries. *Agriculture, Ecosystems & Environment, 9*, 5–24.

Romero, L., & Quental, C. (2014). Research for better health: The Panamanian priority-setting experience and the need for a new process. *Health Research Policy and Systems, 12*, 38.

Ruttan, V. W. (2000). The continuing challenge of food production in the 21st century: From science to sustainable agriculture. *Environment, 42*(10), 25–30.

Tilman, D., Balzer, C., Hill, J., & Befort, B. L. (2011). Global food demand and sustainable intensification of agriculture. *Proceedings of the National Academy of Science, 108*(50), 20260–20264.

Tilman, D., Cassman, K. G., Matson, P. A., Naylor, R., & Polasky, S. (2002). Agricultural sustainability and intensive production practices. *Nature, 418*, 671–677.

Wezel, A., Bellon, S., Doré, T., Francis, C., Vallod, D., & David, C. (2009). Agroecology as a science, a movement and a practice. A review. *Agronomy for Sustainable Development, 29*, 503–515.

Author Biographies

Bruno Borsari is a professor in the Biology Department at Winona State University. He earned his Laurea in Agricultural Sciences (D. Ag. Sc.), from the University of Bologna, Italy in 1986 and his Ph.D. in 2001 from the University of New Orleans. He is an agroecologist with a 25 year experience in west and central Africa, Bolivia, Italy, and various regions within the U.S.

Nuria Peréz De Gracia, MS is the former Director of USMA-Azuero in Chitrè.

Jorge Castro Peralta is the Manager of the Granja Casiciaco Haren-Alde (USMA farm) in Las Minas, Panamà. With a B.Sc. in Animal Science from USMA, he has been working in this capacity since 2013.

Teaching Education for Sustainable Development at University Level: A Case Study from the Philippines

Raquel M. Balanay and Anthony Halog

Abstract

In response to UNESCO's Agenda 21, the Philippine initiative to assimilate Education for Sustainable Development (ESD) in tertiary education is enunciated in the Commission on Higher Education's Strategic Plan for 2011–2016, which contains the roadmap to reform higher education institutions (HEIs) to respond well to the academic pursuits of sustainable development. Over the years, ESD has been instituted with practical strategies hinged on previously-built efforts promoting environmental conservation, climate change mitigation and adaptation as cornerstones of sustainable development among the HEIs in the country. The process of doing so has progressed from social marketing through alliance-building in pushing for eco-friendly and disaster risk reduction programs and community extension activities to enhance social awareness and preparedness to a more academic level through curricular review and development activities. The National Service Training Program (NSTP) is a platform whereby ESD is instituted formally in tertiary education. However, sophistication for ESD to tackle the development of theories of practice is underway but slow. Some universities have been moving forward in this aspect in cooperation

R.M. Balanay (✉) · A. Halog
School of Geography, Planning and Environmental Management,
The University of Queensland, Brisbane, QLD 4072, Australia
e-mail: raquelbalanay@gmail.com

A. Halog
e-mail: a.halog@uq.edu.au

R.M. Balanay
College of Agricultural Sciences and Natural Resources,
Caraga State University, Ampayon, Butuan 8600, Philippines

© Springer International Publishing Switzerland 2016

W. Leal Filho and P. Pace (eds.), *Teaching Education for Sustainable Development at University Level*, World Sustainability Series,
DOI 10.1007/978-3-319-32928-4_11

with two environmental education associations, but knowledge to fast-track the development and study of theories for sustainable development for practical applications is still evidently wanting.

Keywords
Education for sustainable development • Environmental conservation • Climate change mitigation and adaptation

1 Introduction

As a signatory of UNESCO's Agenda 21, the Philippines has joined a host of countries across the world in taking up the call of the *Nagoya Declaration on Higher Education for Sustainable Development*, which was put together on 9 November 2014 in Aichi, Nagoya, Japan. Like its counterparts in the Asian region, the country has been working relentlessly for years to figure out the initiatives that would establish "the transformative role of higher education towards sustainable development" (UNESCO 2011a), especially that environmental problems and climate change impacts have become increasingly unsettling in the Philippines. The commitment of the country towards it has been worked up to include recently the reform on basic education with the implementation of the K to 12 program, which is a defining step in Philippine education to prepare systematically the youths of the country to the challenges in globalization and sustainable development. From then on, the works have moved up to higher levels, where much has been achieved for secondary education institutions to engage in dynamic inter-country collaborations in the development of practical teaching innovations for the promotion and enhancement of socio-cultural and environmental awareness. But consciousness on ESD was developed as early as 1952 in the Philippines, with the "establishment of the Philippine Rural Reconstruction Movement (PRRM) for an integrated program of education, livelihood, health, habitat, environment and self-governance in the development of rural communities," which eventually forged "education for sustainability" (UNESCO 2011a).

At the tertiary level, the Philippine step towards equipping in pursuit of ESD has been articulated in the Commission on Higher Education's (CHED) Strategic Plan 2011–2016. The plan has set out the roadmap for the higher education institutions (HEIs) to do the necessary changes to align the agenda of the HEIs with the global call of strategizing education for sustainable development (SD) in the country (Commission on Higher Education 2012a). The plan calls for a major restructuring process to enable the Philippine HEIs to streamline efforts and resources towards the said goal. Cognizant to what the country had committed in integrating ESD in higher education, series of legislations have helped formalize the framework to carry out relevant interventions in practical formats in the HEIs, which are aimed ultimately to build resilient and climate-smart societies. The anchorage for this framework is built on the previous efforts towards environmental awareness and conservation with major policy support from CHED. As a confluence of all efforts for education to catalyze SD, ESD provides a new face of education, which embodies the "principles of lasting human development" (Granados 2011). To the Philippine universities, these principles provide continually a dynamic but formidable challenge inasmuch as environmental and climate change concerns are seen with calamitous damage on human lives and properties in the past few years. Nonetheless, for "ESD to be quality education," much has to be done to verify its beneficial outcomes and research is wanted for this aspect to produce the solid evidence for such outcomes in the country especially (UNESCO 2012).

2 The Legal Framework for ESD in Philippine Universities

Although the major underpinning for the repositioning of Philippine universities to institute sustainable development through academic means is a commitment of the country in UNESCO's Agenda 21, the framework for carrying ESD out in Philippine universities is with the policies of CHED and republic acts whereby CHED is still the focal driver for implementation. The blueprint for which every action works towards UNESCO's Agenda 21 is contained in the Philippine version of the said agenda [Philippine Agenda 21 (PA 21) and Enhanced Philippine Agenda 21 (EPA 21)], which aptly "represents the national will to pursue a development approach that: (1) implies the balance of growth, equity, and ecological integrity; (2) requires the operationalization of sustainable development (SD) parameters; and (3) is both people-oriented and ecosystem-based" (Philippine Council for Sustainable Development 2015). From it, many policies have stemmed to ensure concerted response to the strategies for ESD and the integration of which in the academic programs of the university. For starters, Republic Act No. 9512 known as the Environmental Awareness and Education Act of 2008" set out the mandate for the integration of environmental education in school curricula at all levels and the incorporation of which in the National Service Training Program under Republic Act No. 9163, "as a Civic Welfare Training Service component required for all baccalaureate degree and vocational courses with at least 2-year curriculum."

As a platform for further promotion of ESD under RA 9512, the aptness of the National Service Training Program (NSTP) institutionalized by virtue of Republic Act No. 9163 in 2002 as a channel for ESD was espoused in the aim of the program, which is towards "enhancing civic consciousness and defense preparedness in the youth by developing the ethics of services and patriotism, and ensuring the various components of which to enhance the youth's active contribution to the general welfare." In consonance with the SD framework, NSTP comprises an ideal vehicle to bring ESD to as many people as possible, inasmuch as similar intentions are being served with the education mechanisms of the program. Accordingly, at CHED's level, a memorandum order was passed to require all HEIs to roll out the implementation of NSTP across the Philippines. CHED has likewise enjoined HEIs to affiliate with the Philippine Association of Tertiary Level Educational Institutions in Environmental Protection and Management (PATLEPAM). The association is anchored in the Environmental Management Bureau (EMB) of the Department of Environment and Natural Resources (DENR), in which its chief function is to streamline environmental education in Philippine higher education. Streamlining in this case subsumes the strategies aimed to pursue practical and theoretical interventions for ESD to flourish in the country's educational system. PATLEPAM with the Environmental Education Network of the Philippines (EENP) is important in the "integration of SD in school curricula as well as in campus administration and organizational culture" (Segovia and Galang 2002). Nevertheless, the National Agriculture and Fisheries Education System (NAFES) came much earlier under the Agriculture and Fisheries Modernization Act (AFMA) of 1997, as a way of "integrating all provisions of international development assistance made for agriculture and fisheries education since 1964 to prepare human resources on the global concerns of development agriculture" (Suemitsu and Mancebo 2007).

3 Approaches Used in Delivering ESD in Philippine HEIs

ESD in Philippine HEIs has to touch-base on their quad functions of instruction, research, extension and production/administration; thus, these functions reflect the key areas for the assimilation of ESD in academic programs relative to the objectives of PA 21 and EPA 21 where the Philippine Millennium Development Goals (MDGs) are articulated (UNESCO 2012). UNESCO (2012) has identified ESD specifically as part of the "major UN-supported education campaigns such as Education for All (EFA) and the UN Literacy Decade (UNLD) including a whole range of other educations that touch upon SD," which goes well with the changing demands of time. Broadly, it considers ESD as an "umbrella concept for emerging educations" targeted at a number of pressing issues such as climate change and risk reduction, as shown in the Philippine case. With it as a welcome opportunity in the Philippine higher education, new curricular programs on environmental studies have come about, which have been patronized by numerous students due to the timely relevance of the programs. For those HEIs with environmental science as a baccalaureate degree course, CHED's memorandum order 35 in 2005 provides the guide on its offering, because it embeds the minimum policy standards for rationalizing the training of the youths under the course.

Based on the memorandum order, a graduate of the said course is expected to earn competencies on:

- Basic skills in biology, chemistry, physics, earth science and mathematics and their applications in an integrated way in the analysis of an environmental problem;

- Understanding of the basic concepts of biology and ecology, qualitative and quantitative chemical analysis, energy and thermodynamics, earth science, mathematics and statistics, and
- Adequate technical writing and oral communication abilities.

Caraga State University in Butuan City, Philippines has offered the same course in consideration of the required competencies about which the academic services are planned. For instance, besides the classroom activities with board and chalk, the students have to undergo field exposures and preparatory training for terrestrial and aquatic assessment activities (e.g. trekking, caving and free diving). Research partnerships have been also practiced to help the students develop their technical writing skills. To broaden awareness on and management of environmental problems, students likewise have to observe such aspects in selected communities. To date, ninety (90) of the 2299 HEIs in the country have environmental courses in their academic programs; most of which are state-owned universities and colleges (Philippines Universities and Colleges Guide, 2015). Overall, CHED manages that number of HEIs, where 1643 are private institutions, 547 are state universities and colleges, 95 are local universities and colleges, and 14 are other government HEIs (Commission on Higher Education 2012b). In 2014, total enrolment had gone up to 3,563,396; of which the highest is in business-related courses with 970,558. Respectively, second and third in enrolment rates are education and teacher training (624,254) and information technology (425,416) (Commission on Higher Education 2014). Although sustainable development agenda are also tackled in other disciplines such as agriculture, forestry and fisheries, the environmental courses that take up those agenda with considerable emphasis are listed under "other disciplines" having an enrolment of 214,277 (Commission on Higher Education 2014), indicating that the said courses still constitute a minority in Philippine higher education. Even so, ESD promotion is assured with NSTP being compulsory to all HEIs in the country. However, in upscaling ESD for research and practical applications, the Philippine HEIs might flounder a bit for reasons concerning the need for more emphasis, experience and expertise.

Also, the Philippine universities in the delivery of ESD had to observe the National Environmental Education Action Plan (NEEAP) 2005–2014. In this plan, the ESD program must be pursued following the strategies identified by the Department of Environment and Natural Resources (DENR), the Department of Education (DepEd), the Technical Education and Skills Development Authority (TESDA) and the Commission on Higher Education (CHED), which are as follows (UNESCO 2011a):

- Establishment of centers of excellence in environmental education in the different regions of the country;
- Provision of incentive support to deserving professionals who wish to specialize in environmental science and management;
- Strengthening of environmental education role and advocacy work of NGOs;

- Improvement in the technical capability of DENR and the education departments in environmental education for the general public and other concerned agencies;
- Mobilization of the youth in environmental enhancement projects; and
- Promotion of an integrated approach in educating the local communities on environmental conservation.

These strategies provide the importance of having a holistic approach in training the students under the Environmental Science and Management courses. In the Philippines, the delivery of ESD through NSTP to various students and audiences is carried out in modular programs, taking on the minimum standard set for the HEIs in reaching out these intended audiences for the learning points aimed to build social capability in disaster risk reduction and environmental protection (UNESCO 2011b). In Philippine universities, the topics are extended to cover issues on women empowerment, gender and development in consonance with Republic Act No. 9710 (*The Magna Carta of Women*). This is to bring women's capability to the fore in the event they need to provide leadership and backstopping measures and NSTP is likewise used in the process. CHED has set out a particular module that contains the corresponding scopes of instruction for the priority topics on disaster risk reduction and management and environmental protection (see UNESCOs 2011b *Education for Sustainable Development Country Guidelines for Changing the Climate of Teacher Education to Address Sustainability: Putting Transformative Education into Practice*).

Early on, the HEIs were supportive of ESD-related social marketing schemes, specifically for programs aimed to instil environmental consciousness among the Filipino people. In 2006, the Search for Eco-friendly Schools in Metro Manila was launched where the top schools were given due recognition for their winning participation (Nomura and Abe 2008). This has become an annual event for all schools in the country in all education levels: elementary, secondary and tertiary (higher education), which advocates the development of eco-schools. In the Philippine context, "eco-schools are environmentally-friendly schools that have initiated and integrated environment-related programmes in their instruction, research, extension and/or administration" or in the quad functions of the HEIs. These eco-schools are strategized to take on the streamlining and mainstreaming of environmental education. As defined, environmental education in the country "shall encompass environmental concepts and principles, environmental laws, the state of international and local environment, local environmental policies, the threats of environmental degradation and its impact on human well-being, the responsibility of the citizenry to the environment, and the value of conservation, protection and rehabilitation of natural resources and the environment in the context of sustainable development. Theoretical and practicum modules shall comprise activities, projects and programs including, but not limited to tree planting, waste minimization, segregation, recycling and composting; freshwater and marine conservation, forest management and conservation; relevant livelihood opportunities and economic benefits and other such programmes and undertakings to aid the implementation of the different environmental protection laws in the Philippines" (ASEAN 2013).

Relative to these initiatives, two education associations/networks have played a great role in harmonizing efforts for the HEIs to grasp easily the process of going about environmental education and ESD, starting from the conceptualization of the country's participation in the furtherance of environmental conservation that is still a central point in sustainable development discourse in the Philippines. PATLEPAM was formed in 1995 as a government-supported network of 380 colleges and universities to deliver environmental education, training and research for sustainable development to local communities. It also endeavors to incorporate sustainable development in university curricula and in administrative/institutional culture (Calder and Clugston 2003). EENP is, on the other hand, of similar understanding with PATLEPAM in the pursuit of ESD in the country. It has introduced the "Dark Green School" program, which has "the objective of producing citizens through college systems who are coherently directed towards environmental education for sustainable development (EESD) and of offering a distinctive "whole institution" approach and accreditation system in line with ESD principles for coherent systemic change and acceleration of the "greening" of the academy" (Galang 2010 as cited by Reyes 2014).

4 Some Documented Practices in Delivering ESD

Teaching ESD in Philippine universities has evolved over the past years, in which the beginning took a bottom-up approach, where at the grassroots level, alliances and partnerships were developed to enhance environmental consciousness and protection and disaster preparedness through NSTP and off-campus extension and education programs (Tan 2012; Unsi 2014). Such approach was credited in terms of practicality in helping communities cope with disasters that had visited the country in the recent past; more so with the development of entrepreneurship through the various projects on waste management. Meanwhile, with ESD to help address societal problems of multiple dimensions, a noteworthy development where universities have a lead role is the contextualization of ESD in spurring development strategies. The following are some accounts on this aspect undertaken beside the NSTP platform of the universities. Cultural sensitivity to mainstream the marginal indigenous people in development efforts is demonstrated by the Xavier-University (XU)-Cagayan-de-Oro-City-supported Apu Palamguwan Center (APC). The center facilitates in the exposure of XU students to a special curriculum of cultural education piloted in the Bendum cultural community. APC's special curriculum is intended for the education of children of the cultural minorities, which allows XU students to see and respect their potentials for development (APC-ESSC 2008).

Similar to this is the innovation made on teaching physics with enhanced cultural and language sensitivity. Morales (2014) of the Philippine Normal University has worked with culturally-profiled student subjects and has introduced the modules of

Culturally-Sensitive Curriculum Material in Physics (CS-CMIP), which were piloted by Pangasinan physics teachers and high-school students with applications found in the local culture of a Pangasinan ethnic group. The subsequent customization of Physics to this ethnic group is found to have contributed to the success of the experiment, which was recommended by Morales (2014) to be validated with other ethnic groups in the country. Culturally-sensitive education is likewise advocated in the pursuits of Abejuela (2007) to broaden social participation in sustainable development. The implementation of Schools for Indigenous Knowledge and Traditions (SIKAT) Programme as documented in his paper has acknowledged the importance of special teacher training institutions for "future teachers to acquire skills to teach in indigenous schools." Discussions on this aspect have encouraged the participation of Bukidnon State College to offer a program on indigenous education based on Bukidnon culture (Abejuela 2007). Another laudable contribution of ESD is education for peace with the Filipino Muslim community, as documented in the case studies of the Asia-Pacific Centre for Education for International Understanding (APCEIU 2007).

In the area of food safety, students in the University of the Philippines-Los Baños could learn the policy and standards in the Bachelor of Science in Food Technology (BSFT) program with the program curriculum set by CHED. The BSFT curriculum requires a 3-unit professional course on Food Safety, which constitutes 3 h of lecture per week. A preparatory stage is also set to infuse knowledge from related sciences as in crop and animal sciences and this is intended to provide "farm-to-fork" perspective of food safety, which lays down the "distinct advantage of food science and technology programs based in universities with a strong agricultural program" (Lizada 2010). The same holistic framework is also observed in the curricular programs of environmental science and management in Philippine universities, because of the many facets that are taken into account in environmental discourses. Under NAFES, ESD for the development of agriculture and environmental conservation in the agri-fishery sector was pursued on the basis of a competency-based curriculum, in which the various competencies are learned through actual experiences in internship programs since the aim is for the youth to receive "occupational preparation for a better life" (Suemitsu and Mancebo 2007).

In the Mindanao State University-Iligan Institute of Technology (MSU-IIT), a cyber portfolio was developed to "introduce innovations with practical and breakthrough solutions against expensive and inflexible vended software." It is intended for "teachers who seek out strategies to integrate technology in their lessons." Tried first in Statistics, the cyber portfolio is viewed as a tool that provides for the management, organization, display and evaluation of the e-portfolio pioneered in use by graduate students who are situated in different places (Robles 2011). According to Robles (2011), "the making of cyber portfolio as a management tool for e-portfolio is one of the practical and effective actions that provide the opportunity for integration of sustainability in education blended with multiple intelligences (MI), higher-order thinking skills (HOTS) and technology." Research about its implementation in the said university has been found to contribute positively to student appreciation on teaching and learning experiences and to the promotion of quality assessment of student outputs that can be posted in the said portfolio (Robles 2011). At the university level, little is yet considered as a concrete accomplishment in terms of delivering ESD effectively—particularly towards greening the Philippine economy while making it climate-smart also. Most of the current efforts are at the level of researching for the intelligent and verifiable ways of integrating ESD in tertiary education relative to intended outcomes. The works of Tan (2004), Khambayat and Majumdar (2010), Reyes (2014), and Necesito et al. (2010) dwell on such aspect where improving the delivery of ESD in the HEIs is of paramount importance to institute the desired transformation in the Filipino youths.

5 Deepening ESD in Philippine Universities

ESD is the kind of education with unquestionable relevance to today's development issues, in which the rigor of getting it to what it should be for sustainable development continues to wheel on in the Philippines. Perhaps the greatest challenge remains on how ESD should be carried out to eventually result to the achievement of the Sustainable Development Goals that countries over the world have vowed to meet. As ESD is looked upon as "education for the future, for everyone everywhere and an essential ingredient to ensure quality education and a successful transition to green societies and economies" (UNESCO 2012), it is approached from different directions at the tertiary education level, as changes due to customization needs based on sustainable development concepts are applied to the different facets of university education. Prof. Tilbury's (2011) recommendations on how universities across the world have to realign their academic services on the basis of sustainable development are accounted for in the on-going initiatives happening on the training of "teachers of today for the learners of tomorrow" (Khambayat and Majumdar 2010; Tan 2004), and on refocusing research and extension directions that are now bent on increasing the production and dissemination of solid evidences on climate change issues and environmental problems and their management strategies (OASERD 2007; UNESCO 2011a, b; Bidad and Campiseño 2010).

There are critical elements and competencies that must be developed and nurtured to befit today's tertiary education in the country to the global definition of ESD. These elements and competencies are implied in the 2012 Report of UNESCO on UN DESD, which are aimed to "refocus lifelong education on knowledge, skills and values, and thought patterns to build a sustainable world." For teacher education, the framework in the development of various competencies is reflected in the report of Comenius 2.1 project for the multidimensional learning processes to address the critical issues in development and the environment (Sleurs 2004). The Comenius 2.1 project ESD framework is comprehensive in accounting for the elements of ESD as in UNESCOs Agenda 21 and thus a good guide to figure out targeted interventions in the development of teachers for the many competencies they have to acquire in relation to ESD. In the Philippines, research for this aspect is yet on-going and progress is likewise slow, especially in the aspect of developing theories of practice that facilitates the assimilation of ESD insights and learning.

Theory development and validation for practical applications in SD efforts is not observable at this point, but learning about these theories (circular economy, industrial ecology, etc.) is gaining ground with the help of scholarships. One reason is attributed to the vague conceptualization of how the approach should be for ESD to produce impacts indicative of the promises made by the country on Agenda 21, since "mainstream societies" in the Philippines have to graduate from being concerned with "short-term growth at the expense of natural capital" (Calder and Clugston 2003). The same is shared with the World Wildlife Fund's document on *Sustainable Development and Learning-inspiration for university teachers*, a guide in the development of efforts at the university level for education to be a catalyst of sustainable development (WWF 2011). It is in this vein that the country is challenged to catch up with global ESD initiatives as shown in the said document, where sophistication is geared higher towards the competencies and modalities in the delivery of ESD. Updates on these efforts are found in the research works of Tan (2004), Talisayon (2014), and others who have wanted to understand the critical elements of making effective changes in various education programs pursuing ESD in the country.

6 Conclusion

The pursuit of ESD in Philippine universities is gaining progress in the way it is delivered for the benefit of the Filipino people. It has evolved through the years of adjustments for implementation to see ESD's outcomes in producing results for the country's responsibilities towards PA 21/EPA 21 and UNESCOs Agenda 21. Looking into the ESD implementation in Philippine universities, it can be said to be grounded with the necessary legal support for it to be pursued seriously. There are quite a number of legal bases that direct the way it should be implemented in all levels of education and to see to it that it should be implemented based on its purpose. As earlier indicated, the intention for ESD is hinged on the priority to withstand or overcome the impacts of climate change in the Philippines, where disaster risk reduction and preparedness is a part. This has helped in a way in reducing losses from human casualties, and damaged properties and livelihoods. The National Service Training Program (NSTP) in the universities has been a good vehicle in delivering education programs at the grassroots, which could push for the learning of strategies about climate change mitigation and adaptation, resilience and disaster preparedness among the local people.

However, in the other aspects of tertiary/university education and responsibilities, not much progress has been made. The delivery of ESD is yet on practical methodologies of aforementioned priority thrusts. The two education associations (PATLEPAM and EENP) have done a great deal in streamlining efforts towards ESD integration in curricular development, which have ensured the significance of the topics being prepared and taught for. But in scaling up ESD in the areas of research and extension, not much progress has been done. Related researches are yet in determining the essential attributes of teaching ESD subjects in the university. Development of theories with practical applications in SD concerns is less explored but necessary for research and policy action objectives in Philippine universities, which can be addressed by furthering international exchange and collaboration efforts. Indeed, the Philippine HEIs have a lot of catching up to do, particularly in joining universities worldwide in changing mindsets and lifestyles and in figuring out the designs of modern industrial systems and societies the sustainable way. Emphasis therefore for this context is set out for Philippine universities to keep track of ESD development in the world and learn for the sensible application of new tools and methods to pursue the country's SD goals efficiently.

References

Abejuela, R. (2007). Indigenous knowledge systems and higher education in the Philippines. *Tribes and Tribals. Special Volume No., 1*, 205–213.

APC-ESSC. (2008). Education for sustainable development. Available at apc.essc.org.ph/index2.php?option=com_content&do_pdf=1&id=24. Accessed 1 Mar 2015.

APCEIU. (2007). Peace and human rights education through education for sustainable development: Lessons from our four case studies in the Philippines. EIU best case study series no. 5. EIU Experiential Learning Programme 2007.

ASEAN. (2013). ASEAN guidelines on eco-schools. Available at environment.asean.org/wp-content/uploads/2013/07/ASEAN-Guidelines-on-Eco-schools.pdf. Accessed 25 Feb 2015.

Bidad, C., & Campiseño, E. (2010). Community extension services of SUCs in Region IX: Basis for a sustainable community enhancement program. *E-International Scientific Research Journal., 2*(3), 235–243.

Calder, W., & Clugston, R. (2003). International efforts to promote higher education for sustainable development. Available at www.ulsf.org/pdf/International_SCUP_article.pdf. Accessed 2 Mar 2015.

Commission on Higher Education. (2012a). Commission on higher education (CHED) strategic plan 2011–2016. Available at www.ched.gov.ph/wp-content/uploads/2014/12/CHED-Strategic-Plan-2011-2016.pdf. Accessed 10 Feb 2015.

Commission on Higher Education. (2012b). Higher education in numbers-enrollment. Available at www.ched.gov.ph/index.php/higher-education-in-numbers/enrollment/. Accessed 11 Sept 2015.

Commission on Higher Education. (2014). Higher education data: 2014. Available at www.ched.gov.ph/index.php/higher-education-in-numbers/higher-education-data-2014/. Accessed 11 Sept 2015.

Granados, J. (2011). The challenges of higher education in the 21st century. Available at http://www.guni-rmies.net/news/detail.php?id=1725. Accessed 10 Feb 2015.

Khambayat, R., & Majumdar, S. (2010). Preparing teachers of today for the learners of tomorrow. *Journal of Engineering, Science and Management Education., 2*, 9–16.

Lizada, M. C. (2010). The role of academe in risk-based national food safety programs for developing countries. *Journal of Developments in Sustainable Agriculture., 5*, 1–11.

Morales, M. P. (2014). Culture and language sensitive physics on student concept attainment. *International Journal of Learning and Teaching., 6*(1), 1–12.

Necesito, M., Santos, R., & Fulgar, J. I. (2010). A results-based monitoring and evaluation framework to determine performance and success of ESD in TVET: The case of the Philippines. Available at www.focusintl.com/RBM077-23.%20A%20Results-Based%20Monitoring-%20Necesito.pdf. Accessed 25 Feb 2015.

Nomura, K., & Abe, O. (2008). *The status of environmental education in the ASEAN region: Survey results and analysis*. Rikkyo University, Tokyo, Japan: Working Paper E-1. Education for Sustainable Development Research Center.

Philippine Council for Sustainable Development. (2015). Rio in retrospect: The Philippines and global agenda 21 1992–1996. Available at http://www.psdn.org.ph/agenda21/rio001.htm. Accessed 1 Mar 2015.

Philippines Universities and Colleges Guide. (2015). Schools offering environmental studies and ecology courses in the Philippines. Available at www.finduniversity.ph/environmental-studies-schools/. Accessed 14 Apr 2015.

Reyes, J. A. (2014). Environmental attitudes and behaviors in the Philippines. *Journal of Educational and Social Research., 4*(6), 87–102.

Robles, A. C. M. (2011). Graduate school cyber portfolio: The innovative menu for sustainable development. *Advanced Computing: An International Journal., 2*(6), 1–11.

Segovia, V., & Galang, A. (2002). Sustainable development in higher education in the Philippines: The Case of Miriam College. Available at www.sciencedirect.com/science/article/pii/S0952873302000132. Accessed 3 Mar 2015.

Sleurs, W. (ed). (2004). Competencies for ESD (education for sustainable development) teachers. Comenius 2.1 Project 118277-CP-1-2004-BE-Comenius-C2.1. Brussels, Belgium.

Suemitsu, K., & Mancebo, S. (2007). Philippines' rural human resource development for sustainable development: Changing issues and approaches. Education for sustainable development (ESD) on agricultural production and environmental conservation, 2007. Tokyo, Japan: Obihiro Asia and the Pacific Seminar on Education for Rural Development.

Talisayon, V. (2014). Development of scientific skills and values in physics education. Available at https://web.phys.ksu.edu/icpe/publications/teach2/Talisayon.pdf. Accessed 25 Feb 2015.

Tan, M. (2004). Nurturing scientific and technological literacy through environmental education. *Journal of International Cooperation in Education., 7*(1), 115–131.

Tan, M. (2012). *Promoting public understanding of sustainable development: Opportunities for science education. Biology Education for Social and Sustainable Development*. Rotterdam, The Netherlands: Sense Publishers.

Tilbury, D. (2011). Higher education for sustainability: A global overview of commitment and progress. Available at insight-dev.glos.ac.uk/sustainability/Education/Documents/GUNI%20HE%20in%20the%20World%204%20HE%27s%20Commitment%20to%20Sus.pdf. Accessed 25 Feb 2015.

UNESCO. (2011a). Country reports on education for sustainable development: Centred on the five cluster countries of UNESCO office, Jakarta. UNESCO House, Jl. Galuh (II) No. 5, Kebayoran Baru, Jakarta 12110, Indonesia.

UNESCO. (2011b). Education for sustainable development country guidelines for changing the climate of teacher education to address sustainability: Putting transformative education into practice. UNESCO House, Jl. Galuh (II) No. 5, Kebayoran Baru, Jakarta 12110, Indonesia.

UNESCO. (2012). Shaping the education of tomorrow: 2012 report on the UN decade of education for sustainable development, abridged. UNESCO, 7, place de Fontenoy, 75352 Paris 07 SP, France.

Unsi, A. (2014). Envisioning education for sustainable development in the post-2015 agenda in the Philippines. *ASPBAE Ed-lines Quarterly Newsletter* 11.

WWF. (2011). Sustainable development and learning-inspiration for university teachers. Available at www.wwf.se/source.php/1395535/Sustainable_development_and_learning.pdf. Accessed 25 Feb 2015.

Integrating the Global Dimension in Engineering Education: Experiences from a Collaborative Project

Rhoda Trimingham, Boris Lazzarini, Agustí Pérez-Foguet, Neil Noble, Alejandra Boni, Manuel Sierra-Castañer, Francesco Mongera and Guido Zolezzi

Abstract

The '*Global Dimension in Engineering Education*' (GDEE) network is an initiative that aims to increase the awareness, critical understanding and attitudinal values of undergraduates and postgraduates students in technical universities across Europe related to Sustainable Human Development (SHD) and its relationship with technology. This is being dealt with by integrating SHD as a cross-cutting issue in teaching activities by improving the competences of academics and through engaging both staff and students in initiatives related to SHD. The GDEE started as a collaborative project between a consortium of European Universities and NGOs. The chapter presents a

R. Trimingham (✉)
Loughborough Design School, Loughborough University, Leicester, UK
e-mail: R.L.Trimingham@lboro.ac.uk

B. Lazzarini · A. Pérez-Foguet
Universitat Politècnica de Catalunya, Barcelona, Spain
e-mail: agusti.perez@upc.edu

N. Noble
University of Warwick, Coventry, UK

A. Boni
Universitat Politècnica de Valencia, Valencia, Spain

M. Sierra-Castañer
Technical University of Madrid, Madrid, Spain

F. Mongera
University of Trento, Trento, Italy

G. Zolezzi
Training Centre for International Cooperation—TCIC, Trento, Italy

© Springer International Publishing Switzerland 2016

W. Leal Filho and P. Pace (eds.), *Teaching Education for Sustainable Development at University Level*, World Sustainability Series,
DOI 10.1007/978-3-319-32928-4_12

common understanding of how best to establish effective education for global development, and presents a pedagogical approach to facilitate the connection between theoretical knowledge (lecturers and students from universities) with practice (through NGOs). It discusses this approach through the analysis of case studies of best practice from those already working in this area within higher education across Europe. It concludes with the presentation of a continued professional development (CPD) approach for academics that uses a series of online training courses, with support from a series of contextual case studies written by NGOs to support teaching human development within engineering courses.

Keywords
Global development • Pedagogy • Academic training

1 Introduction: Global Development and Higher Education

It can be argued that the knowledge and skills required for engineers are the same all over the world, and it is often expected that an engineer will work in a range of countries and cultures during their career (Bourn 2014). The effect of this increasingly global profession has changed the nature of learning. This change naturally has consequences on the Higher Education (HE) Engineering curriculum, with many universities reconsidering the nature and content, covered in courses. The need for this is not new, it has long been realised that there is a need for a new kind of engineer; one who is equipped with the skills to deal with the societal aspects of technologies (De Graaf and Ravesteijn 2001, cited in Segalàs et al. 2010). Indeed, in the 70s Schumacher states that for education to impact on sustainability, it would have to be 'education of a different kind: an education that takes us into the depth of things' (1973, preface). Sterling (2005) agrees stating the need for a fundamental shift in education to address the nature of sustainability. Concurrently, our world is in a constant state of change in which we face new challenges that require new solutions. Engineering must respond to these changes, with education being at the heart of the response (Gathercole 2014).

One proposed method is to incorporate a Global Dimension as an integral part of engineering education. A Global Dimension is one which encourages students to think of themselves as global citizens and thus promote a sense of global social responsibility (Bourn 2014). In particular, the focus is on the incorporation and understanding of international development, human rights, along with equality issues, and the environment. This does not stand alone within engineering education as there are already relationships with other agendas, such as; sustainability, humanitarian engineering and ethics (Gathercole 2014). However the benefits of including a global dimension is that it can help students make links to the real world, and enable engineers to play a role in poverty reduction, human rights issues, and conflict resolution (Gathercole 2014).

Previously, the traditional response from engineering academics has been that through the use of technology we can find solutions to society's problems. This assumes that a solution can always be found, and does not necessarily account for the views of people and the cultures it effects (Bourn 2014). Some universities have already begun to recognise the impact that engineering has on; societies, ethics and ones' individual value-base. An example of this is current recognition of, and the accepted role of Sustainable Development (World Commission on Environment and Development 1987). This definition is still widely used today, by different groups and has ultimately led to the proposal of the Sustainable Development Goals, a successor to the Millennium Development Goals. Target 4.7 states that by 2030 all learners should a have acquired knowledge and skills to promote sustainable development (United Nations 2012). Abundant literature has already substantially improved scientific contribution on sustainable development teaching strategies in higher education, specifically in engineering studies (Mulder et al. 2012; Holmberg et al. 2008; Segalàs et al. 2010; Watson et al. 2013; Lozano et al. 2014). Furthermore, universities have begun to recognise the impact of globalisation pedagogy, typically under the heading of 'internationalisation'. Although some previous work was done with a humanitarian and human development focus (Boni and Pérez-Foguet 2008), the drive for the globalization of higher education has increased momentum in this direction. In recent years there has been a growing debate about the implications of such policies and practices, which has resulted in academics investigating the process of learning. One manifestation of this can be seen in the sharing of knowledge, which has increased due to the willingness to learn from other nations and the increased mobility of staff and students. As a result, there is a growing demand from students to re-think the content and form of engineering degree courses.

In order to address this, in 2012, academics came together in a collaborative consortium known as Global Dimension in Engineering Education (GDEE), which aims to increase the awareness, critical understanding and attitudinal values of undergraduates and postgraduate students related to Sustainable Human Development (SHD). Roots of the thematic and methodological approaches followed by the project are found in Pérez-Foguet et al. (2005), Boni and Pérez-Foguet (2008), Pérez-Foguet and Cruz (2011). The consortium comprised of five technical universities and four NGOs from three EU countries: United Kingdom, Spain and Italy.

During the two year initiative the consortium has established an understanding of best practice for effectively integrating global dimensions into the engineering curriculum. Consequently, this paper presents the pedagogical theory which underpins this understanding. It discusses this approach through a discussion of pedagogical theory derived from prior art plus a review of best practice from those already working in this area within higher education across Europe. It concludes with the presentation of a CPD approach for academics that uses a series of online training courses, with support from a series of contextual case studies written by

NGOs to support teaching human development within engineering courses. It argues for integrated active learning pedagogies and for Universities to actively seek engagement with experts in the field.

2 Goals, Competences and Pedagogical Approach

Referring to curriculum design, Sterling points out that if engineers are to contribute truly to Sustainable Development, then sustainability must become part of their everyday thinking. This can only be achieved if Sustainable Development becomes an integral part of engineering education programmes, not a mere 'add on' to the 'core' parts of the curriculum (Sterling 2005).

In 2008, 'The Global Engineer' report laid out a conceptual methodology to incorporate the competences of a 'Global Engineer' onto the professional accreditation standards (in the UK), comprising 5 sequential stages (Bourne and Neal 2008). However, this list has grown to 10, as others have been added to reflect new understandings of effective education for global development. The additions have come from the outcomes of a review of papers which reflect on best practice submitted during the course of the GDEE project (Trimingham 2014, see also below). It also embeds learning from a recent publication on Internationalising Higher Education from the Higher Education Academy (2014). The 10 key objectives are:

1. Develop a faculty wide philosophy and base of knowledge and understanding
2. Identify areas within the curriculum where global development can enhance current teaching
3. Introduce students to global development
4. Integrate the idea of systems thinking in relation to global development
5. Convey an appreciation of the commercial, institutional, legislative and social motivations for implementing global development
6. Demonstrate knowledge and understanding of the concepts of global development and how it exists within discipline specific contexts
7. Advance practical understanding of the pressures facing industry in terms of integrating global development
8. Acquaint students with the current range of tools and resources available for integrating global development and understand how to use some of the most common
9. Allow students to generate solutions through active learning.
10. Develop a view of future directions for global development engineering (Trimingham 2014).

Such an approach would enable greater integration of Global Development criteria into the curriculum. It promotes learning outcomes that enable graduates to establish a clear connection between engineering and Global Development and helps them in practising sustainable engineering.

But within this methodology a reorientation on pedagogy and learning processes is essential to achieve effective Education for Global Development. The Barcelona declaration states: "*teaching strategies in the classroom and teaching and learning techniques must be reviewed*" (Barcelona declaration 2004). But what is needed to achieve an effective Education for Sustainable Development (ESD) in higher education, and specifically in engineering education? What pedagogy is especially good for Sustainable Development?

The level of adaption required by engineers to enable them to produce globally appropriate outcomes is large, therefore engineering students (and academics!) need to be made more aware of the issues and given the skills with which to deal with such change. Best practice approaches all follow the same pattern. They begin by building momentum within their HE establishment, then they introducing concepts of global development and build global development knowledge, they then move to supporting learners who are expected to be working on live projects. This approach promotes learning that emphasises independence of mind and the ability to make sense of, rather than reproduce information (Khan 1995). Engineering for global development must involve the key characteristics of a transformative educational approach (where the learning constructs meaning, Sterling 2001). It involves creative, solutions-focussed learning; self-directed team work; learning by doing (commonly 'live' projects); iterative refinement and reflection; and drawing from a range of disciplines to inform outputs. Since the introduction of the concept of Education for Sustainable Development there has been wide ranging discussion regarding the knowledge, skills and values needed to contribute to SD, and what competencies should be obtained in Universities (Segalàs et al. 2010; Svanstrom et al. 2008; Mulder et al. 2012). Effective Education for Global Development should promote the development of the following competencies (see Table 1).

In relation to teaching engineering for global development most authors do not opt for one specific learning technique, but for using a wide range of pedagogical tools and strategies. Important aspects of pedagogy include encouraging students to explore issues within contexts relevant to them and their communities. This involves student-centred and interactive enquiry-based approaches to teaching and learning. There are pedagogical approaches that promote dialogue and community, higher-order critical thinking and problem-solving. Some strategies to facilitate integrative teaching and learning are as follows:

- Team-teaching and team planning
- Collaborative learning and learning communities
- Clustered and linked courses
- Core seminars at introductory and capstone levels
- Theme or problem focus in courses
- Proactive attention to integration and synthesis
- Models of interdisciplinary and integrative process
- Theories and methods from interdisciplinary fields

Table 1 GDEE competencies (GDEE 2015, adapted from CSCT 2008; Wiek et al. 2011; Segalàs et al. 2010; Svanstrom et al. 2008; Mulder et al. 2012)

Competence	Description
Systemic thinking	Ability to recognize and analyse the complexity of development issues across different domains (society, environment, economy, etc.) and across different scales (local to global). Ability to identify locally and globally relevant SHD issues and to connect the local and global aspects. Ability to analyse and explain the role of technology and engineering in a globalized context connecting local and global aspects
Knowledge acquisition	Ability to acquire relevant knowledge about SHD challenges and issues. Ability to select educational goals for SHD, taking into account the prior knowledge of students, and the diversity within the group of learners. Ability to find partners outside the school community and to co-operate with organizations which promote SHD
Ethics and values	Ability to include and embed in teaching SD Ethic and values, principles and goals. Ability to encourage students to question their beliefs and assumptions on SD values such as justice, solidarity, dignity, participation, etc. in order to clarify their thinking. Ability to work with students on contradictory beliefs, assumptions and values, as well as moral dilemmas, specifically about the role of technology and engineering in sustainable development issues
Action	Ability to introduce SHD as cross-cutting issues in teaching (introductory courses). Ability to advice students who are actively participating in the resolution of sustainable development issues. This could be through field-work or other extension activities during B.Sc. projects or M.Sc. thesis, typically within a formalized International Cooperation Project (mid-level courses). Ability to design and implement a subject in the field of SHD (advanced courses)
Emotion	Ability to motivate students towards Sustainable Development issues through Leadership and Empathy. Motivate and facilitate participative problem solving and Teamwork. Build capacity to understand diversity across cultures, social groups, communities

- Projects and case studies
- Dyads, triads, and small groups for discussion
- Game and role playing
- Inquiry- and discovery-based learning
- Learning portfolios
- Case studies
- Active participation
- Total immersion (for example managing a site)
- Balancing the far and near (making content relevant)
- Experiential- and service-learning, internships, and fieldwork
- Residential living-learning experiences (developed from Segalàs 2014; Wals and Corcoran 2005).

As well as integrating global development into HE, there is also a need to place it within an industrial context and to highlight the importance of business, innovation and enterprise skills. Teaching techniques in order to accomplish this include work placements, brought in speakers/tutors and strong links with industry, NGO's and community organisations (Trimingham 2014).

Finally it is important to understand the future direction of Global Development in Higher Education. This is important for both academics and students as it helps to guide current activity through a lens of future possibilities. From an academic perspective this includes becoming involved in research related to Global Development and keeping up to date with current thinking within the GDEE agenda. New principles and understanding, as well as new tools and techniques can then be integrated into teaching via regular curriculum reviews.

3 Overview of an Initiative to Engage Engineering Academics with Global Development: The GDEE Project

Roots of the methodological approach on which this initiative is based can be found in the previous works of project partners (Boni et al. 2004; Pérez-Foguet et al. 2005; Boni and Pérez-Foguet 2008; Pérez-Foguet and Cruz 2011). Diverse initiatives for improving SHD teaching have been separately promoted among project partners at a local and national level in Italy and Spain such as: case studies (Oliete-Josa and Pérez-Foguet 2005, 2008), faculty empowerment (Archetti et al. 2007), networking and awarding best practices (Cabrera et al. 2006). In the UK, it is worth mentioning a namesake initiative *The Global Dimension of Engineering Education* project coordinated by the NGO Engineers Against Poverty, alongside Engineers Without Borders, a project partner on the current initiative.

The main aim of the GDEE initiative is to integrate different approaches on engineering education issues, reflected by consortium composition, in order to transcend the national level and encourage a European vision of this issue. From one side, previous approaches more focused on engineering education for SHD, mainly implemented in Spain and Italy and, from the other side, the UK approach that goes back to the concept of Global Engineer (Bourn and Neal 2008). This integrated approach is broadly reflected in different project outcomes, such as training materials and on-line courses.

In order to increase competencies among academics to engage with the global development agenda training materials alongside a set of 9 open source online courses were developed to train academics, teachers or researchers throughout Europe (and internationally as it transpired!). More than forty academics from sixteen European universities and twelve experts in the field of development (from NGOs, development training centres, and engineering organizations, among others) have closely collaborated in developing materials, and nine separate publications,

Table 2 Course outline (GDEE 2015)

Block A—the global engineer	Addressed to those academics that want to introduce cross-cutting issues in their activities; i.e., including a session related to SHD within, typically, a B.Sc. course *Course A.1*: *Making the case for a critical global engineer* *Course A.2*: *Key elements for addressing the global dimension of engineering* *Course A.3*: *The global engineer in Sustainable Human Development*
Block B—supervising BS/MS thesis with fieldwork	Addressed to those academics who want to advice students involved in field-work or other extension activities during B.Sc. projects or M.Sc. thesis, typically within or close to a formalized International Cooperation Project *Course B.4*: *Supervising Engineering Students* *Course B.5*: *Knowing the context and partners* *Course B.6*: *Knowing International Cooperation*
Block C—integrating GDE into teaching and research	Addressed to those academics (or professionals) who want to design a course relating Technology and SHD, from their own technical expertise *Course C.7*: *Integrating GDE into the academic* *Course C.8*: *Integrating GDE into Teaching: Theory and Practice* *Course C.9*: *Integrating GDE into Research*

one for each course, have been published and disseminated as Open Educational Resources (GDEE 2015; see Table 2).

To maximise participation, courses have been implemented through distance learning in the three European countries; Italy, Spain and the United Kingdom. In parallel, participants engaged with one another through collaborative tools and through discussion forums. Evaluation consisted of three types of assessment tools: (i) assessment quizzes at the end of each session; (ii) two academic activities, with the aim of putting in practice notions learnt through the sessions; (iii) a final multiple choice assessment. The open source nature of the online materials also allowed interested academics (and others) to 'dip in' without completing the courses (these materials can be found at www.gdee.eu).

4 The Impact of GDEE Academic Training

From January 2014 to January 2015 the Europe wide online web portal (GDEE 2015) saw just under 8000 visitors, with 39 % of those visitors returning more than once after their first visit. There were over 750 resources and course papers downloaded and over 42,000 page views. In total there were 295 participants across all three training centres (Spain, UK and Italy). The following discusses the impact the academic training has had in Spain.

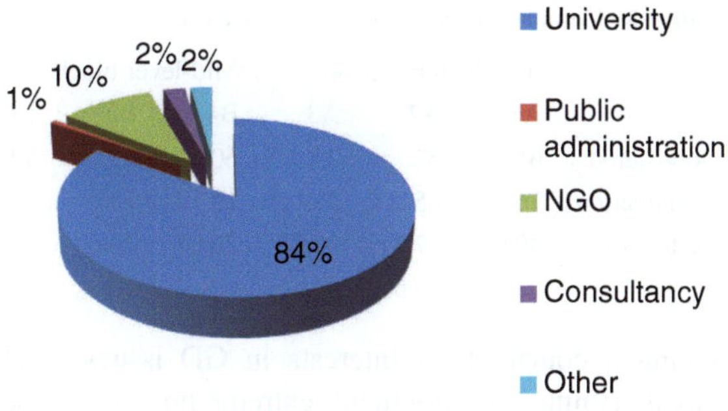

Fig. 1 Participants' affiliation

In Spain courses run from March 2014 to April 2015. Overall, a total of 129 participants enrolled, mostly to more than one course, with a median average of 70 participants per course. Females appear to be more interested, representing the 58 % of participants.

As shown in Fig. 1, the majority of participants (84 %) are linked to a University, with more than hundred participants. NGOs workers and volunteers represent the second largest group (10 %). But other categories (Public Administration, Consultancy firms, etc.) showed an interest in the GDEE training initiative. Enrolled professors come from 36 different universities: 30 Spanish, 2 Portuguese, 2 Colombian and 1 Danish.

The completion rate can be defined as the percentage of enrolled participants who satisfied the courses' criteria in order to earn a certificate. Completion rates of GDEE courses vary across different courses and thematic blocks. The highest rates of completion were seen during the introductory block (A1, A2 and A3, see Table 2). The trend indicates a decrease for courses of the mid-level block and then a slight increase for the advanced group of courses. Time availability also has to be taken into account here however, since academics have limited time for professional development training. Courses for the Mid-Level block (B4, B5, and B6, see Table 2) ran during the months of June and July; notoriously busy months for university professors. Besides, to meet the project timelines, courses were scheduled one after another with a very short break (or sometimes no break at all) between courses. This overload might have affected participants' motivation to complete all course activities.

Since the goal of the majority of academics enrolled wasn't to earn credit (each course was worth 1 ECT), and given the varied background and the broad range of motivation of participants, completion rate may be not the right indicator to measure the impact of the courses. Nevertheless, it can still be argued that GDEE completion rates are higher than other free on-line courses. Research on MOOCs shows that the majority of courses have completion rates of less than 10 %, with a median average of 6.5 % (Jordan 2014). The GDEE courses showed completion rates between 14.86 and 40 % (see Table 3).

According to the answers of anonymous surveys launched at the end of each GDEE course the training initiative had a positive impact on participants. Specifically, a very high percentage of participants (77–100 %) agree that, as a result of

Table 3 Completion rates for online GDEE courses

	Introductory block			Mid-level block			Advanced block		
	A1	A2	A3	B4	B5	B6	C7	C8	C9
Registered	65	67	73	60	63	74	66	73	84
Completions	26	25	21	16	13	11	11	13	14
Rate (%)	40.00	37.31	28.77	26.67	20.63	14.86	16.67	17.81	16.67

taking a course, their interests in GD issues (such as Millenium Development Goals, Human Development, extreme poverty, climate change, etc.) has increased. Moreover, a high percentage of participants (69–100 %) agree that courses were useful for integrating cross-cutting issues in teaching activities. It is worth highlighting that the introductory courses, that dealt with topics in a more theoretical way, are perceived as less useful for integrating cross-cutting issues.

5 Contextual Case Studies

By 'training the trainers' (academics) in global development issues, it is hoped that there will be an increase in academic staff' competences to integrate Sustainable Human Development issues in curricular teaching. However, in addition to this there is evidence of an increasing need to tackle the shortage of adequate tools to implement effectively the acquired competences. With this in mind, another aim of the project was to provide academic staff with specific materials to be used with students. This has been done in two main steps: initially, case studies of real development projects were provided by project partners, as well as external NGOs and universities. The selection process, which led to the choice of twenty-seven case studies, was carried out using the following criteria; geographic context; technology area affected by the project; and subject into which the final material could be used by academics. Finally, each case study was assigned to a specific academic who developed the teaching material following a standardised template.

Following previous experiences of Pérez-Foguet et al. (2005), each case study combines practical/contextual information on the specific project from which it is drawn (the context) with more academic-oriented content specifically designed to be used in class and during self-directed study (activities). The combination of practice and theory in the available materials allows lecturers to overcome the distance between traditional academic teaching and the evidence in the field. As part of a "standard" academic subject, students are also provided with a set of information, both technical and socio-economic, which allows them to understand the multiple variables present in a specific context (as well as practice critical thinking skills!). On the basis of this information a set of activities is provided, designed to provide students with technical problems related to the context. The case studies, which are published under a Creative Common Licence, can be adapted by each academic to suit their own teaching agenda. This process has involved more than 50 authors, from 14 universities.

6 Best Practice

An additional role of the GDEE project was to recognise best practice within Higher Education on the integration of sustainable human development into technology education through 2 editions of a 'best practice award'. The motivation for the best practice awards was two-fold; firstly it allowed the project team to reflect on, and learn from existing academic engagement with the global development agenda (reported on at the beginning of this chapter); and secondly it allowed the project team to motivate and reward activities that stemmed from the training initiative.

The award was presented through two different calls, the first one in 2013 and the second one in 2015. It focused on University academics and awarded the best examples of teaching that contributes to extend the education Global Development through technical courses within European Universities. Submissions, that could be either theoretical or applied, had to focus on:

- Innovative methods for integrated SHD into the curriculum.
- Converting existing experiences in development education into technology/engineering studies.
- Making materials for the integration of SHD available to the Academic Community.
- Innovative methods for the support and supervision of a Ph.D. Thesis, Master Thesis, Bachelor Thesis, or equivalent (GDEE 2015).

Submissions were evaluated through a competition panel. The panel was composed of both Academics and NGO's. Each submission was evaluated against the following criteria:

- Innovation of the work, including novel educational aspects.
- Quality, coherence and sustainability of the work.
- Impact of the work on the academic activities of the European Universities.

During the two periods, 46 proposals were delivered (22 for the first edition and 26 for the second edition). In total 10 submissions were awarded prizes (see Table 4).

It is observed that they cover a very wide range of technological disciplines and focus on a number of different topics including; integration of SHD in the formal curricula, promotion of practical works among the students, computer games for promoting sustainable development, strength of educational capabilities, among many others. All of these examples of best practice follow all, or most of the pedagogical theory presented above.

Table 4 10 Best practise awards

Initiative title	Academic and affiliation
Beyond Traditional Education in Engineering: A Systemic Approach to Strengthen Development	Politecnico di Milano (Italy)
B.E.S.T. (Best Environmental Sustainable Technologies) for International Cooperation	Università degli Studi di Brescia (Italy)
Real-world Water and Sanitation M.Sc. Thesis Research with Cranfield University	Cranfield University (UK)
SHD—Tackling Interdisciplinary Early: Transforming Technical Expertise into Global Citizenship	Imperial College London (UK)
Incorporating Sustainable Wool Processing using Engineering Solutions into the Academic Curriculum	Manchester Metropolitan University (UK)
The Integration of Education for Development in the Civil Engineering School of the University of Granada	Universidad de Granada (Spain)
A global perspective. Environmental Sustainability and Cooperation Workshop in southern Morocco	Universidad de Alcalá (Spain)
ECOLOGY: A Game-experiment to Approximate Engineer Students to Sustainable Human Development and the Limits to Growth Concepts	Universidad de Valladolid (Spain)
Integrated Development Aid Awareness into Architecture	Universidad Politécnica de Madrid (Spain)
Strengthening the Education Capabilities of University of Makeni (Sierra Leona)	Universidad San Pablo CEU (Spain)

7 Conclusions

This chapter has highlighted characteristics of best practice pedagogical strategies and their role in Global Development Engineering Education. It also outlines an approach for training academics within this field which has shown high levels of engagement and motivation from academics (and others!).

It highlights that imparting knowledge is an important activity, but not a guarantee for change. Learning about Global Development does not guarantee realisation of actions and activities supporting changes necessary for effective sustainable development. Learning for change needs a deep knowledge of the basics of Global Development and the development of specific competencies and values through active participatory methods for both students, and training academics within this field. Furthermore, it has to capacitate students with the appropriate competences in relation to their future profession, but also arm them with capabilities in systemic thinking and multi-disciplinary working. To create a pedagogical approach that optimises systemic thinking the understanding of flows of relationships between concepts of all kind is needed.

The need to address global challenges and provide a more rounded and relevant curriculum for engineering education has brought together academics and practitioners from across Europe who have worked together to develop a new pedagogy. By designing courses to engage academics with Global Development a deeper understanding of effective pedagogy has been explored. The skills and knowledge developed can be used to address current curriculum failings, though tweaks and changes to the existing education structure. The overarching aim and consensus from GDEE partners is that the integration of this Global Dimension would not be an 'add on' to existing curriculum development, but should be fully embraced and embedded into the core content.

It is recognised that Global Development requires core competencies, such as, systemic thinking, knowledge acquisition, the ability to question beliefs and assumptions, show leadership and empathy, and get involved in solutions through participatory problem solving. Multi-disciplinary team working and the use of transdisciplinary research is fundamental to the development of Global Engineering students and desired by industry leaders. These skills do not only meet the requirements of the profession, but will help change the mind-set of an engineer towards developing future solutions which are globally appropriate. It is also clear that the Global Development agenda is a 'fast moving beast', and as such regular reviews, underpinned by continued research in this field, are required.

The main limitations of this study are twofold. The first is related to data availability to contrast the real impact of activities; results presented are biased on Spain since no comparable results are currently available. Furthermore, only impact data on GDEE courses are provided as the diffusion of case studies is still on going. The second is related to the methodology adopted to evaluate the changes in participant's interest and ability; a highly quantitative approach was followed during the initiative. More qualitative data is now required to further understanding of the success of the pedagogical approach.

It is worth highlighting that special attention has been given to enhance replicability of this experience at different levels. Courses' content and structure, contextual case studies, and supporting resources are available at the webpage (www.gdee.eu) along with a number of other Global Development resources for academics. All academic resources have been published under a Creative Commons license. Therefore they can be translated, improved and adapted to different contexts. While all training materials are directly downloadable from the webpage, files with the courses' structure are available under request.

Acknowledgements European Commission, Non-State Actors and Local Authorities in Development, Raising public awareness of development issues and promoting development education in the European Union Reference: EuropeAid/131141/C/ACT/MULTI, Number of proposal: DCI-NSAED/2011/63, Barcelona City Council, Team GDEE.

References

Archetti, C., Zolezzi, G., & Pérez-Foguet, A. (2007). Ingeniería ambiental apropiada para los Objetivos del Milenio. Mesiano Sostenible 2015 en 1r Congrés UPC Sostenible 2015: 12 i 13 de juliol de 2007 (pp. 231–235). Barcelona: Centre per a la Sostenibilitat.

Barcelona Declaration. (2004). *Engineering Education in Sustainable Development Conference*, Barcelona, October 29, 2004. Available at: https://www.upc.edu/eesd-observatory/who/declaration of-barcelona.

Boni, A., Acebillo, M., Visscher, J. T., Hidalgo, S., Pérez-Foguet, A, & Del Cañizo, C. (2004). Estrategias para el impulso de la educación para el desarrollo en la universidad. La experiencia del curso de Formación de Formadores universitarios: Educando en Tecnología para el Desarrollo Humano. In II Congreso Nacional Universidad y Cooperación al Desarrollo. Universidad de Murcia. Servicio de Publicaciones. Murcia. http://hdl.handle.net/2117/26700

Boni, A., & Pérez-Foguet, A. (2008). Introducing development education in technical universities: Successful experiences in Spain. *European Journal of Engineering Education, 33*(3), 343–354.

Bourn, D. (2014). The global dimension to engineering education. In Integrating GDE into the Academia, GDEE (Eds.), *Global dimension in engineering education*, Barcelona. Available from http://gdee.eu/index.php/resources.html

Bourn, D., & Neal, I. (2008). *The global engineer*. London: Institute of Education. Available from http://eprints.ioe.ac.uk/839/1/Bourn2008Engineers.pdf

Cabrera, M., Ortiz, I., Mataix, C., Sánchez, E., Gómez, M., Calabuig, C., et al. (2006). Estrategia para el impulso de los trabajos final de grado y doctorado sobre Cooperación Internacional y Tecnología para el Desarrollo Humano. In X Congreso Internacional de Ingeniería de Proyectos. Universidad Politécnica de Valencia, Valencia. http://hdl.handle.net/2117/26656

CSCT. (2008). Curriculum, sustainable development, competences, teacher training project competencies for ESD teachers. A framework to integrate in the curriculum of Teacher Training Institutes. Comenius 2.1 project 118277-CP-1-2004-BE-Comenius-C2. Available at http://www.ensi.org/Projects/Former_Projects/CSCT/

Gathercole, C. (2014). The role of engineering education in relation to the global dimension. In Integrating GDE into the Academia, GDEE (Eds.), *Global dimension in engineering education*, Barcelona. Available from http://gdee.eu/index.php/resources.html

GDEE (Eds.). (2015). *Global dimension in engineering education*, Barcelona. Available from http://gdee.eu

Higher Education Authority (HEA). (2014). *Internationalising higher education framework*. Available at https://www.heacademy.ac.uk. Accessed september 28, 2014.

Holmberg, J., Svanstrom, M., Peet, D. J., Mulder, K. F., Ferrer-Balas, D., & Segalas, J. (2008). "Embedding sustainability in higher education through interaction with lecturers: Case studies from three European technical universities. *European Journal of Engineering Education, 33* (3), 271–282.

Jordan, K. (2014). Initial trends in enrolment and completion of massive open online courses. In *The International Review of Research in Open and Distributed Learning, 15*(1). Available at http://www.irrodl.org/index.php/irrodl/article/view/1651

Khan, A. S. (1995). *Taking responsibility: Promoting sustainable practice through higher education curricula*. London: Pluto Press.

Lozano, R., Ceulemans, K., & Scarff Seatter, C. (2014). Teaching organisational change management for sustainability: Designing and delivering a course at the University of Leeds to better prepare future sustainability change agents. *Journal of Cleaner Production 106*, 205–215.

Mulder, K. F., Segalàs, J., & Ferrer-Balas, D. (2012). How to educate engineers for/in sustainable development: Ten years of discussion, remaining challenges. *International Journal of Sustainability in Higher Education, 13*(3), 211–218.

Oliete-Josa, S., & Pérez-Foguet, A. (2005). Cooperació per al desenvolupament a l'aula: casos aplicats de tecnologia per al desenvolupament humà, Associació Catalana d'Enginyeria Sense Fronteres, Barcelona. Available from http://upcommons.upc.edu/handle/2117/2287

Oliete-Josa, S., & Pérez-Foguet, A. (2008). Cooperación para el desarrollo en el aula: casos aplicados de tecnología para el desarrollo humano, Ingeniería Sin Fronteras, Asociación para el Desarrollo, Madrid. Available from http://upcommons.upc.edu/handle/2117/3045

Pérez-Foguet, A., & Cruz, Y. (2011) UPC's institutional transformation towards sustainabilit. In *Higher education in the world 4. Higher education committed to sustainability: From understanding to action* (pp. 301–307). Basingstoke: Palgrave-Macmillan. ISBN: 978-0-230-53555-8.

Pérez-Foguet, A., Oliete-Josa, S., & Saz-Carranza, A. (2005). Development education and engineering: A framework for incorporating reality of developing countries into engineering studies. *International Journal of Sustainability in Higher Education, 6*(3), 278–303.

Schumacher, E. F. (1973). *Small is beautiful. Economics as if people mattered.* London: Blond & Briggs Ltd.

Segalàs, J. (2014). Key learning theories in GDEE. In Integrating GDE into the Academia, GDEE (Eds.), *Global dimension in engineering education*, Barcelona. Available from http://gdee.eu/index.php/resources.html

Segalàs, J., Ferrer-Balas, D., & Mulder, K. F. (2010). What do engineering students learn in sustainability courses? The effect of the pedagogical approach. *Journal of Cleaner Production, 18*, 275–284.

Sterling. S. (2001). *Sustainable education: Re-visioning learning and change. Schumacher Briefing No. 6: Scumacher Society*. Dartington: Green Books.

Sterling, S. (2005). Higher education, sustainability, and the role of systemic learning. In P. B. Corcoran & A. E. J. Wals (Eds.), *Higher education and the challenge of sustainability: Problematics, promise and practise* (pp. 49–70). Boston MA: Kluwer.

Svanstrom, M., Lozano-Garcia, F., & Rowe, D. (2008). Learning outcomes for sustainable development in higher education. *International Journal of Sustainability in Higher Education, 9*(3), 339–351.

Trimingham, R. (2014). Teaching and assessment methods. In Integrating GDE into the Academia, GDEE (Eds.), *Global dimension in engineering education*, Barcelona. Available from http://gdee.eu/index.php/resources.html

United Nations. (2012). *The future we want: Outcome document adopted at Rio+20*. Available www.uncsd2012.org/content/documents/TheFutureWeWant, June201230pm.pdf

Wals, A. E. J, & Corcoran, P. B. (2005). Sustainability as an outcome of transformative learning. Drivers and Barriers for Implementing Sustainable Development in Higher Education. Education for Sustainable Development in Action. Technical paper 3. UNESCO

Watson, M. K., Lozano, R., Noyes, C., & Rodgers, M. (2013). Assessing curricula contribution to sustainability more holistically: Experiences from the integration of curricula assessment and students' perceptions at the Georgia Institute of Technology. *Journal of Cleaner Production, 61*, 106–116.

World Commission on Environment and Development (WCED). (1987). *Our common future* (p. 27). Oxford: Oxford University Press. ISBN 019282080X.

Wiek, A., Withycombe, L., & Redman, C. (2011). Key competencies in sustainability: A reference framework for academic program development. Sustainability Science, *6*, 203–218. doi:10.1007/s11625-011-0132-6

Author Biographies

Dr. Rhoda Trimingham is a senior lecturer in the Design School at Loughborough University, UK. She is currently the UK Academic on the GDEE project, a large collaborative, EU funded initiative that aims to increase the awareness, critical understanding and attitudinal values of students in technical universities related to Sustainable Human Development (SHD).

Boris Lazzarini (1969) works as project manager at the Research Institute of Sustainability Science and Technology at the Universitat Politècnica de Catalunya—Barcelona Tech (UPC). He graduated in Political Sciences and holds a M.Phil. in Sustainability by UPC. He's currently managing the European project GDEE.

Agustí Pérez-Foguet is an associate professor in the Civil Engineering School of Barcelona, Universitat Politècnica de Catalunya. He is also researcher of the University Research Institute for Sustainability Science and Technologies of the UPC, and member of the advisory board of the Cooperation for Development Center of the university. He has been the academic coordinator of the GDEE Europeaid project.

Neil Noble has worked for Practical Action since 1998 initially as a technical advisor and currently as Knowledge Services Business Developer. Previously he worked at the Rural Industries Innovation Centre in Botswana and studied Engineering Design and Appropriate Technology at the University of Warwick. He has a background in mechanical engineering.

Alejandra Boni, Associate Professor at the Department of Projects Engineering at the Universitat Politécnica de Valencia. Director of the Master in International Cooperation and Convenor of the PhD Programme in Local Development and International Cooperation at the same university. Main research interests are in human development, education and project planning.

Manuel Sierra-Castañer is Doctor in Telecommunications Engineer since 2000. He is Associate Professor at Technical University of Madrid (UPM) since 2002. Since 2010 he is the Director of Cooperation for Development of the University and since July 2014 member of the Spanish Advisory Board of Cooperation for Development. He has been researching and teaching in cooperation for development related to ICT topics since 2001.

Francesco Mongera collaborates with the Training Centre for International Cooperation—TCIC since the beginning of 2012. He has worked as tutor of training courses and as project officer on the GDEE project. He holds a master's degree in International and European Studies, with a focus on development cooperation and global education.

Guido Zolezzi is an associate professor at the University of Trento, Italy. He is the Director the SMART International Ph.D. funded as an Erasmus Mundus Joint Doctorate (www.riverscience.eu) and the Chair holder of the UNESCO Chair in Engineering for Human and Sustainable Development. He represents the University of Trento within the Training Center for International Cooperation (www.tcic.eu) and within the Italian Network of Universities for Development Cooperation (CUCS; www.cucs.net).

Hopeful, Local, Visionary, Solutions-Oriented, Transformative, Place-Based Sustainability Stories and Service-Learning as Tools for University-Level Education for Sustainable Development: Experiences from University of Vermont

Thomas R. Hudspeth

Abstract

Promoting and building capacity for education for sustainable development (ESD) at institutions of higher education requires engaging numerous stakeholders involving various sectors. This chapter aims to provide learning opportunities on how to implement university-level ESD by reporting on two promising practices for engaging stakeholders—sustainability stories and service-learning—and reflecting on how they are used in two courses, their impact and replicability, and useful lessons learned from them.

Keywords

Education for sustainable development · Sustainability · Higher education · Service learning · Community engagement · Stories/narratives

1 Introduction: ESD and HE

Through their roles in teaching, research, and service, institutions of higher education (HE) around the world have a crucial role to play in advancing the goal of a desirable, just, healthy, peaceful, sustainable society (Barlett and Chase 2013; Corcoran and Wals 2004; Cortese 1999; Filho et al. 1999; Filho 1998, 2000, 2002;

T.R. Hudspeth (✉)
Environmental Program and Rubenstein School of Environment and Natural Resources, University of Vermont, 153 S. Prospect St., Burlington, VT 05401, USA
e-mail: Thomas.Hudspeth@uvm.edu

© Springer International Publishing Switzerland 2016

W. Leal Filho and P. Pace (eds.), *Teaching Education for Sustainable Development at University Level*, World Sustainability Series,
DOI 10.1007/978-3-319-32928-4_13

Orr 1994; Wals 2014). And many colleges/universities, recognizing their responsibility, have undertaken ESD initiatives dealing with both curriculum and campus operations (Hudspeth 2010), thereby helping to shape beliefs, values, attitudes, and behaviors/lifestyles of students as well as providing a role model for various community stakeholders. They offer majors, minors, concentrations, certificates, and general education requirements for all students in sustainability. They have developed faculty scholars programs, providing ESD training and financial incentives to develop or revise courses by infusing/incorporating sustainability concepts into them for faculty members in numerous academic fields. And they have established offices of sustainability to improve campus practices and link facilities operations and academics, often treating their campuses as living/learning laboratories and even interpreting features of their green buildings.

Yet, as the United Nations Decade on Education for Sustainable Development (UNDESD) concluded at the end of 2014 and transitions into the Global Action Program, it is clear the overall goal of the DESD has not been achieved in the HE sector; there are major gaps that need to be filled. Filho (2015) reports the lack of any formal commitment to sustainability by many universities; lack of training; lack of funding specifically targeted to support sustainability initiatives at many universities; and "the lack of systematic means to document and disseminate the wide range of experiences available across the world (p. 1)". While they are supposed to be on the leading edge, many of the ~4706 universities/colleges in the United States are behind the curve and moving slowly, with only some doing anything appreciable to advance ESD on their campuses.

Often there is a culture of resistance on college campuses from faculty members, administrators, staff, board of trustees, etc. There are silos on campuses, and turf battles. Strong disciplinary bias is a hindrance, and many faculty members fail to see how sustainability relates to their discipline. While there are far more Sustainability Studies/Sciences programs in HE than in the past, many universities are not adept at administering interdisciplinary programs. And some Sustainability Studies/Sciences programs that do exist tend to reflect just the technical and scientific aspects of sustainability while downplaying/totally ignoring the humanities, ethics, social justice, etc. And those programs that address social science aspects of sustainability often emphasize structural and institutional changes in the polity and economy, overlooking the importance of behavioral change addressed by psychologists and sociologists who consider both extrinsic and intrinsic motivation strategies for influencing individuals to adopt more sustainable behaviors.

The challenges facing us in combatting climate change and creating a more sustainable world are too complex and wicked for any one academic discipline or sector to solve; yet many universities try to "go it alone" in their ESD efforts, rather than collaborating/developing valuable partnerships/networks linking them with other sectors—non-governmental organizations/civil society, government/public sector, business/private sector, K-12 education, faith community, media—for the benefit of all. Institutions of HE are an integral part of the broader communities in which they are based, and it is important that—as they promote and build capacity for ESD—their sustainability initiatives extend beyond the campus to help society as a whole through outreach activities, civic engagement, etc. Service-learning courses foster partnerships between university students and their local communities to effectively solve sustainability issues while preparing future leaders in sustainability.

Even 28 years after *Our Common Future* (1987), critics continue to claim that sustainability is: too abstract to grasp and put into action; vague and imprecise; merely a buzzword or rhetoric, the phrase of the day, without any substance and holding power; just a theoretical concept but not something that is actually happening here and now; and does not offer a positive vision of what is desired, but only decries the negative aspects of our present situation.

2 Two Courses

Two University of Vermont (UVM) courses—ESD and Creating Environmentally Sustainable Communities (CESC)—incorporating two promising practices—service-learning and stories—address these concerns. The courses have many common features:

1. Participants in both are primarily seniors in Environmental Studies with concentrations in Sustainability Studies or self-designed majors in ESD. Many of the students take both courses.
2. For both courses, 40–50 % of the total course grade goes toward term projects, in which students apply what they learn in their courses and from their research to a topic in their community related to the subject.
3. Reasonable Person Model (RPM) offers theoretical framework: R. and S. Kaplan offer an explanatory theory underpinning approaches for providing sustainability solutions. It draws on advances in the behavioral sciences and how they relate to sustainability initiatives, addressing such questions as: Why do people behave as they do? Under what circumstances are we not reasonable? What is needed for us to become more reasonable? (i.e., What conditions help to bring our better behavior?) The Kaplans theorize that reasonable people can learn, communicate, engage, solve problems, work with others, achieve change; and that people are more likely to act in a reasonable and cooperative way when environments meet their informational needs. They provide a framework with three interrelated components—model building, being effective, and meaningful action—that can foster reasonableness by creating supportive environments for bringing out our best. RPM is applicable to many different contexts involving sharing information, communication, and engaging others in seeking answers (Kaplan and Basu 2015). Working toward sustainable futures does not necessarily require making sacrifices, but rather reaching toward a positive vision that brings out the best in people.
4. Wilson (1980) asserts: "*The future is up for grabs. It belongs to any and all who will take the risk and accept the responsibility of consciously creating the future they want.*" Envisioning, creating alternative futures, and being "practical

visionaries" are essential in ESD, since to create a positive and sustainable future, we must first envision it. Both courses engage students and community stakeholders in creating shared visions of a more sustainable future and in identifying strategies, policies, and values for transitioning toward the kind of world we really want.

5. Regarding pedagogy, both provide active, engaged, authentic, "hands-on" learning opportunities for students; utilize broad array of teaching methodologies given the diversity of learning styles and multiple intelligences of students; and, given the developmental level of students, both emphasize higher-order thinking skills in ESD: critical-thinking, problem identification/solving, decision-making, analysis, synthesis/integrative-thinking, interdisciplinary-thinking, systems-thinking, solving-for-pattern, futures-thinking, creative-thinking.
6. They are place-based, cultivating students' "sense of place" and connection to their local community in the state's largest urban area, Burlington, where UVM is located; simultaneously, they highlight local-global interrelationships and connections, addressing planetary-scale/global Anthropocene challenges—often termed 21st century "grand challenges"—at the local level.
7. Both employ High Impact Educational Practices (Kuh 2008) in which students are actively engaged in the educational process, when their learning goes beyond the classroom to be applied in their personal and work lives: capstone course; learning community; writing-intensive course; service-learning/ community-based learning and research.
8. Both emphasize community engagement, Boyer's "scholarship of engagement": Boyer (1996) believed that universities need to re-commit to "*scholarship of engagement, which means connecting the rich resources of the university to our most pressing social, civic, and ethical problems, to our children, to our schools, to our teachers, and to our cities.*" (p. 11) He claimed that higher education should be related to the "humane application of learning to life," and viewed campuses as "staging grounds for action," as opposed to isolated islands. Academic and civic cultures need to communicate more continuously and creatively with each other. Therefore, it is important that universities not work in isolation on their sustainability initiatives, but extend beyond the walls of academe and link with other stakeholders in the broader community. Service-learning partnerships/collaborations between university students and their local communities to work towards sustainable futures provide a mechanism for doing so; service-learning is the way in which "scholarship of engagement" actualizes itself in the curriculum. It gives students a chance to see how their skills can be applied, and offers a reconfiguration of how we involve education and citizenship in the U.S.
9. Both employ multi-sector, multi-capitals approach to sustainability, partnering students with various community stakeholders via service-learning projects which offer benefits to both students and their community

3 Service-Learning, Campus-Community Partnerships for Sustainability

"*Service-Learning is a form of experiential education in which students engage in activities that address human and community needs together with structured opportunities intentionally designed to promote student learning and development. Reflection [structured time for students to reflect on the service experience is included] and reciprocity are key concepts of service-learning*" (Jacoby 1996, p. 5). John Dewey provides the basic theory of service-learning: the interaction of knowledge and skills with experience is key to learning. It is integrated into and enhances the academic curriculum of students and helps foster civic responsibility. Key elements of service-learning include: focused pre-service preparation, reciprocal partnerships, intentional learning goals, and meaningful reflection.

Service-learning is infused into the term projects for all students and considered an integral element of the ESD and CESC courses, not an optional add-on. Students are told that the service-learning activities: are deliberate/intentional; are integrated into their coursework as an essential learning tool; help them to further understand what they are learning in class; help to address community needs; help them think about what they are learning on a different level; and enhance what is taught at the university by extending student learning beyond the classroom and into the community, allowing them to apply and test what they learn in new situations. Further, they are told that structured time for critical reflection on and analysis of service experiences in the context of the course learning is provided, thus enabling the community learning to be harvested and to serve as an academic learning enhancer, blending the experiential and the academic in learning. The service allows them to: gain hands-on experience in their field in the "real world"; see how things they are learning can be put into practice to help others; broaden their understanding of what they are studying; engage them in conversation with others—in the class and in the community—about the work they are doing; and help them to think about their role in the community. Some of the benefits of service-learning for them as a student: it applies concepts from the classroom to their service; provides platforms to analyze and discuss civic values; increases their sense of self-efficacy, analytical skills, and social development; and develops meaningful involvement with the local community.

4 The Power of Stories

Craven (2010) claims: "*We live by our stories, individually and collectively. They are how we learn and how we pass along to each other the idea of who we are... They are in our DNA....Because our brains retain stories better than any other form of information, we develop shortcuts to handle all the information we need in a modern world. The most important shortcut is the narrative. It's the way we store and organize the information.*" Because we are storytelling animals who understand things better if they are told to us in a story, compelling narrative captures peoples' imaginations and connects them.

Stories were the primary way our ancestors transmitted knowledge and values. "*Since earliest times most of our stories have related to our earth, how it was created, the relationship between it and its human inhabitants, and problems that arise when we fail to remember the importance of living in harmony with it and each other….We all love good stories, because they not only entertain but also hold our attention while we learn important concepts, skills, values, and attitudes*" (Fien et al. 2010). Further, stories—especially with characters readers/listeners can identify with—can put a face on sustainability challenges and allow people to care on an emotional level far more than any facts and figures/statistics/reports/graphs/charts/diagrams or "50 simple ways" types of books about how to live more sustainably. The powerful emotional responses evoked by stories help us to clarify the way we feel and can fuel the desire for change.

Stories are important from an educational perspective for the messages that can be learned from them. Not only are stories of indigenous/traditional societies living sustainably valuable in ESD, but also success stories of groups working at various levels to ensure a sustainable future; these demonstrate practical solutions to today's sustainability problems, thereby providing hope and inspiration. Storytelling also helps cultivate a sense of place and builds community, both key aspects of sustainability.

Storytelling is an effective pedagogical approach as well as powerful social transformation tool for addressing, confronting, and seeking solutions to profoundly serious planetary-scale Anthropocene challenges at the local level, offering hope by bringing about paradigm shifts and envisioning and working toward more sustainable futures.

5 Need for a New Story: Sustainability

In *Dream of the Earth* (1990) Thomas Berry claims: "*For people, generally, their story of the universe and the human role in the universe is their primary source of intelligibility and value. … The deepest crises experienced by any society are those moments of change when the story becomes inadequate for meeting the survival demands of a present situation.*" Korten (2013) builds on that notion, asserting: "*We are a self-reflective, storytelling, choice-making species gone astray for want of a sacred story adequate to the needs of our time….a shared story reflecting our responsibility to….bring ourselves into balance with the generative systems of a living Earth…. before the economic, social, environmental, and political system failure wrought by inadequate stories becomes irreversible*".

Every culture has its own story about itself, its myth, its paradigm. We live through our stories. Our culture is going through a crisis because its story is no longer adequate to explain. All the trends about environmental degradation and social instability are a result of our failing cultural story. Our present myth is simplistic, simple-minded, and naïve, yet many of us subscribe to it. It is a reductionist myth, focusing on infinite economic growth in a finite world, on the accumulation of more and better material goods or "stuff," regardless of the toll this quest is taking on the environment, our personal happiness, public health, equity and social justice, and even our sense of citizenship and democracy. It equates human welfare and quality of life with income/money/equity/creation of monetary wealth—a single variable. It treats Economy and Ecology as opposites rather than two sides of the same equation. It emphasizes individualism and independence over community and interdependence. We need to deconstruct outdated/inappropriate notions/narratives/worldviews, reconstruct the old model, revise our myth, and reimagine/generate a new story that better describes what is going on in the world, that reflects our creation of positive and empowering possibilities/opportunities from our envisioning.

Lappe (2010) believes we can create the world we want by aligning our mental maps with conditions that bring out the best in people and for which we evolved: cooperation, empathy, compassion, efficacy, being courageous and doing rather than being fearful and feeling powerless, being active citizens instead of just consumers, and recognizing possibilities rather than decrying scarcity or lack. An enduring understanding of ESD is that it all begins with a change in thinking, and storytelling is a valuable means of shifting mental models.

When she spoke and talked about leverage points, or places to intervene in a system to transform it for the better, Meadows (1999) claimed that the most effective is to change the mindset or paradigm out of which the system—its goals, power structure, rules, its culture—arises. This is similar to what Joanna Macy, David Korten, and others term "The Great Turning," a paradigm shift, telling a new story or myth: a story of sustainability. Giving a name to the world we want—sustainability—helps us create it, to "*tell the world of the future into being*" (Flowers 2013), and sustainability stories are a powerful means of doing so.

6 ESD Course

ESD course is intended for prospective teachers of ESD for youths or adults in formal or non-formal education venues. Students develop and field-test ESD curriculum units with their service-learning partner (K-12 school class, NGO, etc.) after learning about ESD, Environmental Education, Place-based Education; and critiquing many existing ESD curricula. Some of their term projects focus on typical ESD topics such as renewable energy, green buildings, etc. But many—in which students often draw ideas from their other courses (Ecological Design, Ecological Economics, Local Food Systems, Climate Change Adaptation/Resilience, etc.)—are unique to the "sense of place" of UVM and Burlington. See Box 1.

Box 1. ESD Term Project Topics in Recent Years

Community-based agriculture/local food systems in Vermont
Climate change adaptation/resiliency
Genetically Modified Organisms (and labeling in Vermont)
Cooperatives
Overconsumption
Local and slow movements (food, money, democracy, living)
Green roofs
Ecomachines
Human-powered train
Genuine Progress Indicator
Valuing ecosystem services re: pollinators
Commons
Rethinking the role of corporations in democracy
Civic education/political transparency/campaign finance reform

7 CESC Course

In CESC course, students make sustainability come alive by collecting sustainability stories featuring positive sustainability role models/examples from their local community.

Prior to working on their term projects, students gain a strong background in sustainability through readings, seminar discussions (each student leads a class discussion), lectures, guest speaker presentations, and DVD/video presentations, supplemented by field trips in the greater Burlington area. The students become familiar with definitions of sustainability, principles of sustainability, some tools for sustainability (personal and community visioning, creating alternative futures, indicators such as ecological footprint analysis and carbon footprint analysis and Genuine Progress Indicator or GPI, life cycle analysis, full cost accounting/getting the price right, valuing ecosystem services, and unlearning consumerism). They also become familiar with various models of change/transformation and consider the power of stories and the need for a new story.

For their term projects, students produce videotapes (with accompanying papers) to tell *Sustainability Stories* (Hudspeth 2010) about individuals/groups in the Greater Burlington area who can serve as role models/examples for others to emulate in transitioning/downshifting to more environmentally-sustainable communities; people who inspire, encourage, and empower others; "practical visionaries" who have a positive vision of a sustainable future environment—an alternative to the dominant social paradigm, the status quo—and take action to achieve that vision, to turn that vision into reality. The papers are written in the same fashion as some of CESC course readings, and their videos are modeled after DVDs shown and discussed in class.

The students serve as "credible biographers" for these pioneers or visionaries, these unsung local sustainability heroines and heroes, by profiling and celebrating such individuals/groups—utilizing such qualitative research methodologies as semi-structured interviews and analysis of documents and materials—and by spreading the word to others about these examples/role models in the community, so that these others can respond by giving them encouragement and helping them to get their jobs done or by starting their own initiatives for finding solutions to global sustainability problems and for healing the earth and for living more sustainably.

8 Students' Sustainability Stories

The stories include a wide range of examples, and deal with natural, built, human, and—especially—social capital, which involves the norms of behavior that bring us together as a community and help us be more productive and function better.

They draw on all the various stakeholders/sectors mentioned previously. And they address the "4 Es" of sustainability. Some emphasize the *ecological integrity* aspects of sustainability (e.g., ecomachine); others its *economic feasibility* (e.g., Vermont Businesses for Social Responsibility and many of its member businesses); others its *equity or social justice* features (e.g., Peace and Justice Center, Champlain Housing Trust, Good News Garage, Hunger Free Vermont); and others its *educational* aspects (e.g., Sustainability Academy at Barnes, Greenhouse Residential Learning Community at UVM); and some, like ReSOURCE and Vermont Family Forests, give equal emphasis to all aspects.

Box 2. Main Categories of Sustainability Stories

1. Community-based agriculture, food systems, nutrition (e.g., Shelburne Farms, Intervale Center, numerous farmers and composters, Burlington Farmer's Market, City Market Food Cooperative)
2. Sustainability education (e.g., Sustainability Academy at Barnes, the only elementary magnet school in the U.S. using sustainability as an integrative tool to teach all subject disciplines)
3. Renewable energy (e.g., Vermont Energy Investment Corporation; Renewable NRG; All Earth Renewables; cow power; Burlington Electric Department with its 100 % renewables portfolio)
4. Green building, such as UVM's Aiken Center, a national model for green renovation of a campus building, awarded LEED Platinum certification for its efforts, including: John Todd-designed ecomachine for treating human wastes, green roof used for research, etc.

5. Green design (e.g., architect William Maclay in Waitsfield)
6. Green businesses
7. Ecological economics
8. Climate change adaptation
9. Alternative transportation (e.g., Local Motion, CarShare Vermont)
10. Events (e.g., Vermontivate, Vermont International Film Festival, Earth Charter Festival at Shelburne Farms in 2001, Sustainable Communities conference in 2004).

Most of the stories fall into 10 main categories (see Box 2). They consider people and topics to which mainstream print or electronic media devote little or no attention. That is why is up to all of us as concerned citizens—not just UVM students—to help spread the word about such efforts, to celebrate individuals and groups involved in sustainability initiatives in our own communities.

Vermont is justifiably recognized as a leader in the transition to sustainable futures. Its high levels of social capital and sense of community, strong town meeting tradition, and manageable size and scale allow for interaction and cross-fertilization that do not seem to happen as well in larger places. The positive role models featured in the *Sustainability Stories* are *not* presented as being exceptional or outstanding. Undoubtedly such examples exist in every community; one just might have to scratch a little deeper to uncover them in other places.

Collecting and sharing place-based sustainability stories to build sustainable communities may seem like an unlikely and even overly simplistic pedagogical approach or tool for broad-scale social change; yet evidence of the results of utilizing this approach—from the limited perspectives of community members as well as university students—is impressive. Many students comment that focusing on *positive solutions* to the daunting sustainability problems we face and featuring success stories and role models/examples offers an antidote to the feelings of despair/apathy/anxiety/fear/ecophobia/helplessness/powerlessness/depression, even paralysis they had felt from other classes which focused entirely on identifying sustainability problems, the enormity and complexity of our current predicament, and doom-and-gloom approaches. They report that their term project inspired them with hope, empowered them, helped them to consider alternatives to our current unsustainable practices, and showed them that they—and the people/groups they found out about and celebrated—can make a difference. They enjoyed getting out in the real world and meeting real people who are doing exciting things and affecting change, and sharing their stories with others… and a few have even received job or paid internship offers from the sustainability heroes/heroines they featured. They felt good about being part of the bridge between UVM and the community, about sharing with the larger community the insights and knowledge and skills they had gained from their undergraduate education—not just learning for the sake of learning, but learning to communicate with and serve others and to work as change agents. Finally, the positive feedback they received from reviewers of their ESD curricula and viewers of their CESC videotapes left them feeling more optimistic; and the subjects of the students' videos/papers appreciated being asked to share their stories.

The *Sustainability Stories* model developed over two decades in CESC course has been presented to other classes at UVM, other colleges/universities, schools, and conferences in the U.S. and abroad. It has been shown to have replicability/transferability; it has been used effectively in urban or rural settings, in a variety of cultures and bioregions, and by K-12 youth and their teachers and non-governmental organizations as well as by university and college students. And it was one of the major features cited when the United Nations University Institute for Advanced Studies of Sustainability recently recognized the Greater Burlington Regional Center of Expertise on ESD because of its collaborative and ground-breaking ESD programs.

9 Conclusion

Transitioning toward the kind of world we really want—a more sustainable, just, ethical, secure, peaceful future; that challenges the dominant social paradigm and offers an alternative future to business-as-usual; that recognizes that our economic institutions and governance can be redesigned to address the ecological degradation and economic inequality produced by capitalism; that breaks our addiction to overconsumption, fossil fuels, an economic paradigm predicated on continual growth in a finite world, and a cultural presumption that bigger and faster is always better; and that has the potential to satisfy a wide range of human needs not being effectively met by the present consumerism-based society—has no charted course.

Managing such a transition toward a sustainable society that mimics the natural systems all around us, in which we accept limits, live gently and responsibly, and treat our fragile planet with dignity and reverence, will necessarily involve discussion, dialogue, debate involving all cultures and drawing on all academic disciplines. Recognizing that a much better future, an ecologically resilient and socially equitable world, *is* possible and that we already have working demonstrations and examples of aspects of it that need to be taken to scale and replicated, HE needs to play a central role in ESD—not working in isolation but cooperating/collaborating, partnering/linking with numerous stakeholders involving various sectors via creative approaches. Campus-community service-learning partnerships and sustainability stories—that present positive role models and, by operationalizing sustainability, make it more concrete, make it come alive, humanize it, and put a face on it, offer powerful antidote to the "vague, amorphous concept" critique of sustainability—provide such approaches that can inspire and empower others, creating hope and optimism rather than despair and doom-and-gloom, and work toward a paradigm shift and change in mental models to sustainability that will help society achieve a smooth landing instead of overshoot and collapse. They are promising ESD practices/working demonstrations/examples that can be taken to scale and replicated to realize more environmentally-sustainable communities.

While service-learning courses may take more time (to build trust with the partner, arrange logistics, develop deep reflection activities linking classroom learning with partnership activity), the enhanced student learning and skills development—as well as the benefits to the community—are worth the extra effort. These service-learning partnerships for a sustainable future are not a panacea or silver bullet; however, they do provide valuable experience and training for the next generation of sustainability leaders.

References

Barlett, P. F., & Chase, G. W. (2013). *Sustainability in higher education: Stories and strategies for transformation*. Cambridge: MIT.

Berry, T. (1990). *The dream of the Earth*. San Francisco: Sierra Club.

Boyer, E. (1996). The scholarship of engagement. *Journal of Public Outreach, 1*(1), 11–20.

Corcoran, P. B., & Wals, A. E. J. (Eds.). (2004). *Higher education and the challenge of sustainability*. Boston: Kluwer.

Cortese, A. D. (1999). Education for sustainability: accelerating the transition to sustainability through higher education. *Second nature*. http://www.secondnature.org

Craven, J. (2010). Importance of Narrative. *Vermont Public Radio commentary*, November 29, 2010.

Fien, J., Cox, B., & Calder, M. (2010). "Storytelling", UNESCO http://www.unesco.org/education/tlsf/mods/theme_d/mod21.html

Filho, W. L. (Ed.). (1998 and 2000). *Sustainability and university life*. Frankfurt: Peter Lang.

Filho, W. L. (Ed.). (2002). *Teaching sustainability at universities: Towards curriculum greening*. Frankfurt: Peter Lang.

Filho, W. L. (2015). Sustainability 2.0: A new age of sustainable development in higher education. *International Journal of Sustainability in Higher Education, 16*, 1.

Filho, W. L., et al. (Eds.). (1999). *Implementing sustainable development at university level*. Carnforth: Parthenon.

Flowers, B. S. (2013). *The American dream and the economic myth*. Posted July 10, 2013 on The Huffington Post.

Hudspeth, T. (2010) Stories as a social transformation tool to work toward a sustainable future: Sustainability stories help put the pieces together, connect the dots, and build sustainable communities. *Ometeca, XIV–XV*, 77–106. http://www.ometeca.org/HTML/journal/ome28.htm

Jacoby, B. (1996). *Service-learning in higher education*. San Francisco: Jossey-Bass.

Kaplan, R., & Basu, A. (Eds.). (2015). *Fostering reasonableness: supportive environments for bringing out our best*. Ann Arbor: Michigan Publishing.

Korten, D. (2013, July 13). It's a story problem: What's behind our messed-up economy. *YES Magazine*.

Kuh, G. D. (2008). *High-impact educational practices: What they are, who has access to them, and why they matter*. Washington DC: American Association of Colleges and Universities.

Lappe, F. M. (2010). Why are we creating a world that no one wants? *TEDx Talks*. https://www.youtube.com/watch?v=w_Lw5lt3J6c

Meadows, D. (1999). *Leverage points: Places to intervene in a system*. Hartland, VT: The Sustainability Institute.

Orr, D. (1994). *Earth in mind: On education, environment, and the human prospect*. Washington DC: Island.

Wals, E. J. A. (2014). Sustainability in higher education in the context of the UN DESD: A review of learning and institutionalization processes. *Journal of Cleaner Production, 62*, 8–15. doi:10.1016/j.jclepro.2013.06.007.
Wilson, R. A. (1980). Interview by Neil Wilgus from science fiction review 37 (Vol. 9, No. 4), November 1980. http://rawilsonfans.org/1980/11/
World Commission on Environment and Development. (1987). *Our common future*. Oxford: Oxford.

Author Biography

Thomas R. Hudspeth is Professor of Environmental Studies and Natural Resources and Fellow, Gund Institute for Ecological Economics, University of Vermont. His scholarship and teaching address: sustainability education, sustainable communities, environmental interpretation, eco-tourism, citizen participation, community-based conservation, international environmental issues, behavior and environment.

[illegible]

Engaging Students with Environmental Sustainability at a Research Intensive University: Examples of Small Successes

Dianne P. Chambers, Clare Walker, Kathryn Williams, John Rayner, Claire Farrell, Anne-Maree Butt and Danielle Rostan-Herbert

Abstract

The University of Melbourne's Vision for Education for Sustainability is "To develop graduates who will lead change for a sustainable future" (University of Melbourne 2011). This goal is for all graduates and many aspects of a student's experiences will cumulatively contribute toward this outcome. While the individual experiences of students will vary, in particular in the formal curriculum depending on that student's specialization, there are elements of sustainability in the formal and hidden curriculum that all students will experience or can access. This chapter will first explore students' perceptions and concerns regarding environmental sustainability, as gauged through a biennial survey, and then discuss some examples of ways that students of the University of Melbourne engage with aspects of environmental sustainability, including through research, the formal curriculum, the hidden curriculum of the campus, and campus operations.

Keywords

Environmental sustainability · Student engagement · Curriculum · Hidden curriculum · Campus operations · Sustainability integration · Embedding sustainability

D.P. Chambers (✉) · C. Walker · K. Williams · J. Rayner · C. Farrell · A.-M. Butt · D. Rostan-Herbert
University of Melbourne, Melbourne, VIC, Australia
e-mail: d.chambers@unimelb.edu.au

© Springer International Publishing Switzerland 2016

W. Leal Filho and P. Pace (eds.), *Teaching Education for Sustainable Development at University Level*, World Sustainability Series,
DOI 10.1007/978-3-319-32928-4_14

1 Introduction

Sustainability challenges are complex and have many facets and they can be understood in a range of ways by the various stakeholders, who sometimes have conflicting values and interests (Lukman and Glavič 2007). Ratner (2004, p. 62) suggests that:

> When construed not as a fixed end, but as a dialogue of values among competing actors, the sustainability concept acquires a complexity that is more fitting to the diversity of ways in which the idea is applied and contested in practice.

A major aspect of engaging students with sustainability thus is that, in addition to specialist expertise in their chosen discipline, students develop an appreciation for, and a greater understanding of, the values and perspectives of stakeholders outside their own specialty area. Ideally students will also develop knowledge and skills that will prepare them to work in cross- and inter-disciplinary teams to understand and address sustainability challenges. However, it was found in a study of four universities in New South Wales, Australia, that relatively few students engaged directly in sustainability initiatives and it was suggested that "many students appear to be focused on completing their courses and surviving economically rather than on getting involved with university sustainability programmes" (Butt et al. 2014, pp. 802–3). This suggests that integrating student engagement with sustainability into a student's formal studies and in ways that all students connect with, such as experiencing the campus, may increase student engagement with sustainability. The case studies presented here support students developing this broader view of sustainability challenges and enable students to develop knowledge and skills that will prepare them for future challenges. Case studies include examples where the engagement opportunities are through formal studies, some through the lived experience and culture of the university (the 'hidden curriculum', Orr 1992) and other opportunities for student engagement are through extra-curricular activities. The presentation of the case studies is structured around the dimensions of university sustainability defined by Calder and Clugston (2003).

The seven key dimensions of university sustainability functions, as defined by Calder and Clugston (2003), are:

- Research & Scholarship
- Curriculum
- Student Opportunities
- Operations
- Faculty & Staff Hiring, Development & Rewards
- Outreach and Service
- Institutional Mission, Structure and Planning

This chapter will not address all of these dimensions, although all are acknowledged and accepted as being important aspects of a university's journey to sustainability. Of particular relevance to this chapter are: Research & Scholarship, Curriculum, Student Opportunities, and Operations, as these are the dimensions that most closely engage and empower students in regard to sustainability. The chapter will look at student engagement in these dimensions and where the dimensions intersect. It is particularly at the intersections of various dimensions of sustainability that universities and other educational institutions have rich opportunities to engage their students (Chambers 2015). Sustainability is complex concept and taking an interdisciplinary approach to sustainability is derived from a broad consensus that sustainability issues cannot be sufficiently understood in isolation (Jones et al. 2010). Although the chapter is structured around individual dimensions, it will be evident that the case studies described bring together multiple dimensions. An important aspect of student engagement is going beyond the obvious, though frequently neglected, aspect of curriculum and considering the hidden curriculum (Orr 1992) of the campus and how it can be utilized in student engagement. The infrastructure and daily operations of the campus, as well as the culture of the university, act as a hidden curriculum that teaches students about what the university values. Through the approach of 'campus as laboratory' and a whole-of-university approach (McMillin and Dyball 2009) our students are engaging with sustainability simply through being on the campus, whether in class or not.

The other dimensions of sustainability, though not discussed explicitly in this chapter, create the conditions and the culture within which student engagement with sustainability can occur, and thus provide the necessary backdrop for the case studies presented here. For example, the University's goal ('Institutional Mission') of developing "graduates who will lead change for a sustainable future" (University of Melbourne 2011) means that the activities explored in this chapter have been prioritized and invested in by staff of the university. Similarly, staff with expertise and interests in sustainability (*Faculty and Staff Hiring*, *Development & Rewards*) are a prerequisite for the student engagement explored in this chapter.

1.1 Context

The University of Melbourne is a large research-intensive university situated in the city of Melbourne (population approximately 4 million) in Victoria, Australia. In the 2013 *Universitas Indonesia* Green Metrics ranking (see http://greenmetric.ui.ac.id) the university was ranked ninth worldwide for urban campuses and ranked 18 (out of 301) for overall excellence in campus sustainability. The main campus covers 22.5 ha adjacent to Melbourne's central business district and there are six other campuses, both urban and rural. The university has approximately 45,000 students and approximately 8000 academic and professional staff.

In 2012 the University developed a paper positioning its research over the coming decade and defined three 'Grand Challenges' facing society that universities can contribute to and that the University will have as centerpieces for its research endeavors in the coming decade (University of Melbourne 2012). These three Grand Challenges are: 'Supporting sustainability and resilience', 'Health & wellbeing', and 'Place & purpose'. Thus, sustainability is a centerpiece of the University's research efforts for the coming decade.

In addition to placing sustainability as a focus of research, the University has made commitments to sustainability in its operations and in the education of its graduates. The University's strategy document, *Growing Esteem* (University of Melbourne 2010) states that by 2015 the University will have made substantial reductions to its environmental impact, and progress towards these achievements is well underway and is reported elsewhere (University of Melbourne 2013). The *Growing Esteem* strategy document also sets the goal of the University to 'establish itself as a model of sustainability' (University of Melbourne 2010) and undertakes this challenge through the integration of sustainability principles and practices throughout its operations, teaching, research, and community engagement. The University of Melbourne has thus chosen to position itself as a leader in research into sustainability, in the operations of its campuses, and in the education of its graduates. Student engagement with sustainability is undertaken in a variety of ways that together contribute to our graduates being better prepared to lead change for a sustainable future (University of Melbourne 2011) as is aspired to by the University. It is in this context that this chapter will explore how the University has been, and is, engaging students with sustainability. Case studies included in this chapter have been selected to demonstrate a range of approaches and ways that sustainability engages our students and that illustrate ways that various teams within the university can come together to contribute to this engagement.

2 Student Views

Student environmental groups, increasing enrolments in environment-related courses, conversations with students, and student activism around environmental issues are indications of tertiary students' interest in environmental issues, though a recent study at four New South Wales universities suggested that students at those universities did not have a substantial influence on sustainability-related decision-making (Butt et al. 2014). The University's sustainability team sought to quantify environmental attitudes, priorities, and concerns of students and staff at the University through an online survey (now undertaken biennially) to assist with planning engagement activities. Students and staff were invited to participate via invitations through numerous University communication channels and 1246 students responded in 2012 and 532 in 2014.

Environmental sustainability and climate change were identified by respondents to the 2014 survey as the two most important issues facing Australia today. These two issues were ranked more highly than education, health care, and the economy, and support the assertion that the environment is a major concern for our students and staff. One key issue highlighted by students in both 2012 and 2014 was the importance of strong environmental sustainability leadership and culture at the University. In 2014 sustainability leadership was highlighted as the third most important area of focus for the University (behind waste management and reduction of the University's carbon footprint).

Convenience appears to be a key element of engaging students with sustainability. University sustainability initiatives that engage students include recycling (96 % participation) and use of sustainable transport (90 %). With increased provision and promotion of water fountains for re-filling water bottles on campus, more students were using water fountains on campus (75 %, up from 67 % in 2012). However, whilst many students are motivated to undertake sustainability for altruistic reasons (82 % do so because they believe it is the right thing to do, whilst 76 % do so because they believe it will make a difference), their stated barriers to participation focus on a lack of information (52 %) and the perceived inconvenience of sustainability-related initiatives (34 %). Completing the survey also provided students with a formal channel to make suggestions to University leadership about sustainability initiatives that they feel should receive greater focus.

The Sustainability Survey Report 2014 (University of Melbourne 2014), which is based on this survey, provides valuable data to inform future decisions and to focus efforts in the specific areas of greatest importance to students. Areas identified as important to students are to actively engage students and demonstrate the University's performance in sustainability leadership, reducing the University's carbon footprint and active waste management. Survey results have also highlighted student demand for greater dissemination of sustainability information and more effective promotion of sustainability initiatives and events to increase awareness across the University.

Further work is required so that we can work towards understanding the factors contributing to results and to identify longitudinal trends and ensure that the views of a representative sample of students are gained.

3 Research & Scholarship: Using the Campus as a Laboratory

As a means to engage both specific groups of students and the wider student body, one approach taken by the University is built around using the campus as both a site for research about aspects of sustainability and as a space to showcase the outcomes of research. This section illustrates using the campus as the site for research opportunities at an urban and a rural campus. At an urban campus the green roofs initiative investigates how green roofs can ameliorate the heat island effect, while at the rural campus research across numerous disciplines within a farming community is undertaken.

3.1 Green Roofs: Research Influencing Campus Design

The 'Campus as a Laboratory' philosophy is exemplified by the green roofs at the University's Burnley campus, a small urban campus located 7 km from the city centre. The three green roofs of the Burnley Green Roofs project are located on the main administration building at Burnley campus and comprise the main demonstration green roof, the research roof, and the biodiversity roof. The green roofs are used for research and as a demonstration and teaching resource for students and courses conducted at the Burnley Campus. This includes a new post-graduate program, the *Specialist Certificate in Green Roofs and Walls*. Taught by industry experts and academic staff, the course integrates green roofs and walls research with real world experience across a number of disciplines. The teaching aims to provide students with exposure to cutting edge ideas and research innovation, coupled with design and management problem solving, all critical in an area where transdisciplinary thinking and practice is required.

The subject '*Designing Green Roofs and Walls*' explores design and specification of green roofs and walls and engages students in green infrastructure as it relates to the University campus. Students apply their learning to design a proposed green roof for a building at the University's main campus that has been evaluated by a structural engineer. Students use the structural capacity information to design green roofs with appropriate and achievable design outcomes. Students also consider key stakeholders in their designs and many of the green roofs are designed as outdoor classrooms or meeting areas. This requires students to engage with academic and professional staff to ascertain needs and concerns and integrates sustainability-related learning into campus development. Project outcomes include enhancing the broader student experience through providing well-designed spaces, together with the direct participation of students in campus development. By greening the campus, students are also helping to address the 'urban heat island effect', a contributor to extreme summer temperatures in Melbourne, and reducing the risk of flooding in central Melbourne.

3.2 Dookie Campus: Innovations to Influence Others

The rural campus at Dookie, 220 km north of Melbourne, comprises a large working farm and bushland reserves on a 2500 ha site and has a primary focus on agricultural education. Many cross-disciplinary projects are undertaken in collaboration with other faculties, government departments, and the local community and utilize elements of the campus farm estate and the campus is used as a demonstration site to "demonstrate the new paradigm in agricultural production by engaging with industry partners, government, the local community and global collaborators" (http://www.dookie.unimelb.edu.au/dookie21/).

A recently completed robotic dairy, only the third of its kind in Australia, embraces state-of-the-art technology that demonstrates innovative dairy practices to farmers and students and will facilitate future research experiments. The dairy includes a solar array and water recycling and was developed with government support to demonstrate more sustainable farming methods. Projects currently underway include a biodigester for the piggery and an algal ponds project to generate bio fuels (currently at tender stage), methane measurement and trialing of lower emissions feedstock, and a demonstration micro-hydro system is under development. These projects involve the schools of Chemical and Biomolecular Engineering, Agriculture and Food Systems, and the University's Property & Campus Services.

The diversity of the University's campuses enables students and staff to undertake a wide range of research projects and research-led teaching across many disciplines. The rural setting of Dookie campus provides opportunities for land-based technological research that would not be possible at urban campuses. These projects directly address the University's grand research challenges in a very visible way and exposes students and the local community to the University's commitment to sustainability.

4 Curriculum: Sustainability in Coursework

This section describes a subject where sustainability practices at the University have been incorporated into coursework curriculum and lead to credit points for students and link to other aspects of the wider student experience, such as the infrastructure and operations of the university. The impacts of this subject are experienced by many students beyond those who undertake it, as they live and work within the campus environment and the outcomes of the subject inform the operations of the campus. These opportunities where our students have the empowering experience of contributing to change, not just learning about it, are likely to play a significant role in developing the graduate attribute of 'leading change for a sustainable future'. Partnerships between the University's operational and academic arms provide rich opportunities for students to engage in sustainability through the formal curriculum.

4.1 Subject: Interdisciplinarity & the Environment

Interdisciplinarity & the Environment is a capstone subject, taken by approximately 120 students each year in the Master of Environment, which is a cross-faculty program that prepares graduates to work in a variety of interdisciplinary environmental professional roles. The subject focuses on the 'knowledge challenges' experienced by sustainability professionals, particularly the challenges of framing sustainability to support decision-making and integrating knowledge across traditional boundaries of disciplines and professions. The subject requires students to integrate knowledge from across their studies, extend their professional skills in collaboration and integration, and apply their knowledge and skills to environmental decision-making. Each year students grapple with one or more 'real world' dilemmas of making decisions for sustainability. In 2014 all students worked on a single project as the coursework requirement for the subject.

In 2014 students contributed to the University's deliberations around the Green Building Council of Australia's 'Green Star Communities' (GSC) sustainability rating tool (Green Building Council of Australia 2014). Students undertook discussions with Property and Campus Services (PCS) and assignment work in *Interdisciplinarity and Environment* was developed around the Green Star Communities accreditation process. Students explored how a sustainability issue (climate change, environmental risk, or community resilience) was framed by the GSC accreditation documents and then worked in a multidisciplinary team to develop recommendations for PCS on whether and how they should pursue the relevant GSC credit points.

In this project, PCS took the role of briefing agency, while students took the role of environmental consultants. PCS prepared a briefing paper to help students understand the University's decision-making context and priorities in relation to Green Star Communities. PCS staff attended tutorial classes early in semester to discuss the brief with students and throughout the semester students could communicate with PCS staff through the subject's online discussion board. PCS was the target audience for collaborative briefing papers, and—with student permission—the best papers were shared with the University to help inform its response to the Green Star Communities program.

From the perspective of students and academics, projects that facilitate engagement with 'real world' sustainability challenges and professional sustainability practitioners offer clear and real benefits. For students, such projects enable deeper understanding of theory in practice, and a safe environment in which to try out emerging professional skills and more clearly imagine their future professional practice. For academics, projects established in partnership with sustainability agencies facilitate the design of authentic and meaningful assessment tasks that are both information-rich and relatively open-ended in the manner of so many professional projects. Sustainability agencies can provide access to key documents and data, can introduce students to the particular political and social context in which decisions must be made, and help students appreciate the uncertainties and active boundary setting that are so critical to professional activity. For these reasons, it is very valuable to develop academic assessment through a partnership between a subject coordinator and an industry partner.

This kind of partnership adds further value for the University through contributing to achieving the University's sustainability goals, both operational and educational. The focus of sustainability is not just on reducing operational impact, but also integrating sustainability principles and practices through the University's core activities. Sustainability leaders at the University argue that the greatest positive impact we can have is not in operational efficiencies but in the degree to which we can empower our students as future leaders. Property and Campus Services therefore seeks out opportunities to satisfy operational objectives in ways that engage and empower staff and students through curriculum and research. Property and Campus Services are involved in a wide range of research-related projects (described elsewhere in this article and in Chambers 2015) and in small student projects, however this project was the first to engage a large group of students with particular expertise in sustainability who devoted a significant portion of assessment tasks to focus on a key deliverable for PCS.

A curriculum and operational innovation such as this is not without challenges, and staff and students noted several aspects they would like to sharpen in future partnerships. For example, the timing of semester and the external constraints of the project were not well matched, which created challenges and limited genuine student contributions to outcomes. However, the project provided an additional opportunity for the University's operations team to formally and meaningfully engage with students and to access their environmental expertise and enthusiasm. Beyond the value of the submitted material, this experience established a process of engagement between academic and operational units that aligns directly with the University's sustainability aspirations and has generated capability and confidence to seek out and develop similar opportunities in the future.

This subject demonstrated that students from a range of disciplines engaging with a common problem under the guidance of academic staff and consulting with staff from PCS can lead to meaningful student engagement with sustainability and its complexities at the University. By incorporating projects such as this into coursework subjects, students gain valuable learning and cross-disciplinary experiences that prepare them to be more effective practitioners and advocates that can lead change for a sustainable future.

5 Student Opportunities: Workplace Experiences

In addition to coursework subjects, in many courses students take on projects in authentic workplaces, both within the University and beyond. In the subject entitled, the *Melbourne Business Practicum*, the Faculty of Business & Economics offers opportunities for students to work in small groups on challenging projects in a workplace environment. Each student group acts as consultants on a project. Projects described here were located within the Property & Campus Services unit of the University and addressed sustainability issues. These projects benefit students by giving them exposure to contemporary sustainability issues in the 'real world' environment of the University, with all the challenges and constraints of such a complex organization, and in working with others to achieve meaningful change. The University benefits greatly from having our very capable students undertaking these projects.

5.1 Review of Fair Trade Practices

In May 2012, the University became a certified Fair Trade University (http://www.fta.org.au/fair-trade-universities.html), committing to increasing the use of Fair Trade products in University kitchenettes and at events and by encouraging cafés and shops on campus to offer Fair Trade products. An important component of the

Fair Trade initiative is to embed student involvement across many areas of the initiative. This included a student-led consulting project in the *Melbourne Business Practicum*, in which a group of students reported on the uptake of Fair Trade around the University. The results and recommendations within the report provided the University with valuable information on perceptions about Fair Trade on campus and provide a solid foundation to build on the initiative, especially in regards to cafés and the student body.

The 'Fair Trade Ambassadors' program is an example of further student engagement in raising awareness of Fair Trade, in which six student volunteers were selected to join the University's Fair Trade Steering Committee. The students now take an active role in making University decisions relating to Fair Trade. This is a teaching and learning opportunity that works to enhance the student experience while engaging with the wider community. This particular program offers a 'win-win' situation whereby students are empowered to actively support and lead change in their University while enhancing operational outcomes for Fair Trade at the University.

5.2 Developing a Framework for Integrated Sustainability Reporting

The need for the University to develop an integrated reporting framework for sustainability at the University has been recognized for some time and the University's Sustainability Executive provided strong support for this framework to be developed by students, rather than through external consultants. A proposal was submitted for the initial student project through the *Melbourne Business Practicum*. A project team was established and a framework was developed through an information gathering process that included a review of contemporary sustainability reporting in the higher education sector; gathering of key data; identifying of information gaps; and developing recommendations.

The students involved were accounting and finance specialists with no previous exposure to sustainability principles and practices. After undertaking the project they all reported a strong and new interest in sustainability. This project demonstrates how commercial principles can be applied to provide structure around sustainability practices and has established a foundation for further development regarding integrated reporting at the University.

6 Operations: The Hidden Curriculum of the Campus

Students and staff experience the campus on a daily basis and it is a 'second home' to students for the three or four years that they are studying for a degree. The daily experiences and interactions that students have while on campus send a profound message to students about what the University values. This has been elegantly summed up by Orr (1992) as the 'hidden curriculum' of a university.

> We think that education occurs mostly in buildings, yet apparently we believe that the design and operation of those same buildings have nothing to do with education… The design of academic buildings is a kind of crystallized pedagogy full of hidden assumptions about power, about how people learn, how they relate to the natural world, and how they relate to one another… the design and operation of buildings provide an educational opportunity as well… (Orr 1992 p. 7).

Thus, the infrastructure and the operations of a university, though not a part of academic services or explicitly thought of as part of the teaching program of a university, sends powerful messages to its students about what it really values with respect to sustainability, and many other matters. The manner in which the physical campus is presented and the engagement of students in its development and operations is central to the students' experience of sustainability during their time at the University.

6.1 Recycling & Waste: Messages in the Bins

Waste and recycling bins are a visible and daily reality of a campus landscape and can send messages to students, staff and visitors to the campus. In 2010 the University developed a Waste Management Plan and set a 2015 target of 50 % of waste to be recycled (from a baseline of 16 % recycled in 2009) and appointed a Waste & Recycling Coordinator to drive the changes necessary to achieve this ambitious target. A research project (Gilmour et al. 2013) that involved PCS staff and academic staff was undertaken to investigate the availability and placement of bins and human behaviors, with a goal of informing campus practices to minimize waste going to landfill.

Data from bin audits enabled an understanding of how location, labeling, and distance to the nearest recycling/landfill bin influenced behaviors of people disposing of waste and provided evidence of the importance of labeling and of co-locating landfill and recycling bins. The study demonstrated that the provision of suitable infrastructure can lead to dramatic improvements in rates of recycling and less recyclable materials going to landfill. The results of the study led to the replacing of waste bins and recycling bins across the campus with clearly labeled and twinned waste and recycling bins that are a visible and daily reminder about not only what to do with waste, but also that the University sees waste minimization as a priority. Thus the placement and the labeling of something as commonplace as bins can make real contributions to both operational targets and in sending clear messages to students through this aspect of the hidden curriculum.

6.2 Geothermal Installation at the Campus Sustainability Centre

In 2013 a shallow geothermal facility was installed in the building that houses the Office for Environmental Programs (OEP) and Campus Sustainability Centre. The 25 kW facility acts in both an operational and educational capacity—it provides efficient heating and cooling to the ground floor of the building and provides teaching and research opportunities.

The planning, approvals and implementation phases of this project involved the collaboration of numerous stakeholders, predominantly academic staff and doctoral students from the Infrastructure Engineering department within Melbourne School of Engineering, staff of PCS, staff of the OEP (as the major building tenant), and external stakeholders who provided technical services and parts.

This project creates many benefits through the integration of research activities with the operations of the University. Public display screens in the Campus Sustainability Centre capture system performance and act as a visible reminder to the community of efforts to operate the University in a sustainable manner. System monitoring enables ongoing research and teaching opportunities. The project has also informed the design of an 80 kW shallow geothermal facility as part of major construction works elsewhere on campus.

While the processes involved in this project were challenging and resource-intensive, the long-term benefits are considerable. Engagement across organizational boundaries enabled the benefits of an otherwise purely operational implementation to provide fertile opportunities for ongoing research and teaching. The expertise of academic staff and students in the field of infrastructure engineering enabled an outcome that would have been unachievable solely through operational means.

7 Conclusions

Examples presented here illustrate a range of initiatives and activities through which students engage with sustainability across a number of the dimensions of sustainability defined by Calder and Clugston (2003). Some examples directly affect relatively small numbers of students, such as in the specific subjects discussed, although the impacts of the outcomes of those subjects may affect a much wider student population through the work of those students informing campus infrastructure or operations, and some initiatives will directly impact many students. As has been explored elsewhere (see Chambers 2015) most of the initiatives do not fit neatly into a single dimension of sustainability, but rather cross a number of the dimensions, although for convenience they have been presented under a single heading here.

Student engagement with various aspects of sustainability within curriculum, research, and operations enables students to gain valuable experience and rich learning through these authentic challenges of sustainability in the complex environment of a university. This leads to substantial benefits for both students and the university. Students have rich interdisciplinary and authentic experiences to draw on when applying for jobs after graduation. The university gains the many benefits from the efforts of the students, who are the elite of their generation, as do other students through their daily experience on the campus.

While each university has its own history and characteristics, the circumstances and culture of the university in which the case studies are set is not particularly unusual—it is subject to the usual tensions and pressures experienced by large research-intensive universities. Thus, the types of initiatives described here could be replicated elsewhere if there is a desire and a willingness to set and support ambitious goals and if there is support for staff to cross traditional boundaries and to explore new ways of engaging and empowering students in pursuit of these goals.

The sustainability initiatives and activities described here are all aspects of the University's core activities of research, teaching and learning, and community engagement and they are collectively, and with initiatives not outlined here, helping to shift the culture of the University. This is a slow process that is achieved both through governance decisions and through the daily lived experiences on campus. As the title of the chapter suggests, the examples explored in this chapter are small wins where individual staff have created alliances and developed relationships, often across traditional boundaries, to create opportunities for engaging students with sustainability. There is much scope for a more structured and systematic approach to developing further opportunities for students to have more active engagement with sustainability through the formal and hidden curriculum. The University's goal for its graduates to be able to 'lead change for a sustainable future' applies to all graduates, and so an active engagement with sustainability, rather than only passive engagement, is not only desirable, it is necessary. The university has much scope for expanding these active opportunities and celebrating the early successes may encourage more work in this important area that is valued by both students and the University.

References

Butt, L., More, E., & Avery, G. C. (2014). The myth of the 'green student': Student involvement in Australian university sustainability programmes. *Studies in Higher Education, 39*(5), 786–804.

Calder, W., & Clugston, R. M. (2003). Progress toward sustainability in higher education. *Environmental Law Reporter, 2003*(1), 10003–10022. http://www.ulsf.org/pdf/dernbach_chapter_short.pdf

Chambers, D. (2015). Maximising sustainability outcomes by amalgamating dimensions of sustainability. In *Transformative approaches to sustainable development at universities* (pp. 195–206). Berlin: Springer International Publishing.

Gilmour, P., Alcorn, J., & Moore, G. (2013). *Build it and they will recycle: The critical importance of infrastructure in changing recycling behaviour.* A Melbourne Sustainable Society Institute

Report. http://www.sustainable.unimelb.edu.au/files/mssi/UoM%20Waste%20Mangement%20Draft%20Report.pdf
Green Building Council of Australia. (2014). *Green star—Communities.* http://www.gbca.org.au/green-star/green-star-communities
Jones, P., Selby, D., & Sterling, S. (2010). More than the sum of their parts. In P. Jones, D. Selby, & S. Sterling (Eds.), *Sustainability education: Perspectives and practice across higher education* (p. 2010). London: Earthscan.
Lukman, R., & Glavič, P. (2007). What are the key elements of a sustainable university? *Clean Technologies and Environmental Policy, 9*(2), 103–114.
McMillin, J., & Dyball, R. (2009). Developing a whole-of-university approach to educating for sustainability linking curriculum, research and sustainable campus operations. *Journal of Education for Sustainable Development, 3*(1), 55–64.
Orr, D. (1992). *Environmental literacy: Education as if the earth mattered.* Twelfth Annual E. F. Schumacher Lectures October 1992, Great Barrington, Massachusetts. Available at http://sfsf.com.au/Education.As.If.The.Earth.Mattered.pdf
Ratner, B. D. (2004). "Sustainability" as a dialogue of values: Challenges to the sociology of development. *Sociological Inquiry, 74*(1), 50–69.
University of Melbourne. (2010). *Growing esteem 2010.* http://growingesteem.unimelb.edu.au/_data/assets/pdf_file/0003/322437/GrowingEsteem2010.pdf
University of Melbourne. (2011). *Education for sustainability.* http://sustainablecampus.unimelb.edu.au/curriculum/educationForSustainability.html
University of Melbourne. (2012). *Research at Melbourne: Ensuring excellence and impact to 2025.* https://www.unimelb.edu.au/research/docs/research-paper-2012.pdf
University of Melbourne. (2013). *University of Melbourne Annual Report 2013* (pp. 81–86). http://unimelb.edu.au/publications/docs/UoM_ANNUAL%20REPORT%202013_VOL%201&2_REV.pdf
University of Melbourne. (2014). *Sustainability Survey Report 2014.* http://sustainablecampus.unimelb.edu.au/news_items/survey2014.html

Author Biographies

Dianne Chambers is a Senior Lecturer with the Melbourne Graduate School of Education at the University of Melbourne and teaches in Education for Sustainability and ICT in Education. Her research areas include education for sustainability in higher education, the uses of technology in teacher education, and technology-enriched problem based learning.

Clare Walker is the Principal Advisor for Sustainability at the University of Melbourne. She is involved in developing strategic and governance structures to achieve the University's sustainability targets in energy, water, waste and transport, and in developing initiatives to link educational and operational activities.

Kathryn Williams is Director of the Office for Environmental Programs and oversees a large cross-faculty graduate program at the University of Melbourne. She is also Associate Professor in environmental psychology in the School of Ecosystem and Forest Sciences.

John Rayner is a Senior Lecturer in Urban Horticulture at the Burnley Campus of the University of Melbourne. John's research and teaching interests are focused around the design and use of plants in the landscape, particularly green roofs and walls, climbing and ground cover plants, children's gardens and therapeutic landscapes.

Claire Farrell is a Lecturer in Green Infrastructure, based at the Burnley Campus of the University of Melbourne. Her main research interest involves using plants to make cities more livable. Claire's current research looks at using green roofs for storm water mitigation and improving biodiversity in Australian cities.

Anne-Maree Butt manages the market research program at the University of Melbourne and has worked in the higher education sector for more than five years. She has expertise in strategic market research, across both client-side and agency roles.

Danielle Rostan-Herbert is the Sustainability Manager at the University of Melbourne. Danielle currently has a responsibility for University-wide targets to reduce energy, carbon, water and waste. She has produced a Sustainability Implementation plan which engages and empowers staff, students and the community on sustainability issues.

Teaching Towards Sustainability Literacy in Art, Design and Fashion

Antony Johnston, Rebecca Leach and Heather Sproat

Abstract
This chapter explores how teachers can engage art and design students with sustainability. Different perspectives are drawn upon to reflect upon the barriers that exist in implementing curriculum change to increase students' sustainable literacy in higher education. A co-operative inquiry approach is used as a model for participatory pedagogy and shows how practitioner-based research can lead to the enhancement of ESD. Findings suggest that exploring the relationship between ESD and art and design 'signature pedagogies' can be fruitful, especially as the former provide creative and playful approaches that allow complexity and anxiety inherent ESD and transformative learning to be expressed.

1 Introduction

This chapter explores how teachers and supporters of learning, engage art and design students with sustainability. The authors draw upon a number of different perspectives in order to reflect upon some of the barriers that exist in implementing curriculum change to increase students' sustainable literacy in a higher education

A. Johnston (✉)
Teaching and Learning Exchange, University of the Arts London,
272 High Holborn, London WC1V 7EY, UK
e-mail: a.johnston@arts.ac.uk

R. Leach · H. Sproat
Central Saint Martins, University of the Arts London, Granary Building,
1 Granary Square, King's Cross, London N1C 4AA, UK
e-mail: b.leach@csm.arts.ac.uk

H. Sproat
e-mail: h.sproat@csm.arts.ac.uk

© Springer International Publishing Switzerland 2016

W. Leal Filho and P. Pace (eds.), *Teaching Education for Sustainable Development at University Level*, World Sustainability Series,
DOI 10.1007/978-3-319-32928-4_15

setting. Barriers to implementing sustainability have been charted elsewhere, for instance, in terms of capacity, authenticity and space within the curriculum (see Dawe et al. 2005), in terms of the anxiety that the ecological crisis evokes (Buzzell and Chalquist 2009), the breadth, complexity and abstractness of the problems and concepts and the difficulty teachers experience in taking up a position in relation to sustainability and their teaching (Johnston 2015). A number of attempts have been made in order to address these (see Sterling 2013); however these can fall short in terms of addressing how teachers approach sustainability within art and design disciplines, a notable exception is Stibbe (2009).

A key issue within teaching education for sustainable development (ESD) is the difficulty of effecting change in the individual, where he/she is not only cognitively committed to sustainable action, but also realises this in practice. When calls are made for educators to teach appropriate values, lifestyles and behaviours to support a sustainable world (Wals 2009) this is far from unproblematic. If we consider the UK context, then we must acknowledge the unsustainable nature of our society and our place within it. The significance of this for learning and teaching ESD is that the scale and scope of the problems we face require transformational learning; which is neither easy to structure nor without personal risk (Barnett 2007). This can be considered as both a learning problem and a teaching problem and it is perhaps advisable to approach it from both directions. Henry (2009) notes the difficulty for learning theory to address learning appropriate for sustainability as many theories prioritise either individual or social learning; ESD in turn requires a theory that can encompass both types of learning. Furthermore, Henry notes that agents have strong accuracy goals; which suggests the difficulties of revising normative values and beliefs (2009). In effect people do not like being wrong and whilst this experience is individual it is informed by the values and beliefs that are learnt socially. The challenge therefore for teaching ESD is that it needs to support individual learning, for example, systems mapping, understanding complexity, material use, waste etc.; and social learning, for example values of stewardship, respect for all beings, etc.

Participatory pedagogy represents a powerful attempt to meet this challenge and does this through a form of dialectical mediation of realist and idealist perspectives (see Sterling 2004). These perspectives, which are ideal types are inadequate for conceiving of an effective sustainable education (ibid.). Educational development often segments teaching approaches as either teacher- (realist) or student-centred (idealist) with the former considered 'bad' and the latter 'good'; however such a distinction is rather crude. For instance, a stereotype of idealist/constructivist teaching is that students will be able to 'discover' all knowledge with little reference to socio-historical and cultural contexts, whereas realist/didactic stereotypes suggest students merely parrot back what teachers tell them. In response, Sterling articulates 'participatory pedagogy' which aims to overcome the limitations and weaknesses of each approach whilst drawing on their strengths (2004). This leads to a relational and participative model where learners are engaged through meaning making and, individual and wider contexts, while grounded in knowledge and evidence. Learning therefore, is grounded in practice and a critical appraisal of ontology that requires a collaborative, multidisciplinary and systemic approach to epistemology. Sterling (2003) conceives of 'invitational leadership' as an approach that teachers may adopt to support students and to bridge the gap between realist and idealist approaches. The strength of this approach is that it is holistic and provides a framework to think about individual and social learning and to consider this in relation to empirical and normative forms of knowing.

The authors draw on this work to explore how participatory approaches can support ESD teaching and to investigate the role of professional development for teachers. A model of practitioner-based research was drawn upon to structure the investigation and is outlined below, this is followed by three short cases that are descriptive and evaluative illustrations of stages in the inquiry. The discussion section then draws out the relationship between art and design pedagogies and ESD and how each can inform the other.

2 Methodology

The aim of the investigation is to consider, the effectiveness of reflective practice to support sustainability literacy of teachers, and whether art and design approaches can enhance students' sustainability literacy. The method developed to address these concerns had to negotiate two significant tensions; that researchers would be researching their own practice and that they would be addressing research questions as a group, each tension will be discussed in turn.

Practitioner research methods have a long tradition within art and design research and educational practice programmes; which are congruent with an ESD approach to praxis (Wals 2009). While a number of approaches are contained within the umbrella of practitioner research, reflective practice here represents an important approach. Reflective practice enables researchers to investigate a world in which they are directly implicated in, by critically investigating their own practice (Finlay 2008). Reflective practice can be seen as primarily an approach to learning from experience, rather than a research method (McMahon 1999). The primary limitation of reflective practice is that despite its similarities with action research that it lacks a 'strategic action', that is, a predefined area for investigation. Furthermore, a common criticism of reflective practice is that it can mean all things to all people, therefore it is important to establish what it means in this context. Reflective practice broadly involves a description of an event/experience that is evaluated and analysed; which leads to conclusions that can inform future action. A challenge to reflective practice is the difficulty in adopting an approach that is critical and reflexive, rather than purely reactive and/or intuitive. Within the context of ESD and art and design it is useful to consider Brookfield's four lenses; which he believes supports teachers' critical reflection; an autobiographical lens representing the practitioner's self-reflection, peer and student lenses where data and feedback is gathered from others and finally a scholarly lens that draws upon literature to aid in reflection (Brookfield 1995). In order to address some of the issues related to reflective practice this was situated within a co-operative inquiry process.

Co-operative inquiry is drawn upon as it provides a structured approach to participatory research. It is a way: of working with others with similar concerns and interests, to understand the world and to engage others in positive action (Heron and Reason 2001). There are therefore strong links between reflective practice, action research and co-operative inquiry. Co-operative inquiry involves research *with* people rather than *on* people, as such it embodies the ethos of pedagogic approaches in teacher education and art and design, including reflective practice and action research. Moreover it is an approach that is congruent with ESD as it can facilitate relationships and support communities by addressing particular problems that are beyond an individual's sphere of influence.

Co-operative inquiry (Heron and Reason 2001) follows four phases that are iteratively cycled through. Phase 1 concerns the group formation of co-researchers around a common interest, defining the scope of the research and planning. Phase 2 involves co-researchers testing agreed actions and observing what happens. Phase 3 is distinct as it has the potential for transformative learning, it is a creative and generative point where knowledge may be generated in relation to research questions, but new concerns, questions and directions may emerge. This is particularly useful for practitioner research which can take place in complex and messy settings where all variables cannot be accounted for. Phase 4 is the point at which co-researchers share findings and the original questions are reconsidered in light of new experience and understanding. Co-researchers then repeat phases 2–4, whilst the number of times this should happen is not prescribed, three times has been suggested as a lower threshold. While cooperative inquiry allows for a variety of data to be collected (Heron and Reason 2001), co-researchers drew upon Brookfield's (1995) critical lenses. This was seen as holding fidelity to the phenomena under study and therefore appropriate for a qualitative study (Hammersley and Atkinson 2007).

Co-researchers were drawn from 9 participants on an 'Education for Sustainability' module which forms part of a MA Academic Practice; a professional development course for in-service lecturers and supporters of learning in a predominantly arts University. Co-researchers are both teacher and student, which places them in a "wonderfully reflexive position" (Hesse 1993: 225), as student-teachers have the capacity to reflect both on their own experience of learning sustainability and to consider this in light of teaching sustainability. The first case study briefly outlines how the module draws upon co-operative inquiry as a form of participatory pedagogy and this relates closely to phase 1. The following two case studies illustrate phases 2 and 3 through two co-researchers' investigations into their own teaching. The 'findings' of this process are then presented in the discussion which relates to phase 4.

3 Establishing an Inquiry

The first case study describes how an 'Education for Sustainability' module to in-service Higher Education teachers as part of a MA Academic Practice draws upon cooperative inquiry as a form of participatory pedagogy. Students who take the module are typically referred to as participants in recognition of their dual status. Sustainability often evokes strong responses, positive and negative, from participants; which are reflective of the broader student body. Furthermore, if these responses can be thematised, then the module provides the opportunity for teachers to reflect upon their position as both students and teachers in relation to teaching ESD. Teaching is informed by ESD, in particular a model of participative pedagogy articulated by Sterling (2004). The unit has developed over a period of 4 years directly in relation to formal/informal feedback, evaluation data, peer observation and personal reflection, data collection and evaluation.

Participative pedagogy is drawn upon through numerous teaching strategies that aim to promote engagement, active and experiential learning and to set-up the module as a form of inquiry in which participants reflect upon their own experience of ESD teaching. The curriculum of the unit is negotiated through a collaborative approach that results in a mix of teacher-led and student-led activities. 'Invitational leadership' is modelled through the introduction of key issues and what is known about them, whilst also facilitating a space in which participants can share problems and define the questions that the group will investigate as part of their inquiry. The inquiry leads to participants/co-researchers investigating their own teaching practice in response to ESD and to test out ideas in which they gather data to determine its success or not. The participants' inquiry becomes reified as a piece of reflective writing and portfolio which serves as an assessed piece for the module.

3.1 Count Your Blessings

This inquiry focused upon sustainability and fashion design by investigating participant's relationship to textiles, in particular clothing. The investigation was prompted by a questioning of our fast-paced, modern and consumption-led society and how this has impacted upon a loss of 'love' and appreciation for the textiles and garments that clothe us. With the advent of a 'fast fashion' culture there has been a reduction in both the economic value of garments and with their personal significance; which has led to a throw-away culture. Individual garments are increasingly seen as disposable; which when taken to its extreme, leads to single use garments that are worn once and then discarded. Part of this growth in consumption is linked to an increase in speed, which in turn is only made possible by the hidden exploitation of people and natural resources (Fletcher 2007). Where has the meaning and value of clothing gone and is it possible to get it back? The authors believe we need to start by growing a sense of curiosity in student designers, those who will create meaning and value. The inquiry addresses this by considering how teaching through a creative, playful and mindful approach can raise difficult issues with students in a non-threatening way. The inquiry led to the development of a workshop to investigate whether the emotional significance and personal value of clothing can be recovered. One approach, is to start by growing participants' awareness of the relationships they have with clothing.

3.2 Aspects of Learning

To address these issues a student-centred and experiential workshop was delivered that would allow participants the time to invest in the creation of their own unique wearable fabric piece, in this example a scarf. Participants would attach sentiments to their garment via a process of reflecting on positive thoughts relating to their life, writing these down on a template and using this to cut a pattern of holes on their garment. Through this process, the workshop would investigate the theory of emotional durability (see Chapman 2007), by encouraging design students to engage with the concept of emotional attachment in relation to textiles.

In the field of ESD, there is a broad consensus that participative and experiential learning methods have the capacity to engage learners in ways that make a real difference to learners' understanding, thinking and actions (Sterling 2013). The workshop worked with an affective dimension by providing time and space for participants to reflect on their 'blessings', all the things in their life that they could be grateful for. The workshop structure was designed to allow participants to hold those positive thoughts during the creation of their scarf; which would impact on how they invested in the garment emotionally. It was expected that participants would feel less likely to discard the item; which would raise broader questions concerning waste and attachment to belongings.

3.3 Evaluation

Directly after a trial workshop, participants were asked to reflect on their engagement by completing a short open questionnaire. The questionnaire was designed to collect participants' responses, to determine their relationship to the created piece, whether that had any effect on their sense of well-being, if an attachment had developed and whether this would effect their retention of the piece. A majority of participants felt relaxed and/or calm after the workshop, so overall it had a positive effect on their immediate wellbeing. The whole group felt that it would remind them of the feelings that they had during the piece's creation and as a result everyone said they would keep it. A clear limitation however when collecting data at this point is that it cannot be used to make judgements about long term behaviour change.

3.4 Implications

The case illustrates how facilitating students to feel emotionally connected during the process of learning and making can facilitate behaviour change. As James and Brookfield note, "it is pedagogically important to find imaginative ways of helping students discover personal meaning in learning" (2014, pp. 8). When considering the holistic nature of learning introducing a workshop where the participants could engage in the development of their awareness of ESD through the process of creation and self-reflection proved to be a positive experience.

4 A Case for Sustaining Stories

This inquiry drew upon a co-researcher's practise as a storyteller in order to explore how work with story and myth can contribute to fine art teaching practice and support ESD. Story can be a powerful tool for transformative learning and provide students with a structure to explore uncertainty. Here, uncertainty is used to describe the elements of the unknown, not knowing and ambiguity that are inherent within sustainability and creative practice (Fisher and Fortnum 2013). The inquiry led to the development of a 'sustaining stories workshop' that aimed to support participants to create and reflect on a fictional story concerning sustainability. The story is created through an improvised spoken-word storytelling game. Individual participants were asked to create a symbol representing a sustainability issue important to them. These symbols were then pooled together and drawn blind by participants in turn in order to collaboratively create a story about sustainability. This touched on several key areas within ESD including meaning-making, uncertainty and reflective learning.

The workshop reveals how metaphor, meaning-making and dialogue can be used as a tool for reflective learning and can lead to transformative learning. Storytelling techniques were used to create a verbal exploration of meaning through dialogue and reflection, drawing on individual and collaborative responses to metaphor within the creative work. This recognises the comparative 'pedagogies of uncertainty' (Shulman 2005b) and subsequent learner anxiety within ESD and fine art pedagogy and starts to explore ways to reflectively address these tensions through story. The majority of learning is dialogic and reflective and emerges from the discussion about the story, themes and the emotions that arise in response to its creation.

4.1 Metaphor and Meaning-Making

As Abrams (1997) notes, there is the potential to satisfy humans' emotional desire for symbolic meaning in the non-material world through an engagement with metaphor; which is significant given our changing relationship with material possessions, as partially illustrated by the above case study. By identifying personally important issues within sustainability and symbolising them, learners can take ownership of an abstract issue and imbue it with symbolic meaning: "I liked that we could pick characters/issues" (Participant F). As James and Brookfield (2014, p. 117) argue, the role of metaphor and meaning can be strengthened through sensory engagement. Within the workshop the embodied act of creating a symbol deepens learning: "[the] power of visualisation as a learning strategy is highly accessible" (Participant E).

4.2 Dialogue and Reflective Learning

The Sustaining Stories workshop relies on a storytelling technique called 'feeding the story' (Shaw 2014), which supports listeners to make personal connections with a story and to develop an appreciation and understanding of their own symbolic language. This process asks listeners to reflect openly on a key image within the story that resonated with them. Subsequent group discussion allows listeners to draw on each other's responses to feed into a wider discussion and to develop an understanding of their own response in relation to that of others: "Reflecting on the key images helped to find key issues" (Participant F). 'Feeding the story' draws on a dialogic approach to explore the relationship between metaphor and reflective learning. Reflective learning fosters participants' conscious awareness of their thought processes and actions that is intrinsic to ESD (Sterling 2004) and through which we can "educate our students to consciously cultivate their ability to think in tandem with their other three ways of knowing… feeling, sensing and intuition" (Harding 2009, p. 93). Reflecting as a group allowed participants to simultaneously reflect individually on their experience, and to collaboratively evaluate the experience of creating a story together. Collective reflection can creates a safe space for participants to discuss their feelings associated with sustainability and may deepen their engagement with the subject.

4.3 Evaluation

Storytelling techniques can be used to support learners to use metaphor, meaning-making, dialogue and reflective learning to deepen their relationship with sustainability. Furthermore, they have the capacity to facilitate transformational learning towards sustainability and provide a structure for students to explore uncertainty. Evaluating the potential for a short workshop to provide a transformative learning experience is problematic, as realistically this takes time; however it is possible to consider two markers of this experience: anxiety and active learning. Anxiety is inherent to significant learning experiences (Barnett 2007) as they challenge participants by asking them to engage with new ideas and skills. The workshop facilitated participants' exploration of a subject matter riddled with uncertainty whilst gaining confidence in new skills and providing a structure that allowed them to face the anxiety. The role of story as a helpful container for anxiety is particularly relevant to ESD as it is a subject matter fraught with anxiety for learners (Buzzell and Chalquist 2009). Engagement in the workshop provided an example of active learning, as participants were required to accumulate and use knowledge as the game evolved. Active engagement is demonstrative of deep learning and education.

4.4 Implications

As demonstrated by the above discussion, there is huge scope for using storytelling techniques to support explorations of meaning-making, uncertainty and reflective learning within ESD and art and design education. Collective acts of creation rely on collaboration and research has also shown that working with others can also provide increased emotional wellbeing that can act as a desired "incentive" (Haque 2010) to increase citizen engagement with sustainability. Furthermore, there is potential to use models of collaboration and storytelling to explore empathy, complexity and an understanding of interconnection. Despite the wide range of literature on the relation between storytelling and ecology, there is a significant lack of research on the role storytelling can play in ESD specifically. There is huge scope for further research and exploration of how storytelling techniques can be used to support transformational learning within ESD for art and design.

5 Discussion

An important aspect of the case studies has been to illustrate dimensions of art and design pedagogic practice that represent 'signature pedagogies' of art and design. A signature pedagogy is the type of teaching practices that "leap to mind when we first think about the preparation of members of particular professions" (Shulman 2005a, p. 52). Art and design signature pedagogies are characterised by dialogic practice, student-centeredness, experiential learning and typically involve a material and spatial dimension (Shreeve et al. 2010). In turn these are seen as supporting the development of the individual, of making learning visible and of living with uncertainty. While this theorisation seems to privilege the individual in dialogue with others and their own development, the notion of uncertainty provides an important bridge with anxiety of learning generally and in relation to ESD. Teaching ESD is complicated by such barriers to learning where teachers and students are asked to consider inequalities and unsustainability where the scope of problems become too large and complex. Along with complexity and anxiety there also exists a 'learning problem' in that learners are predisposed to reinforce their existing understanding and behaviours, especially where these relate to values (Henry 2009). The problem of teaching ESD is perhaps two-fold as not only do learners want to re-enforce existing habits and understanding, but when values are altered this may not necessarily translate into meaningful action (Sterling 2004). Such issues have led to theorisations of pedagogic approaches, such as participative pedagogy and alternative epistemological approaches that acknowledge complexity and the importance of multidisciplinary and collaborative approaches to systems mapping.

A number of issues are brought to light by the co-operative inquiry in general and the particular case studies. The study reinforces the notion that cooperative inquiry can be a powerful approach to supporting participatory pedagogy for ESD academic development (see Grayford 2003; Chave 2015). Co-operative Inquiry provides a framework which encourages participation, collaboration and active learning. An important dimension of both reflective practice and co-operative inquiry is their emphasis on praxis, the ability to critically theorise one's activity in the world; which emphasises agency and our capacity to meaningfully address issues, an important ESD learning outcome (Wals 2009). The challenge here however is to resist oversimplification and reduction of complex problems, to be able to face complexity and the unknown without foreclosing it. Co-operative inquiry, as a collaborative and practitioner research method, is able to mitigate against reductivity where co-researchers have to consider how their particular experiences resonate with others and in turn reflect broader problems and issues related to ESD. Furthermore, the notion of teachers' authenticity, in terms of practicing what one preaches is seen as important for modelling practices for others (see Dawe et al. 2005). Clearly an incongruence would be set-up if academic development didactically instructed teachers in participatory approaches to ESD.

More broadly the case studies illustrate the way in which creative practice can help to mediate and articulate participants' experience in ways that raise broader questions. The two workshop examples demonstrate how a focus on the here and now can help participants articulate their experiences and share them with others. Furthermore, this goes beyond mere description and in doing so is able to explore the tacit dimensions of our experiences, whether it is the relationship with garments or with the kinds of metaphors used to describe sustainability. The strength of the approaches outlined here is that they have attempted to draw upon disciplinary and ESD pedagogies to raise sustainable issues with students. It is the authors' contention, that creative practice as a playful and potentially mindful approach to learning can help students bear the anxiety they feel regarding sustainable issues. Furthermore, the concern with material practice in which values and ideals become reified in an object can be helpful by providing a critical distance that aids reflection, discussion, evaluation and facilitate change (Cain 2010).

To support learning and motivation it is essential to be able provide positive associations with learning (Tomkins 1963). As there is an ethical responsibility to prepare academics and students for an uncertain future, it is essential to develop learning experiences that provide connections between individuals and to the more-than-human world (Danvers 2009). Approaches outlined above have encouraged thoughtful and critical action by a return to craft that slows learning and create spaces for reflection. This functions in contrast to standard models of consumption that prioritise speed and the creation of economic value over, social, environmental and emotional value. Intrinsic to art and design is the ability create or inscribe objects with meaning and emotional significance that can confront a culture of disposability by changing an individual's personal relationship to an object (Chapman 2007).

The challenge of the teacher to be empathetic attends to the affective dimension that became apparent through the inquiry. In many ways the learning problem around sustainability might be articulated by both teachers' and students' resistance to issues that make them feel powerless (Clarkson 1996). In each case co-researchers had to negotiate barriers to learning related to ESD, but also to manage the risk of asking learners to engage in creative practices which have a performative element. This performativity is most apparent in the example of participants improvising a story; such an approach can only work where the teacher is successful in creating a supportive learning space. If students' anxieties can be attended to, then there is the potential to support reflection that gives rise to heightened self-awareness that can trigger behavioural changes and is symptomatic of transformational learning (Mezirow 2000). Furthermore, it is significant that these experiences are generated within a social group; which in turn are able to set new social norms and values that can challenge the status quo, at least within the boundary of the workshop. Empathy is important not only because it is increasingly recognised as an important attribute for ESD (Eriksson 2006), but also because it is productive, one person's empathy can develop another's. Each case study demonstrates how learners create personal relevance through participatory experience, when the tension between structure and agency is sufficiently resolved. By asking learners to make decisions that inform the workshop, participants are encouraged to become active and potentially agents for change.

The Final point concerns the relationship between reflexivity, invitational leadership and sustainability literacy. An operative question for all educators, perhaps should be, how can we instil ethical agency in others? The first case study considered this directly in relation to academic development, with one measure of success being evidenced by the following case studies where participants take up the issues critically within their own practice. Here the reflexivity was two-fold in terms of the teacher reflecting and understanding their own position and agency in order to facilitate the same process with their students. Each example demonstrates how participants are encouraged through participative approaches to feed into the learning experience and shape it in varying extents. Where there exists sufficient structure, context and openness learners can be encouraged to think about their own activity in a constructive and meaningful way.

6 Conclusion

This chapter has explored the teaching of ESD in academic practice, art and design through participatory pedagogy. In particular it has attempted to demonstrate how reflective practice and cooperative inquiry can come together for practitioners to explore their own teaching and support them in developing an ethical praxis. The findings relate to the efficacy of the approach as a participatory pedagogy and so supports other work in this area, as well as drawing out some distinctive elements of art and design pedagogy that could be developed. The dimension of art and design pedagogy that has been drawn out here, such as object mediation and creation, indicates how the affective barriers to ESD might be handled in a constructive way. While the emphasis in much literature can be on what the student does, i.e. student-centred learning, the inquiry has explored the extent to which teachers lead learning and have to be attuned to the relational aspects of learning. While the latter point is indicated in theorisations of ESD teaching, the case studies are useful for providing descriptions of this in practice. The conclusions the authors have drawn from this is that participatory pedagogy has to negotiate the tensions between structure and agency and that teachers have a key role in leading this.

As a small-scale, qualitative and practitioner-based study, the research is limited in scope and does not make universal or generalizable claims. Rather it aims to illustrate a process of academic development that participants found helpful for the development of their teaching to engage others with ESD. Furthermore, whilst the research cannot make claims beyond its settings, the case studies indicate some useful approaches that others may find helpful. For example, other educators could consider how they can draw on these approaches to build their own affectively aware, playful and positive active learning experiences for their students. Further work might consider different approaches to exploring these issues both within the arts and beyond; for instance utilising less exploratory methods.

References

Abrams, D. (1997). *The spell of the Sensuous: Perception and language in a more-than-human world.* New York: Vintage Press.

Barnett, R. (2007). *A will to learn: Being a student in an age of uncertainty.* London: SRHE and OUP.

Brookfield, S. (1995). *Becoming a critically reflective teacher.* San-Francisco: Jossey-Bass.

Buzzell, L., & Chalquist, C. (Eds.). (2009). *Ecotherapy: Healing with nature in mind.* San Francisco: Sierra Club Books.

Cain, J. (2010). Practical concerns when implementing object-based teaching in higher education. *University Museums and Collections Journal, 3*, 197–203.

Chapman, J. (2007). *Emotionally durable design.* London: Earthscan.

Chave, S. (2015). Toward temporal conceptions of education as sustainability. In W. Leal Filho et al. (Eds.) (2015) *Transformative approaches to sustainable development: Working across disciplines* (pp. 325–335). Switzerland: Springer.

Clarkson, P. (1996). *The Bystander (An end to innocence in human relationships?).* London: Whurr Publishers.

Danvers, J. (2009). Being-in-the-World. In A. Stibbe (Ed.), *The handbook of sustainability literacy* (Kindle ed.). Totness: Green Books.

Dawe, G., Jucker, R., & Martin, S. (2005). *Sustainable development in higher education: current practice and future developments.* York: Higher Education Academy.

Eriksson, E. (2006). Empathetic understanding of the existential situation of fellow human beings as a field of knowledge. In J. Holmberg & B. Samuelsson (Eds.), *Drivers and barriers for implementing sustainable development in HE.* Paris: UNESCO.

Fisher, E., & Fortnum, R. (2013). *On not knowing: How artists think.* London: Black Dog Publishing.

Fletcher, K. (2007). Designers visionaries and other stories. In J. Chapman & N. Gant (Eds.), *Clothes that.* Connect, London: Earthscan.

Grayford, C. (2003). Participatory methods and reflective practice applied to research in education for sustainability. *Canadian Journal of Environmental Education, 8*, 129–142.

Hammersley, M., & Atkinson, P. (2007). *Ethnography: Principles in practice, 3rd edition.* London: Routledge.

Haque, U. (2010) *Notes on the design of participatory systems—For the city or the planet.* http://www.haque.co.uk/papers/notesonthedesignofparticipatorysystems_eng.pdf. Accessed May 15, 15.

Harding, S. (2009). Gaia Awareness. In A. Stibbe (Ed.), *The handbook of sustainability literacy* (Kindle ed.). Totness: Green Books.

Henry, A. (2009). The challenge of learning for sustainability: A prolegomenon to theory. *Research in Human Ecology, 16*(2), 131–140.

Heron, J., & Reason, P. (2001). The practice of co-operative inquiry. In P. Reason & H. Bradbury (Eds.), *Handbook of action research: Participative inquiry and practice* (pp. 179–188). London: Sage.

Hesse, D. (1993). Teachers as students, reflecting resistance. *College Composition and Communication, 44*(2), 224–231.

James, A., & Brookfield, S. (2014). *Engaging imagination: Helping students become creative and reflective thinkers*. San Francisco: Jossey-Bass.

Johnston, A. (2015). From consumer to citizen. In W. Leal Filho et al. (eds.) (2015) *Integrative approaches to sustainable development at university level* (pp 245–257). Switzerland: Springer.

McMahon, T. (1999). Is reflective practice synonymous with action research? *Educational Action Research, 7*(1), 163–169.

Mezirow, J. (2000). *Learning as transformation: Critical perspectives on a theory in progress.* San Francisco: Jossey Bass.

Shaw, M. (2014). *Snowy tower*. Oregon: White Cloud Press.

Shreeve, A., Simms, E., & Trowler, P. (2010). 'A kind of exchange': Learning from art and design teaching. *Higher Education Research and Development, 29*(2), 125–138.

Shulman, L. S. (2005a). Signature pedagogies. *Deadalus, 134*(3), 52–59.

Shulman, L. S. (2005b). Pedagogies of uncertainty. *Liberal Education.* Berlin: Spring.

Sterling, S. (2003). *Whole systems thinking as a basis for paradigm change in education: Explorations in the context of sustainability.* England: University of Bath.

Sterling, S. (2004). An analysis of the development of sustainability education internationally. In J. Blewitt & C. Cullingford, (Eds.) (2004) *The sustainability curriculum* (pp 43–62). London: Earthscan.

Sterling, S. (2013). *Future fit framework: An introductory guide to teaching and learning for sustainability in HE.* York: QAA and HEA.

Stibbe, A. (Ed.). (2009). *The handbook of sustainability literacy: Skills for a changing world.* Totnes: Green Books.

Tomkins, S. (1963). *Affect, imagery, consciousness: II.* The Negative Affects, Oxford, England: Springer.

Wals, A. (2009) *Review of contexts and structures for education for sustainable development.* Paris: UNESCO.

Understanding Our Urban Environment Better: Using Archival Research and Digital Photography in the Classroom

Julian C. Chambliss and Mike Gunter Jr.

Abstract

This pedagogical project focuses on urban environmental issues, encouraging students to explore historical events that inform contemporary environmental challenges through archival research, digital photography, and critical analysis. By examining social, economic, political, and cultural dimensions, students better understand the complex interdisciplinary nature of environmental issues and gain valuable field experience that bolsters engagement and facilitates action. Building on intellectual and reform traditions that recognize a link between narrative and action, this experiential education project encourages students to explore, define, and understand historic and contemporary environmental challenges in an urban context.

Keywords

Urban environment · Experiential education · American environmental history · Digital pedagogy · Superfund · Environmental justice · Sample assignment

J.C. Chambliss (✉)
Department of History, Rollins College, Box 2762–1000 Holt Avenue, Winter Park, FL 32789, USA
e-mail: jchambliss@rollins.edu

M. Gunter Jr.
Department of Political Science, Rollins College, Box 2762–1000 Holt Avenue, Winter Park, FL 32789, USA
e-mail: mgunter@rollins.edu

© Springer International Publishing Switzerland 2016

W. Leal Filho and P. Pace (eds.), *Teaching Education for Sustainable Development at University Level*, World Sustainability Series,
DOI 10.1007/978-3-319-32928-4_16

1 Introduction

Since the days of American educator John Dewey scholars have articulated the benefits to experiential education (Dewey 1938). Indeed, well before the early twentieth century philosophers such as Jean-Jacques Rousseau have espoused the value to learning through direct experience (Rousseau 1979). Within this intellectual tradition, our pedagogical project focuses upon urban environmental issues, encouraging students to explore for themselves historical events close to home by researching the social, economic, political, and cultural dimensions that continue to surround it.

More specifically, this pedagogical project requires students to explore historical events that inform contemporary environmental challenges through archival research, digital photography, and critical analysis. By examining social, economic, political, and cultural dimensions, students better understand the complex interdisciplinary nature of environmental issues and gain valuable field experience that bolsters engagement and facilitates action. Building on intellectual and reform traditions that recognize a link between narrative and action, this experiential education project encourages students to explore, define, and understand historic and contemporary environmental challenges in an urban context.

This is a segmented, semester-long assignment (Appendix I) where successive weeks purposely build upon earlier work in the classroom. As such, it highlights how learning is a continually evolving process, while providing opportunities for deeper reflection on the interdisciplinary nature of specific environmental issues such as Superfund sites. Students will build general research and writing skills, including an appreciation for both the power of creative narrative and the necessity for critical analysis of it.

This interdisciplinary curriculum assignment expressly recognizes the modern urban development debate grew out of concerns surrounding our complex infrastructure and the numerous systems designed to deal with urbanization's effects. Early environmentalism rested in preservation arguments grounded in aesthetic or recreation interests as well as a conservationist mentality espousing the need to harvest resources sustainably, enabling those resources to be utilized for years to come. From the mid-20th century work of (Leopold 1949) to later seminal texts by Carson (1962) and Commoner (1971) as well as the activism of Lois Gibbs at Love Canal (Gibbs 1994), modern environmentalism moved in a different direction, one recognizing ecological interdependence and the degree to which human health depended upon a healthy environment too.

Over time, the natural progression of industrial urban activities, furthermore, produced larger and larger amounts of waste that required disposal or containment. This project encourages students to explore this development while recognizing key historical antecedents that continue to effect contemporary cultural and policy debates (Tarr 2011).

The class also studies key moments in American environmental history such as the early 1970s, when the environmental costs to industrialization and urbanization in the United States were increasingly evident and combined with a more enlightened and politically empowered public to generate calls to safeguard air, water, and land. Indeed, an array of environmental laws from the National Environmental Policy Act in 1969 to the 1970 Clean Air Act and the Clean Water Act of 1972 to the Safe Drinking Water and the Endangered Species Acts of 1973 were enacted in this period. The search for balance between economic industrial activities and environmental health became and continues to be a mainstay of contemporary urban policy debate. This is what drives much of the current sustainable development discourse, for example.

Still, all too often, the failure to safely dispose of urban waste created environmental hazards that challenged communities in every state of the union. (Bullard 1993), for one, points out the degree to which these hazards disproportionately affect minority and lower income populations. Indeed, an entire literature emerged over the last twenty plus years on environmental justice, from here in the states to abroad (Shiva 2005).

Modeled on the ThirdSight History digital humanities project that combines photography and archival research developed by Julian Chambliss and its application in a history course on social issues during the 1950s and 1970s, this modified version is intended for upcoming courses on urban planning and sustainable development (Chambliss 2014). It is specifically designed to explore the complicated historical and political consequences of urban industrial waste problems. Urban populations produce significant refuse with limited viable options for disposal. Diffusion with poorly planned long-term containment represents the historic approach to the urban waste problem, and even then, with each "solution," environmental problems remain common. Not coincidentally, for instance, the infamous disposal of hazardous waste within the Love Canal neighborhood in Niagara Falls, New York, led to the Superfund legislation of today. It is in this context that our assignment addresses both historical and contemporary anxieties linked to urban environmental concerns.

2 Why History?

As the story of Love Canal further illustrates, to fully understand contemporary environmental concerns, students require a strong historical foundation. They need to understand how we arrived at this point. To understand hazardous waste disposal problems today, one needs to know from where such waste originated. One needs to know why the products that produced it were made in the first place. One needs to know how laws evolved with issues of uncertainty and inherently flawed calculation of risk as the driving force, not to mention racism and economic exploitation. One needs to understand critical scientific and health issues such as bioaccumulation and greater susceptibility to toxic agents within the young and elderly.

In short, one needs to know their environmental, social, political, and economic history.

This is true beyond the classroom as well, particularly considering the effectiveness of activist movements as they agitate for change. It's an obvious point, but one worth spelling out explicitly. The past shapes our future. It doesn't determine it in a Calvinist, predetermined sort of fashion, but rather, molds options, shaping what is both possible and impossible. It sets the table so to speak.

Those that fail to incorporate historical context, then, greatly restrict their potential for success in any activist movement. You simply cannot successfully agitate for change without a deep understanding what you are changing from. Too often, this crucial component is neglected. We pay too little attention to historical context. We repeat the mistakes of the past. With this in mind, this pedagogical project highlights an assignment that directs students through the process of connecting the past to the present. Students utilize historical archives, reading and writing about a past event, then visit that location in their community themselves to flesh out more of the how and why in the contemporary context.

3 Why Digital History?

Dialogue about digital tools and the history classroom also informed yet another precursor to this project, one generously funded by the Associated Colleges of the South and entitled "Urban Dreams and Urban Disorders." (Associated Colleges of the South 2012) That project, as well as this one, employed the American Association of Colleges and Universities' (AAC&U) learning outcomes for the 21st century to dictate its structure and goals. In part, this work is informed by the possibility of narrativizing the historical dimensions of contemporary concern through visualization. More specifically, this is a semester-long assignment that incorporates benchmarks activities that build knowledge linked to urban environmental policy, increase information fluency linked to environmental data, and promote civic awareness through site specific exploration and documentation. These efforts are achieved through archival research, experiential field engagement, and in-class readings focused on urban environmental problems. In adopting this model, the assignment follows the path described by historian David Staley that advocates for historical composition to take advantage of "…simultaneity, multidimensionality, pattern, and nonlinearity" found in visualizations (Staley 31).

While the discipline of history is rarely perceived to be at the forefront of dialogue around community engagement, technology, or experiential learning, the reality is that, since the 1990s, the American Historical Association (AHA) has recommended that courses within the history major should include substantial requirements that focus on text analysis and employ varying techniques (Giagano 2007). In recent years, the emphasis on technology transforming education further prompted some colleges and universities to integrate new techniques into to the classroom (Lewin and Markoff 2013). Despite initial efforts, recent studies challenge to what degree these have succeeded and considerable dialogue remains about the best way to integrate the benefits of digital tools into the classroom (Ayers 2013).

This work recognizes the growing opportunities to utilize technology for pedagogical projects that place students at the center of a dynamic interdisciplinary assignment exploring various strands of political, economic, social, and cultural issues within their own community. Building on the concept that digital history creates frameworks for the audience "to experience, read, and follow an argument about a historical problem," this project asks students to critically assess archival materials to create a digital narrative that addresses traditional disciplinary questions, but simultaneously offers the chance to learn and understand scholarly interpretations within a community context (Cohen et al. 2008). In form and function, this assignment blends the outcome associated with photo essay and spatial narratives built on maps to provide interpretative and critical assessment of urban environmental problems. In this way, this assignment recognizes the visually oriented experience informing contemporary student experience and leverages the "visual and digital literacy" found in the "digital native" student in contemporary college classroom. Recent work has emphasized that digital native students naturally express themselves visually through digital devices (Oblinger and Oblinger 2005). This tendency makes contemporary students ideally suited to engage with pedagogical activities designed to facilitate learning through the creation of multi-layered narratives in a digital environment.

Rather than be defined by the software or hardware, this assignment leverages the flexibility of the Wordpress content management system to create a platform to support an inquiry driven assigned aligned with urban history's traditional focus on process, practice, and consequences (Corey and Boehm 2010). The approach moves away from policy-centered analysis to a more holistic approach that incorporates social justice frameworks to create narratives grounded in local history and heightened by spatial awareness. In this way, this assignment incorporates the deep epistemological understanding generated from creating and interpreting maps. As such, this project is an example of using mapping for what Todd Presner, David Shepard, and Yoh Kawano describe as overcoming "historical erasure and silences" found in traditional static histories (Presner, Shepard, and Kawano 2014, 107). Moreover, incorporating mapping builds on a legacy of social survey documenting human behavior, identifying group need and assets, and recognizing the experience of disenfranchised communities (Hillier 2007).

This assignment also highlights the roots of modern civil betterment activism that reacted to urban waste problems at the turn of the twentieth century. Between 1900 and 1917, civic betterment efforts combined aesthetic concerns, social reform, and policy changes championed by individuals and organizations that prompted the government to address urban environment and safety concerns (Wilson 1994). A key tool in these activities was to narrativize the challenges associated with urban waste through photography and personal accounts (O'Donnell 2004). Leveraging those historic patterns in the modern classroom through the application of digital tools bolsters both student understanding and public engagement. A survey of student participants conducted in April 2015 affirmed students found this digital

Table 1 Student responsiveness to digital pedagogy

	Question	Total response	Mean	Stand dev
1	Allowed me to develop my academic reading skills	7	5.14	1.07
2	Deepened my engagement with historical primary sources	7	6	1
3	Allowed me to explore historical concerns that interested me	7	5	1
4	Facilitated my understanding of how local events were linked to state/nation	7	5.86	1.07
5	Were enhanced by use research databases in the Olin library	7	6	1.15
6	Were enhanced by engagement with the college archive	6	5.83	0.75
7	Enhanced my understanding of how historians discussed these issues	7	5.43	0.79
8	Bolstered my engagement with the community and the college	7	5.43	0.53

pedagogy increased their learning. When queried whether a digital project "Deepened my engagement with historical primary sources" student responses scored a mean of 6 on a Likert response scale of 7. On the question of whether or not this process "Facilitated my understanding of how local events were linked to state/nation" student responses scored a mean of 5.86. Utilizing this 7-point Likert scale with 1 equaling strongly disagree and 7 strongly agree, Table 1 reflects positive student responsiveness to digital pedagogy.

4 Assignment Explained

This assignment first asks students to create stories rooted in the environmental history of the region using The History Engine (Nelson 2013). The History Engine is a database project developed by Ed Ayers, Andrew Torget, Scott Nesbit, and Robert K. Nelson that utilizes traditional techniques associated with history education in a digital platform. Made up of the collective efforts of students from colleges across North America, this project asks students to use a primary source and secondary sources to "engage in a modest but challenging exercise" of historical storytelling (Nelson 2013). The goal of a History Engine episode is to understand the past from the perspective of the people who lived it. The History Engine brings the benefits of digital technology into the classroom, but the relationship between teaching and learning is enhanced. The cumulative database is the result of a dialogue between student and professor and subject to a review and screening process.

This assignment orients the student investigations around an environmental narrative in the community. The resulting episodes offer the foundation for the second part of the assignment. Having completed two episodes about the environmental history in their community, students craft an argumentative photo essay inspired by the research in their History Engine episodes. Photo essays traditionally are defined by original photography exploring place and making connections while incorporating a short critical writing component. The photo essay created in this assignment differs by incorporating both historical and spatial awareness. The photo essay contains both historical and contemporary images to create a compelling narrative around urban environmental concerns. Students must write the History Engine episodes before they complete the photo essay. Creating the narrative for the History Engine provides students with the tools to craft a critical argument through the photo essay. Pedagogically, students also learn the difference between writing a creative/contextual narrative in their History Engine episodes and the critical analysis of the photo essay.

5 Conclusions

This pedagogical project demonstrates the continuing merits of community-based experiential education, that how students learn matters. Students too often separate theory from action in their studies. To them, theory remains some distant academic interpretation of an historical event. The connection of theory to the modern world, to their daily life, is poorly understood.

As seen in this iterated assignment, archival research and digital photography are valuable tools to help address this deficiency. In a traditional class setting, for example, many students fail to draw the connections between hazardous waste disposal and the lack of political access points within many minority or disadvantaged communities. Placing students out in the field taps into the power of experiential education as espoused by Dewey and Rousseau before him. It highlights how history continues to remain relevant, particularly within the context of public policy analysis. And finally, it allows students to uncover themselves the legacy of past political power differentials, namely how they continue to shape political, economic, and social justice issues today.

Appendix I: Course Assignment

This is a segmented, semester-long assignment where successive weeks purposely build upon a student's earlier work. As such, it highlights how learning is an evolutionary process while providing opportunities for deeper reflection on the interdisciplinary nature of specific environmental issues. Students will build general research and writing skills, including appreciation for both the power of a creative narrative and the necessity for critical analysis of it.

Week 1: Explanation of Project
Presentation of sample assignment by professor.

Week 2: Overview of Urban Perspective on Society and Environment
Students gather information from the Environmental Protection Agency to identify a superfund site in their area: http://www.epa.gov/oswer/riskassessment/whereyoulive.htm.

Week 3: Local Environmental Context
After identifying local superfund sites, students conduct primary source research by examining newspaper or other archival sources linked to the designated site. Students work closely with a reference librarian to identify sources. If possible, one class session is devoted to working with archival sources in the college library as an experiential exercise.

Assignment: Research Journal

> Students begin keeping a research journal that documents their activities and reflects on the narrative attached to their archival documents. Students record their impression of the environmental narratives they are reading about.

Week 4: Personalize the Historical Narrative
Students identify the primary source that will serve as the foundation for their first History Engine episode.

Week 5: History Engine I Rough Draft
Initial draft of History Engine Episode I based on a local environmental narrative due. Meet with professor during office hours to discuss.

Assignment: History Engine Episode I

> History Engine episodes are short (400–500 words) narrative stories that spotlight the past by telling a story linked to a primary source document. Beyond a primary source, this assignment requires the student to rely on three (3) secondary sources. The secondary sources should include one (1) peer-reviewed academic journal article and one (1) academic encyclopedia entry and one (1) book chapter (or another peer-reviewed academic article).

Week 6: History Engine I Due
Completed version of History Engine Episode I due.

Week 7: Documenting Urban Environment
Students assigned urban theme photo essay as well as readings on the history of documentary photography.

Assignment: Photo Essay

> Students create a short photo essay using archival images of the local community.

Week 8: History Engine Episode II
Utilizing their first History Engine Episode, students focus more expressly on the environmental history of the region in their second History Engine episode.

Assignment: Research Journal

> Students add to their research journal, demonstrating a more developed knowledge of archival sources, i.e. more concise search procedure to find relevant material for the project, and broader understanding of the intersection of

economic, political, social, and cultural aspects when it comes to environmental issues.

Week 9: History Engine Rough Draft
Students should identify the primary source they will use for their second History Engine episode and complete a rough draft that explores the local environmental narrative.

Week 10: History Engine II
Complete second History Engine episode based on local environmental narrative.

Week 11: Digital Tools
Students test platform they will use to create their spatial photo essay. Class evaluates different options available and, once format is selected, practices proper upload procedures.

Week 12: Mapping
Students explore the impact of mapping in constructing perception and informing social dialogue.

Week 13: Outline of Spatial Photo Essay
Students develop thesis for their photo essay based on insight from researching and writing their History Engine Episodes.

Essay Components:

1. Map (pinpointing photograph locations).
2. Introduction—200 words.
3. 10 images with one-sentence captions and commentary of 25–30 words.
4. Conclusion—100 words.

Procedure:

1. Collect the images you plan to use for your essay in a single folder.
2. Create an account at flickr.com or picasaweb.com, or log into your existing account.
3. Upload the images from your folder into a single album or set.
4. Using the site's map tools, create a location map of the photos in your album.
5. Using the screen capture function on your computer, save this map as an image. Remember to crop the photograph to remove the browser window frame.
6. Create a legend for your map document explaining how each location relates to your narrative. The map and legend will be placed at the top of your photo essay as they are the first items readers use to orient themselves to your essay.

Week 14: Drafts of Spatial Photo Essay Due
Students present draft of photo essay to class. Peer feedback given during class.

Week 15: **Final submission of Spatial Photo Essay**.

References

Associated Colleges of the South. (2012). *Urban dreams and urban disorder: Transforming travel study and undergraduate archival research with collaborative digital tools* by Lloyd.

Ayers, E. L. (2013). Does digital scholarship have a future? *Educause*. 5 Aug.

Benson, L., Chambliss, J., Gunter, M., Landi, D., Robert K. N., Scott, N., & Mike, W. (2013). Final report, Atlanta. GA: Associated Colleges of the South.

Bullard, R. D. (1993). Anatomy of environmental racism and the environmental justice movement. In B. Robert (Ed.), *Confronting environmental racism: Voices from the grassroots*. Boston: South End Press, pp. 15–39.

Carson, R. (1962). *Silent spring*. Boston: Houghton Mifflin.

Chambliss, J. C. (2014). HIS 120 decade of decision 1970s. Spring, Berlin: http://social.rollins.edu/wpsites/thirdsight/

Cohen, D. J., et al. (2008). Interchange: The promise of digital history. *The Journal of American History, 95*(2), 452–491.

Commoner, B. (1971). *"The social issues", The closing circle: Nature, man & technology* (pp. 178–215). New York: Alfred A. Knopf.

Corey, S. H., & Boehm, L. K. (Eds.). (2010). *"Urban landscape: From social reform to social history". The American urban reader: History and theory* (pp. 3–22). New York: Routledge.

Dewey, J. (1938). *Experience and education*. New York: Kappa Delta Pi.

Giagano, M. J. (2007). *Liberal learning and the history major*. USA: American Historical Association.

Gibbs, L. M. (1994). The entire community seemed to be sick! In R. M. Linda (Ed.), *Ordinary Americans: U.S. history through the eyes of everyday people*, pp. 270–272.

Hillier, A. (2007). Why social work needs mapping. *Departmental papers (SPP)*.

Leopold, A. (1949). *"The land ethic", a sand county almanac: And sketches here and there*. London: Oxford University Press.

Lewin, T., & Markoff, J. (2013). California to Give Web Courses a Big Trial. *The New York Times* 15 Jan.

Nelson, R. K. (2013). Harvesting the Fruits of the undergraduate classroom. *Inside Higher Ed*. 16 Dec, 2013.

O'Donnell, E. T. (2004). Pictures vs. words? Public history, tolerance, and the challenge of Jacob Riis. *The Public Historian, 26*(3), 7–26.

Oblinger, D. G., & Oblinger, James L. (2005). *Educating the net generation*. Boulder, CO: Educause.

Presner, T., Shepard, D., & Kawano, Y. (2014). *HyperCities: Thick mapping in the digital humanities*. Cambridge, MA: Harvard University Press.

Rousseau, J.-J. (1979). *Emile: Or on education*. New York: Basic Book.

Shiva, V. (2005). *Earth democracy: Justice, sustainability, and peace*. Boston: South End Press.

Staley, D. J. (2002). *Computers, visualization, and history: How new technology will transform our understanding of the past*. White Plains, NY: M.E. Sharpe.

Tarr, J. A. (2011). The search for the ultimate sink: Urban air, land, and water pollution in historical perspective. *The search for the ultimate sink: Urban pollution in historical perspective*. Akron: The University of Akron Press.

Wilson, W. H. (1994). *The city beautiful movement*. Baltimore: Johns Hopkins University Press.

Interdisciplinary Problem-Based Learning—A Student-Centered Pedagogy to Teach Social Sustainable Development in Higher Education

Mirjam Braßler

Abstract

This article presents a pilot project at Hamburg University addressing challenges of social sustainability to students of Psychology, Economics, and Business Administration. Especially developed for teaching sustainability, *Interdisciplinary Problem-based Learning* (iPBL) is a student-centered pedagogy, combining two different teaching methods: Problem-based Learning and Interdisciplinary Learning. Fostering a multi-perspective approach to highly complex problems like corruption, health inequality, and social inequity, students work in interdisciplinary teams consisting of 8 to 10 members. After reading the problem, they follow 8 steps to identify solution approaches: (1) clarification of terms and concepts throughout the disciplines, (2) formulation of an interdisciplinary problem statement, (3) brainstorming about monodisciplinary theories, models and methods related to the problem, (4) classification and structuring of brainstorming by identifying possible connections and discrepancies throughout the disciplines, (5) formulation of interdisciplinary learning objectives, (6) self-study by reading papers across disciplines, (7) interdisciplinary post-discussion, and (8) formulation of an integrative team statement. In each team, students assign roles (discussion leader, team member and secretary). Additionally, each team is supported by a tutor. While promoting interdisciplinary thinking to develop innovative solutions, *iPBL* is designed to enhance understanding of and competence in social sustainability.

M. Braßler (✉)
Department of Work and Organizational Psychology, Hamburg University,
Von-Melle-Park 11, 20146 Hamburg, Germany
e-mail: mirjam.brassler@uni-hamburg.de

© Springer International Publishing Switzerland 2016

W. Leal Filho and P. Pace (eds.), *Teaching Education for Sustainable Development at University Level*, World Sustainability Series,
DOI 10.1007/978-3-319-32928-4_17

Keywords
Higher education · Education for social sustainable development · Interdisciplinary learning · Problem-based learning · Psychology · Economics

1 Introduction

Emergent themes of social sustainability are absence of human well-being and freedom, inequity, inequality, lacking in transparency, democratic government and society (Magis and Shinn 2009; Sen 1999; Sen 2013; UNDP 2014). Due to their complexity, those real-world problems cannot be solved within one discipline (Schmidt 2008). Toward a comprehensive understanding of these complex issues, there is a need to put sustainability and interdisciplinarity together (Blake et al. 2013; Newell 2007). Higher education is expected to enhance students' competence in dealing with such complex issues scientifically and professionally (Jacobson and Wilensky 2006), as well as interdisciplinary (Dale and Newman 2005; Newell 2009).

However, several obstacles in interdisciplinary education were identified: Students have problems overcoming barriers of disciplinary differences in epistemologies, discourses, and ways of teaching (Bradbeer 1999), teachers struggle with feelings of uncertainty and chaos in interdisciplinary classrooms (Scheer et al. 2012), and faculties are unable to evaluate interdisciplinary programs (Schilling 2001).

This paper presents a student-centered pedagogy addressing these challenges. Interdisciplinary Problem-based Learning (iPBL) combines two teaching methods: Problem-based Learning (PBL) and Interdisciplinary Learning. PBL is well known for its deliberate structure guiding students to follow seven steps to problem solving while students are assigned different roles in their group (Barrows 2002). However, adding interdisciplinarity makes the pedagogy iPBL more complex. Therefore, intended learning outcomes regarding interdisiciplinarity and sustainability need to be defined (Biggs 2003). Moreover, necessary characteristics of interdisciplinary problem cases need to be identified to equally trigger the interest of all disciplines involved. Also, extended assignments fostering interdisciplinary teamwork need to be elaborated. What do students need to consider while following the steps towards an interdisciplinary integration? What are additional assignments regarding interdisciplinary teamwork in the roles of the team members, the discussion leader and the tutor?

Finally, Biggs (2003) constructive alignment raises the question of appropriate assessment tools.

Following Sternberg's (2008) advice to put problems before the monodisciplinary tools, iPBL allows students across disciplines (exemplary Psychology, Economics and Business Administration) to explore themes of social sustainability.

2 Theoretical Framework: Constructivism

In line with the philosophical founder of constructivism, John Dewey, education should be grounded in real experience in a democratic environment that allows students to take part and decide in one's own learning (Dewey 1938, 1985). Constructivism underlies the assumption that learning is an active process, where knowledge is constructed based on personal experiences and the continual testing of hypotheses. Nowadays, constructivists distinguish between three phases of inquiry of knowledge: Reconstruction (re-production, imitation, reiteration of already existing constructions), Construction (building one's own meanings, values, reality by exploration, experimentation and experience), and Deconstruction (questioning existing constructions and discovering simplifications, incompleteness and the unconscious) (Garrison et al. 2012). Since students are confronted with authentic, challenging, complex problems and formulate questions and answers themselves, PBL is highly associated with constructivism (Marra et al. 2014; Savery and Duffy 1995). In line with social constructivists, students learn within their environment and co-construct new knowledge (Dewey 1938; Vygotsky 1978). Since disciplines can be viewed as cultures (Woods 2007) with shared values, attitudes, ways of behaving, sets of practices and knowledge (Becher and Trowler 2001), interdisciplinary learning is intercultural learning that supports students crossing disciplinary territories (Hean et al. 2012). Combining PBL and interdisciplinary learning, students can reconstruct knowledge by reproducing constructions of foreign disciplines, construct new knowledge by innovatively integrating content across disciplines, as well as deconstruct knowledge by discovering limitations of one's own discipline.

3 Empirical Results: Advantages of PBL and Interdisciplinary Learning

Originally developed in medical school programs (Barrows and Tamblyn 1980; Boud 1985), PBL is a student-centered pedagogy that triggers students with authentic ill-structured problems to express multiple thoughts and to identify and acquire missing knowledge, while teachers act as facilitators (Barrows 2002). Walker and Leary (2009) found in their cross-disciplinary meta-analysis that PBL students either did as well as or better than their lecture-based counterparts. While following a deeper understanding of the learning content (Torp and Sage 2002), PBL students have greater gains in metacognitive skills (Downing et al. 2009), critical thinking (Tiwari et al. 2006), have greater long-term retention, skill development, and higher satisfaction (Strobel and van Barneveld 2009). Moreover, PBL can support the development of "soft" skills, such as research skills, negotiation, teamwork, and reading and writing (Allen et al. 2011). PBL was found to enhance communication skills as well as foster an efficient use of learning resources (Duch et al. 2001). In line with the theory of constructivism, Chin and Chia (2004) found that students' questions facilitate learning in PBL by directing students' inquiry and scaffolding their thinking. Additionally, PBL has a positive effect on students' attitude (Veli 2014) and engagement since students consider their gained reasoning and processing skills to be valuable (Ahlfeldt et al. 2005. Murray and Summerlee 2007).

Scientific research into interdisciplinary teaching and learning in higher education was found to be limited and explorative (Spelt et al. 2009). However, more recent research shows that interdisciplinary learning enhances students' awareness of disciplinary and cultural boundaries, strengthens their ability to deal with uncertainty in scientific research, and increases their appreciation of using different perspectives in developing sustainable solutions (Fortuin and Bush 2010). Moreover, qualitative research indicates that students learn each other's scope of practice and build confidence in their communication skills (Solomon and Salfi 2011).

Interprofessional education and PBL have been successfully linked in medical education. Students' perceptions of their own professional competency and autonomy improved (Goelen et al. 2006; Cusack et al. 2012), they were more satisfied in this learning setting in comparison to others (Curran et al. 2008), and developed an appreciation of the roles of others (Solomon et al. 2003). Similar achievements can be expected for interdisciplinary problem-based learning in sustainability development education.

4 Interdisciplinary Problem-Based Learning—*Defining Learning Outcomes*

In line with Biggs' (2003) recommendation to clearly define intended learning outcomes, this curricular aims for two major ones. First, there are general interdisciplinary learning outcomes ranging from recognizing disciplinary limitations, perspectives and connections, dealing with complexity, synthesizing knowledge across disciplines (Kezar and Elrod 2012), and gaining knowledge about interdisciplinary teamwork and collaboration (Borrego and Newswander 2010). Second, there are learning outcomes regarding social sustainability development: Knowing of contemporary issues and understanding responsibility, identifying and applying available knowledge related to sustainability within one's own discipline (Svanström et al. 2008).

5 Interdisciplinary Problem-Based Learning—*Constructing Problem Cases*

In PBL literature, there are several guidelines for lecturers to constructing problem cases. Following Hung et al. (2007), PBL problems should confront students with issues that are relevant to them while fostering their development of conceptual frameworks. Moreover, problems should be realistic, challenging (but adjusted to prior knowledge), stimulating, logical, open-ended and designed with images (Azer et al. 2012).

However, iPBL problem cases require an interdisciplinary potential. Even though there is no agreed-upon term of interdisciplinarity (Klein 2010), iPBL builds upon this definition: "Interdisciplinarity is a means of solving problems and answering questions that cannot be satisfactorily addressed using single methods or approaches" (Klein 1990). Therefore, the identification of problems that cannot be solved within one discipline and, at the same time, address different disciplines is a crucial first step. Additionally, the problem should allow not only a scientific approach, but also a personal and ethical approach fostering a discussion and increasing innovation potential.

During one semester, students are confronted with five problems: 'Negotiating conflicts', 'Living and working in a social market economy?!', 'Corruption', 'Healthiness in a modern working world' and 'Change in institutions, organizations and societies'.

Exemplary, the core principle of corruption was presented as a problem case describing three situations: Political corruption in the developing country Pakistan, business corruption at Enron USA, and petty corruption at a German university (a student sleeps with a teacher to get a good grade). Since students have a resistance to learning outside their disciplinary comfort zones (McCalman et al. 2008), iPBL problem cases should include monodisciplinary triggers that are familiar to each discipline involved. In line with the strategy of synthetic interdisciplinarity teaching, iPBL combines theories and concepts from different disciplines, while the contributing disciplines remain identifiable (Lattuca 2001; Lattuca et al. 2004). In the corruption example, psychology students could contribute expertise from social, differential, developmental, and motivational psychology, while business administration and economics students could contribute expertise from development, behavioral, institutional economics, and corporate social responsibility (CSR). Since the problem of corruption in the world is not solved or scientifically fully explained yet, there are no prefabricated solutions, leaving students with a great integrative potential. Before finalizing the problem case, one should seek feedback from other researches/lectures from all disciplines involved, as disciplines differ greatly in their preferred communication patterns and identification of researchable questions (Becher and Trowler 2001).

6 Interdisciplinary Problem-Based Learning—*Participating in Tutorial Groups*

PBL groups consist of a discussion leader (a task that rotates among the participating students), between eight and ten group members (including a minutes secretary), and a tutor, who is either a lecturer or a senior student (van Til and van der Heijden 2010). Each role has to fulfil several tasks that are extended to special interdisciplinary assignments in iPBL.

Starting out with the role of the tutor, s/he is present to support students and provide guidance by motivating students to think more deeply and modelling for them the kinds of questions that they should be asking during problem-solving. In iPBL, tutors need to support interdisciplinary linkages, illustrate interdisciplinary possibilities, identify discipline-based misunderstandings, give feedback to interdisciplinary integration of content and abstain from favoritism to one discipline. Equally to monodisciplinary PBL, iPBL tutors must be trained in the steps, their role, giving feedback, and specific learning content beforehand (Raucent et al. 2010). Additionally, they have to acquaint themselves with content from the foreign discipline and in line with Golding (2009) participate in regularly supervision sessions to deal with interdisciplinary complications.

As a team member, iPBL students take notes, provide and ask for information, listen actively, and provide and receive feedback. Since interdisciplinary communication cannot work by just talking to each other because of actual differences and miscommunication (Klein 2005), team members in iPBL have to actively aim towards reciprocal comprehension and sharing knowledge, while seriously seeking consensus (Holbrook 2013). More precisely, they have to explain technical terms and disciplinary jargon after usage and ask for explanations from foreign disciplines.

As a discussion leader, iPBL students prepare, structure, and stimulate discussions, and give summaries and conclusions. To support interdisciplinary understanding, they also encourage balanced contributions from all disciplines and motivate the integration of monodisciplinary ideas.

7 Interdisciplinary Problem-Based Learning—*Following the Steps*

According to Repko (2008), interdisciplinarity needs dialectical thinking to resolve interdisciplinary conflicts, and to increase the ability to create or discover common ground and interdisciplinary integration possibilities. With the structure of eight steps, including dialectic elements like dialog, hypothesis, and synthesis, iPBL meets this demand. Since iPBL aims toward a development of interdisciplinary thinking on a broad scale (Newell 2007), integration is a constant task in every step. The first seven steps are based on classic Problem-based Learning (van Til and van der Heijden 2010), whereas the eighth step is a supplement to support an interdisciplinary agreement.

(1) *Clarification of terms and concepts across disciplines*

After reading the problem case, iPBL students recognize concepts and terms lacking clarity and provide explanations across the disciplines. This raises students' awareness to the differences across disciplines as well as to the necessity of foreign disciplines in order to gain a holistic approach of the problem case. Language and terminology differences between disciplines have been identified as essential barriers to functional interdisciplinarity (Brewer 1999; Fry 2001; Jeffrey 2003; Repko 2008). Since each discipline has its own patterns, meanings, knowledge traditions, and code of conduct (Frost and Jean 2003), this first step is crucial to frame this issue and attract attention throughout the entire teamwork.

(2) *Formulation of an interdisciplinary problem statement*

In this step iPBL students establish the boundaries of the topic. To foster a collective identification with the problem statement, the formulation should equally include aspects of all disciplines involved. Following Oberg (2009), creating a common ground is necessary to successful interdisciplinary work.

(3) *Multidisciplinary brainstorming*

To activate previous knowledge about monodisciplinary theories, models, and methods related and relevant to the problem, iPBL students collect ideas, explanations, and hypotheses for the underlying problem across the disciplines on a pin board. Especially in interdisciplinary learning, explicit mapping of main tools and concepts was found to be helpful (Woods 2007).

(4) *Interdisciplinary structuring*

Since emphasizing difference rather than similarity leads to fruitful interdisciplinary exchange (Galison 1997), iPBL students identify discrepancies, but also interrelationships and gaps in the classification of their previously collected ideas.

(5) *Formulation of interdisciplinary learning objectives*

iPBL students formulate interdisciplinary learning objectives on the basis of knowledge that is lacking. Moreover, interdisciplinary learning objectives should reflect common interests, and allow learning across disciplines related to the problem.

(6) *Self-study by reading papers across disciplines*

Particularly in interdisciplinary learning, it is important to provide students with time and freedom to weave together seemingly inconsistent perspectives (Stein et al. 2008). Therefore, iPBL students can either choose papers from a pool of papers provided by the lecturer or find appropriate papers in an independent data base research in their own time. Their task is to read, reflect, and prepare a report on one paper from their own and one from a foreign discipline.

(7) *Interdisciplinary post-discussion*

In a discussion with fellow students, answers and learning objectives across disciplines are presented in a report. Besides their summary of their own disciplinary content, each student explains concepts, theories, and research from foreign disciplines. Teaching terminology to peers from other disciplines was found supportive to negotiating shared understandings in interdisciplinary communication (Woods 2007). These understandings are crucial for connecting ideas across disciplines and identifying integrative solutions.

(8) *Formulation of an integrative team statement*

Following Becher and Trowlers' (2001) advice to avoid multidisciplinary results in interdisciplinary work, one should include not only oral but also written manifestation of exchange. Additionally, a task of written fixation forces a mutual agreement and final integration of ideas. Moreover, it increases retention.

8 Interdisciplinary Problem-Based Learning—*Assessing Interdisciplinary Work*

Following Biggs' (2003) principle of constructive alignment, good teaching systems have a high coherence between intended learning outcomes, teaching methods, and assessment. In line with previously defined learning outcomes regarding interdisciplinarity and sustainability, iPBL students follow steps towards interdisciplinary integrative solutions to real-world sustainability problems. Therefore, as an oral group exam, each iPBL team receives a sustainability problem to discuss, while following the practiced steps (2, 3, 4, 7, 8). iPBL students are informed that their teamwork is graded following Boix et al. (2007) criteria for assessing students' interdisciplinary work: (a) being well grounded in the disciplines (quantity of mentioned papers related to sustainability problem across disciplines), (b) having an advancement through integration (quality of elaboration of integrative solutions), and (c) show critical awareness (reflection on limitations of their ideas and practical implications).

9 Conclusion

While combining Problem-based learning and Interdisciplinary Learning, the student-centered pedagogy iPBL enhances students understanding of complex problems regarding social sustainability and facilitates interdisciplinary thinking towards an integrative perspective and a holistic approach to scientific and practical solutions.

However, there are several practical challenges concerning higher education institutions to take into consideration. First of all, PBL is more costly than lecture-based education: Training of tutors, tutor payments, additional rooms and complex problem development (Albanese and Mitchell 1993). One could implement multiple classroom groups to accommodate larger class sizes (Allen et al. 1996), but the other aspects remain a challenge. Moreover, the organization of interdisciplinary education is more demanding. There is additional administrative work to overcome structural barriers within predominantly discipline-based institutions (Pharo et al. 2012) involving coordinating timetables for staff meetings across disciplines and scheduled classes for students across disciplines (Golding 2009), implementing a joint platform allowing all students to enroll in class, finding a common way of granting students credit points while implementing the class in an appropriate curricular module within each discipline, and locating rooms reachable for all disciplines involved. Additionally, there is the question of financial administration (Blake et al. 2013) and who is taking on the main responsibility.

Nonetheless, realizing iPBL might be worth the trouble. Without exception all students showed a positive reaction. In line with the theory of constructivism, students reported that they enjoyed being able to construct their own knowledge, to learn about other disciplines, to recognize boundaries' of one's own discipline while feeling a flow in creating something new. Moreover, dealing with real world problems was seen as highly relevant and motivated students to engage in extra-curricular activities. Students reflected and questioned their own behavior regarding social sustainability. Following the steps helped students to gain insight into theories, models and methods from foreign disciplines without typical issues in Interdisciplinary Learning. Severe chaos (Scheer et al. 2012), unresolvable misunderstandings originated in disciplinary language differences (Jeffrey 2003) and prematurely quitting interdisciplinary teamwork (Repko 2008) could be avoided.

In addition to the benefits for students, iPBL facilitates innovative interdisciplinary integration. Exemplary, during the problem case 'corruption', students formed a concept to implicitly measure intentional corrupt behavior with projective tests. This idea combines Psychology and Economics in an innovative way that would not have been possible by one discipline alone. Using pictures as implicit measurements is well known in Psychology, whereas the identification of incentives towards corruption has a tradition in Economics.

Future iPBL courses could reach a truly holistic approach to social sustainability problems by expanding to more disciplines. For example, the problem of corruption could benefit from scientific impact of sociology, cultural anthropology or linguistics. Moreover, a combination of natural sciences and social sciences might foster new insight to complex problems.

Balancing costs and benefits, iPBL reaches surplus values by exploiting interdisciplinary potential in higher education and sustainable development.

References

Ahlfeldt, S., Mehta, S., & Sellnow, T. (2005). Measurement and analysis of student engagement in university classes where varying levels of pbl methods of instruction are in use. *Higher Education Research and Development, 24*, 5–20.

Albanese, M. A., & Mitchell, S. (1993). Problem-based learning: A review of literature on its outcomes and implementation issues. *Academic Medicine, 68*, 52–81.

Allen, D. E., Duch, B. J., & Groh, S. E. (1996). The power of problem-based learning in teaching introductory science courses In L. Wilkerson, & W. H. Gijselaers (Eds.), *Bringing problem-based learning to higher education: Theory and practice* new directions for teaching and learning. Series no 68. San Francisco: Jossey-Bass.

Allen, D. E., Donham, R. S., & Bernhardt, S. A. (2011). Problem-based learning. *New Directions for Teaching and Learning, 128*, 21–29.

Azer, A. A., Peterson, R., Guerrero, A. P. S., & Edgren, G. (2012). Twelve tips for constructing problem-based learning cases. *Medical Teacher, 34*, 361–367.

Barrows, H. S., & Tamblyn, R. S. (1980). *Problem-based learning and approach to medical education*. New York: Springer Publishing Co.
Barrows, H. S. (2002). Is it truly possible to have such a thing as DPBL? *Distance Education, 23* (1), 119–122.
Becher, T., & Trowler, P. R. (2001). *Academic tribes and territories*. Buckingham: Society for Research in Higher Education/Open University Press.
Biggs, J. (2003). *Teaching for quality learning at university: What the student does*. Buckingham, UK: Society for Research in Higher Education/Open University Press.
Blake, J., Sterling, S., & Kagawa, F. (2013). Getting it together. Interdisciplinarity and sustainability in the higher education institution. *Pedagogic Research Institute and Observatory (PedRIO), 4*, 1–71.
Boix Mansilla, V., & Duraisingh, E. D. (2007). Targeted assessment of students' interdisciplinary work: An empirically grounded framework proposed. *The Journal of Higher Education, 78*(2), 215–237.
Borrego, M., & Newswander, L. K. (2010). Definitions of interdisciplinary research. Toward graduate-level interdisciplinary learning outcomes. *The Review of Higher Education, 34*(1), 61–84.
Boud, D. J. (1985). Problem-Based Learning in Perspective. In D. Boud (Ed.), *"Problem-based learning in education for the professions" Sydney*. HERDSA: Australia.
Bradbeer, J. (1999). Barriers to interdisciplinarity: Disciplinary discourses and student learning. *Journal of Geography in Higher Education, 23*(3), 381–396.
Brewer, G. D. (1999). The challenges of interdisciplinarity. *Policy Sci., 32*(4), 327–337.
Chin, C., & Chia, L. (2004). Problem-based learning. Using students' questions to drive knowledge construction. *Science Education, 88*(5), 707–727.
Curran, V. R., Sharpe, D., Forristall, J., & Flynn, K. (2008). Student satisfaction and perceptions of small group process in case-based interprofessional learning. *Medical Teacher, 30*(4), 431–433.
Cusack, T., O'Donoghue, G., Butler, M., Blake, C., O'Sullivan, C., Smith, K., et al. (2012). A pilot study to evaluate the introduction of an interprofessional problem-based learning module. *Interdisciplinary Journal of Problem-based Learning, 6*(2), 31–45.
Dale, A., & Newman, L. (2005). Sustainable development, education and literacy. *International Journal of Sustainability in Higher Education, 6*(4), 351–362.
Dewey, J. (1938). *Experience & education*. New York, NY: Kappa Delta Pi.
Dewey, J. (1985). *Democracy and education*. Carbondale & Edwardsville: Southern Illinois University Press.
Downing, K., Kwong, T., Chan, S. W., Lam, T. F., & Downing, W. K. (2009). Problem-Based Learning and the Development of Metacognition. *Higher Education, 57*, 609–621.
Duch, B. J., Groh, S. E., & Allen, D. E. (2001). Why problem-based learning? A case study of institutional change in undergraduate education. In B. Duch, S. Groh, & D. Allen (Eds.), *The power of problem-based learning*. Stylus: VA.
Fortuin, K. P., & Bush, S. R. (2010). Educating students to cross boundaries between disciplines and cultures and between theory and practice. *International Journal of Sustainability in Higher Education, 11*(1), 19–35.
Frost, S., & Jean, P. (2003). Bridging the disciplines. Interdisciplinary discourse and faculty scholarship. *The Journal of Higher Education, 74*, 119–149.
Fry, G. L. A. (2001). Multifunctional landscapes—towards transdisciplinary research. *Landscape and Urban Planning, 57*, 159–168.
Galison, P. (1997). *Image & logic: A material culture of microphysics*. Chicago: The University of Chicago Press.
Garrison, J. W., Neubert, S., & Reich, K. (2012). *John Dewey's philosophy of education. An introduction and recontextualization for our times* (1st ed.). New York: Palgrave Macmillan.

Goelen, G., De Clercq, G., Huyghens, L., & Kerckhofs, E. (2006). Measuring the effect of interprofessional problem-based learning on the attitudes of undergraduate health care students. *Medical Education, 40*, 555–561.

Golding, C. (2009). Integrating the disciplines: Successful interdisciplinary subjects. Centre for the Study of Higher Education. Available in electronic form http://www.cshe.unimelb.edu.au/resources_teach/curriculum_design/docs/Interdisc_Guide.pdf

Hean, S., Craddock, D., & Hammick, M. (2012). Theoretical insights into interprofessional education. *Medical Teacher, 34*(2), 78–101.

Holbrook, J. B. (2013). What is interdisciplinary communication? Reflections on the very idea of disciplinary integration. *Synthese, 190*(11), 1865–1879.

Hung, W., Jonassen, D. H., & Liu, R. (2007). Problem-based learning. In J. M. Spector, J. van Merrienboer, M. D. Merrill, & M. P. Driscoll (Eds.), *Handbook of research for educational communications and technology*. Mahwah, N.J.: Lawrence Erlbaum.

Jacobson, M. J., & Wilensky, U. (2006). Complex systems in education: Scientific and educational importance and implications for the learning sciences. *The Journal of the Learning Sciences, 15*(1), 11–34.

Jeffrey, P. (2003). Smoothing the waters: Observations on the process of cross-disciplinary research collaboration. *Social Studies of Science, 33*, 539–562.

Kezar, A., & Elrod, S. (2012). Facilitating interdisciplinary learning: Lessons from project kaleidoscope. *Change: The Magazine of Higher Learning, 44*(1), 16–25.

Klein, J. T. (1990). *Interdisciplinarity: History, theory, and practice*. Detroit, MI: Wayne State University Press.

Klein, J. T. (2005). Interdisciplinary teamwork: The dynamics of collaboration and integration. In S. J. Derry, C. D. Schunn, & M. A. Gernsbacher (Eds.), *Interdisciplinary collaboration: An emerging cognitive science*. Mahwah, NJ: Lawrence Erlbaum.

Klein, J. T. (2010). A taxonomy of interdisciplinarity. In R. Frodeman, J. T. Klein, & M. Mitcham (Eds.), *The Oxford handbook of interdisciplinarity*. Oxford: Oxford University Press.

Lattuca, L. R. (2001). *Creating interdisciplinarity: Interdisciplinary research and teaching among college and university faculty*. Nashville, TN: Vanderbilt University Press.

Lattuca, L. R., Voigt, L. J., & Fath, K. Q. (2004). Does interdisciplinarity promote learning? Theoretical support and researchable questions. *The Review of Higher Education, 28*(1), 23–48.

Magis, K., & Shinn, C. (2009). Emergent themes of social sustainability. In J. Dillard, V. Dujon, & M. C. King (Eds.), *Understanding the social aspect of sustainability*. New York, NY: Routledge.

Marra, R. M., Jonassen, D. H., Palmer, B., & Luft, S. (2014). Why problem-based learning works: Theoretical foundation. *Journal on Excellence in College Teaching, 25*(3&4), 221–238.

McCalman, J., Muir, L., & Soeterboek, C. (2008). *Adventures with breadth: A story of interdisciplinary innovation*. Melbourne: Centre for the Study of Higher Education.

Murray, J., & Summerlee, A. (2007). The impact of problem-based learning in an interdisciplinary first-year program on student learning behaviour. *Canadian Journal of Higher Education, 37*, 87–107.

Newell, W. H. (2007). Decision making in interdisciplinary studies. In G. Morçöl (Ed.), *Handbook of decision making*. New York: CRC.

Newell, W. H. (2009). Interdisciplinarity in undergraduate general education. In R. Frodeman, J. T. Klein, & C. Mitcham (Eds.), *The Oxford handbook on interdisciplinarity*. Oxford: Oxford University Press.

Oberg, G. (2009). Facilitating interdisciplinary work: Using quality assessment to create common ground. *Higher Education, 57*, 405–415.

Pharo, E. J., Davison, A., Warr, K., Nursey-Bray, M., Beswick, K., Wapstra, E., & Jones, C. (2012). Can teacher collaboration overcome barriers to interdisciplinary learning in a disciplinary university? A case study using climate change. *Teaching in Higher Education, 17* (5), 497–507.

Raucent, B., Hernandez, A., & Moore, G. (2010). *Training PBL tutors: How can we meet their needs?*. Working Paper.

Repko, A. F. (2008). *Interdisciplinary research*. Thousand Oaks, CA: Sage.

Savery, J. R., & Duffy, T. M. (1995). Problem based learning: An instructional model and its constructivist framework. *Educational Technology, 35*(5), 31–38.

Scheer, A., Noweski, C., & Meinel, C. (2012). Transforming constructivist learning into action: design thinking in education. *Design and Technology Education: an International Journal, 17* (3), 8–18.

Schilling, K. L. (2001). Interdisciplinary assessment for interdisciplinary programs. In B. L. Smith & J. McCann (Eds.), *Reinventing ourselves: Interdisciplinary education, collaborative learning and experimentation in higher education*. Anker: Bolton, MA.

Schmidt, J. (2008). Towards a philosophy of interdisciplinarity—an attempt to provide a classification and clarification. *Poiesis & Praxis, 5*(1), 53–69.

Sen, A. (1999). *Development as freedom*. New York, NY: Alfred A. Knopf.

Sen, A. (2013). The ends and means of sustainability, Journal of human development and capabilities. *A Multi-Disciplinary Journal for People-Centered Development, 14*(1), 6–20.

Solomon, P., & Salfi, J. (2011). Evaluation of an interprofessional education communication skills initiative. *Education for Health, 24*(2), 616–626.

Solomon, P., Salvatori, P., & Guenter, O. (2003). An interprofessional problem-based learning course on rehabilitation issues in HIV. *Medical Teacher, 25*, 408–413.

Spelt, E. J. H., Biemans, H. J. A., Tobi, H., Luning, P. A., & Mulder, M. (2009). Teaching and learning in interdisciplinary higher education: A systematic review. *Educational Psychology Review, 21*(4), 365–378.

Stein, Z., Connell, M., & Gardner, H. (2008). Exercising quality control in interdisciplinary education: Toward an epistemologically responsible approach. *Journal of Philosophy of Education, 42*(3–4), 401–414.

Sternberg, R. J. (2008). Interdisciplinary problem-based learning: An alternative to traditional majors and minors. *Liberal Education, 94*(1), 12–17.

Strobel, J., & van Barneveld, A. (2009). When is PBL more effective? A meta-synthesis of meta-analyses comparing PBL to conventional classrooms. *Interdisciplinary Journal of Problem-based Learning, 3*(1), 44–58.

Svanström, M., Lozano-García, F. J., & Rowe, D. (2008). Learning outcomes for sustainable development in higher education. *International Journal of Sustainability in Higher Education, 9*(3), 339–351.

Tiwari, A., Lai, P., So, M., & Yurn, K. (2006). A comparison of the effects of problem-based learning and lecturing on the development of students' critical thinking. *Medical Education, 40*, 547–554.

Torp, L., & Sage, S. (2002). *Problems as possibilities: Problem-based learning for K-16 education* (2nd Edition.), Alexandria, VA: Association for Supervision and Curriculum Development.

United Nations Development Programme. (2014). *Human Development Report 2014: Sustaining Human Progress: Reducing vulnerabilities and building resilience*. Basingstoke, United Kingdom: Palgrave Macmillan. Available in electronic form http://hdr.undp.org/en/2014-report/download

van Til, C., & van der Heijden, F. (2010). *PBL Study Skills—An overview*. Department of Educational Development & Research, Maastricht University.

Veli, B. (2014). The effects of a problem based learning approach on students attitude levels. A meta-analysis. *Educational Research Review, 9*(9), 272–276.

Vygotsky, L.S. (1978). *Mind in society: The development of higher psychological processes*. Cambridge, MA: Harvard University Press. (Originally published 1930, New York: Oxford University Press).

Walker, A., & Leary, H. (2009). A problem based learning meta analysis: Differences across problem types, implementation types, disciplines, and assessment levels. *Interdisciplinary Journal of Problem-based Learning, 3*(1), 12–43.

Woods, C. (2007). Researching and developing interdisciplinary teaching: Towards a conceptual framework for classroom communication. *Higher Education, 54*(6), 853–866.

Teaching for Sustainability at University: Constructively Aligned Study Course Design

Eglė Katiliūtė

Abstract

The educational environment created by university lecturers influences student learning, knowledge progress and self-realisation. In the professionally designed educational environment, all knowledge acquirement ways acceptable to students are promoted, a variety of learning forms and methods are tolerated, and evaluation results are used for promoting successful learning and teaching process improvement. To maximise the quality of learning outcomes, courses developed by university lecturers should provide students with sufficient teaching and learning materials, and contain tasks and experiences which are authentic, real-world based and relevant; are constructive, sequential and interlinked; require students to use progressively higher order cognitive processes; are aligned with each other and with the desired learning outcomes; and provide challenge, interest and motivation to learn. Although researchers have recognised that constructive alignment is an important educational tool for study design, the experience of university lecturers revealed various difficulties in applying this approach (Blumberg in Innovative Higher Education 34(2), 93–103, 2009; Biggs in Higher Education 32(3), 347–364, 1996 1996; Biggs in Higher Education Research and Development 18(1), 57–75, 1999; Meyers and Nulty in Assessment and Evaluation in Higher Education 34, 565–577, 2009). In this paper, constructively aligned study course design as an approach and a teaching tool for sustainability implementation practise is analysed. Results of a survey conducted to evaluate the attitude of university lecturers to this approach are also presented. It should be stressed that the constructive alignment approach can significantly increase the quality of teaching in the area of sustainability and change the attitude of university lecturers to sustainability.

E. Katiliūtė (✉)
Department of Management, Kaunas University of Technology,
K.Donelaičio Str. 73, Kaunas, Lithuanian
e-mail: egle.katiliute@ktu.lt

© Springer International Publishing Switzerland 2016

W. Leal Filho and P. Pace (eds.), *Teaching Education for Sustainable Development at University Level*, World Sustainability Series,
DOI 10.1007/978-3-319-32928-4_18

Keywords
University • Teaching for sustainability • Constructively aligned course design • Lecturers' attitude

1 Introduction: Constructively Aligned Course Design and Sustainability

Complexity, chaos and uncertainty of future situations are the keywords that define the state of the modern dynamic society where knowledge and knowing become the main assets instead of material resources. Changes in societal development raise new challenges for education as a whole, including contemporary higher education that is experiencing a period of transformation: higher education is becoming a mass phenomenon (Barnett 1990; Devlin and Samarawickrema 2010); the concepts of research, methodologies and scientific knowledge are changing (Kitchener and King 1989; Barnett 2000, 2011; Gibbons 1994); the quality of studies and teaching demands an orientation to sustainability (Blake et al. 2011; Dawe et al. 2005; Sterling 2004, 2012; Tomkinson 2010; Lozano 2010; Watson et al. 2013).

A fundamental shift in thinking, values and action by all professionals and the general population is needed, and this requires a shift in the university didactic system. Therefore, new challenges emerge for the competence and practice of a university teacher. Special focus is placed on constructivist-approach based learning instead of on traditional teaching practice perceived as a transfer of knowledge and skills. The learning process is treated as active construction of knowledge and meaning that relies on collaboration and reflective inquiry into one's practice. In this sense, the memorization of knowledge has to be replaced by the exploration and transformation of the individual's conceptual understanding, values and attitudes, i.e. teacher and students have to share their ways of seeing the world and in that way to learn from each other. A teacher has to foster a student's innovative reasoning and creativity, to teach a student how to learn and to construct knowledge, to apply meta-learning methods and to organise self-directed learning in order to empower the student for acting in unknown and unforeseen future situations (Gray 1997; Bowden and Marton 1998; Howell 2002; Stanikūnienė 2006).

There are many effective study course design and educational environment elements that can be distinguished: (i) course-content adequacy for study program learning outcomes and sustainable development principles; (ii) variety of teaching methods; (iii) course-content alignment to other courses; (iv) collaboration with lecturers of other courses; (v) objectivity and fairness of assessment; (vi) feedback system; (vii) constructive learning environment; etc. Constructive alignment assumes that intentional alignment of learning objectives, assessment methods, and teaching/learning activities substantially improves the outcomes of learning (Blumberg 2009). The process of constructive alignment emphasises that students are central to the creation of meaning and must be provided with opportunities to actively select and cumulatively construct their own knowledge (Biggs 1996, 1999). Meyers and Nulty (2009) provide recommendations for designing a course based upon Biggs' approach to constructive alignment.

The principles of constructive alignment (Biggs 1996, 1999; Biggs and Tang 2011) have long been promoted as a powerful approach to facilitating improved learning outcomes for a broader range of students. Despite some concern in the science education sector that constructivist approaches undermine the mastery of disciplinary knowledge and independent thinking (Jervis and Jervis 2005), there has been considerable attention in recent years given to the concepts of constructive alignment (Boud and Falchikov 2006) and a general view as to its benefits (Rust 2002; Larkin and Richardson 2013). However, there is little evidence and discussion of its direct and indirect linking with sustainability, implementation for sustainability teaching and evaluation of this approach from a university teacher perspective.

The aim of this paper is to examine how constructively aligned course design contributes to sustainability teaching. The research question that guided the work presented in this paper can be formulated as following: How can a teacher organise the constructively aligned course design for meaningful sustainability teaching? How can university teachers evaluate the use of constructively aligned course design elements in their courses?

2 Constructively Aligned Study Course Design as an Approach and a Tool for Sustainability Teaching

Teaching sustainability is rather challenging, because it is not merely transmitting knowledge, but also learning on critical thinking, complexity, values and ethics (Corcoran et al. 2002; Segalàs et al. 2008). Sustainable development competences are differently reported by several authors, but similar characteristics are used: responsibility (values, ethics, and reflection), system orientation, future orientation, emotional intelligence (empathy, solidarity, and compassion), personal involvement (self-motivation, motivating others, learning) and participatory skills (De Haan 2006; Sleurs 2008; Roorda 2010; Lambrechts et al. 2013). Education for sustainable development means working with students to encourage them: (i) to consider what the concept of global citizenship means in the context of their own discipline and in their future professional and personal lives, (ii) to consider what the concept of environmental stewardship means in the context of their own discipline and in their future professional and personal lives; (iii) to think about issues of social justice, ethics and wellbeing, and how these issues relate to ecological and economic factors, (iv) to develop a future-facing outlook and learning to think about the consequences of actions, and how systems and societies can be adapted to ensure sustainable future (Longhurst et al. 2014). Therefore, a deep approach and meaningful learning become crucial in teaching sustainability. A deep approach "*arises from a felt need to engage the task appropriately and meaningfully, so the student tries to use the most appropriate cognitive activities for handing it*" (Biggs and Tang 2011, pp. 24), while a surface approach "*arises from an intention to get the task out of the way with minimum trouble, while appearing to meet course requirements*" (Biggs and Tang 2011, p. 22). It is necessary, but not sufficient, to integrate sustainability into the intended learning outcomes of a course or a study program curriculum. When university teachers apply constructively aligned course design, they try to ensure a deep approach and meaningful learning.

Constructivist learning theory (Dewey 1933; Piaget 1962; Bruner 1973; Von Glasersfeld 1995; Steffe and Gale 1995; Gray 1997) claims that a human being refers to his previous experience and creates his individual knowing in interaction with the surrounding environment. Learning takes place when a person doubts his beliefs, personal theories and existing understanding. The construction of knowledge is an active process of meaning construction. Learners construct knowledge with their own activities, building on what they already know. Teaching is not a matter of transmitting but of engaging students in active learning, building their knowledge in terms of what they already understand (Biggs and Tang 2011). Moreover, knowledge is socially attributed to the creator of the meaning.

The constructivist ideas bear significance for the higher school teacher in two perspectives: first, in pedagogical activity a teacher has to be able to assist students in learning and developing their meta-learning competence; second, a teacher himself becomes a learner in his activity, since he has to gain skills for applying new learning methods, to know the way his students reason learning process, to know their existing knowledge and experience. Special focus is placed on the teacher's skills for performing reflection, and investigating and evaluating his own existing understanding, and the attitudes and values his activity is based on (Stanikūnienė 2006). Constructive alignment reflects a paradigm shift from teacher-centred to student-centred teaching and learning, which emphasises encouraging and supporting students' construction of their own knowledge inside and outside the classroom instead of the teacher's transmission of the knowledge in class (Tran et al. 2010). Pedagogical approaches that are particularly effective in the context of education for sustainable development tend to have an authentic aspect enabling students to relate their learning to real-life problems and situations. There is likely to be a strong interdisciplinary, multidisciplinary or transdisciplinary element, reflecting the interconnected nature of many issues in sustainable development. Experiential and interactive approaches are also especially well suited to education for sustainable development, particularly where they encourage students to develop and reflect on their own and others' values (Longhurst et al. 2014).

Biggs (1996) outlined the principles of constructive alignment as emerging from a constructivist approach to teaching and learning. The alignment aspect of constructive alignment refers to establishing a teaching environment where the teaching activities support and lead to the achievement of the desired learning outcomes as evidenced by students' engagement with the assessment tasks. Thus, the learning outcomes, teaching methods and assessment tasks are all aligned (Larkin and Richardson 2013). Assessment should provide opportunities for students to demonstrate achievement of graduate outcomes in the core areas of global citizenship; environmental stewardship; social justice, ethics and wellbeing; and future thinking (Longhurst et al. 2014). When assessment is not aligned with the intended or other desired outcomes, or when teaching methods do not directly encourage the appropriate learning activities, students can easily 'escape' by engaging in inappropriate learning activities that become a surface approach to learning. Constructive alignment is a marriage between a constructivist understanding of the nature of learning and an aligned design for teaching that is designed to lock students into deep learning (Biggs and Tang 2011).

Structure of the Observed Learning Outcomes (SOLO) taxonomy (Biggs and Collis 1982; Biggs 1999) describes the level of increasing complexity in a student's understanding of a subject through five stages: prestructural (student demonstrates no understanding of the desired learning), unistructural (student demonstrates understanding of only one item relevant to the desired learning), multistructural (student demonstrates understanding of more than one relevant item, but items are seen as independent or unrelated to each other), relational (items are described as part of an overall structure and interrelated (not necessarily a greater number of items nominated than in multi-structural), and extended abstract [items are described as part of an overall structure, and elements of the structure are seen to be applicable in other situations (i.e. transferable or generalizable)]. The SOLO taxonomy is based on the study of outcomes of academic teaching. SOLO can be used to define intended learning outcomes (ILOs) for sustainable development, forms of teaching that support them, and forms of assessment that evaluate to what extent the ILOs were achieved. It is developed aiming at research-based university teaching as the research activities behind it ultimately converge on real research at its fifth and highest level (Brabrand and Dahl 2009). Teaching, learning and assessment should be constructively aligned, ensuring that the assessment task and pedagogic approaches reflect the learning outcomes, which students are expected to achieve. There are a number of teaching and learning methods that are likely to be particularly effective. Depending upon the discipline or the sustainability challenge to be addressed, these may include one, some or all of the following: case studies, stimulus activities, simulation, experiential project work, and problem-based learning (Longhurst et al. 2014). Implementation strategy of constructive alignment is a continuing action learning cycle of reflection, application and evaluation (Biggs and Tang 2011).

3 The Research Methodology

The research aim is to evaluate university teachers' attitude to constructive alignment and sustainability integration at the course level.

The methodology adopted is quantitative. The total sample consisted of 435 teachers working in a university in one major city (Lithuania) surveyed. Research participants represented 5 science spheres (social sciences, technological sciences, physical sciences, biomedicine science and humanities). The survey format was an electronic self-completion questionnaire with closed-ended questions and scaled responses, which provided the respondents with a defined set of answers. Prior to distributing the questionnaire, a pretesting procedure with twelve people (hereinafter *experts*), was conducted. Experts were university teachers working in managerial positions. As a result of this phase, some items from the questionnaire were eliminated. These experts did not participate as respondents in the further research.

Data were collected between 1 November 2013 and 23 December 2013 by an original questionnaire distributed to 841 (total population) university teachers in one university in Lithuania. The response rate was 52 %. SSPSS 16.0 for Windows was used to process the collected data.

The survey was carried out by applying a non-standardized questionnaire consisting of an introductory part, a block of demographic questions and a diagnostic block of variables (11 statements). To evaluate the factors disclosing the university teachers' attitude manifestation, the 4 point Likert scale was used (from "1"—do not agree at all, to "4"—totally agree). Moreover, the respondents could point out that they do not have opinion on a given question. The initial step in the survey analysis was grouping the answers. In the analysis of the most manifested factors, the answers with "3" (agree) and "4" (totally agree) have been joined. The factors with very low manifestation ("2") or ("1") were also combined in the survey findings.

4 University Teachers' Attitude to Constructive Alignment at the Course Level

The survey results revealed a positive attitude of university teachers to constructively aligned course design. Most university teachers agreed that they are trying to implement constructively aligned study course design elements (see Fig. 1). Almost all university teachers agreed that they always present the course curriculum to students (99 %), try to align learning outcomes with teaching and evaluation methods (98 %), and encourage students to take responsibility for their own learning (96 %). The most challenging area for teachers is responding to recommendations from social partners.

Survey participants were asked to identify where improvements are needed in the same constructively aligned course design elements (see Fig. 2). Most teachers agree that they need improvement in aligning learning outcomes, teaching and evaluation methods (85 %). To create an environment that promotes student learning and to use problem-based teaching are the second and third priorities for improvement.

Areas that require less improvement are the integration of sustainable development principles in the curriculum of the courses, and course curriculum presentation to students.

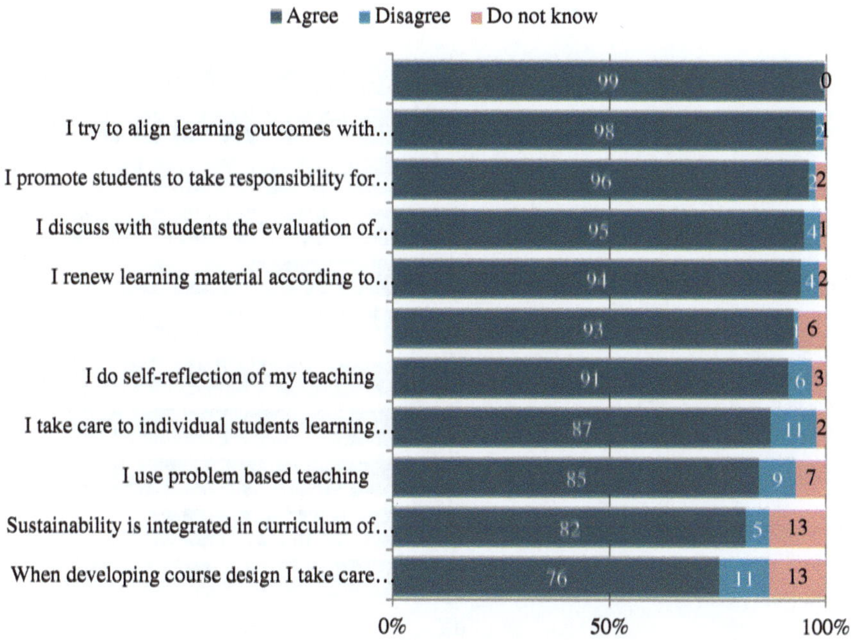

Fig. 1 University teachers' attitude to constructively aligned course design elements (% from all respondents, n = 435)

5 Conclusion

In conclusion, it could be stated that despite the attention given to the importance and relevance of constructive alignment over a number of years, analysis of teachers' perspective on this approach has been limited. This study provides an example for applying constructive alignment in sustainability teaching, and evaluating this teaching and learning approach from a teacher's perspective. Constructive alignment can ensure that each student is able to embrace a deep approach to learning. Therefore, the constructive alignment approach can significantly increase the quality of teaching in the area of sustainability.

The approaches taken by current university teachers to constructive alignment are promising. Teachers agree that they need to define clear learning objectives, to enlist teaching methods, to apply assessment/evaluation expertise, and to align constructively all aspects of the curriculum. The scientific insights in regard to the interaction between sustainability teaching and constructive alignment prescribe the necessity of further research. Additional quantitative studies, and especially qualitative studies, based on theoretical insights into the link between sustainability teaching and the constructive alignment approach, will provide new knowledge on

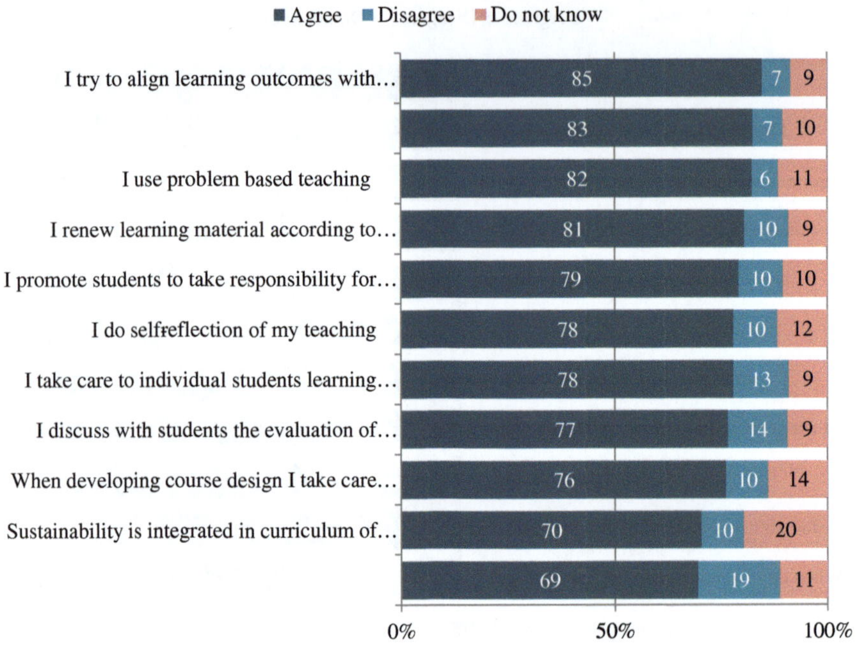

Fig. 2 University teachers' attitude to the need for improvements in constructively aligned course design elements (% from all respondents, n = 435)

the interaction of concepts delivered within the construct based on actual collaboration between teachers and students in the study process that conditions deep understanding of sustainability as well as new attitudes and values.

References

Barnett, R. (1990). The idea of higher education. 1900 Frost Rd., Suite 101, Bristol, PA 19007: Society for Research into Higher Education and Open University Press.

Barnett, R. (2000). Realizing the university in an age of super complexity. New York: McGraw-Hill International.

Barnett, R. (2011). Lifewide education: A new and transformative concept for higher education. *Learning for a complex world: A lifewide concept of learning, education and personal development*, pp. 22–38. Author House.

Biggs, J. (1996). Enhancing teaching through constructive alignment. *Higher Education, 32*(3), 347–364.

Biggs, J. (1999). What the student does: Teaching for enhanced learning. *Higher Education Research and Development, 18*(1), 57–75.

Biggs, J. B., & Collis, K. F. (1982). *Evaluation the quality of learning: The SOLO taxonomy (structure of the observed learning outcome)*. USA: Academic Press.

Biggs, J., & Tang, C. (2011). *Teaching for quality learning at university* (4th ed.). Maidenhead: McGraw—Hill/Open University Press/Society for Research into Higher Education.

Blake, J., & Sterling, S. (2011). Tensions and transitions: Effecting change towards sustainability at a mainstream university through staff living and learning at an alternative, civil society college. *Environmental Education Research, 17*(1), 125–144.

Blumberg, P. (2009). Maximizing learning through course alignment and experience with different types of knowledge. *Innovative Higher Education, 34*(2), 93–103.

Boud, D., & Falchikov, N. (2006). Aligning assessment with long-term learning. *Assessment & Evaluation in Higher Education, 31*(4), 399–413.

Bowden, J., & Marton, F. (1998). *The University of Learning: Beyond quality and competence in university education*. London: Kogan Page.

Brabrand, C., & Dahl, B. (2009). Using the SOLO taxonomy to analyze competence progression of university science curricula. *Higher Education, 58*(4), 531–549.

Bruner, J. (1973). *Going beyond the Information given*. New York: Norton.

Corcoran, P. B., Calder, W., & Clagston, R. M. (2002). Introduction: Higher education for sustainable development. *Higher Education Policy, 15*(2), 99–103.

Dawe, G., Jucker, R., & Martin, S. (2005). Sustainable development in higher education: Current practice and future developments. In K. S. Kitchener & P. M. King (1990). *The reflective judgment model: Ten years of research*. New York (UK): A report to the Higher Education Academy. (http://www.heacademy.ac.uk/assets/York/documents/ourwork/tla/sustainability/sustdevinHEfinalreport.pdf)

De Haan, G. (2006). The BLK '21' programme in Germany: A 'Gestaltungskompetenz'—Based model for education for sustainable development. *Environmental Education Research, 12*, 19–32.

Devlin, M., & Samarawickrema, G. (2010). The criteria of effective teaching in a changing higher education context. *Higher Education Research & Development, 29*(2), 111–124.

Dewey, J. (1933). *How we think*. Boston, MA: Houghton Mifflin Company.

Gibbons, M. (1994). Transfer sciences: Management of distributed knowledge production. *Empirica, 21*(3), 259–270.

Gray, A. (1997). Contructivist teaching and learning. *SSTA Research Centre Report*, 97–07.

Howell, C. L. (2002). Facilitating responsibility for learning in adult community college students. ERIC Clearinghouse for Community Colleges.

Jervis, L. M., & Jervis, L. (2005). What is the constructivism in constructive alignment? *Bioscience Education BEE-j, 6*. http://www.bioscience.heacademy.ac.uk/journal/vol6/Beej-6–5.pdf

Kitchener, K. S., & King, P. M. (1989). The reflective judgement model: Ten years of research. In M. L. Commons, C. Armon, L. Kohlberg, F. A. Richards, T. A. Grotzer, & J. D. Sinnot (Eds.), *Adult development 2: Models and methods in the study of adolescent and adult thought* (pp. 63–78). New York: Praeger.

Lambrechts, W., Mulà, I., Ceulemans, K., Molderez, I., & Gaeremynck, V. (2013). The integration of competences for sustainable development in higher education: An analysis of bachelor programs in management. *Journal of Cleaner Production, 48*, 65–73.

Larkin, H., & Richardson, B. (2013). Creating high challenge/high support academic environments through constructive alignment: student outcomes. *Teaching in higher education, 18*(2), 192–204.

Longhurst, J., Bellingham, L., Cotton, D., Isaac, V., Kemp, S., Martin, S., Peters, C., Robertson, A., Ryan, A.,Taylor, C., and Tilbury, D and Quality Assurance Agency, Higher Education Academy. (2014). *Education for sustainable development: Guidance for UK higher education providers*. Technical Report. QAA: Gloucester. Available from:http://eprints.uwe.ac.uk/23353

Lozano, R. (2010). Diffusion of sustainable development in universities' curricula: An empirical example from Cardiff University. *Journal of Cleaner Production, 18*(7), 637–644.

Meyers, N. M., & Nulty, D. D. (2009). How to use (five) curriculum design principles to align authentic learning environments, assessment, students' approach to thinking and learning outcomes. *Assessment and Evaluation in Higher Education, 34*, 565–577.

Piaget, J. (1962). *The Language and thought of the child*. London: Routledge & Kegan Paul.

Roorda, N. (2010). Sailing on the winds of change. The Odyssey to sustainability of the universities of applied Sciences in the Netherlands. Ph.D. thesis. Netherlands: Maastricht University.

Rust, C. (2002). The impact of assessment on student learning: How can the research literature practically help to inform the development of departmental assessment strategies and learner-centred assessment practices? *Active Learning in Higher Education, 3*, 145–158.

Segalàs, J., Ferrer-Balas, D., & Mulder, K. F. (2008). Conceptual maps: Measuring learning processes of engineering students concerning sustainable development. *European Journal of Engineering Education, 33*(3), 297–306.

Sleurs, W. (Ed.). (2008). Competences for ESD (education for sustainable development) teachers. *A Framework to Integrate ESD in the Curriculum of Teacher Training Institutes (Brussels), 2*, 1–90. Available:www.unece.org/fileadmin/DAM/env/esd/inf.meeting.docs/EGonInd/8mtg/CSCT%20Handbook_Extract.pdf

Stanikūnienė, B. (2006). Reflective teachers in higher education: different perception and acting in their learning environments. *Social Sciences, 53*(3), 0758–1392.

Steffe, L. P., & Gale, J. E. (Eds.). (1995). *Constructivism in education (p. 159)*. Hillsdale, NJ: Lawrence Erlbaum.

Sterling, S. (2004). Higher education, sustainability, and the role of systemic learning. In *Higher education and the challenge of sustainability* (pp. 49–70). Netherlands: Springer.

Sterling, S. (2012). *The future fit framework: An introductory guide to teaching and learning for sustainability in HE*. Retrieved 23 Nov, 2012.

Tomkinson, B. (2010). Education to face the wicked challenges of sustainability. *Journal of Social Sciences, 7*(1), 1.

Tran, N. D., Nguyen, T. T., & Nguyen, M. T. N. (2010). The standard of quality for HEIs in Vietnam: A step in the right direction? *Quality Assurance in Education, 19*(2), 130–140.

Von Glasersfeld, E. (1995). A constructivist approach to teaching. *Constructivism in Education*, 3–15.

Watson, M. K., Lozano, R., Noyes, C., & Rodgers, M. (2013). Assessing curricula contribution to sustainability more holistically: Experiences from the integration of curricula assessment and students' perceptions at the Georgia Institute of Technology. *Journal of Cleaner Production, 61*, 106–116.

Development of the Green-Campus Programme in Ireland: Ensuring Continuity of Environmental Education and Action for Sustainable Development Throughout the Irish Education System

Yvonne Ryan-Fogarty, Deirdre O'Carroll, Michael John O'Mahony and Bernadette O'Regan

Abstract

Ensuring education for sustainable development (ESD) programmes deliver meaningful action within society presents significant challenges including systemic integration, consistency of methods, and safeguarding relevance and quality. The Eco-Schools Programme, intended initially as an international environmental educational initiative, has developed, through thematic implementation processes and extensive collaboration with governmental agencies and non-governmental organisations (NGOs) to embrace both environmental education and ESD. Eco-Schools evolved from the Blue Flag Programme for beaches and marinas and is coordinated at an international level by the Foundation for Environmental Education. The Programme has operated in Ireland since 1997 with over 93 % of all primary and second level schools currently participating. Students from Eco-Schools progressing further through the education system demanded ESD action on reaching university leading to the development of the Green-Campus Programme (GCP). All Irish Universities and more than half of Institutes of Technology are involved to some extent in the programme with many awarded Green-Campus status, meaning these sites engaged with the GCP, committed to continual improvement and self-elected for verification through detailed assessment processes. The GCP was successfully implemented in Cork University Hospital, Ireland's largest teaching hospital and has formed strategic partnerships and action platforms with governmental

Y. Ryan-Fogarty (✉) · B. O'Regan
Department of Chemical and Environmental Sciences, University of Limerick, Limerick, Ireland
e-mail: yvonne.ryan@ul.ie

D. O'Carroll · M.J. O'Mahony
Environmental Education Unit, An Taisce, Unit 5a, Swifts Alley, Dublin 8, Ireland

© Springer International Publishing Switzerland 2016

W. Leal Filho and P. Pace (eds.), *Teaching Education for Sustainable Development at University Level*, World Sustainability Series,
DOI 10.1007/978-3-319-32928-4_19

agencies, supporting NGOs and relevant policy initiatives. The evolution and development of the GCP in Ireland was mainly an organic process, however, evaluation of this case study reveals a flexible, dynamic framework which international policy makers and NGOs can imitate in order to champion enduring ESD programmes that are responsive as well as responsible.

1 Introduction

1.1 Greening Campuses

It is increasingly recognised that the institutions charged with academic research, innovative development and education of the leaders of the future, namely higher education facilities, are contributing significantly to environmental damage and failing in their duty of care toward the environment (Association of University Leaders for a Sustainable Future 2008). Third level campuses have come under increasing pressure to include sustainability into their mission, plans and policies, however the assumption should not be made that inclusion of policy leads to enhanced performance (Velazquez et al. 2006). Transformation of education for sustainable development programmes to meaningful action within society presents significant challenges including systemic integration, consistency of methods, and ensuring relevance and quality. Analyses of planned retrofit of facilities with new technologies and new-build greener campuses suggest future positive outcomes (Li et al. 2014). Recent economic constraints mean that refurbishments, new-builds and technologies cannot be solely relied on to deliver complete environmental improvement (Huesemann 2011), therefore existing facilities must act. Evidence of campus' engagement in sustainability initiatives is growing; some elect for public commitments to act on sustainability through peer agreements e.g. Tallories Declaration (Koester et al. 2006), peer support networks have been established such as the Environmental Association for Universities and Colleges in the UK, whilst more engage with systems to produce metrics and rankings such as UI Green Metric (UI Green Metric 2014). Prior to the emergence of green rankings, concerns had been expressed regarding the use of cross institutional comparison assessment tools, noting that the more useful tools "reflect the transition in thought from environmental management to management for sustainability" (Shriberg 2002). Best practice guidance on greening education are available through international peer reviewed literature and support organisations nevertheless stakeholder attitudes and behaviours contribute most to the environmental performance of an organisation (Porter-O'Grady and Malloch 2010). Therefore, the ultimate realisation of campus sustainability is dependent on a diversity of actors including the campus community, national policy makers, and support organisations.

Notwithstanding the role campuses play in their own realisation of sustainability goals, campuses can serve as "living laboratories" most importantly influencing stakeholders at key life event stages. Many campuses, similar to the Environmental Campus Birkenfeld, Germany build capacity and collaboration through cooperative efforts with local communities to practice sustainability using cutting edge technology to achieve zero emissions and focussing on future-oriented education (Umwelt Campus Birkenfeld 2015). There is growing acknowledgement that key life events can be used to influence behaviour and induce sustainable consumption patterns (DEFRA 2011). The distinctive attributes of educational campus communities have been used in creative ways to enhance sustainability measures (Ongondo and Williams 2011) and grass root, student led initiatives on campus sites have proven effective (Mason et al. 2003; Reidy et al. 2015). However whole systems approaches are required to green campuses; they are complex ecosystems comprising many independent components and successful evolution necessitates consideration of all of these components (Koester et al. 2006). Just as conventional communities and regions have formed their own action plans in response to inadequate actions at national and international level (Desai 2008), campus communities have responded in similar fashion, sometimes supported by NGOs and local agencies. Community led interventions have been shown to have a greater ability to engage and empower local actors and stakeholders than top-down initiatives which in many instances have failed (Forrest and Wiek 2014).

1.2 The Irish Education System

The Irish education system consists of early childhood, primary, post primary, further education and training and higher education (Ireland, Department of Education and Skills 2015). Further education and training and the higher education sectors include 7 Universities, 14 Institutes of Technology (IoTs), 7 Colleges of Education (CoEs), 5 National University of Ireland Colleges and 10 other state aided institutions e.g. Army and Police Education Colleges (Department of Education and Skills 2015). The 26 Higher Education Authority Funded institutions alone employ >17,000 core staff, excluding contractors, and accounts for almost 200,000 enrolled students (Higher Education Authority 2015). Irish third level campuses exert significant effects on the environment, in terms of land occupied, resource use, energy consumption, travel, transport and waste generation. Although these impacts have not been formally verified, both the Irish Environmental Protection Agency and An Taisce suggest that sizable opportunity exists for enhanced resource efficiency within the sector (Environmental Education Unit, An Taisce 2013; Purcell 2011). Although campus management can achieve accreditation to certified environmental management systems, such as ISO 14001 and EMAS, at the time of writing, evidence could not be found of any Irish campus gaining accreditation, although some, UCC for example, hold ISO 5001 energy management system accreditation (UCC Buildings and Estates Office 2015). The most widespread environmental initiative for third level institutions in Ireland is the GCP.

1.3 Eco-Schools and Green Campus Programmes

The Foundation for Environmental Education (FEE) developed the Eco-Schools Programme following the 1992 UN Conference on Environment and Development. The Programmes Seven Steps are based on ISO 14001 (Hens et al. 2010; Nan et al. 2006), and is acknowledged as a model initiative for Education for Sustainable Development by the United Nations Environmental Programme. FEE is also recognised as an NGO in official relations with UNESCO (FEE 2015). In Ireland the programme is known as Green-Schools and coordinated by environmental

Fig. 1 Seven steps of green schools programme

NGO, An Taisce. 93 % of all primary and secondary schools in Ireland are registered on the programme and 79 % have been assessed and awarded at least once. In Ireland a targeted approach has been adopted, where schools implement the Seven Steps first for the target of litter and waste only, then the school progresses sequentially through further environmental education and ESD "themes". The Seven steps of the Green-Schools Programme are outlined in Fig. 1.

Once a school is assessed, and found to have satisfactorily implemented the Seven Steps for the initial theme of litter and waste, a Green Flag is awarded. Schools must undertake new themes and undergo assessments every two years in order to maintain the Green Flag. Figure 2 shows the order of themes and their current distribution amongst registered primary and secondary schools.

Like Green-Schools, the GCP does not reward specific environmental projects, implementation of technologies or capital investments; instead it acknowledges long term commitment to continual improvement from the entire organisation and full implementation of the Seven Step environmental management system. Although Green-Campus (or EcoCampus as it is known internationally) has now been piloted in other FEE member states, Ireland currently has the largest number of registered and awarded campuses (FEE 2015).

This chapter describes practical examples, actions and insights developed from empirical experiences of the establishment and maintenance of the GCP in Ireland since its inception in 2007.

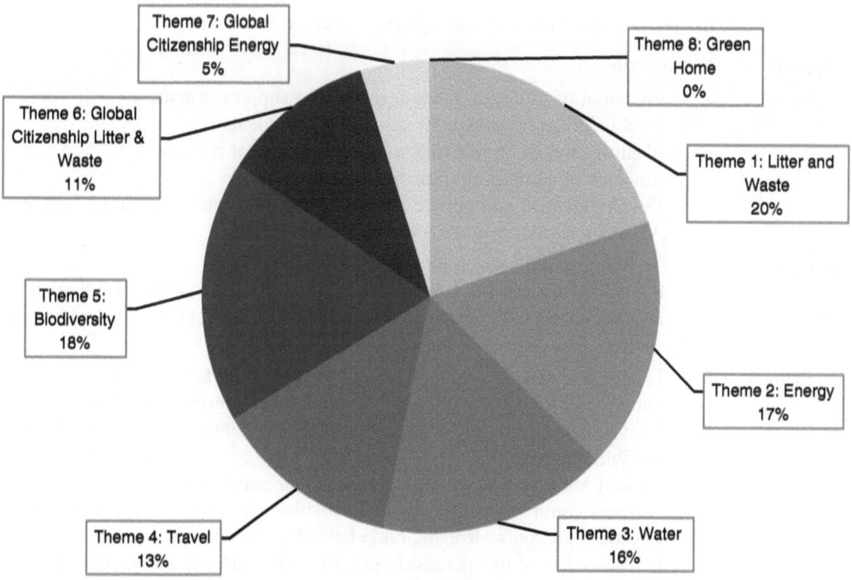

Fig. 2 Theme distribution and order through primary and secondary schools academic Year 2015–2016

2 Pilot Implementation of the GCP

The GCP started in Ireland in 2007 when students from University College Cork (UCC), having previously attended Green-Schools during their primary and secondary education, requested that a programme be developed for higher and third level institutions. Two further campuses also requested that a programme suitable for their needs be developed, all three, UCC, Coláiste Dhúlaigh College of Further Education, Coolock, and Galway-Mayo Institute of Technology (GMIT) Mayo agreed to participate in the trialling and piloting of the GCP. Both UCC and Coláiste Dhúlaigh Coolock were awarded the Green Flag in 2010, whilst GMIT Mayo was awarded in April 2011.

A green campus coordinator was appointed in September 2009 to expedite development of the programme as it became evident that in order to progress the programme the lack of technical expertise and staff on some campuses necessitated structured Green-Campus support as detailed in Table 1. The GCP maintained the use of the Seven Step methodology from the Green-Schools Programme.

The programme was successful in the three pilot sites leading to significant waste, energy and water reductions as well as increased campus community engagement, environmental education activities and wider community involvement. UCC reported a saving of ~€300,000 in waste management costs between 2007 and 2010, reducing waste to landfill by 400 tonnes. Between 2008 and 2011 GMIT

Table 1 Supports provided to campuses through green-campus coordinator

Supports	Description
Technical	• Provision of guidance to management on support structures • Establishment of links between staff and students • Identification of targets following environmental reviews • Reviews of campus environmental impacts • Development of appropriate metrics to monitor trends and target setting • Assist in development of green charters
Education	• Training of students on all aspects of green-campus • Provision of workshops for various groups (students, administrative and academic staff and management on review methodologies, action and target setting
Facilitation	• Facilitation of green-campus committee meetings, for some acting as temporary chairperson until formal committee structures established • Engagement of green-campus committees in scoping exercises to identify feasible strategies • Liaison with student's union and class representatives • Advised committees on methods to involve academic and research staff • Liaison with course leaders, on behalf of green-campus committees to outline potential for increased learning, skills and knowledge outcomes
Organisational	• Provision of contacts and supports and links to national and international programmes • Development of guidance materials, website, social media, networking events and conferences

Mayo reduced paper use by 60 %, diverted 12 tonnes of waste from landfill through improved recycling and composting, and water conservation measures reduced consumption by almost 1000 l daily. Finally Coláiste Dhúlaigh, Coolock devised innovative ways of communicating with students, by not printing student handbooks this small campus prevented over 1.4 tonnes of paper waste annually and improved resource efficiency and waste management reduced waste to landfill by a factor of 34.

3 GCP Development

3.1 Adaptation of Eco-schools Methodology

Through the pilot phase, the differences between implementation of the Programme at primary and secondary education levels as opposed to higher and tertiary levels were identified. Firstly campuses cannot be greened like typical corporate organisations or schools, campuses are complex communities within communities. To illustrate, the largest stakeholder group, students, are enrolled in various courses and faculties, differ in study type e.g. Erasmus, part-time, undergraduate, postgraduate etc., and spend varied amounts time on campus, typically 3–4 years. Students may live on site, nearby offsite or commute daily. Student progression means that awareness campaigns, policies and procedures must be communicated continually and consistently to new entrants. Secondly, the current recruitment embargo in the Irish public sector means that specialists to work on environmental and resource efficiency targets have not been employed, despite student number and campus size increases. These tasks increasingly fall to overstretched facilities management, members of voluntary groups and committees, supporting NGOs and government agencies. On the other hand reduced capital spending in the public sector has renewed interest in low to no cost initiatives and solutions. Thirdly, the diversity of third level campuses in Ireland means that campuses are wide-ranging in size and location: large scale urban sites, small urban sites, suburban and rural sites and sites which encompass or border Natura 2000 designated sites such as Special Areas of Conservation and Special Protection Areas. There exists an array of effects and opportunities available to campuses in transitioning their own, local and collegial communities towards sustainability. These dichotomies not only relate to location and scales but also to function with the Universities and larger institutes of technology engaged in year round research, innovation and laboratory testing, perhaps lending these toward more living laboratory, and 'eco-varsity' type implementations. Lastly, with the exception of energy consumption, for which the Irish Government has set mandatory targets (Ireland, Department of Communications, Energy and Natural Resources 2009), other targets for resource efficiency in the third level education sector have not been established by national policy makers. The GCP made some minor adaptations to the existing Green Schools methodology in order to facilitate and address these challenges and opportunities.

- **Multi-themed approaches**: When UCC embarked on the GCP the Waste, Energy and Commuter Managers attended Green-Campus meetings and became members of the Green-Campus Committee. UCC therefore undertook a multi-themed approach as it had the expertise and data available. Coláiste Dhúlaigh did not have such management available and undertook a themed approach focusing first on the theme of litter and waste. Pre-registration and scoping phases have been included into the Green-Campus methodology where participants meet with the Green-Campus Office to assess an appropriate approach (themed or multi-themed) for the particular arrangements on campus depending on the extent and availability of facilities management and expertise on site.
- **Pre-Registration**: Pre-registration with the Green-Campus office ensures that the campus has the necessary information, committee structure and supports in place to proceed successfully with the programme. The committee must have the support of the head of campus in order to proceed with registration. In addition, the committee must be composed of both students and staff. GCP staff offer guidance and assistance as outlined in Table 1.
- **Assessment of Programme**: Assessment panels are used to assess the campus implementation of the Seven Steps of the GCP in order for a campus to be awarded the Green Flag. The feedback and contacts made through the assessment process assists campuses in furthering their GCP as Committee members are introduced to specialists in areas such as energy conservation, waste prevention and management, biodiversity protection, and environmental management. In order to retain GCP status, annual renewal reports must be submitted with full reassessments required every 3 years.
- **Green Charter**: The Green Code (in Green-Schools) has been replaced by a requirement to develop a Green Charter at Campus level. The Green Charter is designed to be compiled after the action plan has been implemented and the monitoring and evaluation steps have been carried out. It differs from an environmental policy in that the latter is an expression of what the campus intends to do and provides direction at the strategic management level; the former is the means by which the campus community can achieve the aims through specific advice and information. The Green Charter ensures continual involvement and communication with staff and students.

3.2 Current Green-Campus Participants

At the time of writing 20 campuses are formally registered on the programme, 10 of which have been awarded the Green Flag. Table 2 lists current Green-Campus awarded campuses and environmental themes addressed.

The GCP is also recognised as best practice by the Irish Department of Education and Skills which has included Green-Campus in the National Strategy on Education for Sustainable Development in Ireland 2014–2020 (Ireland, Department of Education and Skills Ireland, Department of Education and Skills 2014).

Table 2 Current green-campus awarded sites: targets addressed and student numbers

Campus	Year of award	Environmental themes addressed	Approximate student numbers
UCC	2010 2013	Litter and waste Energy conservation Water conservation and protection Biodiversity Travel and transport Green procurement Climate change	16,000
Coláiste Dhúlaigh College of Further Education, Coolock Campus	2010 2013	Litter and waste Biodiversity Energy conservation	500
GMIT Mayo	2011 2014	Litter and waste Energy conservation Water conservation and protection Biodiversity Travel and transport	1000
Ballsbridge College of Further Education	2012	Litter and waste Energy conservation	500
Trinity College Dublin	2013	Energy and climate change Waste management Water conservation and protection Sustainable transport Resource use and sustainable food Biodiversity Green procurement	17,000
GMIT Letterfrack	2014	Litter and waste Biodiversity	250

(continued)

Table 2 (continued)

Campus	Year of award	Environmental themes addressed	Approximate student numbers
Dublin City University	2014	Litter and waste Energy conservation Biodiversity Water conservation and protection Travel and transport	10,000
Pearse College of Further Education	2014	Litter and waste Water conservation Travel and transport Energy conservation	900
Cork University Hospital	2014	Major: litter and waste Energy conservation Minor: sustainable transport Biodiversity Water conservation and protection Sustainable healthcare	234,202 average Patient bed days per annum (based on 2012, 2013 and 2014)
University of Limerick	2015	Travel and transport Energy Biodiversity	13,000

3.3 Environmental Performance of Participants

Key performance indicators for the GCP have been developed using data provided by awarded and registered campuses. Table 3 presents a selection of both quantitative and qualitative data from a university, a teaching hospital and a small campus site extracted from academic year 2013–2014 campus report returns. A key determinant of the magnitude in terms of quantitative measurements of environmental savings made has been the support of facilities management in driving initiatives envisioned by the community led Green-Campus Committees through staff or investment.

Whist some believe that a lack of formal benchmarks and targets available for use by third level campuses represents a significant challenge in driving sustainability

Table 3 Selected quantitative and qualitative reports from campus reports for academic year 2013–2014

Campus	Key performance outcomes
Dublin City University	– Recycling level on campus maintained at 2011 level – External segregated bins – Reusable cups available on campus – Energy consumption by the campus has decreased by 15.2 % since 2011 – DCU Community Garden introduced on site – Native Irish trees, wildflowers and plants introduced to provide nectar for pollinators and encourage biodiversity – Bee hives introduced on campus
Cork University Hospital	– Reductions in waste: 11 % despite an overall 10 % increase in hospital activity. 205 tonne reduction in waste going to landfill, 21 tonne decrease in clinical waste and 77 tonne increase in recycling rates – 860 MWh decrease in gas consumption – 1185 MWh decrease in electricity consumption – 785 tonne decrease in CO_2 emissions
Pearse College of Further Education	– Waste reduction measures reusing shredded paper in compost bays, improved signage over recycling bins and general waste bins, resulting in a reduction in general waste. Printers and photocopiers programmed to employ paper savings modes while incoming students are informed electronically of Green Charter – Retrofit of water conserving taps and hand dryers – Allotment area features wind turbine and compost bins – A campus branded reusable Eco-Cup is incentivised with a reward system – Ecological niches within the campus grounds preserve wildlife in an urban campus and allotments produce a range of organic fruit and vegetables

(McNeilly et al. 2008), the use of green leagues and international checklist methodologies to "green" universities are also eliciting concern with commentators fearful that without clear targets and stakeholder engagement such leagues may become "hegemonic mechanisms to facilitate inaction" (Jones 2012). As can be seen from Table 3 environmental achievements vary greatly depending on the campuses type, resources available and locations. Increasingly campuses are engaging in sustainability initiatives and tend to value those which produce metrics and rankings such as UI Green Metric. Data are submitted via online forms and a numeric scoring system is used to generate rankings. A number of Irish Universities have participated, with UCC, University of Limerick, Dublin City University, Trinity College Dublin and Dublin Institute of Technology ranked 2nd, 11th, 53rd and 104th respectively of 360 participating institutes (UI Green Metric 2014). Of these the former four hold GCP Awards whilst the latter, DIT, is in the final stages of the GCP award application process. Programmes such as Green-Campus that facilitate all participants, irrespective of size, access to investment capital or onsite expertise, to develop their own goals and objectives based on the unique attributes of the campus site coupled with peer networking mechanisms and supports may ultimately prove most effective in delivering environmental responsibility and action.

3.4 Green-Campus Hospitals

Cork University Hospital (CUH) is the largest teaching hospital and only Level 1 trauma centre in Ireland, containing >40 medical and surgical specialities. Whole time equivalent staff and student numbers totals 3297 and 408 respectively. During 2013 the hospital catered for 234,752 patient bed days, 166,103 outpatient attendances and 15,983 births. The hospital joined the GCP in 2010 and was accepted to participate as a teaching hospital; its academic affiliate, UCC, was the first Irish university to implement the GCP. Teaching hospitals offer unique opportunities to foster environmental education. Graduates move to other healthcare facilities, countries or into private practice. Delivering environmental education to healthcare practitioners creates a ripple effect that filters through the hospital, the wider healthcare system and ultimately society. A recurrent theme in healthcare and environment literature is that healthcare workers are undertrained and uninformed (Harhay et al. 2009; Ozder et al. 2013). Evidence from working with CUH suggests that for the majority of healthcare practitioners, patient safety takes priority and so a wider understanding of how unpolluted environments support patient safety is required. Green Advocates are offered environmental training counting toward continuing professional development on résumés. Opportunities that hospitals and other public buildings can exploit as visible presences in cities can promote environmental sustainability (Redmond et al. 2015). Footfall of visitors and staff through the hospital is high so public engagement was included in CUH action plans. Key life events can be used to influence behaviour and induce sustainable consumption patterns (DEFRA 2011) and some patients groups are particularly receptive to environmental education. Green guides were developed for mothers post maternity and the CUH School for children participates in the Green-Schools programme. The Health Service Executive formed and launched the National Health Sustainability Office in 2014 to coordinate a National Sustainability Plan for the health service (Health Service Executive 2015). The GCP and supports utilised in CUH have become best practice for other hospitals in the Irish health system to emulate.

3.5 Developing Links

The GCP compliments and is complimented by many other environmental and social engagement initiatives. An Tasice has developed experience working with Local Authorities, Government Departments, corporate sponsors, community groups, schools and third level institutes in delivering environmental education through Blue Flag, Clean Coasts, Green Home, National Spring Clean, and Green Schools Programmes. Local Authorities have dedicated environmental awareness staff tasked with engagement of the public and have played pivotal roles in participation on assessment panels and ongoing support of campuses throughout the academic year. This support has been particularly beneficial in the cases of colleges lacking onsite facilities management and ensures campuses are aware of and involved in environmental initiatives ongoing in their local municipality.

The Green-Campus Partner Programme, which is currently under development, arose from the recognition that service providers would benefit from assessing and reducing the environmental impact of their organisational activities, improve their sustainability, and support their clients in applying sustainable best practice associated with their services. This has led to the development of a pilot programme for Green Campus Partner organisations which encourages service providers to third level institutions to develop, adopt and apply the Seven Step environmental management process similar to that of the GCP to their organisation.

New themes are emerging within the GCP, 'Climate Justice', originated from within Green-Campus Committees looking to foster their individual specialities in international aid, development and climatology as is the case with National University of Ireland, Maynooth. A new theme 'Green Information and Communications Technology' was developed as a result of partnerships between the GCP and stakeholders such as HEAnet, Ireland's National Education and Research Network. In this way the GCP has accessed niche expertise and new Green-Campus and Green-Schools themes are evolving using academic outputs and peer reviewed research, meeting national recommendations that higher education institutions should maintain closer links with schools in order to exchange best practice and access specialist expertise available (Ireland, Department of Education and Skills 2014).

The Green-Campus Office has facilitated networking to assist institutions in their implementation of the GCP. Network approaches deliver benefit to participants by providing access to social resources, a means to tap external resources required, and access important information, best practice, advice and innovation in a cost effective manner (Watson 2007). An annual Green-Campus Colloquium offers campuses opportunities to network with other GCP participants, stakeholders, and support programmes. Campuses are invited to make oral and poster presentations to disseminate information and best practice. Many of these have been recorded and are accessible via the Green-Campus website: www.greencampusireland.org.

4 Closing Remarks

- Environmental performance of universities and tertiary education providers has been enhanced through, for example, green building, waste and energy management, and product design. However, unpredictable occupant behaviour, new research outcomes and evolving best practice requires educational facilities to react and respond in an ever challenging and changing environment, and clearly there is no one set of actions appropriate in all jurisdictions.
- Both Green-Campus and Eco-Schools (from which the GCP derived) provide suitable frameworks to bring together voluntary initiatives, governmental and

non-governmental organisation actions, and peer supports to address sustainability challenges.

- Maintaining the link between Eco-Schools, Green Schools and Green-Campus ensures consistency of ESD approaches for students as they progress through the education system. The methodology and symbols are instantly recognisable by both Irish and international students facilitating participation.
- GCP being both a programme and award relies on a networking approach rather than competitions and ranking exercises. Collaboration and partnerships are facilitated amongst participants.
- The GCP builds a strong network for campuses, introduces further support systems and facilitates interactions and learning.
- The involvement of third level campuses and access to cutting edge research has led to improvements across all programmes.
- A limitation of the study presented is that predominantly the experiences of successful campuses are described. More research is required on finding ways to increase participation and retention of those currently in the programme. Development of further relevant indicators is currently under research.

Acknowledgements Dr. Ryan-Fogarty and Dr. O'Regan wish to acknowledge support from the Irish Environmental Protection Agency Research Programme 2014–2020.

References

Association of University Leaders for a Sustainable Future. (2008). *Tallories declaration 1990 report*. Available: http://www.ulsf.org/programs_talloires_report.html. Accessed 7 Oct, 15.

DEFRA. (2011). *Moments of change as opportunities for influencing behaviour*. Food and Rural Affairs, London: Department for Environment.

Department of Education and Skills. (2015). *Providers of higher education*. Available: https://www.education.ie/en/Learners/Information/Providers-of-Higher-Education/List.html. Accessed 30 June, v15.

Desai, P. (2008). Creating low carbon communities: One planet living solutions. *Globalizations, 5*, 67–71. doi:10.1080/14747730701587462.

Environmental Education Unit, An Taisce. (2013). *The green-campus programme*. Available: http://www.greencampusireland.org/. Accessed 30 Jan, 15.

FEE. (2015). *EcoCampus*. Available: http://www.eco-schools.org/menu/about/ecocampus. Accessed 17 Sept 15.

Forrest, N., & Wiek, A. (2014). Learning from success—Toward evidence-informed sustainability transitions in communities. *Environmental Innovation and Societal Transitions, 12*, 66–88. doi:10.1016/j.eist.2014.01.003.

Harhay, M. O., Halpern, S. D., Harhay, J. S., & Olliaro, P. L. (2009). Health care waste management: A neglected and growing public health problem worldwide: Managing health care waste worldwide. *Tropical Medicine & International Health, 14*, 1414–1417. doi:10.1111/j.1365-3156.2009.02386.x.

Health Service Executive. (2015). *National health sustainability office*. Health Service Executive. Available: http://www.hse.ie/eng/services/news/newsfeatures/healthsustainabilityoffice/Aboutus/. Accessed 11 Aug, 15.

Hens, L., Wiedemann, T., Raath, S., Stone, R., Renders, P., & Craenhals, E. (2010). Performance of newly implemented environmental management systems in primary schools in South Africa. *Journal of Environmental Management, 91*, 906–917. doi:10.1016/j.jenvman.2009.11.007.

Higher Education Authority. (2015). *Higher education statistics 2014–2015*. Available: http://www.hea.ie/en/statistics/overview. Accessed 1 July, 15.

Huesemann, M. (2011). *Techno-fix: Why technology won't save us or the environment*. Gabriola, B.C.: New Society Publishers.

Ireland, Department of Communications, Energy and Natural Resources. (2009). *Maximising Ireland's energy efficiency: the national energy efficiency action plan 2009–2020*. Energy and Natural Resources, Dublin: Department of Communications.

Ireland, Department of Education and Skills. (2014). *"Education for sustainability" the national strategy on education for sustainable development in Ireland 2014 2020*. Dublin, Ireland: Department of Education and Skills.

Jones, D. R. (2012). Looking through the "greenwashing glass cage" of the green league table towards the sustainability challenge for UK universities. *Journal of Organizational Change Management, 25*, 630–647. doi:10.1108/09534811211239263.

Koester, R. J., Eflin, J., Vann, J. (2006). Greening of the campus: A whole-systems approach. *Journal of Cleaner Production, Sustainability In Higher education: What is happening? sustainability in higher education: What is happening? 14*, 769–779. doi:10.1016/j.jclepro.2005.11.055

Li, J., Xiao, D. W., Fu, J., He, D. D., & Wei, C. (2014). Research on passive planning and design of green campus in subtropical region. *Advanced Materials Research, 1079–1080*, 252–257. doi:10.4028/www.scientific.net/AMR.1079-1080.252.

Mason, I. G., Brooking, A. K., Oberender, A., Harford, J. M., & Horsley, P. G. (2003). Implementation of a zero waste program at a university campus. *Resources, Conservation and Recycling, 38*, 257–269. doi:10.1016/S0921-3449(02)00147-7.

McNeilly, L., Winters, J., & McKanna, K. (2008). *University of California Berkeley: Campus sustainability*. Berkeley: University of California.

Nan, C., Xiaoqiang, W., & Jin, W. (2006). Development of national assessment criteria for green schools in China. *Southern African Journal of Environmental Education, 23*, 64–77.

Ongondo, F. O., & Williams, I. D. (2011). Greening academia: Use and disposal of mobile phones among university students. *Waste Management, 31*, 1617–1634. doi:10.1016/j.wasman.2011.01.031.

Ozder, A., Teker, B., Eker, H. H., Altindis, S., Kocaakman, M., & Karabay, O. (2013). Medical waste management training for healthcare managers—A necessity. *Journal of Environmental Health Science and Engineering, 11*, 20.

Porter-O'Grady, T., & Malloch, K. (2010). Innovation: Driving the green culture in healthcare. *Nursing Administration Quarterly, 34*, E1–E5. doi:10.1097/NAQ.0b013e3181fb48d3.

Purcell, M. (2011). *How to green your campus or workplace: A step by step guide*. Cork Institute of Technology: Environmental Protection Agency.

Redmond, A., Fies, B., & Zarli, A. (2015). Developing an integrated cloud platform for enabling "holistic energy management" in urban areas. In B. Martens, A. Mahdavi, & R. Scherer (Eds.), *eWork and eBusiness in architecture, engineering and construction: proceedings of the 10th European conference on product and process modelling (ECPPM 2014), Vienna, Austria, 17–19 September 2014*. The Netherlands: CRC Press, Leiden.

Reidy, D., Kirrane, M., Curley, B., Brosnan, D., Koch, S., Bolger, P., et al. (2015). A journey in sustainable development in an urban campus. In W. Leal Filho, L. Brandli, O. Kuznetsova & A. M. F. Paço (Eds.), *Integrative approaches to sustainable development at university level, world sustainability series*. Berlin: Springer International Publishing, pp. 599–613.

Shriberg, M. (2002). Institutional assessment tools for sustainability in higher education: Strengths, weaknesses, and implications for practice and theory. *International Journal of Sustainability in Higher Education, 3*, 254–270. doi:10.1108/14676370210434714.

UCC Buildings and Estates Office. (2015). *ISO 50001 buildings and estates UCC*. Available: http://www.ucc.ie/en/build/energy/iso50001/. Accessed 1 July, 15.

UI Green Metric. (2014). *UI greenmetric world university ranking*. Available: http://greenmetric.ui.ac.id/ranking/year/2014. Accessed 1 July, 15.

Umwelt Campus Birkenfeld. (2015). Green campus concept. Hochschule Trier Umwelt Campus Birkenfeld. Available: http://www.umwelt-campus.de/ucb/index.php?id=7994&L=1. Accessed 2 July, 15.

Velazquez, L., Munguia, N., Platt, A., & Taddei, J. (2006). Sustainable university: What can be the matter? *Journal of Cleaner Production, 14*, 810–819. doi:10.1016/j.jclepro.2005.12.008.

Watson, J. (2007). Modeling the relationship between networking and firm performance. *Journal of Business Venturing, 22*, 852–874. doi:10.1016/j.jbusvent.2006.08.001.

The Inclusion of Elements of Local Social and Environmental Sustainability in Logistics Education: A Case Study from Poland

Joost Platje, Krzysztof Łobos and Krzysztof Wilk

Abstract

The WSB University in Wrocław (WSB) is a private institution of higher education with over 15,000 students, located in the Polish city Wroclaw (650,000 inhabitants). As the practice-oriented study programme focuses on business subjects without clear relation with sustainability issues, the aim of this article is to show how issues of social and environmental sustainability can be included in the curriculum. First, conditions for students' transport behaviour and the WSB car-pooling initiative (environmental element) and an initiative for making study facilities accessible for physically disabled students will be discussed (social element). Then, practical elements of sustainability education in the study programme on logistics will be presented, and opportunities for including these issues in education for sustainability will be identified. In the conclusion, implications for regional development will be discussed.

Keywords

Campus sustainability · Education · Poland · Local sustainable development

J. Platje (✉) · K. Łobos · K. Wilk
WSB University in Wrocław, ul. Fabryczna 29/31, 53-609 Wrocław, Poland
e-mail: johannes.platje@wsb.wroclaw.pl

K. Łobos
e-mail: krzysztof.lobos@wsb.wroclaw.pl

K. Wilk
e-mail: k.m.wilk@wp.pl

© Springer International Publishing Switzerland 2016

W. Leal Filho and P. Pace (eds.), *Teaching Education for Sustainable Development at University Level*, World Sustainability Series,
DOI 10.1007/978-3-319-32928-4_20

1 Introduction

The WSB University in Wrocław (WSB) is a private institution of higher education with over 15,000 students (about 3000 in the location in the city of Opole), and is located in Wrocław, the capital of the Polish voivodship Lower Silezia with about 650,000 inhabitants. It is one of the nine members of the WSB Universities located in different Polish cities. Its mission is the transfer of professional and practical knowledge, guaranteeing the students a strong position on the labour market. One of the aims is that students will consciously and effectively participate in the construction of the modern Polish economy. Its vision is to be the regional leader in teaching students who combine work with studying (WSB 2015a). WSB focusses on quality management (it possesses the ISO 9001 certificate since 2014) with a focus on preparing students for the labour market (WSB 2015b).

The aim of this article is to show how issues of social and environmental sustainability can be included in the curriculum in a business-oriented programme where currently sustainability issues are not explicitly dealt with. Campus sustainability often focuses on environmental performance (Amaral et al. 2015). While environmental issues are less focussed upon, they appear in many subjects dealing with legal requirements to be fulfilled (e.g., transport law), are integrated in part of the logistic chain (e.g., eco-logistics) or introduced by lecturers as an enrichment of the curriculum (e.g., sustainable transport as an element of transport economics) (compare Larán and Andrades 2015). At the moment, the motivation of campus stakeholders to engage in sustainability issues needs to be strengthened, while policies need to be developed (compare Too and Bajracharya 2015). Another issue is that sustainability is not considered to be relevant for economics and business courses by many lecturers (Green 2015). However, as sustainability is only expected to increase in importance and required by labour markets (Leal Filho et al. 2015), it is necessary to consider it for future curriculum development as it is an opportunity for development of business schools (Lambrechts et al. 2015) and to remain competitive on the educational market.

Two issues will be discussed, providing a basis for future research on campus sustainability at WSB—access for the physically disabled (social element) and transport policy (social and environmental element) increasing general accessibility of the campus. The reason is that these two issues are important elements in regional development as well as WSB's marketing strategy and development policy. WSB obtained EU funds for improving access for the disabled, and started a car-pooling initiative, which makes studying more attractive. This is important in the current situation of increased competition for students, as their total number in Poland has been declining during the last years, and are expected to decline during the next few years as a consequence of a demographic low (data from the central Statistical Office).

It can be expected that access for the disabled contributes to social sustainability and development of the region. Participation of the physically disabled not only improves their capability to develop their lives, but also provides an example of good practice which may be followed by business and other universities. The influence of the car-pooling initiative on regional development is more ambiguous.

Although it may reduce the number of cars as well as parking problems, when public transport will not be improved, car use is unlikely to be reduced. A reason is that people using public transport may use this service, as the existing connections by bus and train are less attractive. This negatively contributes to the sustainability of regional transport systems. When including research on such elements of sustainability in the curriculum (e.g., as topics of BA and MA theses), this may not only increase students' knowledge on sustainability issues, and increase interest in dealing with other elements of campus sustainability. It creates an opportunity to link regional development policy and policy implementation with education.

The assessment of accessibility of facilities for the physically disabled students is based on an empirical check of the facilities. The authors visited and controlled all facilities during the month of May 2015, interviewed porters and made pictures for later analysis and control. The car-pooling initiative and conditions for students' transport behaviour were analysed based on research of websites with information on time tables of public transport, as well as the car-pooling initiative. This will be the basis for further empirical research on the issue, also at other universities.

First, the initiatives for making study facilities accessible for physically disabled students will be discussed. Then, conditions for students' transport behaviour and the WSB car-pooling initiative will be discussed. Finally, practical elements of sustainability education in the study programme on logistics will be presented, and opportunities for including elements of campus sustainability in the educational process will be identified.

2 Accessibility of Facilities for Physically Disabled Students

In the period 2013–2015 WSB obtained two grants for carrying out consulting on ecological issues and providing post graduate studies on environmental and ecological issues for small and medium sized enterprises as well as banks (each grant about 375,000 euro). Regarding access of facilities for physically disabled students, the following grants were obtained:[1]

1. Adjustment of buildings to disabled people—installation of elevators. Realization—01.01.2009–31.08.2012. Total sum about 3.3 million euro.
2. Two computer workstations for physically disabled. Realization—01.08.2009–31.12.2012. Total sum about 1.15 million euro.
3. Two computer workstations for physically disabled (one in the computer lab and one in the library). The workstation includes: keyboard in Braille, voice synthesizer, a specialist printer as well as a special computer mouse and desk. Realization—03.08.2009–31.12.2012. Total sum about 1.25 million euro.
4. Appointment of a Representative of the Dean for disabled people, organization of 3 training for teachers on ethical aspects of contacts with disabled people,

[1]Data were obtained from internal documents. As the grants were in Polish zloty, they were calculated in euro according to an exchange rate of 4 zloty for 1 euro.

Table 1 Number of disabled students at the WSB University in Wrocław—2009–2014 (31 December of each year)

Year	Extramural students (weekend studies)	Full-time students	Total
2014	211	51	262
2013	210	66	276
2012	179	51	230
2011	90	33	123
2010	97	41	138
Total	787	242	1029

Source Internal data from the WSB University in Wrocław

organization of a conference for disabled people, placement of Braille markings in WSB buildings. Realization—01.09.2010–30.12.2015. Total sum about 1.8 million euro.

5. Appointment of a Representative of the Dean for disabled persons, developing solutions for facilitating studying for disabled people, adaptation of 2 toilets for the physically disabled. Realization—01.09.2010–30.09.2015. Total sum about 2.72 million euro.
6. Coaching and educational-professional consulting for disabled people, individual classes/meetings with teachers, transport to the location of classes, designation of routes in buildings, purchase of Dictaphones. Realization—01.05.2013–28.02.2015. Total sum about 660,000 euro.

In the period 2009–2015, WSB obtained in total about 11 million euro in order to adapt their facilities to the needs of the disabled. This has facilitated studying for these students, which is exemplified by the increase in their number between 2010 and 2014, in particular among the extramural students[2] (Table 1).

There are 6 buildings where classes are organized: A, B, C, D, H and L. Building L is not considered in the analysis, as this one was acquired through a merger with another private university, after the investments for facilities for the disabled started. While buildings A, B and C are located close to each other on the same campus, buildings D and H are a few minutes walking from this main campus.

In May 2015, the authors inspected all buildings on the accessibility for the physically disabled. Pictures were taken, and interviews with porters on location were made. A preliminary conclusion is that the accessibility for the disabled is very good at first sight in buildings A and B. In the other buildings the situation can be assessed as good. However, there are some issues requiring attention for improvement. This will be researched in more detail in the near future with involvement of physically disabled students.

[2]A specific feature of the education system in Poland, like in many former socialist countries, is the existence of extramural studies during the weekend, where students do the same programme during the same amount of semesters as the full-time students. However, the number of teaching hours is lower, and it is assumed that students do more self-study at home.

In accordance with the projects described, there are elevators in each building. These elevators are accessible for wheelchairs, while there are no significant barriers for people in wheelchairs to enter buildings. In case of problems, there are always porters nearby who can help.

Building A and B are at the heart of the campus. They have 3 parking lots for physically disabled. On the way to the entrance, there are clear yellow lines, facilitating access for the visually impaired. In building A, stairs steps are secured against slipping and highlighted in yellow (first and last step). This is not the case in building B. However, at the back of the building A, stairs are not secured against slipping. Furthermore, first signs of utilization can be observed, and maintenance may be required in the next few years. The moment this has to be paid from the general budget, this creates a challenge as the authors expect that due to increased competition on the educational market pressure to reduce or prevent costs strengthens.

Furthermore, there are clear yellow lines at the edge between the floor and the walls in each corridor. On the ground floor and first floor, at each door there is information in Braille. Also information about changes of classrooms is provided in Braille. However, classrooms in the basement do not have such signs. The toilets are easily accessible for physically disabled. Another issue is that the canteen at the back of the building, while being adapted to the needs of the physically disabled, is difficult to access with a wheelchair when being inside the building. In this case, this person needs to get out via the main entrance, and enter via the back entrance. The computer workstations planned in the grant applications fulfil the requirements.

Near building C, a small building at the other side of the road of building A and B, there is no special parking space for the disabled. The doorstep at the entrance is not made additionally visible by a yellow line, like in the other buildings. While entrance is not a real problem, this may create some challenges. Furthermore, while there are toilets for the disabled at both floors in the building, the one at the first floor is in a dark part of the corridor, and does not have a sign that it is a toilet for the physically disabled. The sink is too high, while there are no handles. Also, in the corridors and on the stairs there are no yellow lines increasing visibility for the visually impaired, while there are no signs in Braille on the doors. The situation for building H is similar. While toilets are better equipped than in building C, some of them have sills. In building D, the toilet for the disabled does not have handles near the sink, and there is only one parking space for the disabled.

3 Conditions for of Students' Transport Behaviour and the WSB Car-Pooling Initiative on Urban Transport

On the campus and the vicinity of the discussed buildings of WSB there are about 600 parking spaces for students. As there are more than 12,000 students, of whom about 80 % study during the weekend (different years of study have classes during different weekend), parking problems during this time exist. Many students park of Fabryczna Street, where this is forbidden. As a basis for further future research, the authors compared public transport and car for travel from 7 cities from which many young people study in Wrocław (Tables 2, 3 and 4). The different modes of transport were compared based on the assumption that a student would start classes at 09:00. The starting point was the railway/bus station in the city of origin.[3] The city of Wrocław itself was not taken into consideration. Although in the city public transport is well-developed, from the point of view of time and costs a car is often more attractive when someone possesses a car. The reason is that at this moment the user rather takes the variable costs (fuel consumption) into consideration when making a transport decision. While a car is often quicker during the weekend, it is on short distances cheaper. A roundtrip by public transport using only one connection costs PLN 6 (about 1 euro 50). The moment that a bus or tram is changed to another line, a new ticket needs to be bought.[4] A day ticket costs PLN 11. For PLN 6, an average car can drive about 15 km.[5]

From Tables 2, 3 and 4 the following observations can be made:

- The car is the most expensive mean of transport in case of one passenger. This difference is likely to decrease in case of car-pooling or car-sharing. In most cases, the travel cost per person is lower that for the train in case of two passengers per car (except for Zgorzelec-Wrocław and Żary-Wrocław[6]).
- In most cases, travel time by car is significantly lower (except for Legnica and Wałbrzych).
- Taking a bus is in most of the cases no option, as the student cannot get on time to classes.
- For five out of seven cities, the student would have to wait more than an hour before classes when travelling by train.

The hypothesis for questionnaire research among students to be carried out in the future is that most of the students from outside the city of Wrocław will travel by car. Furthermore, it can be expected that car-pooling is a good option due to longer travel times by public transport and the need to change the means of transport. Travel time is expected to be important, as the large majority of the students work during the week, increasing the value of their free time.

[3]The travel time home—railway station are not taken into consideration. The farther away a person lives from the railway station, the more attractive the car becomes. This will be in particular the case for people living in small villages.

[4]Another option is the purchase of a time ticked valid for, e.g., 60 min (PLN 4.40 per ticket) or 90 min (PLN 6.00 per ticket).

[5]This is based on the price of a litre of gasoline of PLN 4.80, assuming the car drives 12 kilometres per litre.

[6]The reason is that train tariffs are declining for extra kilometres, which becomes most visible on long distances. Special offers for people travelling together by the railways were not considered in the analysis. However, also in case the second passenger would pay halve the price of the first passenger, the car would remain the most favourable option when considering fuel costs and two passengers.

Table 2 Accessibility of the WSB campus during the weekend (classes start at 09:00)—train and urban public transport

Destination	Jelenia Góra—Wrocław Zachodni	Legnica—Wrocław Nowy Dwór	Świdnica—Wrocław Zachodni	Głogow—Wrocław Kuźniki	Zgorzelec—Wrocław Nowy Dwór	Żary—Wrocław Nowy Dwór	Wałbrzych—Wrocław Zachodni
Train (according to timetable)	04:49–07:04	07:17–07:59	05:56–07:04	06:12–08:01	05:17–07:21	05:25–09:13[a]	06:36–07:22
Type of train	Railcar	Railcar	Railcar	Slow train	Railcar	Railcar	Railcar
Train travel time	2 h 15 min	0 h 42 min	1 h 28 min	1 h 49 min	2 h 09 min	3 h 48 min	1 h 06 min
Time of arrival using urban public transport	About 07:45	About 08:30	About 07:45	About 08:45	About 07:50	About 09:45	About 08:00
Total travel time	2 h 56 min	1 h 13 min	1 h 49 min	2 h 33 min	2 h 33 min	4 h 20 min	1 h 24 min
Cost of travel (roundtrip)[b]	PLN 53.20	PLN 35.20	PLN 33.00	PLN 45.60	PLN 57.00	PLN 57.00	PLN 40.20
Remark	Need to wait more than an hour for classes		Need to wait more than an hour for classes		Need to wait more than an hour for classes	Too late for classes	Need to wait more than an hour for classes

[a]1 h 16 min waiting time in Legnica

[b]Based on price of train ticket + 2 tickets for public transport in Wrocław (PLN 3 each). Costs are based on the assumption of 1 person travelling

Source Authors' own research, based on websites of the Polish Railways, bus companies, Wrocław Public Transport, www.otodojazd.pl, www.googlemaps.pl

Table 3 Accessibility of the WSB campus during the weekend (classes start at 09:00)—bus and urban public transport

Destination	Jelenia Góra—Wrocław Busstation	Legnica—Wrocław Busstation	Świdnica—Wrocław Busstation	Głogów—Wrocław Busstation	Zgorzelec—Wrocław Busstation	Żary—Wrocław Busstation	Wałbrzych—Wrocław Busstation
Bus (according to time table)	05:45–07:45	06:00–08:43[a]	Cannot get there on time	Cannot get there on time	Cannot get there on time	Cannot get there on time	03:05–07:54[b]
Bus travel time	2 h 00 min	2 h 43 min					4 h 49 min
Cost of travel ticket (roundtrip)	PLN 56	PLN 46					PLN 90
Time of arrival using urban public transport	About 08:15	About 09:15					About 08:20
Total travel time	2 h 30 min	3 h 15 min					5 h 15 min

[a] 38 min waiting time in Bolków

[b] 2 h 22 min waiting time in Kamienna Góra

Source Authors' own research, based on websites of the Polish Railways, bus companies, Wrocław Public Transport, www.otodojazd.pl, www.googlemaps.pl

Table 4 Accessibility of the WSB campus during the weekend (classes start at 09:00)—car

Destination	Jelenia Góra—Wrocław Zachodni	Legnica—Wrocław Nowy Dwór	Świdnica—Wrocław Zachodni	Głogow—Wrocław Kuźniki	Zgorzelec—Wrocław Nowy Dwór	Żary—Wrocław Nowy Dwór	Wałbrzych—Wrocław Zachodni
Car travel time—railway station to WSB (googlemaps)	1 h 37 min	0 h 56 min	0 h 48 min	1 h 31 min	1 h 40 min	1 h 51 min	1 h 06 min
Distance (one way) (km)	114	78	65	107	165	175	84
Cost of roundtrip travel (PLN 0.35 /km)[a]	PLN 79.80	PLN 54.60	PLN 45.50	PLM 74.90	PLN 115.50	PLN 122.50	PLN 58.50

[a]Assumption: car drives on gasoline, 7 litres per 100 km, price per litre of gasoline PLN 5. When using LNG or LPG, the costs of fuel will be reduced, as the price of a litre is less than half the price of gasoline in Poland

Source Authors' own research, based on www.googlemaps.pl

Focus in the research will be on the effects of WSB's car-pooling initiative, which has been developed in cooperation with otodojazd.pl (WSB 2015c). Via the online system, students can find a driver with a car going to classes at the same time. The website advertises the initiative as a way to reduce travel costs, protect the environment and to meet new people. The search engine of otodojazd.pl is based on the geolocation along the whole route. This makes it possible to take passengers from locations along the whole route, increasing the probability of finding a driver or passenger.

However, an issue for deeper research, which will be carried out together with students in the framework of classwork and BA or MA theses, is whether this solution will cause side effects. The identification of potential side-effects may increase awareness among students about the importance of system analysis. While car-pooling may be assumed a more sustainable way of passenger transportation, and may create behavioural change, it may strengthen the focus on the use of cars and also may lead to substitution of public transport to car-pooling. As a consequence, the number of cars and the related parking problems may not be reduced. By introducing factors such as the age and type of the car in the research, the students may see the link with accessibility for the physically disabled (e.g., research the accessibility of public transport for the disabled), greenhouse gas emission, local air pollution and other elements of sustainable development.

4 Practical Elements of Sustainability Education in the Study Programme on Logistics and Opportunities for Change

The aim of this article was to show how issues of social and environmental sustainability can be included in the curriculum in a business-oriented programme where currently sustainability issues are not explicitly dealt with.

A general problem in Poland is that education is often quite theoretical, and little practice-oriented. Many textbooks are full of definitions, trying to give an overview of every element, while making no real connection with practice. As a result, students often have to deal with practical situations without understanding many interactions and awareness of side effects of policy and management measures when not taking the whole system or logistic chain into consideration. However, a problem identified in discussions with teaching staff is that teachers need to be aware that practice is more than training standards. For example, dealing with standard logistics programmes does not necessarily prepare students for the labour market, where in a decade or so jobs may appear we never thought about. While "learning how to learn" might be a good approach (a course on "effective learning strategies" is provided), the theoretical thinking and repetition of facts remains strong. This reduces a society's capacity to innovate and solve problems, which negatively influences its competitive economic potential. The study of logistics (BA and MA) were designed in according to the philosophy that studies should be practice oriented. This is a challenge in the context of competitive pressure due to a decline in the number of students at a national level and reduction in teaching hours (a phenomenon that can be observed at many institutions of higher education in Poland). While there is merit in the idea that the student should obtain more effective classes, and be stimulated to do more self-study, practice oriented classes under teacher guidance are more time consuming. Furthermore, in larger groups student-teacher interaction as well as group work on-location becomes more difficult. In such a situation, an interesting idea is stimulating students to do practical class work based on elements of campus sustainability.

The following challenges need to be considered when introducing elements of sustainability into the curriculum and practice of subjects, the following factors need to be considered:

- Knowledge among staff about sustainable development and innovative teaching methods.
- The lack of willingness to change, often caused by scholars' and educators' own beliefs regarding their professional existence (Tuinman 1995).
- The lack of awareness of the usefulness of co-operation with other universities for increase the quality of education (Tuinman 1995).
- Vested interests and different goals of university staff and administration. While young academics should be involved, as they are often closer to students, tenured staff rather develops programmes (Tuinman 1995). In the case of logistics at WSB, the programme was co-developed to a significant extent by young staff members.
- Institutes and departments may often be a king of "closed shops" (Tuinman 1995), where process passed trust created through repeated interaction of its members (see Raiser 1999; Raiser et al. 2001) reduces the willingness to cooperate with outsiders with innovative approaches.

When involving students in research on transport and access for the disabled, this may not only be an occasion for obtaining practical experience. It may also provide knowledge on and strengthen incentives for improving the situation, while having potentially an effect on the students' own behaviour. Another example is identification and assessment of challenges in the supply chain of food products to the university restaurant for sustainability. This may provide a basis for supporting more sustainable production patterns. In fact, all elements of campus sustainability which are related to logistics can be included in the curriculum. However, a limitation is not only that such experience will be content specific, which may sometimes be difficult to use in a business context (for this reason cooperation with business should be extended). Also, relating logistics and sustainability issues to real life practice is an opportunity. Organizing ones' own life contains many features of logistics, where sustainability issues can be easily introduced.

The initiative to produce on-line manuals for students, including instructions for lectures, seminars and laboratories, is instrumental in supporting students' self-study and independent search for information. Besides lecture summaries and practical case-studies, they provide an overview of available literature on the subject. An advantage of the online manual is it can be easily adapted. The manuals are available via the moodle open-source learning platform, enabling communication with larger groups of students (case studies, presentations, papers, etc., can be easily distributed), while student inactivity can be observed.

The ideas presented here are general, and need deeper elaboration. For example, when there is no habit of self-study, introducing a programme based on supporting self-study and learning-by-doing without enough time for guidance may easily lead to a reduction in the quality of education. Another issue is the overemphasis on efficiency improvements in logistic chains, which also can be found in environmental management and projects for improved energy efficiency. Just to mention one example, if sustainability issues are introduced based on the idea that win-win situations are the basis for sustainable development, it may be forgotten that the resilience of the system may be threatened, while rebound effects may lead to increased resource use. Often, students are told that eco-driving, where the driver is trained in order to reduce fuel use while driving a truck, is a way to support environmental sustainability. However, a further system analysis should be made, as eco-driving not only saves fuel and reduces transport costs (improving a company's competitiveness on the market). Reduced costs, in case of competition, leads to a decrease in prices, which in turn may cause an increase in the demand for transport as well as products, in turn leading to increased resource use (compare Sterman 2000).

Thus, including research on elements of sustainability in the curriculum is quite possible. However, the moment that the study itself is focused too much on linear thinking (see Kahneman 2011) where technological solutions are considered to be able to solve different problems, this also may lead to a mechanical approach towards sustainability. Both logistics and sustainable development require a system approach where interactions and potential side effects are studies, and policy and policy implementation are linked with education. A way to develop such an approach is to turn things upside-down. Often, first theory is used in order to analyse and assess real-world phenomena. However, at such a moment, people tend not to focus on issues which the existing theory does not deal with, but may be important for the functioning of a logistic chain as well as sustainable development (compare Taleb 2012). In case of a BA or MA thesis, a student may start with identifying a problem, describe different problems, and then assess them using common sense (such an approach has been applied by the authors in seminars). At this moment, simple theories may be used re-assess the problems, after which the student may analyse more deeply by showing where breaking points/bottlenecks/fragilities appear. This is elementary in the sustainability discourse, as the bottom-line is the survival of a system. And a bottleneck or fragilities (e.g., lack of supply of an input, debts which can be collected by the bank each moment) create threats to survival. Then, a system approach can be introduced, related to issues of externalizing environmental and social problems to third parties (e.g., moving polluting activities to countries with poor environmental regulations or countries with low wages and low labour protection), which makes the link to sustainable development easier (see Platje 2013).

5 Concluding Remarks

While it is quite possible to include issues of social and environmental sustainability in the curriculum of logistics at WSB, there are many challenges to be dealt with which need deeper research. When including sustainability issues in a simplistic way, without considering a system approach, the impact of any type of policy may be contrary to principles of sustainable development due to unexpected side effects.

Discussed were two examples of policy which can be easily included in practical course work and related to sustainability issues. Access for the physically disabled as such empowers these people, and may contribute to similar policies outside the campus due to the example function. However, when focus is only on access of the campus, while car-pooling is supported without dealing with barriers in public transport and the infrastructure (e.g., pavements, bus and tram entrance), the physically disabled will still have to rely on support by others, as specially adjusted cars to travel individually are often too expensive.

As discussed, the car-pooling initiative may paradoxically strengthen the dependence on car transport, weakening the position of public transport. While, of course, public transport policy as well as infrastructural development is outside the competence of WSB, a question is to what extent the university should try to influence local authorities to deal with the issue. This requires a change in the university's strategy, which should be accompanied by a change in the awareness about the responsibility regarding regional sustainable development.

References

Amaral, L. P., Martins, N., & Gouveia, J. B. (2015). Quest for a sustainable university: A review. *International Journal of Sustainability in Higher Education, 16*(2), 155–172.

Googlemaps. www.googlemaps.pl/

Green, T. L. (2015). Lecturers' perspectives on how introductory economic courses address sustainability. *International Journal of Sustainability in Higher Education, 16*(1), 44–56.

Kahneman, D. (2011). *Thinking: Last and slow.* London: Penguin Books.

Lambrechts, W., Van Liedekerke, L., & Rymenams, S. (2015). Connecting sustainability initiatives with efficiency measures: An opportunity for business schools. *Central and Eastern European Journal of Management and Economics, 3*(2), 161–173.

Larán, M., & Andrades, J. (2015). Determining factors of environmental education in Spanish universities. *International Journal of Sustainability in Higher Education, 16*(2), 251–271.

Leal Filho, W., Manolas, E., & Pace, P. (2015). The future we want: Key issues on sustainable development in higher education after Rio and the UN decade of education for sustainable development. *International Journal of Sustainability in Higher Education, 16*(1), 112–129.

Otodojazd.pl. www.otodojazd.pl

Platje, J. (2013). Physical infrastructure and logistics from the perspective of transaction cost economics. *Central and Eastern European Journal of Management and Economics, 1*(1), 35–46.

Raiser, M. (1999). Trust in transition. EBRD Working paper 39, London.

Raiser, M., Haerpfer, C., Nowotny, T., & Wallace, C. (2001). Social capital in transition: A first look at the evidence. EBRD Working paper 61, London.

Sterman, J. D. (2000). *Business dynamics—system thinking and modeling for a complex world.* Boston: Irwin McGraw-Hill.
Taleb, N. N. (2012). *Antifragile—things that gain from disorder.* London: Penguin Books.
Too, L., & Bajracharya, B. (2015). Sustainable campus: Engaging the community in sustainability. *International Journal of Sustainability in Higher Education, 16*(1), 57–71.
Tuinman, J. (1995). Productive co-operation and collaboration among educational institutions of perceived unequal status. Practical fundamentals. *Tertiary Education and Management, 1*(1), 38–58.
WSB. (2015a). Prasowe Centrum Informacyjne. WSB, Wrocław. http://www.wsb.pl/wroclaw/dla-pasy
WSB. (2015b). ISO 9001 w WSB we Wrocławiu. WSB, Wrocław. http://www.wsb.pl/wroclaw/sites/wroclaw.nowestrony.sandbox.dti.teb-akademia.pl/files/default_images/dla_prasy/informacje_prasowe/iso_9001_w_wsb_we_wroclawiu.pdf
WSB. (2015c). Studencka sieć wspólnych dojazdów na uczelnię. WSB, Wrocław. https://www.otodojazd.pl/wsb/front-auth/login/redirect/wsb

Author Biographies

Prof. dr hab. Joost (Johannes) Platje is professor at the WSB University in Wrocław (Poland). He obtained a PhD from the University of Groningen (The Netherlands) and his habilitation thesis (University of Economics, Wroclaw, Poland) dealt with institutional capital as a factor determining capacity and capabilities for sustainable development. His research focuses on institutional foundations of science and sustainable development. He is scientific editor of different journals.

Prof. dr hab. Krzysztof Łobos is rector for scientific affairs and scientific development at the WSB University in Wrocław. He obtained his habilitation in management at the Wrocław University of Economics. His research focuses on efficiency issues in organizations.

Krzysztof Wilk is a PhD student at the WSB University in Wrocław. He obtained a master in construction technology and logistics.

Scaling up the Woven Filigree: (un) Common Systemic Thinking to Embedding Sustainability into the Curriculum in a Large-Scale Higher Education Institution in the UK

Valeria Ruiz Vargas and Graeme Heyes

Abstract

Education for Sustainable Development (ESD) is taking a rich variety of shapes and forms around the globe depending on cultures, resources, and general contexts. In addition, there is a growing but relatively small amount of research and guidance on embedding sustainability into the formal curriculum at a whole institution level. However, some institutions are successfully developing case studies through exploratory approaches, led by emerging roles that vary greatly between institutions. This characteristic seems to be a reflection of the complexities of the ESD agenda in higher education. This paper reports on the "scaling up" of approaches towards embedding sustainability into the curriculum, from one faculty to a whole institution (Manchester Metropolitan University). It analyses the results and achievements of this approach including the potential influence on the ESD agenda in the UK through the National Union of Students (NUS) Responsible Futures Project. Finally, it discusses the role, profile and background of the ESD lead for the vertical and horizontal approaches in large-scale institutions.

Keywords

Higher education for sustainable development · Strategy · Practice · Case study · Environmental management system · Barriers

---

V.R. Vargas (✉)
Centre for Excellence in Learning and Teaching, 1st Floor,
All Saints Building, Oxford Road, Manchester M15 6BH, UK
e-mail: v.vargas@mmu.ac.uk

G. Heyes
Centre for Aviation, Transport and the Environment (CATE), School of Science and the Environment, Manchester Metropolitan University, John Dalton Building, Chester Street, Manchester M1 5GD, UK
e-mail: g.heyes@mmu.ac.uk

© Springer International Publishing Switzerland 2016

W. Leal Filho and P. Pace (eds.), *Teaching Education for Sustainable Development at University Level*, World Sustainability Series,
DOI 10.1007/978-3-319-32928-4_21

1 Introduction

Manchester Metropolitan University (MMU) has a student population of more than 37,000 students of which 70 % remain in the North West of the UK after graduation. Additionally, 44 % of MMU's students come from low-income backgrounds. (MMU 2015) This presents a significant opportunity for MMU to contribute to the Education for Sustainable Development (ESD) skills, values and attitudes of the UK's North West population, because its graduates are likely to have considerable impact on the region's social, environmental and economic sustainability.

MMU has been working to include ESD into its Environmental Management System (EMS) (Tinker and Tzoulas 2015) through a policy area related to Teaching and Learning. The latest MMU's EcoCampus Audit report suggests that MMU is leading the way in this area compared to other universities, which are going through this audit. (Eco Campus 2015). Although teaching and learning might work differently from other policy areas such as waste management, there are several arguments to do so (Nicolaides 2006). However, few Higher Education institutions are committed and actively pursuing environmental and social sustainability beyond operations and teaching and learning is behind campus management in Europe and the US in term environmental sustainability and social responsibility (James and Card 2012).

For these reasons, this is an area with great potential for development. For instance, the practices of other widely defined policy areas need to be adapted for Learning and Teaching. In addition, research and theory on ESD has the potential to underpin approaches to its integration in the curriculum (for example, Lozano 2010). In practice however, individual organisational circumstances and cultures shape the barriers (Sterling 2012; Lozano 2010) to embedding ESD due to its links to values in education.

One of the latest initiatives in this area at MMU is the National Union of Students (NUS) Responsible Futures Accreditation Mark (RF). The RF project is based on the fact that some 60 % of students have either agreed or strongly agreed with the statement 'Sustainable development is something which I would like to learn more about', with 85 % agreeing that 'Sustainable development is something which universities should actively incorporate and promote' (NUS 2015).

The NUS is a confederation of 600 student unions working on behalf of, and accounting for over 95 % of higher education unions in the United Kingdom. The union has a strong history in campaigning for social rights issues, and it has been committed voice for issues such as climate change and sustainable development for many years. In this time, the union has attempted to engage with students on these issues in a number of ways, not least through the recent Carbon Ambassador and Green Impact programmes (circa 2011–present).

The RF project has encouraged or supported the development of several new and established ESD projects related to the formal and informal curriculum, whilst evaluating the MMU approach to embedding ESD into the curriculum. The broad success of the MMU approach has a number of implications for the wider ESD agenda in the United Kingdom. The NUS RF project, with criteria co-created by MMU and other institutions, has been shown to overcome many of the obstacles to ESD such as those identified by Sterling (2010), by conforming to the approaches put forward by Lozano (2012). An example of how the criteria have proved useful is demonstrated by the fact that the auditing process conducted by MMU students highlighted the fact that MMU's community engagement, although evidenced, was an area that could be improved, particularly in light of the institution's other significant achievements in ESD. If implemented nationally, this project has the ability to act as a framework to empower academic institutions to embed ESD across the institution by providing a broad strategic foundation on which initiatives can be developed.

This paper provides an overview of the process and structure of embedding ESD at MMU to date through appreciative enquiry and its evaluation through RF. This sees the ESD co-ordinator focus on asking questions, rather than seeking answers, in terms of the achievements and limitations of this process. The Paper achieves this around a framework of barriers to ESD integration, as identified by Sterling (2012), to illustrate how the approach may overcome such barriers. In doing so, the paper contributes to both wider ESD theory, and its practical application in higher and further education at a local and national level. It is worth acknowledging that this paper is not intended to be a full scientific research case study but a description of one example of the practice of embedding ESD in higher education and some of the complexities in this area.

2 Approach to Embedding ESD at MMU

In my role as ESD coordinator, I have facilitated the MMU approach to ESD. The ESD coordinator role had its origins as Sustainability Intern in the Art School. Early on in that role, I was tasked with developing an approach to embed sustainability into the Art School curriculum. This approach had three main strands (Shuttlewood and Vargas 2014).

1. Interviews with Programme Leaders and students.
2. Curriculum review through a full analysis of unit specifications.
3. The development of a sustainability forum with staff and student participation.

The success of this work saw the post develop into a central position in MMU as ESD co-ordinator where I have been applying a similar approach on a larger scale. Located centrally, the role has to be adapted to a different set of structures and cultures ranging from the subtle to explicit. For instance, diversity between and within faculties includes discipline-specific and organisational language, approaches to developing curriculum, to teaching and to working in general. In terms of curriculum design and development, some programme teams write programme specifications for a group of courses and others for one course, which raises a wide range of questions in terms of reviewing ESD related language in them.

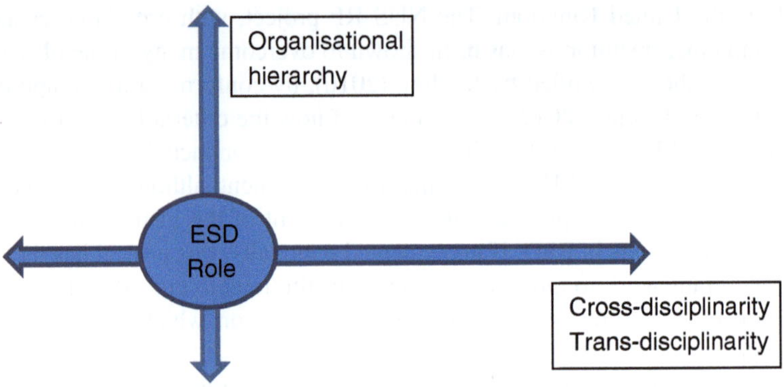

Fig. 1 ESD role in the vertical and horizontal approaches

To help overcome these issues MMU's approach to embedding sustainability into the curriculum is being developed through the "vertical" and "horizontal" domains, which are working paths towards an institution-wide, collaborative-mixed (i.e. horizontal and vertical) approach that aims to adapt to the dynamic nature and diversity of the institution (see Fig. 1).

These two domains are supported by the Strategy for Learning Teaching and Assessment (CELT 2014) and the Environmental Sustainability Strategy (MMU Environment Team 2014) which addresses two themes: Teaching, Learning and Research; and Estates and Operations. This has allowed exploratory activity leading to systemic change within the institution.

Reciprocally supported by the ESD steering group (consisting of academics and non-academics with an interest or time allocation on ESD). I work as the linking point between the vertical and horizontal approach making this one of many instances of the university-wide collaboration. The ESD co-ordinator role is part of a partnership between the Environment Team, the Centre for Excellence in Learning and Teaching (CELT) (which provides education and advisory services to MMU faculties and staff) and the Faculty of Science and Engineering. The steering group is cross-institutional and includes staff and student representatives from all faculties in MMU.

3 The Vertical Approach

The vertical approach is about engaging different hierarchical levels using channels that include reporting through MMU's governance structure (MMU Environment Team 2014). For instance, ESD activity and progress has been reported to the Estates and Services Advisory Group (ESAG), which is one of the committees and advisory groups established by the Board of Governors (Vargas and Prowse 2015). In addition, this activity has been reported to the Environmental Sustainability Board (ESB) and as ESD co-ordinator I have been invited to The Faculty Executive

Groups (FEG), whose membership includes Heads of Departments and Deans. Currently, the ESD steering group does not report to FEG. However, MMU is exploring which would be the best reporting structure through curriculum boards and groups.

4 The Horizontal Approach

The horizontal approach works on the principle of collaboration between different faculties and departments, including Estates and Central departments, such as CELT. This path provides a platform for links between different faculties or disciplines that otherwise would be unlikely to work together; in the process providing benefit to ESD work, improving the student experience, and facilitating a holistic view as to how their degree is related to authentic situation learning.

One example of successful collaboration between faculties emerged from attending the Sustainable and Ethical Enterprise Group (SEEG) and the Sustainability Research Network at MMU. Through these groups a Senior Lecturer in Fashion, Art School; a Principal Lecturer in Electrical & Electronics Engineering, Faculty of Science and Engineering and I developed a project to explore ways to bridge curriculum gaps in the area of sustainable production and consumption whilst addressing priorities for human development. The project named *Incorporating Sustainable Wool Processing using Engineering Solutions into the Academic Curriculum* won the 2nd European Award for Best Practices for the Integration of Sustainable Human Development (SHD) into Technology and Engineering Education (Fernando et al. 2014).

5 Supporting Initiatives and Framework

The MMU approach is strongly supported by a wide range of formal and informal Continuing Professional Development (CPD) activities, and by extra-curricular opportunities for students. These include: a curriculum review tool based on the Quality Assurance Agency's ESD Guidance (QAA 2014); bespoke workshops; and two accredited postgraduate units—*Education for Sustainable Development* and *Global Citizens, Global Learners*. Opportunities for students include support to develop projects and papers, workshop facilitating skills development and voluntary auditing work experience.

In addition, a number of research projects also support the development of the approach to embed ESD into the curriculum of MMU. Examples of this are a Society for Research into Higher Education (SRHE) Scoping Award: *The Potential of the Human Capabilities Approach (HCA) for strategy development in the Higher Education curriculum* and a Higher Education Academy (HEA) funded project: *Integrating strategic goals in the 21st century curriculum: creating a new resource.*

6 National Union of Student (NUS) Responsible Futures (RF) Project

The ambition for RF is to create an externally assessed accreditation mark for academic institutions that is desirable to them—rather than being viewed as bureaucratic or irrelevant (NUS 2015). This accreditation would assess universities on a whole-institution level, based on their approach to environmental and social responsibility, i.e. in line with the broader definitions of Sustainable Development,

Table 1 Overview of MMU's commitments, interventions and outcomes reported to RF, criteria adapted from NUS (2015)

Area	MMU's commitment/intervention/outcomes
1. Knowledge and understanding	Enrolment student surveys, NUS HEA local survey results, global citizenship survey staff and students, curriculum audit
2. Partnership	ESD steering group, SMART action plan, engagement of five key stakeholder groups, senior staff sponsor, graduate attributes, corporate strategy, L&T strategy, sustainability strategy, internal communication strategies
3. Policy and commitment	SU policy commitment, student officer (ESD), time allocation for academic staff, very diverse CPD offer, curriculum review tool based on QAA guidance (2014), HR processes, induction
4. Interventions	Internal events, external change programme, funding opportunities, collaboration between academic staff and estates, student coursework, courses about SD, interdisciplinary experiences for students (faculty, course, unit level), informal curriculum (MMU Futures 2015)
5. Leadership and outreach	Support other institutions on ESD, ESD in community outreach activities and present MMU's work at sector events
6. Progress and positive outcomes for staff and students	1. Society for Research into Higher Education **(SRHE) Scoping Award 2014** 2. Higher Education Academy **(HEA) Enhancement Programme** 3. HEA Integrating strategic goals in the 21st century curriculum 4. **(GDEE) European Award** (Fernando et al. 2014) 5. Result of 100 % in Education for Sustainable Development criteria in the **People and Planet Green League** (2015), which contributed to MMU's 3rd place in this league 6. **Eco campus gold** Eco campus gold awarded to MMU in March 2015 7. Several **blogs and emails from students** about positive outcomes related to ESD 8. **New degrees**: BSc contemporary health and BA food business entrepreneurship

that include the triple bottom line issues of the Environment, Society and the Economy (Elkington 1997).

The whole-institution approach to RF sees the students' union working actively with the institution in a partnership, with the aim of delivering together positive change to both the institution, and to its students (Table 1).

The accreditation process of RF comprises approximately 36 pre-defined criteria in six main areas (Table 1), the completion of which would help facilitate and embed sustainability and social responsibility issues in the core business of participating institutions. These criteria were developed by a number of pilot institutions including MMU, in a series of workshops led by the NUS (2015). Ten of the criteria are mandatory in nature, whilst the rest are optional. In addition there is a number of open criteria where the institution is able to include activities it may have conducted and seen as relevant to RF, but that did not fit into any of the criteria.

Rather than being conducted by an NUS representative, the RF project sees students recruited by the institutions and trained as NUS auditors (under the guidance of an NUS member of staff). Following the audit, members reported to the intuition their findings, followed by an additional report from the NUS on the audit outcomes, and any recommendations that could be made (NUS 2015).

7 ESD Role: Profile and Background

In some higher education institutions, an ESD role similar to the one introduced above is emerging. In MMU, in the role of ESD co-ordinator, I lead the approach to embed ESD into the curriculum as well as the Teaching and Learning policy area within the EMS—developed around the EcoCampus framework towards ISO14001 accreditation (Tinker and Tzoulas 2015). From discussing such role with the pilot institutions working to develop and gain RF (NUS 2015), it seems that such role varies greatly from one institution to another across the UK and these variations occur at different levels. At a very basic level, the ESD role can be part time or full time. The role sometimes sits in the students' union, however in other cases it sits centrally in the institution, in the academic services or estates department. The staff in this role also vary from early career professionals to experienced academics. The focus of the role too may vary; some roles may have a stronger focus on social responsibility, others on environmental sustainability and others having a holistic ESD spectrum goal.

Firstly, this role brings the possibility of uncertainty, because it is not yet an established role in higher education institutions. In MMU, I face the challenge of working through a structure that is not yet fully defined, due to the fact that this is an emerging field. The benefit of this uncertainty is that it allows me, my managers and less directly the staff interacting with the role to shape it and develop it. We would argue that if the role is not linked to academic development when becoming mainstream, it risks becoming more prescriptive which may reduce our ability to develop an adaptive approach.

Secondly, as the role needs to move with ease between the horizontal and vertical axes, or domains, (see Fig. 1) to develop the MMU's approach presented earlier in the paper of this paper, the profile of my role in MMU needs to address the following in each domain:

1. Horizontal domain within the mixed approach:
   I engage with different disciplines through multidisciplinary initiatives, with the view of developing 'transdisciplinarity' (Max-Neef 2005). In order to do this, the role develops or requires flexibility and the ability to provide impromptu ideas on how to embed ESD into a wide range of situations and initiatives.
2. Vertical domain within the mixed approach:
   I also encourage ESD activity and support groups and individuals at various hierarchical levels in the university's structure, with the view of exploring multiple levels of engagement. In order to do this, I need to be able to engage different audiences, and some cases to use subtle influencing skills.

I have the ability to report and communicate directly with senior decision makers, but at the same time be able to work with the silos as in an approachable, collaborative way that is empathetic to their own needs and concerns. Doing so has helped to start establishing trust towards the co-ordinator, and thus 'buy-in' to the ESD agenda; these are two important objectives for any individual looking to implement change in an organisation (Neyland 2008).

Finally, my role at MMU needs to adapt to institutional changes working in an aspirational and adaptive, rather than prescriptive way. For instance, attitudes towards values might change over time amongst individuals, requiring me to manage these changes by asking appropriate questions to develop ESD from a culture of values.

Although several post holders in equivalent roles across the UK in this area have a scientific background, and I do not, the analysis above suggests that some key requirements for my role may be creativity, adaptability, autonomy and engagement.

8 Achievements of the MMU Approach

Despite a number of barriers to embedding ESD in academic institutions (see for example Sterling 2012; Lozano 2010), and to achieving organisational change in general (see Nonaka 1996), the work thus far described in this paper can be considered a success on a number of levels. Organisational change is widely regarded in the literature as a complex and difficult thing to achieve requiring buy-in at senior levels, cross-organisational commitment, and a general high level of awareness about the issues at the root of the change sought (Nonaka 1996). MMU's approach to ESD can be seen as successful in this regard in that the ESD role, with vertical and horizontal flexibility, has empowered me, as coordinator, to communicate at high levels within the organisation.

Lozano (2010) identified a list of barriers (reference) and recommend seven ways in which they might be overcome. Table 1 illustrates how the MMU approach was able to apply these solutions (Table 2).

Table 2 How barriers to ESD may be overcome (adapted from Lozano 2010)

Potential solution	MMU performance
Prioritising teaching of SD concepts	SD concepts being embedded into curricula across the institution, albeit this is typically as a bolt-on to existing course material, rather than becoming a central aspect within each curriculum
Incremental implementation of SD	Rather than demanding that sustainable development principles be deeply embedded into course curricula as a one off exercise, the process has been incrementally focused to ensure that participants find the processes less overwhelming and have the flexibility to adapt and develop it on their own terms
Utilising multiplier effect from first steps	The MMU approach has seen the initial-incrementally focused steps to ESD set the groundwork for further achievements to follow. For example, a project by Fernando et al. (2014) on human and sustainable development led to further projects including a 'wool-counter' device that resulted in an academic paper. Additionally, a range of extra-curricular activities [i.e. the MMU Futures scheme (MMU 2015)], and subliminal and informal curricula (Fig. 2) (such as communication and engagement strategies) help to raise the awareness of ESD in 'soft-touch' ways
Intertwining sustainability in regular courses	At MMU sustainable development principles are starting to become embedded into courses traditionally not associated with such issues. This is well demonstrated in the Business School, where students take part in a sustainable business module that complements other modules rooted in more traditional neo-classical economic theories (Tomer 2002). The idea being to educate students on the failings of the neo-classical economics, and how capitalism can be a force for good by internalising externalities such as the environment The example of the Business School's Sustainable Business module is an example of this
Staff promotion or top-down managerialism	Vertical approach provides top-down facilitation of ESD
Tailor ESD to the nature of each specific course	ESD principles are being embedded on a course-by-course basis to ensure that the materials covered are relevant to the taught material
Using leverage from top management	Vertical approach provides top-down facilitation of ESD to individual departments, facilitated through the institutions overarching corporate and sustainable strategies

9 Limitations and Critique of the MMU Approach and Evaluation

MMU's approach to ESD has been assessed externally through the RF project ran by the NUS. This has seen MMU become accredited through the project for their engagement with ESD. However, a number of limitations to the approach can be observed, through which MMU may be able to improve their ESD approach. From a curriculum perspective, embedding ESD as a 'bolt-on' to the established course material has proved successful in light of the knowledge and resources (particularly time) made available to the ESD coordinator, whilst also facilitating buy-in from course leaders and mitigating the concern that their course and established materials are under threat. From a purely sustainable development perspective however, it could be argued that this approach is not fully efficient as sustainability issues are more likely to be considered as subsidiary to the wider subject matter. For example, if over-consumption is the primary threat to the sustainable development of society (Monbiot 2007; Porritt 2007; Meadows et al. 1972), then it can be argued that this should be a central component in academic fields such as marketing—which are often focused at maximising consumption in the search for enhanced profits (see Tye 2002).

Implementing such initiatives is however limited by the fact that I, as ESD coordinator, have a lack of knowledge regarding the specificities of all courses taught at MMU and certainly how these relate to the often-abstract theories of sustainable development. This is not a critique of my particular capabilities, but rather an observation that it is unlikely that any individual would hold such high-level understanding of such a range of interdisciplinary issues as required for this kind of cross-institutional role. Overcoming this obstacle could be facilitated by having a local coordinator in each department of the university. Such a role would be able to specialise in the pertinent theories within each course, and act as the facilitator of ESD into the curricula as required. This too however could be limited by the fact that as ESD is a relatively nascent field engaging with more established fields, existing knowledge regarding ESD within these departments may be limited. A solution could be for each department to individually recruit staff to new roles rooted in both the sustainable development and standard course literature, with this person acting as lecturer, researcher, and ESD coordinator. The university is aware of the benefits of this approach and they form part the long term plan for the institution, however implementing such ideas is difficult due to barriers of finding such skilled employees, and obtaining the necessary funds.

It should be noted that the MMU Board of Governors has no direct ability to communicate downstream to the individual faculties and other disparate groups of the institution. As ESD coordinator I function in this gap (in terms of vertical flexibility), however the level of engagement I have in this respect is limited. This could be addressed by increasing the seniority of the coordinator role, which would also respond to a further critique of the approach in that the ESD co-ordinator does not have the power of senior management to actively impose the sustainable development agenda across the institution. Whilst my horizontal and vertical flexibility to move around the institution acts in a way to overcome this problem, it is likely that an ESD role with more executive power would have enhanced efforts to embed ESD initiatives into the institution. However, this would warrant testing as it runs the risk of disconnecting the co-ordinator from the individual departments. By acting as an intermediary between senior management and the silos, the coordinator has the ability to apply a 'soft-touch' approach to implement ESD within the institution.

Additionally, the ESD approach taken by MMU to date is somewhat short-term in nature, in that the contract of the coordinator is only on a short-term basis, coupled with an overall short-term strategy towards ESD by the university. A longer term ESD coordinator appointment would allow for longer term projects, and to help facilitate longer term strategies with greater reward potential. This could include, for example, ensuring that ESD at MMU includes the formal and informal curriculum, the subliminal curriculum (i.e. subconscious learning from the campus), and research, and that these are able to facilitate direct impacts within the local community, as illustrated in Fig. 2.

Engaging in this way could be particularly important in light of the fact that a further critique of the current MMU approach regards the institution's engagement with the local community. This is not to say that the university has neglected such groups, indeed, several successes have been achieved; not least working with Manchester City Council and local businesses on a carbon literacy project, and a number of smaller scale initiatives. Longer-term ownership and strategy of ESD within the institution would enable projects with more outreach to be implemented, for example application of a Living Lab framework (Niitamo et al. 2006), that would enable more holistic projects that have the ability to bring together the student body, researchers, academics, and local community groups.

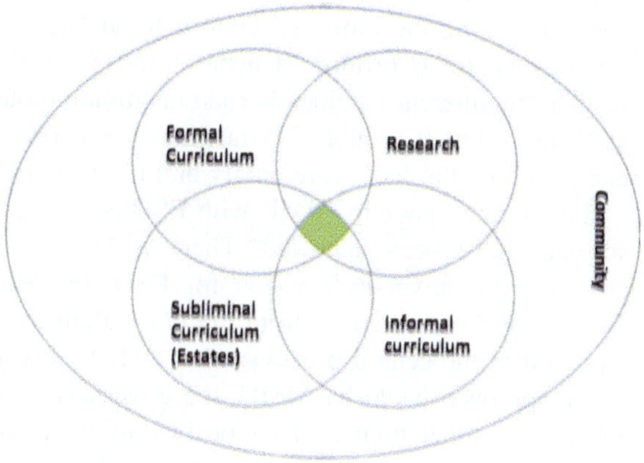

Fig. 2 Student experience domains, adapted from Willmore and Tweddell (2015)

10 Conclusion

The work described has broadly been a success, bringing together the many dispersed efforts of the institution to embed ESD principles throughout the university in a single holistic approach.

The vertical and horizontal approach has helped to facilitate clear and visible change across the institution, empowering me as ESD co-ordinator to report to the Board of Governors, and to support the individual departments across the university. In doing so, these independent groups are brought together in such a way that wider implementation of ESD principles is beginning to be achieved. The vertical approach is limited in its ability to communicate between faculties, and in terms of reporting down from the Board to these faculties—but in the context of a short-term project, this is understandable.

A longer-term strategic approach and vision for ESD would see the linkages between the Board of Governors and the individual faculties strengthened, facilitated by the coordinator. Long-term strategic direction and visioning can be considered an essential process of an organisation's success and so the lack of such a long-term vision can be viewed as something of a failing of the MMU approach to date, despite its evident commitment to tackling the ESD agenda.

The limited seniority of ESD role has been judged as one of the main contributing factors to the role's overall success. It gives flexibility for academics to lead and shape their projects in the most appropriate way for them. Working in this way, combined with vertical and horizontal flexibility, has enabled the co-ordinator to act as a facilitator between senior management and lower level groups.

One of the key elements of a long-term strategy might be the Living Lab Framework (Niitamo et al. 2006); a project designed to link different parts of the institution together in such a way that the campus becomes a living laboratory in which innovation and ESD principles may be implemented and tested together. Discussions are currently in place to link this type of work with both MMU and Manchester University, and could include the businesses that exist between the two, potentially along the proposed Oxford Road Green Corridor into central Manchester city centre (Corridor Manchester 2015). Doing so would not only bring together the different faculties in each institution (potentially improving the student experience), but it would also facilitate cross-institutional working, with direct benefit to both the local community and the local environment.

The progress made by MMU with ESD is the start of a journey, in which many successes have been achieved. There is however a long way to go towards achieving the university's vision for ESD, by seeing it fully embedded in all activities in the institution; from the curriculum it teaches, the research it undertakes, and to the central processes that underlie everything it does.

The approach taken by MMU, the governance structure and the ESD role are replicable to other higher education institutions across the UK and potentially in other countries. However, due to barriers of the culture of each institution these need adaptation in terms of the subtleties and the practicalities of the approach.

Finally, as a nascent field that is still under development, and in the nature of collaboration and shared learning, we welcome and encourage feedback regarding this article, and the MMU approach to ESD described above. In addition, I, as ESD Co-ordinator and MMU as an institution are interested in making links and embedding ESD through partnerships and knowledge exchange. All ESD resources are publicly available for other institutions to use them within their own context. If you would like to share your feedback or get further understanding of the details of this approach—the woven filigree—please feel free to contact the authors using the contact details provided.

References

Corridor Manchester. (2015). Strategic Vision. Available at http://www.corridormanchester.com/_filestore/corridormanchester/cm-strategic-vision-2020-pdf/original/CM_strategic_vision_2020.pdf on the July 10, 2015.

Eco Campus Audit. (2015). Manchester Metropolitan University.

Fernando, M., Langdown, A. & Vargas, V. (2014). *Incorporating sustainable wool processing using engineering solutions into the academic curriculum*. Global Dimension in Engineering Education. Available at http://gdee.eu/images/Awards/Incorporating-Sustainable-Wool-Processing.pdf on the May 27, 2014.

James, M., & Card, K. (2012). Factors contributing to institutions achieving environmental sustainability. *International Journal of Sustainability in Higher Education, 13*(2), 166–176. Permanent link to this document: http://dx.doi.org/10.1108/14676371211211845. Downloaded on July 14, 2015.

Lozano, R. (2010). Diffusion of sustainable development in universities' curricula: An empirical example from Cardiff University. *Journal of Cleaner Production, 18*, 637–644. Available at http://www.esd.leeds.ac.uk/fileadmin/documents/esd/12._Lozano._2010._Diffusion_of_sustainable_development_in_universities__curricula.pdf on the July 8, 2015.

Manchester Metropolitan University. (2015). MMU Futures. Available at http://www.mmu.ac.uk/students/futures/ on the July 6, 2015.

Max-Neef, M. A. (2005). Foundations of transdisciplinarity. *Ecological Economics, 53*(1), 5–16.

Meadows, D. H., Meadows, D. L., Randers, J., & Behrens, W. W. (1972). The limits to growth. *New York, 102*.

Monbiot, G. (2007). *Heat: How we can stop the planet burning*. UK: Penguin.

National Union of Students. (2015). *Responsible futures accreditation criteria version 1*. Retrieved from www.nus.org.uk/responsiblefutures

Neyland, D. (2008). *Organizational ethnography*. Thousand Oaks: Sage.

Nicolaides, A. (2006). The implementation of environmental management towards sustainable universities and education for sustainable development as an ethical imperative. *International Journal of Sustainability in Higher Education, 7*(4), 414–424. Permanent link to this document: http://dx.doi.org/10.1108/14676370610702217. Downloaded on July 14, 2015.

Niitamo, V. P., Kulkki, S., Eriksson, M., & Hribernik, K. A. (2006). State-of-the-art and good practice in the field of living labs. In Proceedings of the 12th International Conference on Concurrent Enterprising (ICE2006): Innovative Products and Services Through Collaborative Networks (pp. 341–348). Nottingham: Center for Concurrent Enterprise.

Nonaka, I. (1996). The knowledge-creating company. In S. Ken (Ed.), *How organizations learn*. London: ITB Press.

People & Planet Green League. (2015). Available at https://peopleandplanet.org/university-league/2015/tables?uni=11329 on the July 16, 2015.

Porritt, J. (2007). *Capitalism as if the World Matters*. London: Earthscan.

QAA. (2014). *Education for sustainable development: Guidance for UK higher education providers*. Gloucester. Available at http://www.qaa.ac.uk/en/Publications/Documents/Education-sustainable-development-Guidance-June-14.pdf on the December 17, 2014.

Shuttlewood, E. & Vargas, V. R. (2014) *Where we are: Manchester school of art's place in the world of sustainability*. Manchester School of Art (internal report), Manchester Metropolitan University.

Strategy for Learning, Teaching and Assessment (CELT). (2014). Manchester Metropolitan University. Available at http://www.celt.mmu.ac.uk/ltastrategy/ on the January 19, 2015.

MMU Environment Team. (2014). Governance structure. Manchester Metropolitan University. Available at https://icred.mmu.ac.uk/collaboration/ESG/Governance%20Structure/EMS%20Governance%20StructureV1.pdf on the May 27, 2015.

Tinker, H., & Tzoulas, K. (2015). The benefits and challenges of developing and implementing an environmental management system using a participatory approach: A case study of Manchester Metropolitan University, UK. In *Integrating sustainability thinking in science and engineering curricula* (pp. 425–438). Berlin: Springer International Publishing.

Tomer, J. (2002). *The human firm: A socio-economic analysis of its behaviour and potential in a new economic age*. Abingdon: Routledge.

Tye, L. (2002). *The father of Spin: Edward L and Bernays & the birth of public relations*. Victoria: Crown Publications.

Vargas, V. R. & Prowse, A. (2015). Education for sustainable development (ESD)/global citizenship progress report January 2015 (internal report). Manchester Metropolitan University.

Willmore, C., & Tweddell, H. (2015). Experiences of 'reflective action': Forging links between student informal activity and curriculum learning for sustainability. In *Transformative approaches to sustainable development at universities* (pp. 541–557). Berlin: Springer International Publishing.

Author Biographies

Valeria Vargas is ESD Co-ordinator at Manchester Metropolitan University and she leads the Environmental Management System policy area on ESD (teaching and learning), which includes the approach to embedding ESD into the curriculum. Valeria has a multi-disciplinary background and explores transdisciplinarity daily. She explores arts based research, action research, autoethnography and case studies as methods to address ESD in different contexts and through subtle approaches.

Graeme Heyes is a PhD student at Metropolitan University, conducting research in sustainable business model innovation, with a range of experience in sustainability, having working in a number of corporate roles in the past before returning to education in 2012. This includes working as the Environmental Manager at Keep Britain Tidy. Graeme has a keen interest in the sustainable development conversation, both in terms of the corporate approach to this challenge, and to how such concepts may be embedded in the education sector.

From Individuation to Autonomy: Enabling Fashion Design Students to See a Bigger Picture

Amanda Langdown and Eleanor Hannan

Abstract

Many UK fashion courses perpetuate the romantic notion of the individuated designer producing unique objects of wonder (Wood in Designers visionaries and other stories: a collection of sustainable design essays. Routledge, London, 2007; Clark in The Journal of Fashion Theory 12(4):427–446, 2008), encouraging and continuing a culture of production unfettered by the concerns of Education for Sustainable Development (ESD). Research shows, however, that there is a need for approaches within Design Education that promote and reward forms of creativity that are adaptive as well as innovative (Manzini in Designers visionaries and other stories: a collection of sustainable design essays. Routledge, London, 2007), and that this is an essential characteristic if curricula are to be developed for ESD. This paper reports on a Fashion Design undergraduate project that has been developed in light of institutional strategies for ESD and employability and for staff development in ESD. The project contributes to a wider, whole-institution approach taken by Manchester Metropolitan University as it takes part in the National Union of Students (NUS) *Responsible Futures* project. The paper explores the merits of implementing a cross-disciplinary approach that focuses on local environmental issues whilst remaining sensitive to globalisation. It analyses the resulting shifts in attitude of students towards sustainable design and adaptive

A. Langdown (✉)
Manchester School of Art, Manchester Metropolitan University,
Benzie Building, Manchester M15 6BR, UK
e-mail: a.langdown@mmu.ac.uk

E. Hannan
Centre for Excellence in Learning and Teaching, Manchester Metropolitan University,
All Saints Building, Oxford Road, Manchester M15 6BH, UK
e-mail: e.hannan@mmu.ac.uk

© Springer International Publishing Switzerland 2016

W. Leal Filho and P. Pace (eds.), *Teaching Education for Sustainable Development at University Level*, World Sustainability Series,
DOI 10.1007/978-3-319-32928-4_22

creative practices. Finally, it discusses the impact that this approach might have on future curriculum design for Fashion Education.

Keywords
Adaptive creativity · Sustainable fashion design · Collaboration

1 Introduction

This paper applies Castells' concept of individuation to autonomy in order to explain the process of transformation undertaken by undergraduate fashion design students as they participate in a project that attempts to enable them to see the bigger sustainability picture.

Castells (2012) distinguishes individuation and autonomy as the key trends affecting social change and cultural transformation since the 1970s. Individuation is characterised by behaviour that places emphasis on the projects of the individual (Giddens 1991; Beck 1992 in Castells 2012: 230) while autonomy is defined by the characteristics of discretion and sound decision making. The autonomous individual has the capacity to become a social actor 'by defining its action around projects constructed independently of the institutions of society' according to their values and interests (Castells 2012: 231).

The aim of the students' project was to reveal the labour behind the label, 'the fibre behind the fabric, the land behind the fibre and the person on the land' (Hawken in Fletcher and Grose 2012: 4). In short, encouraging student to question the dominant linear 'take, make, dispose' model of fashion production (Ellen MacArthur Foundation 2015) and to appreciate the interconnectedness of systems based on the values and concepts of an eco-local framework. Eco-localism is a framework for a sustainable economy and society that values the diversity of natural capital contained within the regions (Curtis 2003). The eco-local movement encompasses the principles and propositions adopted by the 'Slow Design' movement and the Circular Economy. These will be described more fully in the section covering the students' project.

This sustainable design project was offered as an option to first year undergraduate fashion students sitting Manchester School of Art's outward facing unit of study, 'Unit X'. This unit is designed to encourage cross-disciplinary collaboration between students across the school and further afield. 'Unit X' acknowledges the importance of providing projects that support public engagement with local regions and communities, thus creating a learning experience that 'engenders the kinds of shifts in thought and action required to meet the challenges facing the planet' (Cook and Cutting 2014). Scholars contend that place-based learning prompts these shifts in perception by enabling students to better understand their bio-geo-cultural context (Sherman and Burns 2015; Curtis 2003).

These shifts include their perceptions of creativity. Wood (2007) contends that 'creativity' has been 'characterised by the Romantic movement's somewhat theatrical, confident and self-absorbed mode of thinking' (Wood 2007: 104). This is reflected in the following commentary made by a first year fashion student:

> I was unhappy with the idea of upcycling to a waistcoat – I felt as though it didn't reflect me or my sense of design, which is very important to me, as I see fashion as self-expression and therefore a reflection of myself.

These comments illustrate Castells' concept of the individuation trend with its preference for transgressive forms of creativity. This is a form of creativity that can be characterised by an avoidance of context, namely 'social, political or ecological responsibility' (Wood 2007).

Therefore, the project offered opportunities for the individuated fashion student to employ more adaptive and altruistic aspects of creativity, expressed as 'ecological creativity' by Wood (2007: 104). These aspects of creativity enhance the designer's ability to anticipate the unknown and adapt to new contexts and changes within the environment. The autonomous designer is more inclined to use discretion and apply understanding of context to their designs.

The project used learner-centred pedagogies that encourage learning through direct participation (Sherman and Burns 2015) with creative communities and collaborative networks (Manzini 2007: 80). It is the participatory element of collaboration through these networks that trigger the transition to autonomy (Castells 2012: 232) as it introduces the culture of sharing, which is a positive step towards social equity and environmental sustainability.

This paper reports on the transformative process experienced by a group of twelve students as they take part in project designed to enable them to understand the multidimensional nature of sustainability, and recognise their own agency and interconnectedness with all life (Sherman and Burns 2015). The paper goes on to provide a brief background to Fashion's sustainability issues. It will build on the idea of the autonomous design student, drawing upon Castells' concept of autonomy. Greater detail will be provided about the students' project before the research aims and methodology of the paper are outlined. The findings of the research are then presented and discussed before some suggestions are made about the potential impact the research might have for fashion design education.

2 Background

Von Busch (2008) notes that as fashion leaks into every aspect of our lives the fashion system has evolved from a linear top down system; based in Paris and delivering collections of *haute couture* twice a year, to 'an extensive global distribution of multi-layered and complex systems'. The general public have never been so fashion "savvy" and yet for all of its multi-cultural influences and suggestions of a democracy of style it has never been so divisive (Von Busch 2008). Indeed the experience of fashion as a cultural phenomenon has become so commoditised that cultural identity is formed almost exclusively around extreme levels of marketing and consumption (McLaren 1995).

These cultural phenomenon inform a design applicant's motivation for studying fashion at Higher Education. Through informal conversations with applicants for fashion design programmes at Manchester Metropolitan University, interviewers noted that '*creative freedom*', '*freedom of expression*' and '*to be different*' were cited as reasons for selecting their programmes. These motivations strike an accord with Castells' notion of an individuated person, suggesting that students are orientated towards producing concepts and artefacts that are unprecedented. The following quote came from a first year fashion student's self-evaluation form, and provides an insight into student preconceptions about the role of context to the design process.

> I feel that my research needs to be really different, stand out in a crowd and this stops me seeing [sustainability] as something that should inform my work.

The reality facing the majority of fashion design students is far from glamorous. It is participating in the production of 'homogenised 'McFashion'… As unsatisfying, commonplace and utterly forgettable as the fast food equivalent' (Von Busch 2008). To add insult to injury, yesterday's original idea ends up in landfill. In Britain, 350,000 tonnes of clothing worth at least £140 million is thrown away each year, and it is estimated that £30 billion worth of clothes which haven't been worn in the last year hang unused in wardrobes (WRAP 2014).

In a search for the novelty and diversion that fast fashion provides, consumers tend to make decisions based on instant gratification rather than on anticipating long term gains (Offer 2006). Deyan Sudjic, the director of the British design museum, has suggested that one result of this is 'a world drowning in objects' (Sudjic 2008: 5).

3 Students' Perceptions of Creativity

Over the last 40 years, many fashion design students have learned to appreciate a form of creativity that has become overly concerned with image and in a perpetual search for the new and unique (Clark 2008; Manzini 2007; Wood 2007). The idea of creativity as self-expression is not especially pernicious in itself unless it is detached from a shared sense of wholeness (Wood 2007) but it has left some students with a very limited understanding of what creativity is. Here are some responses to the question 'what is creativity in fashion?' from the students on this project:

> … Making something unique to someone else.
>
> …Expressing yourself, having fun.
>
> ..The feeling that I did that, that's what I like.
>
> ..Leaving a legacy behind, to be remembered.

It is true to say that creativity is usually connected to original behaviour, and indeed, originality is necessary for creativity, but it is not enough (Runco 2004). Wood (2007) goes on to suggest that design educators should encourage new design mavericks; the sustainability heroes of the future, to think in ways that enable them to adapt to a variety of contexts. Therefore, in contrast to transgressive creativity, students should be encouraged to practice adaptive creativity that requires individuals to think critically, and to engage with social, political or ecological issues affecting the fashion industry. Runco (2004) suggests that it is this adaptive creativity that affords us 'the capacity to cope with the advances, opportunities, technologies and changes that are part of our current day-to-day lives'. There is a need for a fashion design student who can employ adaptive creativity, to see beyond their own personal projects and act as a force for design activism in order to reinvigorate public debate about the social and environmental values attached to fashion production. These are the characteristics that define an 'autonomous design student'.

The paper continues by describing the practical student design project that integrated a range of sustainable dimensions within its content.

4 Project Context

Before describing the student project, some institutional context for this research is useful. Manchester Metropolitan University (MMU) won the People and Planet Green League Award, naming it as the UK's most green university in 2013 (People and Planet 2013) and recently became an accredited UK National Union of Students (NUS) Responsible Futures institution (2015). It has various key institutional strategies (MMU 2014 and CELT 2014) that place high importance on Education for Sustainable Development (ESD). These strategies, and the resulting staff development opportunities and guidance on implementing ESD within curricula, have provided much of the motivation for this project.

The students that took part in this project had encountered some ESD in previous units. This took the form of lectures on or by sustainable designers or activists and did not have a practical element to them. However, ESD was not present in all units of study and was not specifically assessed. Application of ESD is, therefore, inconsistent across the curriculum.

5 The Students' Project

The student project to which this paper refers is called 'Knitprovisation'. As previously described, it is one of a range of projects that come under the umbrella of 'Unit X', the outward facing unit of study created at Manchester School of Art. 'Unit X' is designed to provide students with an opportunity to enhance their employability skills by encouraging collaboration. Emphasis is placed on enquiry, experimentation and reflection. The assessment criteria for 'Unit X' are listed below:

- Apply and reflect on teamwork and leadership skills.
- Recognise the broad context of art and design practice.

- Generate creative artwork in response to a collaborative, interdisciplinary brief.
- Present solutions and articulate ideas to a peer audience.

These criteria reward engagement with the design *process* rather than concentrating solely on the output of a creative artefact. The unit offered the flexibility to introduce and assess the principles of Education for Sustainable Development (ESD).

The project aimed to foster a more adaptive form of creativity in these students, by broadening their perspectives on fashion systems that sit with an eco-local framework through direct participation.

They were introduced to and engaged with two systems that are in opposition to the dominant linear system of fashion production:

1. 'Slow Design'. In relation to fashion this has been characterised by three main principles (Clark 2008: 427).
    - 'Valuing local economies and distributed economies.
    - Transparent production systems with less intermediation between consumer and producer.
    - Production of sustainable and sensorial products; that have a longer life and are more highly valued than typical consumables.'
2. 'The Circular Economy'. This system 'aims to keep resources in use as long as possible, extract the maximum value from them whilst in use, then recover and regenerate products and materials at the end of each service life'. It is often referred to as the closed loop system (WRAP 2015).

To this end, students were asked to up-cycle or recycle a discarded knitted garment using hand knitting techniques and locally produced woollen yarns. Through their design practice they were able to experience 'Slow Design'. Students were required to document their learning experiences through a blog and it was this reflective element of work that was submitted for assessment.

Scholars have identified that implementing a curriculum that seeks to educate for a sustainable future takes effort and resources (Cook and Cutting 2014), and while the content is important the process by which it is delivered is crucial for effective learner engagement with new values that are packed up in the content (Sherman and Burns 2015). Therefore, the 'Knitprovisation' group were set achievable challenges to promote participatory learning. For example, they were asked to make contact with a farm in their local community in order to connect clothing with the environment. They also increased their knowledge about a range of regional wool types. They were tasked with documenting this activity and to identify the breed of sheep that they had found. This task resulted in students having conversations with farmers and livestock traders about their animals and what their wool was used for.

The project also introduced students to examples of good practice and inspiring advocates of the 'closed loop' system within an eco-local framework. Katie Jones was one such pioneer. She is a young knitwear designer, who reuses the waste from Leicestershire knitwear factories as the main resource for her designs. By identifying good role models, and actually making something using the principles of 'Slow Design', it was hoped that students would begin to appreciate the symbiotic relationship that exists between environmental, economic and social dimensions of society (Winter and Cotton 2012).

In order to provide a more multidimensional and global perspective on sustainability students and staff collaborated with a Liberal arts university in Pennsylvania, which was also engaged in participatory learning about sustainable food production. There were opportunities to experience the concept of a multi local community through, shared learning and this was achieved through a collective blog and Skype discussion.

6 Aims of the Research

The aim of the research presented here was to investigate whether participation with 'Slow Design' and the Circular Economy could develop the capacity of those involved to become autonomous design students 'with skills, values and attitudes required to transition to sustainable society' (Sherman and Burns 2015). Developments would be indicated in the perceptions that the students held about sustainable design in fashion. Another important indicator would be a heightened awareness of environmental, economic and social issues affecting the fashion industry. Finally, students might begin to show attitudes or behaviours synonymous with being an autonomous design student.

To ascertain what the perceptions of students were, and whether they had changed as a result of the project, the students took part in reflective workshops. Details of the method used during this session are introduced in the next section.

7 Method

In order to produce information about the attitudes of students on the project, a method for eliciting reflective responses was necessary. These were generated using a form of Lego® Serious Play™ (LSP). This method comprises of a set of challenges given by a facilitator to which students respond by making models with Lego® bricks. Following each task, participants share their models with the group and reflect on their meaning (McCusker 2014). The approach can be likened to a focus group that utilises the making of artefacts to promote reflective discussion.

Alison James, who has an established practice using LSP with students at London College of Fashion, notes that 'by making reflection hands on and three dimensional through modelling, LSP has been effective in deepening reflection, provoking thought and making recollections more memorable' (James 2013). James also shares a discipline-specific motivation for using a non-traditional means of reflection with students. Reflection is often seen as 'merely being a dull, paper-based review of experience' (James 2013) by students and staff, resulting in shallow reflections. Therefore, in order to gain deeper insights into students' perceptions and attitudes towards sustainability in their discipline, LSP was identified as an innovative and appropriate tool for collecting the reflections that make up the body of data used to inform this paper.

Students were asked to complete a series of tasks, in line with the LSP method (Lego Group 2010), that progressed towards reflecting on their understanding of creativity in fashion, their experience of the project, and their thoughts and feelings towards sustainable design. For the main task, participants built three models that represented their perceptions of sustainable design practice before, during and after the project. Additional questions were used during the sharing process to help participants elaborate on their thinking. The LSP session was recorded as an audio file in order to be recalled in this paper.

8 Findings

Evidence that students' attitudes towards sustainability and their design practice has changed as a result of the project has been identified from the LSP workshop and relayed verbatim here. Where appropriate quotes from students' learning blogs are used as they provide a rich resource for understanding their changing perceptions.

8.1 In a Bubble

While a small portion of students said they knew about sustainability before coming to university, most said they had started the project with next to no knowledge of the subject:

> I knew nothing about sustainability… this is me when I was learning about it and it is like a lightbulb
> this is me at the beginning, in a little bubble, not knowing really what is going on

> This is me at the beginning and I'm not thinking about anything that I use like when I make things, being quite wasteful and not thinking about the environment or anything and just doing anything I want.

Closely related to this was a sense that, although they knew some of what 'goes on' in the fashion industry, they knew they had ignored it:

> Before uni I kind of knew what was going on but I didn't really ask questions, so kind of like a closed window, I just didn't even get involved.

8.2 Limited to Recycling

Perceptions prior to the project of sustainability and what it means for a designer's creative practice were frequently described in terms of being boring and limited to certain materials and styles.

> I used to think of sustainability as like recycling and stuff but now I think about not just recycling, like how I can actually use sustainability in my work

> I think I always thought that it was just about recycling and using biodegradable stuff and that it is always in greens and browns

> [I] had a very closed mind about what [sustainability] actually was and thought everything was kind of like green and hippie

8.3 New Concern for the Traceability of Their Materials

Materials are an inescapable aspect of current fashion education. It is common practice for students to purchase virgin material, which has not been previously used or processed, in order to complete design and make projects. Many students expressed a new concern for the traceability of materials and what happens throughout the lifecycle of a garment. For some this was recyclability, but for others it was informed by social issues, such as animal welfare and working conditions.

> Before I obviously used to use any material just that I liked the look of, whereas now I would probably, obviously think more about what it is made of and if it was to get thrown away, what effects it would have on the earth.

> I think now maybe I will consider more about where materials come from and where they are sourced from and look into more slower processes like what I have been experimenting with throughout the project

> At the start I was just looking at the colour and the fabric or something and that attitude towards sustainability has changed and now at the end it is something I would think about when I buy material

> Before completing this project I felt that sustainability was very limited in terms of what you can design, I felt it would be all organic fabrics and browns and greens, however this is not the case at all and in some ways it makes the designer have to work more creatively by designing with a problem and limited amount of resources.

8.4 Fun and Freedom

Having held ideas that sustainable design was dull and limited, students articulated what they perceived to be surprising, namely that they found it enjoyable! Where a dichotomy had existed between creative freedom and sustainable design, new perceptions had arisen that countered this.

> Sustainably and fun and interesting stuff can co-exist.
>
> you have got more freedom with it than you think you do
>
> I feel like it has opened my eyes more. I have more, you know, [more scope], more options than I did before. I was very closed minded before.
>
> I just thought sustainability was just like biodegradable stuff and things that are like dull and this project has shown me that you can still make whatever you want still, you just have to think about where the fabric comes from.
>
> acting sustainably doesn't have to be restricting. In fact, I believe that having to upcycle and make the most of my limited resources has forced me to be more creative

8.5 Emotional Responses

Two students expressed a change in their emotional response to issues surrounding the environment, particularly the sense that they felt their design practice had been self-centred.

> looking back on it seems that I was quite selfish
> I was thinking about other people so I was happier. I wasn't just selfish about me.
>
> I really truly believe that I will continue to work sustainably wherever possible as it's something that I now feel very strongly about

8.6 Broader Communities

The act of sharing learning through a blog and Skype has enabled students to see they are part of a much broader community.

> We then exchanged information about our project.. Which was called "soil to skin." About the production and process of wool. It was a very interesting lesson and It made me realise that although we're studying completely different subjects.. We're very much alike!! We both care about the production and where our materials are coming from.
>
> The top picture shows our class and the students we Skype in Allegheny … a gold crown to symbolise our realisation that sustainable fashion is the best option and how United if we all commit to it we could make a difference.

8.7 There Is More to Fashion Than 'The Look'

After expressing that sustainability encompasses more than they originally thought, some students reflected that they were thinking about further dimensions to their practice.

> I should think about things other than just the design and what it looks like. I should think about where it is going to be sourced from and like is it more sustainable and does it make a difference

> I have different priorities to kind of think about, what kind of designer should I be looking up to or what should I think about when I source my fabrics

This student spoke about seeing the production of fashion in a different way and shows initial understanding of how adaptive creativity demands a different position for the designer.

> [The model] represents how I became interested in how the hierarchies are broken and it is like designer and consumer are equal

Another noted how the process of designing sustainably could be collaborative.

> These [aspects of model] are like everyone else's ideas pitching in, like the little eyes and the head, like collaborative and bouncing off other people's ideas

8.8 Inconsistencies

Our findings echo with Winter and Cotton's study (2012); students identify inconsistency and 'patchy' delivery of ESD in the curriculum.

> I feel like, at the very beginning, I was getting interested in it but then it completely disappeared and wasn't interested in it anymore and now it has come back but stronger

9 Discussion

Whilst this is a small project and therefore broad generalisations should be avoided, the findings offer some points for discussion and possible wider implications for ESD in Fashion design studies.

The reflective workshop proved to be a useful tool for eliciting responses about the students' perceptions of sustainability. A common process of transformation was revealed: from knowing little or nothing about sustainability, most students described a new level of awareness and a keenness to explore alternative ways of working.

Students' resistance to engaging with social and environment issues prior to the project was wrapped up in the misconception that sustainability was '*just about recycling and using biodegradable stuff*'. It was '*green and hippie*'. These ideas deterred students because they saw this as a restriction on their creative freedom. When one student said '*acting sustainably doesn't have to be restricting. In fact, I believe that having to up cycle and make the most of my limited resources has forced me to be more creative*', they expressed a kind of revelation. The sustainable designer had been liberated from simply recycling to being a resourceful and creative maker. Sustainable design was not a 'style' anymore, but encompasses many appealing traits, and by moving beyond one-dimensional transgressive creativity, they discovered *more*, not less, creative licence.

It is clear that students became more concerned about the raw materials they use in their designs as a result of this project. This demonstrates their engagement with the environmental, economic and social issues as they no longer felt that any fabric would do. They no longer felt that the primary role of the project was to produce an artefact at any cost; without questioning the source of materials used. They indicated that they were more inclined to think critically about the context for their design work and to use a more adaptive approach, both characteristics of the autonomous designer.

Further than this, students felt empowered because acting sustainably was within their control and still allowed them to be creative. Several stated that they intended to change their practice to encompass sustainable materials in the future. This feeling of empowerment is important as it means that they are more capable of becoming agents for sustainable design and forces for design activism.

However, it should be noted that although most of the group said they cared more about the origin of the materials now, it was most definitely a '*maybe*' as to whether they would actually use ethically sourced or locally sourced materials in future projects. It was clear to the authors that students were wrestling with a dilemma of wanting to continue being sustainable, while at the same time knowing this would be difficult to achieve in all projects.

Perhaps not demonstrated in the findings, but apparent from student's blogs was that ESD gained more credibility and relevance with the students when they were able to discover good role models. Signposting students to designers who use adaptive creativity, and work effectively with 'slow design', helps students to gain a deeper understanding and acceptance of sustainable design practice. Furthermore, the element of collaboration seems to have bolstered their confidence, and reoriented them towards a broader world view, beyond their own interests.

However, they noticed when sustainability '*disappeared*' from the curriculum. They lost interest in it because it was not an explicit requirement in their other projects. Therefore, ESD needs to be embedded throughout the curriculum in order to maintain its relevance. This backs up arguments for integrating ESD throughout the curriculum, not just in stand-alone projects.

10 Conclusion

The intention of the student project reported here was to provide fashion students with a multidimensional learning experience that would help to challenge their preconceptions about fashion design. It was hoped that this would enable them to make the transition from the individuation trend associated with self-absorbed projects, to a position of autonomy (Castells 2012), from which they were more able to confront the unsustainable aspects of fast fashion, and to see design as something more than purely cosmetic.

Prior to attending university most participants had little knowledge about the issues of sustainability facing the fashion industry. On the whole, they put their own desire for differentiation before 'real world' issues.

Sustainable design was perceived as dull, and designing sustainably seemed to suggest a curtailing of their creative freedom. There was little incentive for them to engage with adaptive forms of creativity that could provide innovative solutions to real world problems.

The project successfully presented sustainable fashion without its sense of worthy 'hair shirt' and introduced a degree of novelty and playfulness to teaching sessions.

The participating students were guided towards examples and role models who are demonstrating adaptive forms of creativity, as exciting as any presented in fashion media. The students who actively engaged with the project tended to be more willing to let go of preconceived ideas about sustainable design.

A level of autonomy was achieved through the process of collaborating and networking, both within the group and with its overseas partners. This allowed the group to build their confidence and understanding, and 'to have more intense attachments in the world and feel more fully a part of it' (Lenvinson 1978: 195. cited in Tennant 1997: 51).

The students' comments might be interpreted as an indication that they are beginning to realise that they can work within the demands of sustainable practice and still satisfy their desire for self-expression and differentiation. However, the fashion curriculum must be aligned to reward adaptive creativity if progress towards a sustainable future is to be ensured.

References

Castells, M. (2012). *Networks of outrage and hope: Social movements in the internet age.* Cambridge: Polity. ISBN: 13:978-0-7456-6285-3(pb).

Centre for Excellence in Learning and Teaching. (2014). *MMU strategy for learning, teaching and assessment.* [Online] http://www.celt.mmu.ac.uk/ltastrategy/LTA_strategy.pdf. Accessed on May 15, 2015.

Clark, H. (2008). Slow fashion—An oxymoron—Or a promise of the future? *The Journal of Fashion Theory, 12*(4), 427–446.

Cook, R., & Cutting, R. (2014). 'Low-impact communities' and their value to experiential Education for Sustainability in higher education. *Journal of Adventure Education and Outdoor Learning* (Special Issue: Space, Place and Sustainability and the Role of Outdoor Education), *14*(3), 247–260 [online], June 20, 2015.

Curtis, F. (2003). Analysis. Eco-localism and sustainability. *Ecological Economics, 46*(1), 83–102 [online]. Accessed July 19, 2015.

Ellen Macarthur Foundation. (2015). http://www.ellenmacarthurfoundation.org [Online]. Accessed July 20, 2015.

Fletcher, K. (2007). Clothes that connect. In J. Chapman (Ed.), *Designers visionaries and other stories: A collection of sustainable design essays.* London: Routledge. ISBN-13: 978-1-84407-412-9.

Fletcher, K., & Grose, L. (2012). *Fashion & sustainability: Design for change.* London: Laurence King Publishing. ISBN-978 185609 754 5.

Fuad-Luke, A. (2007). Re-defining the purpose of (sustainable) design: Enter the design enablers, catalysts in co design. In J. Chapman (Ed.), *Designers visionaries and other stories: A collection of sustainable design essays*. London: Routledge. ISBN-13: 978-1-84407-412-9.
James, A. R. (2013). Lego serious play: A three-dimensional approach to learning development. *Journal of Learning Development in Higher Education,* (6). http://www.aldinhe.ac.uk/ojs/index.php?journal=jldhe&page=article&op=view&path%5B%5D=208 [Online]. Accessed on May 15, 2015.
Manchester Metropolitan University. (2014). *MMU environmental sustainability strategy 2014–2020.* http://issuu.com/mmuenvironment/docs/final_mmu_ess_issuu [Online]. Accessed on May 15, 2015.
Manzini, E. (2007). The scenario of a multi-local society: Creative communities, active networks and enabling solutions. In J. Chapman (Ed.), *Designers visionaries and other stories: A collection of sustainable design essays.* London: Routledge. ISBN-13: 978-1-84407-412-9.
McCusker, S. (2014). Serious play: Thinking about teaching and learning. *International Journal of Knowledge, Innovation and Entrepreneurship,* 2(1), *27–37.* Available http://www.ijkie.org/IJKIE_August2014_SEAN%20MCCUSKERv3.pdf, June 01, 2015.
McLaren, P. (1995). *Critical pedagogy and predatory culture: Oppositional politics in a postmodern era.* London: Routledge.
People and Planet. (2013). *People & planet green league 2013 Tables.* http://peopleandplanet.org/green-league-2013/tables [Online]. Accessed on May 26, 2015.
Runco, M. A. (2004). Creativity. *Annual Review of Psychology, 55*, 657–687.
Sherman, J., & Burns, H. (2015). Radically different learning: Implementing sustainability pedagogy in a university peer mentor program. *Teaching in Higher Education, 20*(3), 231–243 [online]. doi:10.1080/13562517.2014.993962. Accessed July 05, 2015.
Sudjic, D. (2008). *The language of things: How we are seduced by the objects around us*. London: Penguin.
Tennant, M. (1997). *Psychology and adult learning*. London: Routledge.
The LEGO Group. (2010). *Open-source introduction to LEGO(R) serious play(R).* http://seriousplaypro.com/docs/LSP_Open_Source_Brochure.pdf [Online]. Accessed on May 15, 2015.
Von Busch, O. (2008). *Sustainable: Hacktivism and engaged fashion design. Dissertation in design.* http://www.konst.gu.se/english/ArtMonitor/dissertations/otto_von_busch/ [Online]. Accessed on May 24, 2015.
Winter, J., & Cotton, D. (2012). Making the hidden curriculum visible: Sustainability literacy in higher education. *Environmental Education Research, 18*(6), 783–796.
Wood, J. (2007). Relative abundance: Fuller's discovery that the glass is always half full. In J. Chapman (Ed.), *Designers visionaries and other stories: A collection of sustainable design essays.* London: Routledge. ISBN-13:9781844074129.
WRAP. (2014). *Experts in the circular economy and resource efficiency.* http://www.wrap.org.uk/ [Online]. Accessed June 24, 2015.

Author Biographies

Amanda Langdown is a senior lecturer in fashion design at the Manchester School of art. Her research and design practice are primarily to do with education for sustainable development.

Eleanor Hannan is the Multimedia Resource Developer in the Centre for Excellence in Learning and Teaching. She studied at the Manchester School of Art, graduating from BA (Hons) Interactive Arts in 2013. She has a personal interest in sustainability through making.

The Development and Evaluation of a Sustainable Tourism Module Addressed to Student Hotel Managers

Mark C. Mifsud

Abstract

The study is an evaluation of a module addressed to student hotel managers entitled—'Sustainable Tourism'. The module was carried out through a face to face teaching environment and in the field with student hotel managers. The main aim of the module was to improve the environmental knowledge and technical abilities of hotel managers and increase their awareness on sustainable development and its application in the tourism industry. The study involved the use of a mixed method approach. The qualitative data was supplied through the use of a number of open ended questions in which the students could write down their feelings and opinions, while a questionnaire with a number of close ended questions supplied quantitative data. The research also utilized a number of sessions in which the participants had to come up with a thematic project that focused on evaluating the current sustainability of a hotel and formulating a strategic plan to move the hotel towards improved sustainability. The research identifies a number of areas in which the module was very effective (such as in the fieldwork) while it also highlights a number of areas which require improvement (less scientific verbiage). Overall, the module was found to be very effective in increasing the knowledge, awareness and attitudes of the students towards sustainable hotel management in the Maltese Islands. The individual project was seen as being highly effective in nurturing the skills required by student managers in order to properly guide the industry towards sustainability. The study proposes changes to the curriculum, in the pedagogy and methodology so as to increase the effectiveness of the module in developing tourism

M.C. Mifsud (✉)
Centre for Environmental and Education Research, University of Malta,
Msida MSD 1252, Malta
e-mail: mark.c.mifsud@um.edu.mt

© Springer International Publishing Switzerland 2016

W. Leal Filho and P. Pace (eds.), *Teaching Education for Sustainable Development at University Level*, World Sustainability Series,
DOI 10.1007/978-3-319-32928-4_23

managers which are not only knowledgeable and aware of sustainability and its application in the industry, but which are also able of positively influencing the knowledge, attitudes and behavior of tourists and staff towards the environment.

Keywords
Student hotel managers • Course development • Course evaluation • Sustainability mixed methods

1 Introduction

The usefulness or otherwise of a 'sustainable tourism' module for student hotel managers at diploma level has never been studied in the Maltese context. This study is an evaluation of the delivery of the unit and an analysis of student perceptions on this innovative module in the Maltese context. The module was mainly delivered through the use of lectures and a fieldwork session. The main aim of the module was to improve education for sustainable development knowledge, skills and values in student hotel managers and it mainly addressed local students through its contextualization. The perception of environmental issues, attitude and knowledge of students following such a course is of great importance as knowing what students think about environmental issues will encourage pro-environmental education (Pawlowski 1996) and also because the involvement of students in decision-making and the implementation of environmental and developmental programmes is critical to the long-term success of Agenda 21 (UNCED 1992).

2 Background to the Study

2.1 The Maltese Environment

The Maltese islands are a small archipelago located in the centre of the Mediterranean. The Maltese archipelago comprises three inhabited islands—Malta, Gozo and Comino—with a number of uninhabited smaller islands. The most serious environmental problems arise from the fact that Malta is one of the smallest states in the world and one of the most densely populated. The high population density is augmented further by high tourist arrivals of about 1.2 million yearly (Mallia et al. 2002). The main environmental issues on the island include waste production and management, reliance on fossil fuels for energy production, high private motor usage and freshwater production requiring a high energy input.

2.2 Local Environmental Education Development

Environmental education in Malta started off with environmental NGOs in the 1960s, mainly in response to the major environmental issues on the island. The awareness raising campaign was a very long affair, hindered in its development by a number of factors that lead to the slow growth of environmental education in the islands (Mifsud 2009). These factors include:

- the highly competitive educational system;
- the non-committal policy of the government;
- the colonial mentality.

In the formal education sector one of the major problems is the dominant educational ideology that suppresses creativity and rewards rehearsed words in examinations. Individual teachers who are interested in the environment may attempt to highlight environmental education, but the majority of teachers are hampered with little timetable time and lack of locally produced resources. Some materials currently used in schools were produced for use in other countries, and their transferability in the local context should be cautiously studied (Mifsud 2012).

With regards to the local government, it is apparent that the Maltese government mainly funds projects that have short term goals. Additionally, the lack of a clear national policy on environmental education has resulted in a waste of human resources and the shelving of long-term environmental education initiatives. Due to the fact that Malta was a colony for a long time, a number of anthropologists have indicated that the Maltese people seem to have a problem realising they own the island itself and its environment (Boissevain 1990). Subsequently, they do not attach much importance to the outside environment. Furthermore, although the Maltese native language is taught and understood by everyone, the English language is still considered to be more prestigious. The situation started to improve mainly in response to the requirements imposed on the country by the European Union. The government is now realising that the environmental education is an effective and long-term solution to ensure environmental sustainability. Many government officials speak of their commitment towards sustainability, but their concern is mainly short-term (Mifsud 2011).

2.3 Sustainable Development and Higher Education

Sustainable development has increased in importance both as a concept and as process within higher-education institutions in these last years. Such efforts include highlighting sustainability as a key theme within teaching, learning and research policies; increasing course content addressing sustainability; promoting initiatives encouraging sustainable energy and waste practices among students and teachers (Djordjevic and Cotton 2011). Nonetheless, evidence of efforts to include sustainable development related to the student hotel managers within institutes of

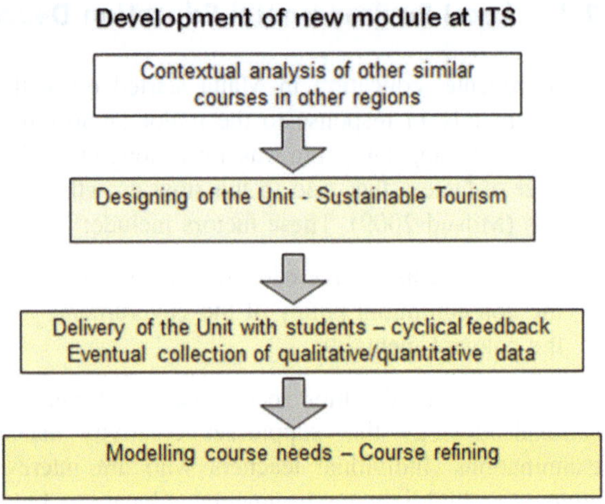

Fig. 1 The developmental process of the sustainable tourism module

higher education appears to be limited, with most of the courses having a more general focus. Notable efforts include courses such as those by the University of Manchester which offers a wide range of sustainability courses including courses addressed to hospitality professionals which emphasise positive change rather than on the threats posed by global environmental problems (Dobson and Tomkinson 2012).

2.4 The Institute of Tourism Studies and Education for Sustainable Development

The Institute of Tourism Studies (ITS) was established in 1987 and focuses on the changing needs of the Travel, Hospitality and Tourism Industry. ITS aims to produce professional personnel who are able to guarantee an excellent standard of products and services within the Hospitality Industry. The institute provides a range of courses at different levels and aimed at different tourism professionals including in the culinary arts, tourist guiding and in management. Each course is made up of a number of modules and a new module termed 'Sustainable Tourism' was designed, developed and introduced in 2013. Figure 1 illustrates the main processes involved in its formation. This particular module and its first participants are the focus the present study.

3 The Module Structure

The Module aims at instilling in students the significance of sustainable tourism. Sustainability issues are discussed from the social, the economic, the cultural and the environmental perspectives. The issues presented are coupled with field

Topic Number	Study Area
1	The Environment – An Introduction
2	The Environment – Introduction to the main global issues
3	The Environment - Waste/Water/Energy/Pollution
4	The Environment - Land Use Management/Social and cultural Issues/CSR
5	Case Studies
6	Sustainable Development
7	Case Studies
8	Sustainability Principles
9	Case Studies
10	Carrying Capacity, Limits to Acceptable Change
11	The Physical Impacts of Tourism
12	Strategies for managing Impacts
13	Eco-Certification
14	Global Synoptic Case Seminars
15	Field Activity

Fig. 2 The structure of the sustainable tourism module

observations. The module is structured (see Fig. 2) through a philosophy that will enable students to study tourism related sustainability issues in practice and in different contexts and encourages students to access and critically evaluate research and to develop the skills and attitudes necessary to promote sustainable lifestyles.

The module starts by exposing the students to the main current global environmental issues and then focuses on the local environmental issues which may be produced by tourism and tourism related activities. The unit then moves on to discuss the nature of sustainable development and the various principles of sustainability. Furthermore it lays down the principles of intergenerational equity, carrying capacity, resilience, consensus building, mitigation, viable economy, indigenous culture and quality of life. The unit also examines a large number of case studies, both local and global that portray both successful and inadequate attempts at sustainable tourism in order to understand the underlying frameworks. The unit then moves on to discuss the current local state of tourism and the tourism industry with a special focus on sustainability. This also includes current management practices with regard to water, waste, electricity generation and corporate social responsibility. A number of local tourism related concerns are scrutinized, including important areas such as Hotels, Natural Parks, Agro-tourism activities, travel agencies, Natura 2000 sites, eco-tourism, green tourism plans, sustainable tourism projects and eco certification. Although the local arena is the main focus of the unit, opportunities are provided to help students frame local issues within a global perspective. A main component of the course is the actual fieldwork in which the students choose a hotel and evaluate its sustainability drawing up a report and a list of recommendations to move the hotel towards more effective sustainability.

4 The Study

The study involved the use of questionnaires that focused on gathering the general socio-demographic student picture and an in depth student evaluation through open ended questions during term time. The main thrust was to find out how effective the module was being at promoting ESD and what avenues should be taken in order for the module to become more effective. The reponses were categoried and a number of themes emerged. The questionnaire was constructed following the examination of other instruments in the literature (e.g., Mifsud 2010; Barrett and Kuroda 2002; Eagles and Demare 1999; Gambro and Switzky 1996, 1999; Hodgkinson and Innes 2001; Kuhlemeier et al. 1999; Makki et al. 2003; Mogenson and Nielsen 2001; Fien et al. 2000; Pawlowski 1996). The research identifies a number of different areas which were effective in imparting knowledge, skills or values, while it also highlights areas which can be improved, changed or realigned in order to make the module more effective and operative.

5 Outline of the Methodology

There were thirty six participants in this study which represent the whole cohort of the students following the hotel managers course in Malta. The participants were forwarded a questionnaire to locate their socio-geographical characteristics, and eventually through a number of open ended questions they were allowed to write their feelings and perceptions.

The analysis of the open ended was carried through an adaptation of the approach identified by Vaughn et al. (1996) who suggested four processes:

1. identifying the big ideas—the participants' words and ideas and the intensity with which the participants responded provide an initial framework;
2. unitising the data—identifying units of information from the text that will later become the basis for forming themes;
3. categorising the units—bring together the units of data identified above that are related to the same content;
4. identifying the themes—after considering the big ideas and the categorisation of the units the main themes are identified and refined.

The selection of the 'quotes' to include was informed by a professional judgement of what was important and significant for the context of the study. This, in turn, was based on the considerations of trustworthiness and transparency in qualitative studies, insights gained from the literature and the existing knowledge of environmental education in Malta and the Maltese environmental-political-educational context.

6 Limitations of the Study

One of the limitations of the study was the issue of time management as delivering the questionnaire and collecting qualitative data used valuable course time which had to be continuously sensible to the needs of the students. Another limitation was the effect of the study on the participants responses as the study had to be carried out during the course. This may have influenced the participants to be more sympathetic in their answers to the course parameters. This limitation was partly addressed by carrying out the research after the publication of the assignment results.

Figure 3 illustrates the students' socio demographic backgrounds. A number of trends emerge:

Students N=36	Male	Female
	47.2%	52.8%

Age	16	17	18	19	20 and over
Students	2.7%	33.3%	25%	16.6%	22.2%

Geographic Location	Students
South	25%
North	25%
Central	41.6%
Not specified	8.4%

Fig. 3 Socio demographic characteristics of students

- The main entry qualification are a number of ordinary level subjects
- Most students' mothers and fathers not employed in tourism industry
- The students' geographic origin was spread across the islands, but a peak was registered in the Central region.

7 The Findings

7.1 Results of the Findings from the Quantitative Analyses

No previous study had ever been made on students following the diploma for management in tourism. The present study was of a mixed design. A short questionnaire with a number of course parameters was designed in order to give an overview of the course and to act as a precursor to a more 'personal' qualitative analysis. The quantitative results indicate a variety of responses from students in most of the course dimensions which were examined.

Nonetheless, it is clear that students did find that the individual work was not very effective (0 %), that the module was interesting (66.6 %) and the feedback was effective and useful (69.3 %). A clear weakness in the course was identified as the individual work, which was also corroborated in the qualitative analysis. Conversely, students appear to be much better off when working in teams and in collaboration on their projects as more than 82 % agreed with this statement. Other areas of the course structure had an average response throughout the continuum, such as; course structure and the suitability of the teaching environment. An illustrative set of quantitative findings from the study are found in Fig. 4.

7.2 Results of the Findings from the Qualitative Analyses

The present study has brought to the surface quite a range of views regarding the module, its effects and the relation between tourism and the environment in general. With no direct influence from the researcher, the participants introduced several broad themes, the main points of which are summarised below.

7.3 Main Themes

- Our Project
- Changes in Perception
- A New Dawn
- Strengths and Weaknesses
- The Future.

	Strongly agree	agree	Not certain	Disagree	Strongly disagree
The module covers the outlined scope, aims and objectives	33.3%	30.6%	30.6%	5.5%	0%
The module as a whole was well-structured	30.6%	66.6%	2.7%	0%	0%
The intellectual demands made on you were appropriate for the level of the course	33.3%	33.3%	33.3%	0%	0%
Were you satisfied with your own level of preparation and participation	16.6%	33.3%	50%	0%	0%
The module materials were adequate	30.6%	63.9%	5.5%	0%	0%
The feedback was adequate	69.3%	30.6%	0%	0%	0%
Teaching methods were adequate	50%	33.3%	16.6%	0%	0%
The availability of reading materials listed in the bibliography was reasonable accessible	33.3%	33.3%	33.3%	0%	0%
The course was interesting	66.6%	30.6%	2.7%	0%	0%
The course was difficult	16.6%	33.3%	25%	25%	0%
The course required too much effort	66.6%	30.6%	2.7%	0%	0%
Adequate support was provided	66.6%	30.6%	2.7%	0%	0%
The teaching environment was adequate	33.3%	33.3%	16.6%	16.6%	0%
Project supervision was adequate.	33.3%	33.3%	16.6%	16.6%	0%
Tutor interaction during feedback was adequate	66.6%	30.6%	2.7%	0%	0%
Group work was effective	16.6%	66.6%	8.3%	8.3%	0%
Individual work was effective	0%	0%	69.3%	30.6%	0%

Fig. 4 Selected quantitative results

7.3.1 Our Project

Many students reported that the project was a very important part of the module and that it relates theory to practice. Another advantage of the project was the fact that the students had to work in teams and collaborate together to achieve the desired outcome. Collaboration appears to be very important for this particular group of students. Most students also exhibited a sense of pride and ownership when they collectively presented the project.

> I came to learn about the sustainability of some local hotels, and the hotel I studied in much more detail, have developed a more insightful outlook towards the environment and have acquainted myself with some local indigenous creatures and their danger of extinction.
>
> The project allowed us to work as a team and study a hotel we wanted to study We were also able to propose some ideas on how the hotel can become more sustainable.

7.3.2 Changes in Perception

Many students reported a variety of changes in their knowledge, awareness or belief systems that occurred throughout the module and because of the module. Nonetheless, most of the students did not focus on any particular attitude or action and just mentioned that there was a positive change.

> Yes, I learned stuff I didn't know before that made me aware of some situations. I improved my knowledge.

I got to know how the environment and the hospitality industry are related and in the future when I will have my restaurant, I will have an ecological one that will care for the environment.

I am now more aware on what humans are doing and how it is affecting our planet.

7.3.3 A New Dawn

A number of students reported a number of changed behaviours or personal world views due to the teaching and learning that occurred during the module. Some students mentioned a positive change in lifestyle while others mentioned the development of leadership skills and the increased importance of being environmentally friendly.

Yes, because now I try and be more environmentally friendly and aware.

If everyone does something to change our lifestyle it could really help the environment.

Yes, because it made me more into a leader (environmental) and helped me to take care of the environment and others.

7.3.4 Strengths and Weaknesses

Students mentioned a large number of areas which were considered to be strengths and others that were considered to be weaknesses. The following points illustrate the wide ranging strengths and weaknesses as identified by the participants:

Strengths

- Increase in environmental awareness
- Discussions on environmental issues
- Ideas on pollution reduction through simple changes in workplace
- Teamwork during lectures and project
- Presentations about fieldwork done collaboratively.

Weaknesses

- Sometimes difficult to see applicability to the industry so early in the course
- Not enough practical lessons
- More useful if these lectures are held at the end of the course rather than in the first year
- More outdoor activities
- Module too broad when compared with other modules.

7.3.5 The Future

When discussing their opinion on the future of the module, most students mentioned that the module should increasingly cover the issue of food waste in the tourism industry, an area which was not adequately covered in this initial module. Other students mentioned the importance of increased field visits and some also talked about the importance of reducing some scientific detail to make the module more approachable to all students.

Increase the parts that have to do with food waste and food production and the tourism industry. Like I said, it is important to emphasize more on food waste as it is very important in our sector.

There is a big need for much more outdoor activities to see everything with our eyes rather than to examine them only through a picture.

There was too much detail about the environment when maybe with less detail we can still understand how to make a change for the better in our workplace.

8 Conclusions

The research has identified a number different areas that need to be addressed in order to make the 'sustainable tourism' module more relevant and effective with students in the management side of the tourism industry. These areas include:

1. a more effective and meaningful starting time for the module—which should be later on in the course so as students would be able to more easily make the connection between sustainability and the tourism industry.
2. a change in the module content to afford increased importance to food, in particular food waste and the importance of local food in the tourism industry in order for it to remain sustainable.
3. an increase in field activities—a more practical, hands on approach will lead to a better understanding of how the tourism industry is trying to infuse sustainability principles in its operation.
4. increased importance afforded to collaborative activities and a reduction in individual work—from the study, collaboration appears to be key in the formulation of solutions toward sustainability in the industry.
5. streamlining of the module in order to reduce scientific jargon and make the module more accessible to students.

All these suggestions must be examined for incorporation in the next module in order to increase effectiveness. A visual model that illustrates the necessary changes is depicted in Fig. 5.

This baseline study identified essential matters that need to be addressed in order to improve links between sustainability and hotel managers. The qualitative and quantitative methodology employed to uncover these findings may be applied in other countries following careful contextualization. Further research should be carried out on future student cohorts of this module to further improve the effectiveness of its teaching and learning model. Comparative research with other similar

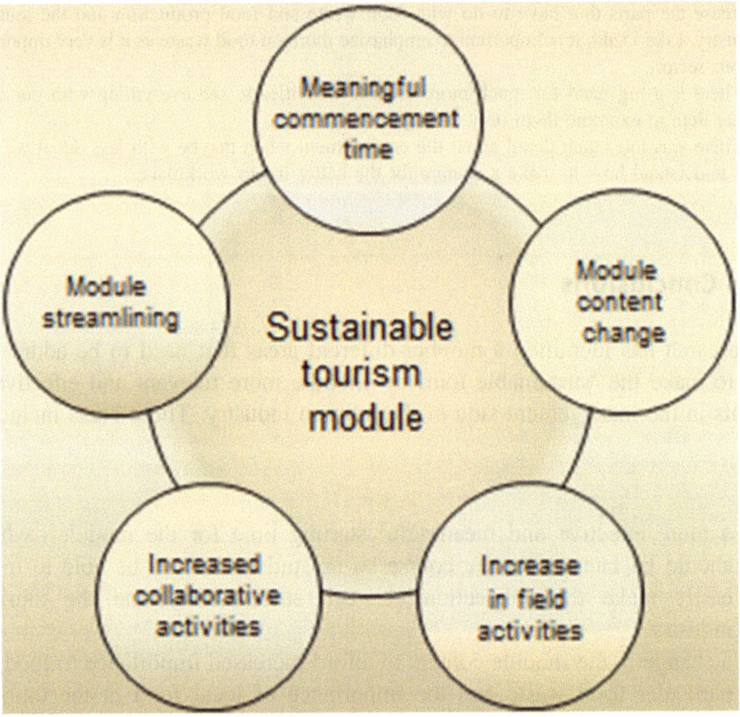

Fig. 5 Modelling of course evolution

modules in the Mediterranean, European and World regions would help to build a more universal module which should nonetheless be properly contextualized in each region in order to make it more relevant to the different realities.

References

Barrett, B. F. D., & Kuroda, A. (2002). Ecological modernisation, environmental knowledge and societal change: Attitude and behaviour of young people in Japan. *International Research in Geographical and Environmental Education, 11*(3), 237–261.

Boissevain, J. (1990). Why do the Maltese ask so few questions? *Education, 3*(4), 16–18.

Djordjevic, A., & Cotton, D. R. E. (2011). Communicating the sustainability message in higher education institutions. *International Journal of Sustainability in Higher Education, 12*(4), 381–394.

Dobson, H. E., & Tomkinson, C. B. (2012). Creating sustainable development change agents through problem-based learning: Designing appropriate student PBL projects. *International Journal of Sustainability in Higher Education, 13*(3), 263–278.

Eagles, P. F. J., & Demare, R. (1999). Factors Influencing children's environmental attitudes. *Journal of Environmental Education, 30*, 33.

Fien, J., Yencken, D., & Sykes, H. (2000). *Young people and the environment. An Asia Pacific perspective*. London: Kluwer Academic Publishers.

Gambro, J. S., & Switzky, H. N. (1996). A national survey of high school students' environmental knowledge. *Journal of Environmental Education, 27*(3), 28, 6p.

Gambro, J. S., & Switzky, H. N. (1999). Variables associated with American high school students knowledge of environmental issues related to energy and pollution. *Journal of Environmental Education, 30*(2), 15–22.

Hodgkinson, S. P., & Innes J. M. (2001). The attitudinal influence of career orientation in 1st year university students: Environmental attitudes as a function of degree choice. *Journal of Environmental Education, 32*(3), 37–40.

Kuhlemeier, H., Huub, V. D. B., & Nijs, L. (1999). Environmental knowledge, attitudes and behaviour in Dutch secondary education. *Journal of Environmental Education, 30*(2), 4, 11p.

Makki, M. H., Abd-El-Khalick, F., & Boujaoude, S. (2003). Lebanese Secondary School Students' environmental knowledge and attitudes. *Environmental Education Research, 9*(1), 21–33.

Mallia, A., Briguglio, M., Ellul, A. E., & Formosa, S. (2002). *Physical background, demography, tourism, mineral resources and land use.* In: State of the Environment Report for Malta, 2002. Ministry for Home Affairs and the Environment.

Mifsud, M. (2009). A critical review of the global events that have shaped the development of education for sustainable development. *Environmental Scientist, 18*(1). ISSN-09668411.

Mifsud, M. (2010). Focus groups effectiveness in studying youth environmental behaviour. In *Proceedings of the 6th International Conference on Education*, ISBN: 978-960-466-060-5, ISSN: 1790-3859.

Mifsud, M. (2011). Factors influencing environmental knowledge of Maltese youth. Environmental Scientist, *20*(2). ISSN-09668411.

Mifsud, M. (2012). A contextual study of the events that have shaped the development of environmental education in Malta. *Journal of Teacher Education for Sustainability, 12*(2), 110–128. ISBN: 978-960-466-060-5, ISSN: 1790-3859.

Mogenson, F., & Nielsen, K. (2001). Students' knowledge about environmental matters and their belief in their Own Action possibilities. *Journal of Environmental Education, 33*(1), 33, 3p.

Pawlowski, A. (1996). Perception of environmental problems by young people in Poland. *Environmental Education Research, 2*(3), 279–285.

UNCED. (1992). *Agenda 21: Programme of action for sustainable development.* N.Y, United Nations: Rio Declaration on Environment and Development.

Vaughn, S., Schumm, J., & Sinagub, J. (1996). *Focus group interviews in education and psychology.* Thousand Oaks, CA: SAGE Publications.

Author Biography

Mark C. Mifsud is a Senior Lecturer at the Centre for Environmental Education Research at the University of Malta. He is a Chartered Biologist, a Chartered Environmental Scientist, a Chartered Science Teacher, a Certified Wildlife Photographer and a Prince II Certified Practitioner with more than 20 years experience in Environmental Sciences, Environmental Education and Sustainable Development. Mark is presently the coordinator of the Masters in Education for Sustainable Development and his main areas of research include youth and the modelling of environmental knowledge and behaviour.

Dies Oecologicus—How to Foster a Whole Institutional Change with a Student-Led Project as Tipping Point for Sustainable Development at Universities

Miriam Block, Mirjam Braßler, Vincent Orth, Martin Riecke, Juan Miguel Rodriguez Lopez, Grischa Perino, Wey-Han Tan and Moritz Lamparter

Abstract

The student-led project organizing the event *Dies Oecologicus*, which aims for a whole institutional change by initiating a bottom-up sustainable development process, is described. Driven by the need for a more prominent role of sustainability in the university's curriculum, the daily lives of its members, and the governance and administration of the organisation, the initiative started off as an interdisciplinary student-led project. The university-wide event was realised based on an assessment of conducted interviews with change agents (at the University of Hamburg and other universities) at all levels of the university from several disciplines and faculties. The event *Dies Oecologicus* has been acknowledged as a single contribution to the UN Decade Education for Sustainable Development (DESD). During the event *Dies Oecologicus* participants from multiple backgrounds reflected on, discussed and created possible

M. Block (✉) · V. Orth · M. Riecke · M. Lamparter
AStA (Allgemeiner Studierenden Ausschuss, Student Union),
University of Hamburg, Von-Melle-Park 5, 20146 Hamburg, Germany
e-mail: miriam.block@posteo.de

V. Orth
e-mail: orth@chemie.uni-hamburg.de

M. Riecke
e-mail: martin.riecke@campusgruen.org

M. Lamparter
e-mail: moritz@dies-oecologicus-uhh.de

M. Braßler
Department of Work and Organizational Psychology, University of Hamburg,
Von-Melle-Park 11, 20146 Hamburg, Germany
e-mail: mirjam.brassler@uni-hamburg.de

© Springer International Publishing Switzerland 2016

W. Leal Filho and P. Pace (eds.), *Teaching Education for Sustainable Development at University Level*, World Sustainability Series,
DOI 10.1007/978-3-319-32928-4_24

concepts of a curriculum on ESD, student-led projects and the reduction of the ecological footprint of universities. The possible concept(s) for a curriculum on ESD was based on sessions focusing on identifying essential content, adequate didactical methods and feasible curricular realisations and integrations. Results of the project were summarised in an evaluation booklet, distributed throughout the university. This participative process has proven to be a successful strategy to overcome resistance to change, influencing current reforms, empowering change agents and establishing a network. Several changes on a personal, personnel, institutional and regional level are described.

Keywords
Student-led project · Sustainable development · Institutional change at university

1 Introduction

Society faces many connected and interdependent crises, e.g. climate change and loss of biodiversity (Rockström et al. 2009). Humanitiy faces a second reversal of the relation between humans and nature: To survive, humanity needs to care for nature and not fight against it as it has done in the past (Stengel 2011). To overcome these crises, a huge transformation is needed (WBGU 2011). Key factors are education for sustainable development (ESD) and whole institutional change everywhere (UNESCO 2015). SD has been a key term for any institutional change since the Brundtland report pushed the concept into the limelight (UNESCO 2015). In the spirit of the claim 'think global, act local' there are many topics and problems to act on locally, for example Universities need transformation, e.g. integrate

J.M.R. Lopez
Centre for Globalisation and Governance/KlimaCampus, University of Hamburg, Grindelberg 5, 20144 Hamburg, Germany
e-mail: miguel.rodriguez@uni-hamburg.de

G. Perino
Department of Socioeconomics, University of Hamburg, Welckerstr. 8, 20354 Hamburg, Germany
e-mail: grischa.perino@wiso.uni-hamburg.de

W.-H. Tan
Interdisciplinary Centre for Learning and Teaching in Higher Education (IZuLL), University of Hamburg, Schlüterstr. 51, 20148 Hamburg, Germany
e-mail: wey-han.tan@uni-hamburg.de

interdisciplinary studies, environmental education and push awareness (United Nations Conference on Environment and Development 1992). Universities play an important role and have a special responsibility in this process for transforming cities, regions and the world because they can analyse the drivers of unsustainability, develop sustainable alternatives, broaden the minds of future decision-makers as well as educate change agents and be role models for other public institutions (e.g. Drupp et al. 2012; Tappeser and Meyer 2011). But the progress within universities is seen as slow (Müller-Christ 2014). To bring new momentum and action to the process, a small interdisciplinary group of students at the University of Hamburg (UHH) started a movement for SD, aiming to implement sustainability in the university's curriculum, the daily lives of its members, and the governance and administration of the organisation itself. The group focused its activities on ecological aspects because this was recognised both as a deficit and as a key issue.

In this article the authors report on the student-led project as a best practice example for SD in higher education institutions (HEIs). The project took advantage of several windows of opportunity that had emerged in the form of curriculum and administrative reforms at different levels of the university. The project is backed by experiences from other institutions and recent research which confirms that ESD is a key driver for SD in society at large.

The project aiming to realize the event *Dies Oecologicus* was based on four principles: inclusion, learning-by-doing, voluntariness and grassroots democracy, and living our vision. It went through three different phases: grounding, planning and realisation, and summarizing. Each principle and phase is presented in more detail below. Furthermore, it is pointed out how each of them contributed to the project's success. While a direct measurement of success is not feasible, there is no doubt that the movement for SD at the UHH is flourishing—and that the event *Dies Oecologicus* played an important role in making that happen.

2 Scientific Framework on Sustainability in Higher Education Institutions

Before reporting on the project, the relevant literature on sustainability in HEIs is briefly reviewed. The discussion about sustainability in HEIs was triggered by important decisions at the international level. The first step was taken at the United Nations Conference on Environment and Development in Rio de Janeiro in 1992, and it was followed by the confirmation of the need for sustainable development in education through the UN DESD between 2005 and 2014 (Barth 2013). The concept of sustainability and SD has been gaining importance for academic life (Leal Filho 2010), and in particular there is an ongoing discourse about how to create sustainable HEIs (Leal Filho et al. 2015). Two different approaches have been proposed: top down and bottom up (Brinkhurst et al. 2011). Endorsers of the top down approach argue in favour of the advantages of projects that are borne by the highest level of the HEIs' management, while the bottom up approach promotes a grass roots movement increasing engagement, interaction, and critical reflection of students and hence supporting a broad learning process within HEIs (Biedenweg et al. 2013). Many HEIs have started sustainability programs (Shields et al. 2014), and report on them with explicit reference to the top down (Bilodeau et al. 2014) and bottom up approaches. However, many initiatives have been a mixture of both approaches called 'intrapreneurship' (Brinkhurst et al. 2011). Intrapreneurs are actors who move within the boundaries of large institutional structures, bringing together grass roots ideas and swaying the direction of future projects; their ideas start from the bottom but are supported by the leaders (Lee and Schaltegger 2014). From this intrapreneurship perspective, the persons making these sustainability initiatives successful are at the middle levels of the HEIs' management (Brinkhurst et al. 2011).

The literature on SD at HEIs has developed a conceptual framework and conducted case studies and comparative analyses (Karatzoglou 2013). The more conceptual literature argues that SD should be pushed in all the dimensions of the HEIs, i.e. education, research, outreach and campus operation (Amaral et al. 2015). Implementation of sustainability at HEIs (Fadeeva and Mochizuki 2010) and their role in transforming society have received special attention (e.g. Stephens et al. 2008; Ferrer-Balas et al. 2008).

Several case studies report from projects implementing sustainability at HEIs from around the world (López 2013; Chikami and Sobue 2008). A prominent example is the Research Centre of Expertise (RCE) in SD that has been created to tackle the challenges and opportunities of the UN Decade of SD. Experiences from participating institutions have shown how cooperation between various actors of society (e.g. HEIs, governments, communities, schools, etc.) improve sustainability within these regions (van Dam-Mieras and Leman Stefanovic 2008; White and Petry 2011; Sedlacek 2013; van Dam-Mieras et al. 2008a, b). Lehmann and Fryd (2008) study how HEIs and cities could work together to implement SD.

All in all, sustainability initiatives have played an important role in changing students' perceptions. These have often been driven by the teaching side, i.e. by courses covering SD. Broadening the minds of future decision makers is crucial, but changes in the curriculum are more likely to be effective in the long-run (Zeegers and Francis Clark 2014).

Many courses and programmes on sustainability from top down, bottom up and mixed approaches have been evaluated (Wiek et al. 2014), and for the most part the assessments have been positive. Yet it has to be noted that most of the evaluations have been carried out by the persons in charge of the course or programme, which might produce a biased perspective. Nevertheless, the literature recommends introducing the ideas of SD into the curriculum to foster SD within the HEI and more importantly of the society at large (Davison et al. 2013). The United Nations Conference on SD in 2012 stated that it is crucial to "teach sustainable development concepts, ensuring that they form a part of the core curriculum across all disciplines [...]" (UNCSD 2012).

Teaching on SD should be complemented by making sustainability a core objective of the university's administration and governance, and by sustainability playing a prominent role in the values and the mission statement of the university (UNESCO 2015). Especially students have a unique role and potential in transforming universities. They can start projects and do conceptual work which would be done slower or not at all by other members of the university (Drupp et al. 2012). Looking from an organizational perspective it is important to understand Universities as "loosely coupled systems" in the sense of Weick (1976), orientated on professionals and organized anarchy (Hüther 2010). In planning projects aiming to transform universities it is important to understand this aspect of their internal decision-making processes (Hüther 2010).

3 Principles

In preparation, realisation and post-processing of the event *Dies Oecologicus* the project team followed four principles: Inclusion, Learning by Doing, Voluntariness and Grassroots Democracy, and Living our Vision.

3.1 Inclusion

The first guiding principle was to be inclusive toward people, perspectives and positions. The 'whole-of-university' approach was chosen to include not only students but also lecturers and administrative staff throughout the institution. To link research, educational and operational activities toward sustainability, a 'whole-of-university' approach was found to be effective to build trust among status groups as well as creating an identity as a university of sustainability (Brinkhurst et al. 2011; Mcmillin and Dyball 2009). Like successful initiatives on sustainability some elements of top-down and bottom-up approaches were mixed (Wiek et al. 2014). Following Kezar (2011) the project team used networks and created coalitions with other groups to strengthen bottom-up elements of institutional change, but also the support from the board committee of the university was actively sought. Having a key role as students the project team was able to cross boundaries of hierarchy and to engage in informal dialogues (Drupp et al. 2012). Additionally, inclusion prevents resistance to change: Feeling included and being an active part of the decision making process has been identified to be a key factor in change processes (McKay et al. 2013). Moreover, sustainability is a field with a high interdisciplinary potential (Leal Filho 2010). The vision of the project team for ESD involves all disciplines, since future problems are complex and cannot be solved by one discipline alone (Dale and Newman 2005; Blake et al. 2013). Therefore, the inclusion of as many people as possible representing a wide range of disciplines was desired to foster a dialogue without predefined results.

Müller-Christ (2014) suggests using the format of conferences because it is well established within the scientific community and allows reflecting on oneself and observing others. The aim should be to listen to each other and to start a constructive dialogue with stakeholders in politics and society. It is important that from watching and analysing changes the members of a university move on to transform their institution and inspire others to do the same (Müller-Christ 2014). In line with the principle of inclusion, the conference format of the event *Dies Oecologicus* includes key elements of bottom-up processes and has been found to substantially increase the acceptance of change within institutions. This is especially relevant for loosely coupled organisations in the sense of Hüther (2010). Since each discipline has its own patterns, meanings, knowledge tradition, and code of conduct (Frost and Jean 2003), interdisciplinary exchange and finding a common interdisciplinary way of thinking is necessary (Schäfer and Schnelle 1983). The event format meets these needs.

The project team early on managed to attract a small number of patrons that helped to identify and get in touch with key players relevant for the success of the project at all levels of the university. This network greatly facilitated the objective of making the project inclusive by allowing the project team to approach the different status groups of the university and to identify interview partners that formed an essential part of the grounding phase of the project.

3.2 Learning by Doing

Secondly, the principle of Learning by Doing was followed, in line with Aristotle, who once said

> For those things which we must do after learning, we learn to do by frequently doing; as by building houses, we become house-builders, and by playing on the harp, harp-players; thus by doing just things we become just, by temperate things temperate, and by valiant things valiant.

Following Reese (2011) rather 'trial and error' was used instead of instruction, practical experience instead of book learning and doing instead of excessive theorisation. Moreover, learning by doing includes constant reflection. On the one hand, the teamwork including responsibilities, work capacities, occurring conflicts and future strategies was reflected. On the other hand, the development and learning of definitions, ideas, and concepts regarding sustainability was deliberated. Furthermore, the project team kept an open mind to internal and external opinions, ideas and recommendations. Also, learning by doing includes a high degree of flexibility to change involving team constellation, windows of opportunities and availability of support. In line with Drupp et al. (2012) student initiatives foster students' learning as an independent knowledge acquisition on sustainability in a communicative environment.

3.3 Voluntariness and Grassroots Democracy

An important feature was the way the project team was formed and how it organised its work. Open membership guaranteed that all interested parties were able to participate and due to the grassroots democratic decision making were able to make their voice heard in the goal setting, implementation and evaluation of the project. Voluntariness ensured that no one had to do anything they did not like to do, which helped to keep up the high spirit that is essential for a student-led, unpaid project. The project team also assigned specific roles to individual team members that thereby became responsible for implementing a particular task or to represent the project team at specific occasions or functions. Taken together these organisational choices allowed the project to harness the mix of motivations and abilities of a team drawn together by a combination of personal and political sympathies. With the principle of voluntariness and grassroots democracy it was tried to reduce and deal with typical challenges of student initiatives and projects like high fluctuation of volunteers and a small number of participants (Drupp et al. 2012; Spira 2012).

In line with the project team's wish for a democratic dialogue inspiration was taken from the event "*Dies Academicus*", a day of discussing and reforming the curricula that is well established at universities throughout Germany.

3.4 Living Our Vision

Establishing a commonly agreed goal of the project, to work toward a more sustainable university, and sharing common values and the other guiding principles of inclusion, learning-by-doing as well as voluntariness and grassroots democracy has been pivotal in successfully completing the project. This common basis allowed solving the unavoidable internal and external conflicts generated by an ambitious project aiming for institutional change. Articulating a vision also turned out to be crucial in activating people and to motivate them to become a part of the change process (Boehm and Staples 2005) in contrast to people using sustainability as an empty shell. Moreover, the project team tried to work and live as sustainable as possible ("walk our talk"), e.g. by using recycling paper, separating waste, a green bank account etc.

4 Implementation

The idea for the project was created within a small interdisciplinary group of students. As a first step, financial support of 3800€ for travel expenses, equipment, flyers etc. was applied for and granted at a student initiative funding program at UHH. Early on the DESD acknowledged the event *Dies Oecologicus* as an individual contribution. The overall project surrounding the event *Dies Oecologicus* was divided into three phases: grounding, planning and realisation, and evaluation.

1. *Grounding*

In the first phase the common motivation and objective as well as what could be learned from other universities was identified and what the state of affairs was at our university. Starting from a group of four students that came up with the idea the first important step was to attract more members and to discuss and agree upon a common understanding of sustainability in general and the objectives and guiding principles of the project in particular. At that point the project team was neither familiar with the scientific discourse on sustainability in HEIs nor did it know much about sustainability definitions. The project team needed to focus the project and as explained above it was started with a focus on ecological aspects of sustainability. Different definitions were discussed and an agreed-upon definition was put down in writing. It was revised several times in the course of the project. At the end of the project it read:

> Ecological sustainability requires dealing with nature in a respectful and long-sighted way and transferring this into one's own lifestyle. As a result, resources can only be used at a rate equal to their regenerative capacity or in non-destructive ways. This includes effects on both current and future generations. Ecological sustainability requires education. As a consequence, impulses to act both for individuals and for society as a whole are created. This is a process and not an outcome. Ecological sustainability is closely connected with social responsibility and economic sustainability. However, there are strict limits to the extent these different dimensions are to be traded off against each other in situations where they are in conflict.

Based on this definition the possible ways to implement SD in the university's curriculum as well as in everyone's daily life was discussed. Within regular courses sustainability could be covered by discussing different definitions of the concept, teaching and testing strategies to educate on sustainability, studying specific applications in real-world contexts, reflecting on personal habits and life-styles, investigating the causes of excessive resource use including historical examples and by highlighting the relevance of discipline specific theories and concepts for sustainability. Reading an existing student-prepared sustainability report for the UHH (oikos hamburg 2012) allowed identifying further change agents. The report also showed that the current transformation process was mainly top-down and lacking effort. The report also raised a number of questions that helped designing the questions to be asked in the interviews that formed a crucial part of the project. Furthermore, the project team cooperated with an interdisciplinary seminar called "Energy transition at universities in northern Germany" and learned more about the sociological and physical aspects of sustainability as well as decision making at universities.

Using the information acquired the questions for the interviews with different change agents were developed: students, academic and administrative staff working on sustainability. The interviews were conducted to establish the state of affairs on sustainability at the UHH. This included people involved in different board committees. The interviewees were identified by suggestions from experts and sustainability as well as reform process involvement. The interviews were more than just tools to collect relevant information on perspectives, motivations and existing projects and reforms on SD. They also established a broad network of change agents that knew about the project, its objectives and to some extend started identifying themselves with it.

Based on experiences during the first set of interviews the questions were modified to include specific examples.

1. How would you define sustainability?
2. Do you do something for sustainability
   - as a person?
   - as part of your function within the university/institution?
3. If yes why and what? If no, why?
4. Can you identify and apply available knowledge related to sustainability within your own discipline according to universities' curriculum, daily lives of its members, and the governance and administration of the organisation itself?
5. Where do you see (a) possibilities and (b) necessities to act sustainably at universities?
   - Which decisions have to be made and by whom?
   - How can the different status groups at universities contribute to sustainable development?
6. Which change agents work on sustainability at universities?

In order to learn from change agents at other universities, the universities of Tübingen, Potsdam, Lüneburg, Bremen and Kiel, which are well known for working on sustainability throughout Germany, were selected for our external interviews. They were chosen, because each of them was interesting in several aspects, e.g. the university was recognized for excellence in research by a federal initiative ("Exzellenzinitative"), examples of established courses on SD, successful student initiatives, eco-management-system, pilot projects. The universities of Bremen and Kiel were additionally analysed by Hackstedt and Walz (2014).

2. *Planning and Realisation*

Secondly, the results of these interviews were analysed and discussed. In order to get feedback and an external view on the data, results were presented in the seminar "Energy transition at universities in northern Germany". Mayor topics that guided the planning of the event *Dies Oecologicus* were identified: The curriculum, the students and the institution itself. To start a whole institutional change it was decided to structure the workshop into different sessions (see Fig. 1). Teaching was covered by four separate sessions because it is a very complex topic and the main focus: (1) "Sustainability inflation? We need content!" about what content is

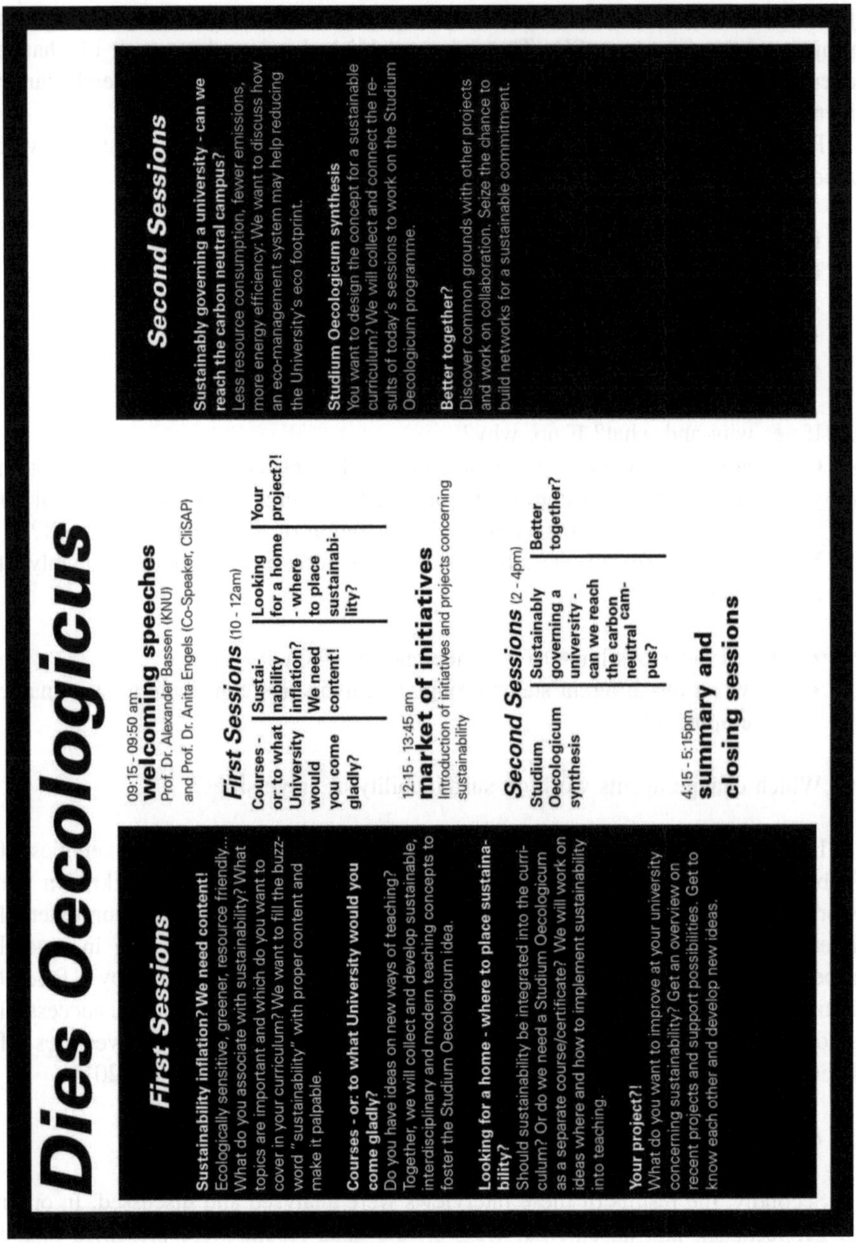

Fig. 1 Structure of the event *Dies Oecologicus*

currently missing and what courses are needed. (2) "Courses—or: to what University would you come gladly?" about identifying adequate didactical methods. (3) "Looking for a home—where to place sustainability" about administrative challenges in implementing sustainability in teaching and (4) "Studium Oecologicum synthesis" where the results of the other three sessions where combined. Following up on the results of Walz and Hackstedt (2014) on the institutional aspects, the session on a university's ecological footprint and eco-management systems was created. It had the title (5) "Sustainably governing a university—can we reach the carbon neutral campus?" During the grounding it was found that student-led projects are often facilitators for institutional change as has been reported in the literature (e.g. Drupp et al. 2012). That is why the session (6) "Your project?!" gave space to develop new student-led projects and to collect ideas. The session (7) "Better together" focused on connecting existing projects because many interviewees talked about being alone.

Each session was supported by an internal and an external expert/change agent/stakeholder that the project team got to know during the grounding phase. They were chosen due to their scientific expertise and/or their function within the university. Moreover, a buffet of organic and fair trade food supported by a local society educating and advising on organic food was organised. Participants could have brunch while meeting others and exchanging ideas.

3. *Summarising*

The last phase of the project was dedicated to summarising main results. The minutes and products of all sessions were collected and more descriptions (and reflections) added to an evaluation booklet (Dies Oecologicus 2014), which was handed over to most of the internal interviewees. Based on the results of the project new steps, strategies and projects were planned.

5 Results and Discussion

It is quite difficult to define the outcome of the project, and even more difficult to measure the impact of the day on SD at the UHH. The results are therefore seen as part of the overall reform process, with the project team and the event *Dies Oecologicus* having been (major) players therein. The sessions produced more approaches and possible action points than can be named here. In what follows a number of recent developments are listed that at least to some extent were brought about by the event *Dies Oecologicus* and the change process it started.

5.1 Personal and Personnel Change

First of all, the project team gained new ideas on how to implement sustainability in the university's curriculum, the daily lives of its members, and the governance and administration of the organisation itself.

The project team members became multipliers for their aims and principles: They attended the *2nd WSSD conference* September 2014 in Manchester, the

Conference of the network of sustainability initiatives October 2014 in Bochum and the *European Green Office Summit* October 2014 in Berlin. Also, the project team was invited to present their project and their specific issues at a national education conference organised by the *German Council for Sustainable Development*, November 2014, in Berlin.

Certainly one of the most important results is the establishment of a working group ("*Studium Oecologicum*") as a follow-up project to implement SD in HEIs. The group consisting of students and lecturers develops new courses with topics related to sustainability and using new ways to teach, focused on education through scientific research in groups, e.g. problem-based or project-based learning. This illustrates how a student-to-university project transforms to a student-and-staff-project according to Spira (2012) and through that confirms the initial principle of inclusion.

Moreover, more people got involved and established their own working groups. This development represents a new form of connecting members groups and shows the effectiveness of boosting a movement by connecting existing players, adding new ones and being visible to the public. People involved in the event *Dies Oecologicus* and the project carried the ideas, especially on ESD, into their departments and spread them among friends and colleagues. This enlarged community is of course able to further create ideas, new projects and add momentum to the university's transition process towards SD. Furthermore, sustainability was the topic of this semesters' university-wide "*Dies Academicus*". Hence, the project started as a bottom up movement and quickly received positive and supportive top down resonance.

5.2 Institutional Change

The project revealed some of UHH's forgotten roots from the 80s and 90s and finally raised awareness for ESD and the need for a suitable governance structure, e.g. a coordination position. Moreover, a new university-wide funding scheme for student-led projects on SD was established. Funding student-led projects helps overcoming typical barriers to student engagement (Drupp et al. 2012; Spira 2012). Such projects increase quickly the number of people working on a topic and strengthen the bottom-up approach. Furthermore, students are now involved in a committee working on SD at UHH, and hopefully more participation is yet to come.

5.3 Regional Change

Due to intensive press coverage, the project has been highly recognized within the region. The project triggered several urban gardening and greening initiatives. Furthermore, currently developed courses on ESD will be open to all members of society.

Moreover, two students most active in organising the project were rewarded with a prize of the council of future development of Hamburg (Zukunftsrat Hamburg), a network for SD following Agenda 21.

6 Conclusion

The overall success of the event *Dies Oecologicus* is being the tipping point for sustainable development at the University of Hamburg. The event *Dies Oecologicus* has accomplished to build up a critical mass and momentum for the long and potentially burdensome process of implementation and integration into existing processes of institutional change.

The outline of the event *Dies Oecologicus* is transferable to other universities and this paper strongly suggests strengthening students' possibilities to participate in university's change process and encourages students to actively take part.

By following the principles of inclusion, learning by doing, voluntariness and grassroots democracy while living the vision of a sustainable university, the project team was able to take a first step into realizing this vision.

Acknowledgments The authors gratefully acknowledge the financial support from the funding line for student-led projects by TP 27/STIF of the Universitätskolleg of the University of Hamburg. The authors would also like to thank everyone involved in running the project and the patrons, interview partners, session organisers and speakers as well as the Center for a Sustainable University (KNU) and everyone else who actively contributed to the success of the project and the event *Dies Oecologicus*.

References

Amaral, L. P., Martins, N., & Gouveia, J. B. (2015). Quest for a sustainable university: A review. *International Journal of Sustainability in Higher Education, 16*(2), 155–172.

Barth, M. (2013). Many roads lead to sustainability: A process-oriented analysis of change in Higher Education. *International Journal of Sustainability in Higher Education, 14*(2), 160–175.

Biedenweg, K., Monroe, M. C., & Oxarart, A. (2013). The importance of teaching ethics of sustainability. *International Journal of Sustainability in Higher Education, 14*(1), 6–14.

Bilodeau, L., Podger, J., & Abd-El-Aziz, A. (2014). Advancing campus and community sustainability: Strategic alliances in action. *International Journal of Sustainability in Higher Education, 15*(2), 157–168.

Blake, J., Sterling, S., & Kagawa, F. (2013). Getting it together. Interdisciplinarity and Sustainability in the Higher Education Institution. *Pedagogic Research Institute and Observatory (PedRIO), 4*, 1–71.

Boehm, A., & Staples, L. (2005). Grassroots leadership in task-oriented groups: Learning from successful leaders. *Social Work with Groups: A Journal of Community and Clinical Practice, 28*(2), 77–96.

Brinkhurst, M., Rose, P., Maurice, G., & Ackerman, J. D. (2011). Achieving campus sustainability: Top-down, bottom-up, or neither? *International Journal of Sustainability in Higher Education, 12*(4), 338–354.

Chikami, S., & Sobue, K. (2008). Creating a sustainable city through a system of citizen-based learning: ESD at Nagoya open university of the environment. *Journal of Education for Sustainable Development, 2*(2), 127–139.

Dale, A., & Newman, L. (2005). Sustainable development, education and literacy. *International Journal of Sustainability in Higher Education, 6*(4), 262–351.

Davison, A., Brown, P., Pharo, E., Warr, K., McGregor, H., Terkes, S., et al. (2013). Distributed leadership. *International Journal of Sustainability in Higher Education, 15*(1), 98–110.

Dies Oecologicus. (2014). *Abschlussbericht Dies Oecologicus.* Available at https://dies-oecologicus-uhh.de/wordpress/wp-content/uploads/2014/11/DiesOec_Bericht-aktuell.pdf

Drupp, M. A., Esguerra, A., Keul, L., Loew Beer, D., Meisch, S., & Roosen Runge, F. (2012). Change from below—student initiatives for universities in sustainable development. In W. Leal Filho (Ed.), *Sustainable development at universities: New Horizons*. Frankfurt: Peter Lang Scientific Publishers.

Fadeeva, Z., & Mochizuki., Y. (2010), Competences for sustainable development and sustainability. *International Journal of Sustainability in Higher Education, 11*(4), 391–403.

Ferrer-Balas, D., Adachi, J., Banas, S., Davidson, C. I., Hoshikoshi, A., Mishra, A., et al. (2008). An international comparative analysis of sustainability transformation across seven universities. *International Journal of Sustainability in Higher Education, 9*(3), 295–316.

Frost, S., & Jean, P. (2003). Bridging the disciplines. Interdisciplinary discourse and faculty scholarship. *The Journal of Higher Education, 74*(2), 119–149.

Hackstedt, C., & Walz, K. (2014). Universitäten zur Nachhaltigkeit managen? Eine exemplarische Analyse des Umweltmanagement-Systems EMAS an Hochschulen. In A. Engels (Ed.), *Global transformations towards a low carbon society*, Vol. 9 (Working Paper Series). Hamburg: University of Hamburg/KlimaCampus.

Hüther, O. (2010). *Von der Kollegialität zur Hierarchie? Der New Managerialism in den Landeshochschulgesetzen*. Wiesbaden: VS Verlag.

Karatzoglou, B. (2013). An in-depth literature review of the evolving roles and contributions of universities to Education for Sustainable Development. *Journal of Cleaner Production, 49*, 44–53.

Kezar, A. (2011). Grassroots leadership: Encounters with power dynamics and oppression. *International Journal of Qualitative Studies in Education, 24*(4), 471–500.

Leal Filho, W. (2010). Teaching sustainable development at university level: Current trends and future needs. *Journal of Baltic Science Education, 9*(4), 273–284.

Leal Filho, W., Evangelos, M., & Pace, P. (2015). The future we want. *International Journal of Sustainability in Higher Education, 16*(1), 112–129.

Lee, K.-H., & Schaltegger, S. (2014). Organizational transformation and higher sustainability management education. *International Journal of Sustainability in Higher Education, 15*(4), 450–472.

Lehmann, M., & Fryd, O. (2008). Urban quality development and management. *International Journal of Sustainability in Higher Education, 9*(1), 21–38.

López, O. S. (2013). Creating a sustainable university and community through a common experience. *International Journal of Sustainability in Higher Education, 14*(3), 291–309.

McKay, K., Kuntz, J. C., & Näswall, K. (2013). The effect of affective commitment, communication and participation on resistance to change: The role of change readiness. *New Zealand Journal of Psychology, 42*(2), 29–40.

Mcmillin, J., & Dyball, R. (2009). Developing a Whole-of-University Approach to Educating for Sustainability. Linking Curriculum, Research and Sustainable Campus Operations. *Journal of Education for Sustainable Development, 3*(1), 55–64.

Müller-Christ, G. (2014). Konferenzen für Nachhaltigkeit an Hochschulen - die akademische Art der Vernetzung? In UNESCO (2014), *Hochschulen für nachhaltige Entwicklung* (pp. 62–63). Available at http://www.bne-portal.de/fileadmin/unesco/de/Downloads/Dekade_%20Publikation_national/20140928_UNESCO_Broschuere2014_web.pdf.

oikos Hamburg. (2012). *Nachhaltigkeitsbericht für die Universität Hamburg*. Available at http://hamburg.oikos-international.org/fileadmin/oikos-international/chapter/hamburg/oikos_Hamburg_Nachhaltigkeitsbericht.pdf.

Reese, H. W. (2011). The learning-by-doing principle. *Behavioral Development Bulletin, 11*, 1–19.

Rockström, J., W., Steffen, K., Noone, Å., Persson, F. S., Chapin, III, E. et al. (2009). "Planetary boundaries: exploring the safe operating space for humanity". *Ecology and Society*, 14(2), 32.

Schäfer, L., & Schnelle, T. (Eds.). (1983). *Ludwik Fleck: Erfahrung und Tatsache*. Suhrkamp: Frankfurt a.M.

Sedlacek, S. (2013). The role of universities in fostering sustainable development at the regional level. *Journal of Cleaner Production, 48*, 74–84.

Shields, D., Verga, F., & Andrea Blengini, G. (2014). Incorporating sustainability in engineering education. *International Journal of Sustainability in Higher Education, 15*(4), 390–403.

Spira, F. (2012). Sowing sprouts to engender greener universities—A qualitative study exploring the projects, challenges and strategies of sustainability student groups. *Maastricht Journal of Liberal Arts, 4*, 41–54.

Stengel, O. (2011). *Suffizienz—Die Konsumgesellschaft in der ökologischen Krise*. München: oekom_verlag.

Stephens, J. C., Hernandez, M. E., Román, M., Graham, A. C., & Scholz, R. W. (2008). Higher education as a change agent for sustainability in different cultures and contexts. *International Journal of Sustainability in Higher Education, 9*(3), 317–338.

Tappeser, V., & Meyer, A. (2011). Change-agents in sustainability governance: Institutional transformation at three institutions of higher education. In W. Leal Filho (Ed.), *Sustainable development at universities: New Horizons*. Frankfurt: Peter Lang Scientific Publishers.

UNCSD. (2012). *Commitment to sustainable practices of higher education institutions on the occasion of the United Nations conference on sustainable development in Rio 2012*. UNCSD, United Nations, Rio de Janeiro.

UNESCO. (2015). *UNESCO Roadmap zur Umsetzung des Weltaktionsprogramms "Bildung für nachhaltige Entwicklung"*. Available at http://www.bne-portal.de/fileadmin/unesco/de/Downloads/Dekade_Publikationen_international/2015_Roadmap_deutsch.pdf

United Nations Conference on Environment and Development. (1992). *Report of the United Nations Conference on Environment and Development, Rio de Janeiro, 3–14 June 1992*. New York: United Nations, 1993.

van Dam-Mieras, M. C. E., Ferrer-Balas, D., & Buckland, H. (2008a). Mutual learning for sustainability. *International Journal of Sustainability in Higher Education, 9*(4), 450–468.

van Dam-Mieras, M. C. E., Itoh, M., Suemoto, M., Matsuoka, K., Ito, A., Yui, K., et al. (2008b). Contribution of Kobe University to the regional centre of expertise (RCE) on education for sustainable development (ESD) Hyogo-Kobe. *International Journal of Sustainability in Higher Education, 9*(4), 479–486.

van Dam-Mieras, M. C. E., & Leman Stefanovic, I. (2008). Educational alliance for a sustainable Toronto. *International Journal of Sustainability in Higher Education,* 9(4), 416–427.

WBGU (2011). *Welt im Wandel: Gesellschaftsvertrag für eine Große Transformation [Hauptgutachten]*. Berlin: Wiss. Beirat d. Bundesregierung Globale Umweltveränderungen (WBGU-Hauptgutachten 2011).

White, P., & Petry, R. (2011). Building Regional Capacity for Sustainable Development through an ESD Project Inventory in RCE Saskatchewan, Canada. *Journal of Education for Sustainable Development, 5*(1), 89–100.

Weick, K. E. (1976). Educational organizations as loosely coupled systems. *Administrative Science Quarterly, 21*(1), 1–19.

Wiek, A., Xiong, A., Brundiers, K., & van der Leeuw, S. (2014). Integrating problem- and project-based learning into sustainability programs. *International Journal of Sustainability in Higher Education, 15*(4), 431–449.

Zeegers, Y., & Francis Clark, I. (2014). Students' perceptions of education for sustainable development. *International Journal of Sustainability in Higher Education, 15*(2), 242–253.

MIX
Papier aus verantwortungsvollen Quellen
Paper from responsible sources
FSC® C105338

If you have any concerns about our products,
you can contact us on
ProductSafety@springernature.com

In case Publisher is established outside the EU,
the EU authorized representative is:
Springer Nature Customer Service Center GmbH
Europaplatz 3, 69115 Heidelberg, Germany

Printed by Libri Plureos GmbH
in Hamburg, Germany